Sir James McGrigor

Sir James McGrigor

The Scalpel and the Sword:
The Autobiography of the Father of Army Medicine

edited by Mary McGrigor

First published in 2000 by

SCOTTISH CULTURAL PRESS

Unit 13d, Newbattle Abbey Business Annexe
Newbattle Road, Dalkeith EH22 3LJ
Tel: 0131 660 6366 • Fax: 0131 660 4757
Email: info@scottishbooks.com
website: www.scottishbooks.com

British Library Cataloguing in Publication Data
A catalogue record for this book is available from the British Library

ISBN: 1 84017 035 2

Printed and bound by Colour Books Ltd, Dublin

Acknowledgements

My deepest thanks for his invaluable help and encouragement to Mr Alec Adam M.B., F.R.C.S.(Ed), F.S.A. Scot., Honorary Librarian of the Medico-Chirurgical Society (Medical Centre, Aberdeen).

Also to Dr Brian D. Keighley M.B., ChB., F.R.C.G.P., D.F.M.; Colonel Robert Thornton of the R.A.M.C. Headquarters (Millbank, London); Captain Peter Starling, Curator of the Army Medical Services Museum (Keogh Barracks, Aldershot); Sir Julien Paget Bt., C.V.O.; Mrs Caroline Robot (for translating the French material relating to Baron Larrey); Miss Helen Wakely, Assistant Archivist, Contemporary Medical Archives Centre, The Welcome Institute for the History of Medicine (Euston Road, London); Miss Sally Harrower, Assistant in Manuscripts Division, National Library of Scotland; Miss Avril Gray and Mr Brian Pugh of Scottish Cultural Press; Mrs Howard Bennett of the *Oban Times*; and Mr Roy Summers and Mr Gordon Ross Thomson, Photographers.

Contents

Knight, his character, &c. – Office of Inspector-General – Regimental and general hospitals – Improvement in the army medical officers – Views on army medical reform – Deputy Inspector of Northern District – Headquarters at Beverley, Yorkshire – Introduces many reforms in the military hospitals – Treatment of typhus fever and ulcerated legs – Sir Everard Home, and Drs Currie, Jackson and Baynton – Excitement in York on the death of a soldier from typhus – Bad feeling in York against the government – Promotion from York to the South-West District – Low state of the army medical profession – Comparative advantages of the civil and military practitioner – Progress in the army medical profession during the last forty years – Temptation of the young medical officer at mess – Studious habits

INTRODUCTION

The Boy Born at Cromdale in Strathspey

'I've won! I've won!'

The boy tore down School Hill, where the Grammar School then stood, his boots thumping on the hard surface of the road. 'I've won! I've won!' The words spun through his mind.

> I ran to my father's house, at a quicker pace than ever I ran in the course of my life to announce my success in having obtained the highest prize in the fifth or high class . . . My heart did not swell with more pride when, nearly half a century afterwards, I was elected Lord Rector of my Alma Mater and of the University of Aberdeen.

So wrote Sir James McGrigor in his *Autobiography*, published after his death. James, the eldest of three sons of Colquhoun McGrigor and his wife, Ann Grant, was actually born in Lethendry in Strathspey, Inverness-shire, his mother's home. The status of the family was by then greatly changed from that of Colquhoun's great great grandfather, Gregor McGrigor (or MacGregor – the names are synonymous) who had come to Strathavon in Banff in 1624 virtually as a refugee.

The MacGregors of Roro, of whom he was one, had lived in Glenlyon since 1490 but without feudal rights to their land. Their chief, Alasdair MacGregor of Glenstrae, who likewise had no legal claim, was refused possession of his inheritance by Sir Duncan Campbell, 7th of Glenorchy, in 1588. Subsequently, Alasdair was blamed for the lawlessness of some of his clansmen and Sir Duncan Campbell, appointed as head of a list of commissioners, was empowered to bring them to trial. In 1603, the MacGregors defeated the Colquhouns in Glenfruin and Alasdair, arrested on the charge of treachery, was convicted and hanged.

Following his execution, the entire clan was proscribed. It became legal to shoot a MacGregor. Men were hunted down with bloodhounds and killed; women were branded with irons. The name being forbidden, most took the surnames of relations, or of people who risked prosecution by allowing them to live on their land. Some who gave sanctuary to the MacGregors did so for personal gain. Cattle-raiding was then endemic throughout Scotland and the old adage of setting a thief to catch one applied to desperate men.

In 1624 the Earl of Moray (who also held the Lordship of Doune in Perthshire), fearing repercussions from people of Clan MacIntosh whom he had evicted, brought some 300 MacGregors from Menteith and Balquhidder to Strathspey. Certainly, Gregor MacGregor and his wife, Christian (great grandparents of Sir James), who came from Glen Lyon are known to have settled in Strathavon at this time.

Shortly after that it is recorded that the MacGregors, who supported the Earl of Huntly in a feud with the Crichtons, were commanded by a son of MacGregor of Roro and by MacGregor of Glengyle early in the following year.[1]

The River Avon (pronounced 'aan') rises in Loch Avon at a height of 2,370 feet and runs thirty miles through Kirkichael, the highest parish in the Highlands. From Tomintoul, the highest village at 1,000 feet, built c.1775, it descends for eight miles through the floor of a narrow glen before entering the parish of Inveraven still at 700 feet. During the seventeenth century, Strathavon was described as a haven for outlaws 'where they have ane peacable and ordinarie abode and rest unmolested . . . as if they were lawful subjects'.[2] The MacGregors, or McGrigors, who lived there married into local families, mostly Grants and Gordons, whose surnames they adopted as their own. Thus, the accounts of the Duke of Gordon's estate show Grigor Grant (great grandfather of Sir James) as the tacksman of Dellaworar (sic) in 1708. As such he paid 'a tack dutie of two hundredth and fourtien merks. The said fourtien merks being allowed as Forrester'.[3] Significantly, he appears in these records four years later as Grigor Grant, or MacGregor, when holding the same office of Forester, or keeper of the Duke's deer.

James, who was Grigor's second son, called himself Gordon. In 1737, he paid a rent of £866-13-4 as the tenant of Campdelmore and the Forest of Glenaven. He married a daughter of Grant of Abernethy and they settled at Milton of Duthill in 1761. Their son Colquhoun, maintaining the family tradition, married Ann, daughter of Lewis Grant of Lethendry in Cromdale where, in the following year of 1771, their eldest son James was born. An entry in the records of the Gordon estates of this year states: 'Colquhoun MacGregor, innkeeper at Cromdale, Strathspey, has been invited to offer for the tacks but requires to know if Torrans is to be added to Camdel' (a place notoriously short of grass).[4]

Colquhoun, who was obviously struggling to farm on poor upland ground, is also described as a merchant, but this business also appears to have been unprofitable due to unpaid debts. Writing to James Grant, Clerk at Castle Grant, from Cromdale, on 13 September 1775, he asks him to settle the outstanding account of Sir James Grant of Grant for a shilling's worth of figs which was long overdue. Also, he begs him to send him fifteen shillings sterling 'as the compriesing of the Corn diestroyed in Tim [time] making the roads . . . and I hop that you will be so Good as not to let me lous this for I have no way to Recover it unless you do it . . . I do ashour you that I never hade more ous for money than I have at this time.' He signs his name Colquhoun MacGregor, an indication of the fact that proscription of the clan surname had been withdrawn that year. The writing must have been smudged, for a postscript runs 'Excaus me for want of wafers for none can be had in this please.' Plainly, he was winding up his business. The Strathspey 'Minutes of Tacks of 1772–75' state that: 'As Colquhoun MacGregor, Merchant in Cromdale, is to give up or leave the country [i.e., Strathspey] at Whitsunday first [in 1775] the Minister of Cromdale would wish to get the lands of Achroisk possessed by Colquhoun as he cannot live quietly with any Neighbour there except he was under himself.'

The tone of Colquhoun's letter, ending with his contemptuous reference to a place where no blotting paper could be bought, suggests that as a young man, ambitious and with a family to raise, he had but little regret in leaving the wilds of Strathavon to seek his fortune in the city.

Today Sir James McGrigor is remembered as the 'Father of the R.A.M.C.'. His greatest achievement, however, was that he transformed the poorly regarded profession of a surgeon into one accorded great respect. Medical men of his day included physicians, surgeons and apothecaries who adhered to a strict set of rules. Physicians were forbidden by law either to practise surgery or to dispense medicines; surgeons were regarded as craftsmen – even though some, particularly in the army and navy, were little more than butchers – but they could not call themselves doctors and did not have the same social standing accorded to them as the result.

The Royal College of Surgeons in Scotland was founded in Edinburgh in 1505 when the town council granted its Seal of Cause, or Charter of Privileges, to the Barber Surgeons, allowing them to practise surgery within the city boundaries. This seal was finally ratified by James IV, and in 1567 his granddaughter, Mary Queen of Scots, gave the Barber Surgeons a special exemption from carrying arms in battle, on condition that they treated the wounded.

In 1694, William and Mary granted the Incorporation a Gift and Patent, giving the surgeons sole control over surgery in south-east Scotland and the responsibility of teaching anatomy. Subsequently, the first Surgeon's Hall was built in Edinburgh and even now remains (greatly altered) as the Department of Oral Medicine and Oral Pathology in Edinburgh University.

Originally only Fellows, who had to be Burgesses of the City of Edinburgh, were admitted to the college but in 1770 a new examination called the 'Licentiateship' was introduced, this being the qualification which, eighteen years later, the young James McGrigor aimed to obtain.[5]

McGrigor himself, 'such a shy chap' as Wellington said, gives only the briefest details of his childhood and education. I have, therefore, attempted to describe the circumstances of his youth from sources concerned with his times. The early days of the Aberdeen Medico-Chirurgical Society are taken from the records held within the library of the Society in Aberdeen.

In the last decades of the eighteenth century, an ancient loch, weed-filled and almost a bog, lay in the centre of Aberdeen. The city, however, was beginning to extend beyond the Denburn, formerly its boundary to the west. Beyond lay open moorland. An area round Foresterhill was cultivated, as was much of the Loanhead slopes where some fine houses stood. Gilcomston was still a village, but the suburb of Hardgate was beginning to emerge. In 1780, the burgh from the Bridge of Dee to the river's mouth was described as 'one continuous village' and the same writer reported that 'improvements' were taking place. Foremost amongst these was the North Pier. Ten years previously, in 1770, the Town Council had asked John Smeaton, the most distinguished harbour engineer of his day, to advise on what could be done to prevent the harbour entrance being silted up by sand blown in by north and north-east winds. Subsequently on his advice, the granite pier had been built.

The 'New Town' of Aberdeen was centred round the harbour, nucleus of its trade. The city was renowned for its shipyard where great wooden ships were built. Tall-masted, high-rigged merchantmen, which sailed to and from the Continent and even as far as North America, lay at anchor. They towered above the fishing smacks with their short masts and lug sails.

At the head of the harbour, the Fish Market was important as it is today. From the time of its foundation, salmon had been the city's staple trade. The fish, salted or preserved in vinegar, were exported at a rate of over a thousand barrels annually from the river Dee (only slightly less came from the Don).

During this century, Aberdeen developed into a pioneer town for the textile trade. As early as 1618, Taylor, the 'Water Poet', mentions the home-made linen which was spun from locally grown flax. He was also impressed by the home-made hose which excited his admiration almost as much as the local whisky! The making of stockings was a home-weaver's job. By 1770, there were no less than twenty-two merchants, who bought wool from the south and distributed it among thousands of women in the countryside where it was made into stockings and women's gloves. Some pairs of stockings sold for as much as £5. In 1760, Aberdeen Town Council presented James Keith, Frederick the Great's Field Marshal in Potsdam, with a pair of stockings of the highest price and fine enough to be drawn through a thumb ring.[6]

The raising of Highland regiments during the European Wars had produced a great demand for the woven kilt hose, which was worn by both officers and men, and despite the trade restrictions imposed by governments of hostile countries, there was much demand for them abroad.

Colquhoun McGrigor, described by his son as 'a general merchant', established a line in hosiery that eventually became his main concern. His business premises were in the Gallowgate, where he most probably lived. The Gallowgate, one of the two northern city gates, or bows, had been removed in 1768, but in many respects the district maintained the aspect of medieval times. The Town Council was only slowly succeeding in banishing the citizens' pigs; the animals foraged everywhere, creating havoc in churchyards where they rooted up corpses from the earth. The streets were inches deep in filth and 'in addition to the noisome solids of the midden . . . there were the equally odoriferous liquids of the gutters. These ran full, summer and winter, down the braes of the Gallowgate . . . the largest of these streams was known as the Braid Gutter, which carried off the foul water that flowed down the Gallowgate round the north eastern end of Marischal College to West North Street and into the Powcreek Burn.'[7] There was no water supply and sturdy women carried buckets of water from house to house. Nonetheless, some of the noblemen and gentry still lived in the Gallowgate, despite its insalubrious surroundings.

The houses of the well-to-do citizens were simple and homely. Oatmeal and milk formed the staple diet and most clothes were home-made. Children went first to a dame's school, such as Miss Hogg's school for young children, where the boys learned scripture texts and the girls did 'shanking' or stocking knitting. Boys were then sent to an English, or writing school, as elegance in penmanship (never a strong point with James McGrigor) was considered the mark of a gentleman.'

Mr Bower's Academy in Long Acre – known for the dapperness of the body of its master as 'Bodsie Bower's School' – became famous for having Lord Byron as a pupil. Byron then went on to the Grammar School, where amongst the senior boys he must have found James McGrigor.

An etching of the 'new school', built almost on the site of the old one on the Schoolhill in 1757, shows that it formed three sides of a square. The main building, topped with a belfry, contained the public hall, where the boys assembled, and four teaching rooms lay on one side. The Rector was Dr James Dun who, having joined the staff in 1732, had become Rector in 1744. He retained his post until he died in 1798, at the age of ninety. At that time education had to be paid for. Only in a few special cases did the parish meet the cost. The curriculum included Latin and Greek as well as reading, writing and arithmetic, each subject priced separately by the term.

The young James McGrigor, having entered the Grammar School when he was nine, left aged only fourteen. He describes the occasion of the prize-giving at the end of a five-year course as 'the most joyous . . . of any in my life'. The annual event, which took place at the end of October, was the highlight of the school year. The floors were newly sanded. The Rector, resplendent in a robe, looked as grand as a professor. The procession was headed by the red-coated town sergeants. The questions were set and the pupils wrote their answers. The crowd then retired to return at night with the sergeants bearing lanterns before it. The town-clerk's powdered head towered, when he sat down, between a blaze of lights. The prize names were read amid cheers and then the assemblage parted, but not before a general smash of windows on the part of the junior members of the company, after which quiet returned to the town.[8]

James McGrigor, who avoided the last part of the proceedings as he rushed home to his parents, gives a more sober version of the occasion (see page 27).

Aberdeen, with two universities, could boast of having more seats of learning than any other city in Great Britain. One was King's College, named in honour of James IV, the other Marischal College, established by a charter of James VI. The buildings of the latter were gifted by George Keith, Fifth Earl Marischal, who saw it as a Protestant rival to the other Catholic foundation. Two hundred years later the buildings of Marischal College had disintegrated to the point of becoming 'an ugly edifice of four storeys high, with a wing at one end and at the other a huge clumsy tower meant as an observatory. On the central building was a clock . . . Within there was a large hall on the ground floor of the middle building called the "Public School", where the students met at eight o'clock in the morning, and when it delighted the wilder spirits to enter while the Lord's Prayer was being finished, in order that they might be fined, as the Reverend Principal hastily concluded with the words "Pay down a penny, sir – for ever and ever Amen".'

'Boys will be boys', as the old saying goes, and a favourite prank of the chemistry students was to put miniature glass-bombs into the candles hanging from the roof of the classroom. The bombs, exploding from heat, put out the candles while yells of 'terror' from those involved in the conspiracy rang through the darkened hall. James McGrigor, apparently uninvolved in such skulduggery, entered the First, or Greek, class of Marischal College. Writing that the professors had been numbered amongst the foremost scholars for over three hundred years, he names those of his day: Dr Beattie, the philosopher and poet; Dr Hamilton, the mathematician; Dr Gerard; and others 'all well known for their writings'. Foremost amongst them was 'Principal Campbell' otherwise known as the Reverend George Campbell, Professor of Divinity and Principal of Marischal College, and 'author of the work on "Miracles" which originated in his controversy with Hume.' Here, James is, in fact, referring to Campbell's 'Dissertation on Miracles', written in 1763, in which he accepted the challenge to Christian belief thrown down by the philosopher David Hume, who asserted in his 'Philosophical Essays' of 1748 that witnesses of miracles are more likely to lie or be mistaken than miracles are to occur.

Campbell, a small quiet man, who all but died of tuberculosis as a boy, had a large and domineering wife. One day, when she was busily preparing for a party, they collided. 'Oot o' the wye, ye bodie! Ye're aye in the road in a steer!' she shouted, to which he meekly replied, 'Weel, Gracie, if I were oot o' the wye, maybe there wouldna be sae muckle steer!' Famous for his 'Philosophy of Rhetoric', his 'Translation of the Gospels', and his 'Lectures on Ecclesiastical History', Campbell died in 1796, having been Principal of Marischal College from 1758 to 1795.

The problem then paramount in the McGrigor family involved James's choice of a career. One can picture the family discussions and sense the affection of both parents for their clever son. Plainly, his parents accepted that James had ideas of his own. The medical profession, so long restricted by ignorance, was now, thanks to improvements in science, proving a source of advancement to ambitious young men.

Students at Marischal College, encouraged by their mentors, had been quick to recognise the chance of making a successful career. However, they found themselves faced with the near impossibility of gaining anything but the most basic knowledge of medicine in the city of Aberdeen. There were no medical classes in either Marischal College or King's, and boys wishing to become doctors, who could not study elsewhere, usually began as apprentices to a qualified physician in the town.

One such was William Ross, son of a weaver in Aberdeen, who indentured himself as servant and apprentice to Dr William Chalmers, physician and Professor of King's College. For the term of five complete years he condemned himself to slavery, being forbidden to absent himself without leave and 'that I shall do all the business of an ordinary house servant in and without doors'. He was bound to conceal from his master nothing that tended to his prejudice, and to reveal to none the secrets of his business.' Ross's father, the weaver, was to supply him with shirts, stockings and washing while, for his part, Chalmers agreed to instruct his apprentice 'in everything related to his business that he himself knows' a penalty of ten pounds being incurred by either side for breach of contract. [9]

Dr Chalmers had a chemist's shop on Mount Hoolie, where his apprentice was required to take down the shutters every morning. Medicines, which were far from cheap, could also be obtained from the laboratory of Neil MacLean, on the south side of the Castlegate, the most important shop in Market Place. He sold senna leaves at 3s 3d per lb.; borax at 4s.; and hog's lard at sevenpence halfpenny. Mrs Thomson, the bookseller, sold Mr Spillburn's pills (which cured rheumatism and the measles) at 5s. Otherwise, medicines of various kinds could be bought from advertisements in the news sheets, again at an exorbitant price.

The suffering of the poorer people, who could not afford to pay for a physician, let alone buy medicine, was recognised and a dispensary, financed by the chief citizens, was opened in 1781. It worked in close connection with the Infirmary, despite the fact that the funds of the latter were so poor that the chaplain volunteered to do without his stipend for half a year. The Infirmary managers, aided by the townsmen, worked hard to improve the healing of the sick by every means in their power. Nonetheless, despite all their efforts there was neither a clinical lecturer nor a clinical ward in the hospital. Students had to learn what they could from the twice weekly lectures given by the doctors for six months only in the year, and by accompanying them on their rounds of the wards.[10]

The work of the students in the hospital must have been fairly menial – holding cups for blood-letting, pulverising ingredients such as rhubarb for powders and the like. Yet they talked amongst themselves of adventure and of the chance of advancement overseas. McGrigor's idea of becoming a soldier, sparked off by young Farquhar strutting about in his cocked hat, was furthered by his meeting with Ensign David Stewart of Garth, resplendent in the officer's uniform of 'The Gallant 42nd' (The Black Watch). Stewart, who became a major-general and well-known author, remained a life-long friend. One wonders if the impending greatness of her two young guests ever entered the mind of the good old lady who entertained them to tea!

However, despite his liking for Stewart, James became increasingly determined to become a doctor rather than a soldier. The study of medicine enthralled him and it seems that he visualised a lucrative practice in London where so many Aberdeen doctors had already made their name. Not all, however, were successful. His teacher, George French, renowned for his shortness of temper, was an embittered man. Nephew of the Fordyce brothers, he had followed them to London, but despite their patronage had failed as a practitioner. Returned by his uncles to Aberdeen, he found himself frustrated by the provincial life. Renowned as a grumbler – he regularly complained of faulty apparatus to his class – he was also persistently controversial to the point where, on Sir Humphry Davy inventing the miner's safety lamp, he called him 'a very dangerous person!' French, nonetheless, ran a profitable sideline with a shop in the Upper Kirkgate advertised as 'provided with an assortment of the most reputed patent medicines and several perfumery articles'. He also supplied Aberdeen Infirmary with medicines and wines at what some of the managers considered to be double the price, an accusation he did not bother to refute. Thought to be very learned, he terrified the ignorant, who believed him to be a wizard, tampering with chemical experiments. Yet some clever young men admired him, among them James McGrigor, who wrote that 'he sustained a high professional reputation to the close of his long life'.

Dr French's instruction, however, was limited to chemistry and for tuition in anatomy it was necessary to go elsewhere. James went to Edinburgh, walking there from Aberdeen. Once in the city his first problem was in finding somewhere to live. Lodgings in Edinburgh were four times the cost of the equivalent in Aberdeen. Less fashionable areas were cheaper, however, and a snug little room with a boxed bed in it could be got for 2s. a week in places like Potter's Row; dinner in an 'ordinary' cost 6d.

McGrigor gives no indication as to how he addressed his problem. Perhaps by the time he wrote his *Autobiography* such details had left his mind. He says simply that: 'I attended Dr Monro's class of anatomy, Mr Fyfe's Demonstrations and Dr Gregory's Practice of Physic.' [11]

The men whom he thus mentions were among the most brilliant lecturers of their day. Monro 'Secundus', as his name implies, was the second of the three generations of Professors of Anatomy in Edinburgh who were world famous. Professor Struthers, in his book on the Edinburgh Medical School, wrote that 'Monro "Secundus" had a clearness of style that thrilled his audience like an electric shock.' [12] Professor James Gregory, a fellow Aberdonian, made an impact of a different kind. A household name, thanks to his invention of Gregory's mixture (a laxative compounded largely of rhubarb), he was a big, heavy-featured man, with a wig tied with a ribbon in a queue on top of his large head. He loved nothing more than an argument, which sometimes got out of hand. On one occasion he gave a fellow physician a good thrashing with his gold-headed cane and the man took him to law. Nonetheless, despite his temper and abusive language, Dr Gregory was greatly beloved. 'His mind was sagacious and straightforward, he was forgiving of injuries, of broad and enlightened views, and scorned like smaller persons to court public favour.' [13]

The young McGrigor at this stage was a bit of a firebrand himself, as he openly admits, although he adds that his ideas were 'entirely changed after my entering the army.' His political involvement gave way to his increasing immersion in his work to the point where he appears to have had a physical, and perhaps partly mental, breakdown, brought on by overwork.

He returned home to Aberdeen where, during the months of enforced idleness, he began to plan constructively on ideas forming in his mind. While in Edinburgh he had been elected a member of the Medical and Chirurgical Society and now, together with James Robertson, his greatest friend, McGrigor assembled a meeting of the students in Aberdeen to suggest the formation of a medical society of the city. Thus, twelve young men, aged from seventeen to twenty, founded the Aberdeen Medical Society on 14 December 1789. They met first in the houses of their parents, all substantial burghers of the city. Colquhoun McGrigor, James's father, was particularly supportive, being not only a stocking and general merchant but a founding director of the Gaelic Church.

James McGrigor and James Robertson, as the instigators of the society, laid down a set of rules. The members were to meet on Tuesdays, at three in the afternoon. Each of the twelve was to be president for a week at a time. A paper on some medical subject was to be read every evening and criticised. A seal designed by James McGrigor, showing the head of Hippocrates surrounded by the date, 14 December 1789, and the words 'Societas Aberdoniae Medicae' with 'Res Medica Floreat' underneath, was engraved on copper by an artificer in King's College.

They could not afford a library but seven of the members pledged themselves to lend a book every fortnight until one could be formed. The office of treasurer was permanent. The price of membership was fixed at half-a-crown annually and the funds of the Society boosted by an ingenious method of fines. Absence at a meeting cost sixpence while the president had to cough up a halfpenny for each minute he was late. Making faces, or in any way upsetting the president, incurred a penalty, and finally, when all else failed, the members had to pay equal shares until the necessary money was raised.

The subject of the first meeting was 'How far is the knowledge of mathematics consistent with and useful to medicine?' (preses Alexander Mitchell; proposer James Robertson). This was followed by 'Is an accurate knowledge of anatomy absolutely essential to medicine?' (as suggested by James McGrigor).

Some books being given for a library, the librarian, John Grant, was entrusted with three volumes of the writings of Sydenham and the works of Hippocrates in Greek and Latin as well as other volumes. Gifts for a museum then also appeared: the skeleton of a dried snake from James McGrigor, and 'a polypus from Janet Carnegie's heart' presented by the Infirmary.[14]

The Minutes of all the first meetings, in the upright handwriting of James McGrigor, are in the Library of the Medico-Chirurgical Society of Aberdeen. They show that the serious discussions sometimes ended in fun. The birthday of the celebrated surgeon, John Hunter, was an ideal excuse for celebration and McGrigor writes: 'We proceeded to the tavern, where we spent the greater part of the evening in mirth and jollity.'

Brothers William and John Hunter were among the first to raise the profession of surgery to one of eminent respect. John Hunter, younger of the two, and McGrigor's idol in his student days, had been an army surgeon in Belleisle and in Portugal during the Seven Years' War. The experience he gained there resulted in his treatise on 'The Blood, Inflammation and Gunshot Wounds' published after his untimely death from the then common disease of syphilis in 1793.

As the Medical Society became more popular, another twelve members joined in the spring of 1790 and, perhaps at the request of parents, kept awake on Tuesday nights, it was decided to approach Marischal College for accommodation. Professor Beattie had already allowed the Literary Society to use his classroom and now that gentle philosopher, first of the academics to encourage the medical students, gave them the regular use of his classroom for a period of eighteen months. What went on in that room can only be guessed at now. It has to be remembered that before x-rays were invented the only possible way in which any knowledge of anatomy and subsequent attempts at healing could be gained was by the dissection of bodies, regardless of how they were obtained. Mrs Ella Hill Burton Rodger, in her book, *Aberdeen Doctors*, claims that James McGrigor actually incited the medical students to the crime of body-snatching . . . 'On one occasion the Aberdeen students, who had an efficient means of digging up a coffin quickly, got a great shock on opening the coffin as they found that the mortal remains were those of about the last person they had wished to practice on. Him they quickly reburied without mutilation.' (Tantalisingly, she does not explain the identity of the deceased!)

In London, largely at the instigation of the fashionable surgeon, Sir Astley Cooper, the violation of graves had become a lucrative trade. The professional resurrectionist, having prized the corpse from the grave with a crowbar at dead of night, usually put the body, doubled up, into a square of green-baize cloth, crossed and tied the corners, and left it in some ruined building or other secret place until morning when, dressed as a porter, he carried it through the crowded streets to the hospital. The horrible trade was well paid – bodies sold from £10 to £20 depending on the freshness of their state – but it was also dangerous on account of the public hatred it caused.

In Aberdeen Infirmary, where a dog was dissected every week, the professor of medicine sent out his students to do the ghastly work. It had to be kept a close secret. Payment was made by the Medical Society which safeguarded itself with the motion that 'a person who can betray the secrets of the Society forfeits his word of honour, and ungratefully renders obnoxious to the laws of this country those persons who had risked their own lives partly for his improvement and instruction.' Expulsion from the Society followed betrayal but nothing remains to indicate that such punishment ever had to be enforced.

Many years later, Sir James, as he had then become, wrote of his own amazement at the success of the institution he had founded when a fairly impecunious student aged eighteen. Academics and other men of importance in Aberdeen were asked to become honorary members of the Society. Professor Beattie and William Livingstone, who had just become professor of medicine at Marischal College, were among those honoured to accept. Nonetheless George French, now professor of chemistry, contrary as ever, resolutely refused. The cantankerous former physician to the County Infirmary, despite his own failure in London, now urged his former pupil, for whom he seems to have had a secret liking, to follow the path of many other Scottish doctors who were forging successful careers in the city. Acting, therefore, upon the doctor's advice, and also influenced by his mother (who probably on account of his health did not wish him to go abroad) James McGrigor decided to go to London to find his fortune, as so many of his countrymen had done.

Before leaving, he made a farewell speech to the Medical Society, which, according to the minutes: 'if the author had done it justice by a good delivery, might have brought tears to our eyes'. But McGrigor, for all his brilliant gifts, was never a good speaker. Shy by nature, words were inclined to fail him when faced with a public address. Later, when as a major witness he was cross-examined before parliament during the public enquiry into the Walcheren disaster, the strain of speaking affected him to the point where he simply 'dried up'.

The Medical Society, probably at their founder's instigation, voted to confer honorary membership upon the Reverend Mr Wynne, private chaplain of the Prince of Wales (later George IV). Mindful of the Society's poverty, James volunteered to deliver it to save the price of a stamp.

He graphically describes the voyage that involved the near loss of his precious box of bones, so it is, therefore, all the more surprising that Sir James's *Autobiography* makes no mention of the loss of his mother, who died on 22 December 1792, just a few months before he set sail for London. Perhaps he felt that it was too personal a family matter to relate, or he may have not wished to recall it even after many years had passed. His father remarried in 1785, but his second wife, a widow named Grizel Gordon, died a year later. Colquhoun himself died on 1 January 1797. He is buried in St Nicholas Churchyard, Aberdeen, in the shadow of the Gaelic Chapel which he founded, and where his second son, Robert, who inherited the family business, followed him a year later, aged only twenty-seven.[15]

Arriving in London, James found that his letters of introduction from Scotland were of little use. A few people befriended him but none offered employment in a practice as he had hoped.

Eventually, it would seem in desperation, he apprenticed himself to an elderly surgeon in Islington. Writing to his uncle David Grant in Aberdeen, on 14 September 1793, he tells him 'I am now situated as assistant to the surgeon one-and-a-half miles from London and a very pretty village. He is an old gentleman and the first man in this place . . . but what with ye gout . . . he lets a good deal of his practice evolve on me. The salary with bed, board, and lodging which he allows me is reckoned equal to be £70 per annum – not much here.'[16] The old doctor in his top hat and frock coat, bad tempered from his gout, was soon to loose the assistant who thought himself overworked.

The War of the First Coalition had broken out with France. McGrigor's friends in London, some of whom came from Aberdeen, were talking excitedly of enlistment and the chance to gain rapid promotion in the armed forces abroad. He, too, longed for a life of adventure and 'stimulated by everything around me, I determined on serving as a medical officer in the army'. Thus, largely through circumstance, his choice of career was made.

NOTES

1 McGregor, A. M., *A History of Clan Gregor*, Vol. II, p. 37.

2 *Register of the Privy Council of Scotland*, 2nd Series, Vol. V1, p. 209.

3 Gordon Castle *Papers*, pr.V.a.15.

4 *The Lordship of Strathavon*, p. 152.

5 For information on the Royal College of Surgeons, see Collins' *Encyclopaedia of Scotland*, edited by John and Julia Keay.

6 Keith, A., *A Thousand Years of Aberdeen*, p. 307.

7 Ibid, p. 336.

8 McGrigor, Sir James, *Autobiography* (1861), p. 2.

9 Hill Burton Rodger, E., *Aberdeen Doctors*, p. 51.

10 McGrigor Family Letters.

11 McGrigor, Sir James, *Autobiography* (1861), p. 2.

12 Hill Burton Rodger, E., *Aberdeen Doctors*, p. 103.

13 Ibid. p. 104.

14 Ibid. p. 58.

15 A. S. Maxwell, *Monumental Inscriptions: St Nicholas, Aberdeen* (Aberdeen, 1792), Section D, p. 6, entry 27.

16 McGrigor Family Letters.

Sir James McGrigor
(painted by Andrew Geddes A.R.A.,
reproduced by kind permission of the Aberdeen Medico-Chirurgical Society)

The Autobiography

of

Sir James McGrigor

(b. 26 March 1770 – d. 2 April 1858)

CHAPTER 1

I am the eldest of three sons of Colquhoun McGrigor, Esq, a merchant of Aberdeen, by Ann the daughter of Lewis Grant, Esq, of Lethendry in Strathspey, Inverness-shire, where I was born. My brother Robert followed his father's occupation and my youngest brother, Lieut. Colonel McGrigor, who served with distinction in the East and West Indies, America, and other quarters, particularly at the capture of Seringapatam, died at Nottingham in 1841.

I was educated at the Grammar School, Aberdeen, which had at that time a high reputation as one of the first of the public schools in Scotland; Dr Dun being the Rector, with able teachers for the five classes. At the conclusion of the five years' course, there was an examination and on that occasion an event occurred, the most joyous to me, as I often recounted, of any in my life. In the evening of the day, the whole of the pupils were assembled in the public hall, in the presence of the Lord Provost, Magistrates, Professors of the University and the clergy of the city, and my name being called aloud by the Rector he announced to me, in a Latin oration, that the first prize had been awarded to me. He then presented me to the Lord Provost, who complimented me in a Scottish address; and I left the public school amidst the applause of the assembly; from which I ran to my father's house, at a quicker pace than ever I ran in the course of my life, to announce my success in having obtained the highest prize in the fifth or high class. It has since been my good fortune to obtain various distinctions and honours, but with none of them have I been more elated than by the prize which I then gained, when it was presented to me by the Lord Provost. My heart did not swell with more pride when, nearly half a century afterwards, I was elected Lord Rector of my Alma Mater and of the University of Aberdeen.

Having pursued my studies during the usual period of five years at the Grammar School, I entered the first, or Greek class, of Marischal College. This college has numbered among its professors, during the last three centuries, some of the most distinguished men the country has produced. At the periods adverted to, the names of Principal Campbell, the author of the work on Miracles which originated in his Controversy with Hume; Dr Beattie, the philosopher and poet, Dr Hamilton the mathematician, Dr Gerard, &c., &c., were well known by their writings.

Having with the fourth or magistrand class finished the prescribed course of study and taken the degree of A.M., which was then obtained after an examination not the most severe and searching, I left college.

For a year or more before I left college, the question as to what profession I should follow had often been mooted to me, both by my excellent father and beloved mother.

Marischal College, Aberdeen. The obelisk to Sir James McGrigor (foreground) is now in Duthie Park (painted by James Giles, reproduced by kind permission of Aberdeen University)

Although it was the wish, and I believe the earnest desire of my father, that I should follow his profession and succeed him in it as a general merchant; yet as I evinced a disinclination to it, he readily fell in with my excellent and amiable mother's advice not to urge me.

Of my early associates and friends a large proportion had entered on the study of medicine. With these young men I spent much of my time; I accompanied them to the Royal Infirmary and, as their books fell in my way, I felt much interest in medicine and more especially in works on physiology, and even on anatomy. This brought me immediately to a decision as to the profession which I would follow and my parents did not baulk my choice.

One of the senior students, a Mr Farquhar, obtained through his friends the appointment of assistant surgeon to a regiment stationed in Jamaica. The moment he obtained it, he exchanged his round hat for a smart cocked hat, mounted a cockade in it and strutted to the Infirmary where, at twelve o'clock daily, all the medical students usually attended to accompany the physicians and surgeons of the hospital through the different wards. He attracted the attention of all, and the admiration of some.

Although I said nothing to my father on the subject of the army, yet the cockade and cocked hat, with the smart appearance of Farquhar, took hold of my fancy and were not entirely effaced from it for several years after I joined the army.

Another circumstance occurred which tended to strengthen the impression which Mr Farquhar's martial appearance had made upon me. At the house of a relative (an excellent, hospitable old lady), I met frequently, among others, the late General David Stuart, of Garth, who then joined the gallant 42nd Regiment as ensign and with whom to the end of his life I continued on terms of friendship. It will readily be believed that the splendid Highland uniform of Ensign Stuart did not diminish the impression which Mr Farquhar had left on me; still I had no ardent desire for the military profession, to which I may add that, by this time having warmly entered upon the study of medicine, I was delighted with it and had become enthusiastic about a profession; for I had often heard the name of Dr Fordyce, of his brother Sir William Fordyce, a medical officer in the army, of Sir Walter Farquhar and Dr Saunders, and others, all of whom had in early life studied in Aberdeen and gone to London where they obtained the highest eminence in the profession.

Having therefore decided on the profession of medicine as that which I intended to follow, I commenced the study of it under Dr French, physician to the County Infirmary, and attended the few lectures then in existence on the different branches. After three years' attendance at the infirmary and the dispensary, I proceeded to Edinburgh in company with two English students who had passed through the college course at King's College, Aberdeen. In the autumn of the same year, we set out on our tour, a very agreeable pedestrian one, visiting the ancient university of St Andrew's and other notable places by the way, and we reached Edinburgh in a week after leaving Aberdeen.

At Edinburgh I attended Dr Munro's class of anatomy, Mr Fyfe's Demonstrations and Dr Gregory's Practice of Physic.

During the Christmas vacation I went to Glasgow, chiefly to see that state of the university there. I heard several of the professors' lectures, but was most pleased with Dr Hope, then a young man and professor of chemistry, who performed the experiments with singular success, never failing in one.

Refreshed by my trip to Glasgow, I returned to Edinburgh and resumed my studies with such intense application that my constitution gave way. By the end of the session, my friends became alarmed and I returned to Aberdeen accompanied by Mr Evans, one of my fellow travellers in the pedestrian tour to Edinburgh. Several months passed before I recovered my health.

On my return from Edinburgh, where I had been elected a member of the Medical and Chirurgical Society, in concert with Dr Robertson, we laid before a meeting of the students at Aberdeen the plan of a medical society for that city. Inconsiderable as it was on its first formation in 1789, its growth has been extraordinary since and it now takes a considerable place among the literary institutions of Aberdeen.

From the earliest period of the institution of the Medical Society of Aberdeen, in whatever quarter of the globe I was stationed, I never ceased to entertain the warmest interest in its prosperity. I watched its advancement and its success with the anxiety of a parent. By my own subscriptions, donations of books and continued warm importunities to my numerous friends, I obtained no small proportion of the funds required for the erection of the handsome building which the society now possesses and which contains its valuable library, museum, &c.

Having now finished my education for the profession of medicine, it at last became a question how I should enter life in the practice of it and different views were taken of this. Dr French, who had been educated in London under his two uncles Dr George Fordyce and Sir William Fordyce, had himself entered the profession as a general practitioner in London, but was soon after appointed surgeon to the Northern Fencible Regiment, quartered at Aberdeen, of which the Duke of Gordon was Colonel. However, on the disbandment of the Northern Fencible Regiment, flattering prospects were held out to Dr French of success in Aberdeen as a physician, which he embraced and maintained a high professional reputation till the close of his life. He strongly inculcated on my father the course originally projected for himself, and after full consideration I consented to adopt it. I did so the more readily as it met the wishes of my beloved mother, who was ardently desirous that I should not go abroad.

I may here advert to an important event of the times. While I was at

Edinburgh, the French revolution broke out, which was at first hailed with joy by no small portion of the students by whom its merits were warmly discussed, and I brought the contagion of republicanism with me to Aberdeen, where I found it warmly advocated, particularly in the university. I associated so much with those who advocated the revolution as to give uneasiness to some of my friends and I was strongly cautioned against giving expression to my opinions on the subject, which were in no long time, however, entirely changed after my entering the army.

At length, in 1793, having taken leave of numerous kind friends, my departure by a vessel for London was at hand. I proceeded on board and we sailed immediately after I had bidden adieu to my father and brother. The passage was a cheerless one. I was the only passenger; we had rough weather and with only the master and mate of the vessel, both very homely personages, my society on board was by no means enviable. One day, while it continued to blow very hard, my baggage got loose and along with my trunks was a small box which contained a skull and some bones of the human subject, the different parts of which it had formerly cost me some trouble to connect and to denote by writing. When the frail box burst open with all its contents, the sailors declared that the cause for the bad weather was now apparent and insisted on throwing all the bones overboard; but as I stoutly resisted, and the master of the vessel at length sided with me, I was allowed to retain and re-pack my bones. After this, contrary to the expectation of the sailors, we had fair weather till we cast anchor in the Thames.

As might have been expected, my letters of introduction to various individuals were of little service to me in London; some of them, nevertheless, procured me kind attention and hospitality. I remember especially with pleasure the kindness of the late Dr Saunders, of Sir Walter Farquhar and Sir Gilbert Blane.

By this time the war of the revolution commenced against France. In London I met many of my friends from Aberdeen and, stimulated by everything around me, I determined on serving as a medical officer in the army.

CHAPTER 2

Purchases surgeoncy in the 88th Regiment (or Connaught Rangers) — Joins at Chatham — Duels — Ordered to Jersey — Typhus fever — Sails for Ostend — Fire on board ship — Siege of Bergen op Zoom — The Duke of York — Siege of Nijmegen — Retreat — Sufferings of the army — Second outbreak of typhus — Return to England

From colonels of regiments, who were then in every quarter of the kingdom raising new corps for the service, I learned that General De Burgh, afterwards Earl of Clanricarde, was similarly engaged. I wrote to my father so earnestly upon the subject of the purchase of a surgeoncy, that he consented and gave me a draft on his bankers in London. I negotiated for the purchase with the late Mr Green, then of the army-agency house of Cox and Greenwood, and I can never forget what passed at that negotiation. Having heard that General De Burgh's would be an Irish regiment, I urged that as an objection to Mr Greenwood, saying I would prefer a Scottish corps. He told me with a smile that I was very wrong and that he would recommend me to go into any regiment rather than a Scottish regiment. Your prudent countrymen, he said, will soon make their way in an English or Irish regiment, but in one of their own corps there are too many of them together; they stand in the way of each other. In the course of my military career, I often met Mr Greenwood and he never failed to remind me of this admonition, asking me always jocosely: 'Do you repent the advice I thought it wise to give you?'

James McGrigor, a well-set-up young man of above middle height, must have cut a fine figure as an officer in his red coat with its yellow cuffs and collar, its lacing of buttonholes and epaulettes of silver. In addition, he would have worn a crimson sash round his waist and a white sword-belt over his shoulder. His trousers were grey in winter and white in summer and, to crown all, he wore one of the shakos that had recently become army issue.

The purchase of the surgeoncy of General De Burgh's regiment being completed, I was gazetted and ordered to join the corps then forming at Chatham. I arrived at a small inn, then within the gates of the garrison, which

I observed to be crowded with young officers, like myself, joining the army for the first time. I soon equipped myself and paid my respects to Major Keppel [later Colonel], the officer in command of General De Burgh's regiment, and I have never forgotten his salutation on my presenting myself: 'Well, Mr McGrigor, I believe you are north of the Tweed. I am south of it and here we stand alone; all the other officers are from the sister isle: every one of them from Galway. Therefore we must be on our good behaviour.' In fact, the officers were not only all Irish, but almost all of one sept or family; all more or less nearly related to the colonel; all of them having raised men, Connaught Rangers, for their rank. But I must say there never was a finer set of young men, with more appearance of being the sons of gentlemen, congregated in any corps in His Majesty's service.

On the morning after my arrival at Chatham, I was awakened about daylight by a great noise in the house. On inquiry, I found that two of the inmates, two young officers, who like myself had arrived the day before, had been out, in consequence of a dispute on the way, and one of them was killed. The bringing in of the body was the noise that had disturbed me. Neither of the combatants was a Connaught Ranger, although both were from the Emerald isle. This incident, in the house where I lodged, on the first day after my joining the army, took great hold of my mind and no doubt influenced my after life by making me cautious and studious to avoid brandy-and-water parties at night.

Another incident which took place soon after I cannot omit, as it had a strong influence in confirming the impression which the previous one had made on me, and which in no small degree tended greatly to regulate my conduct, ever after, in the army.

While the corps was assembling and forming at Chatham, and before it was completed and became numbered as a regiment, there was no regular regimental mess. For some time the officers of General De Burgh's regiment formed a part of the general detachment mess of the garrison at Chatham and officers, as they joined, became members of this mess. I did as my brother officers did; I joined with them the detachment mess, which was composed of very gentlemanly men of various corps. Among the members of this mess who took a lead was a Captain Sparrow, of what regiment I now forget, but as Colonel Sparrow he became afterwards the husband of Lady Olivia Sparrow and their daughter is now the Duchess of Manchester. The officers of the Connaught Rangers being, as I have already said, almost all of them relatives in some degree, and of one family, were a most regular and orderly conducted set of young men. It having been observed among ourselves that there were some late sitters at the detachment mess, we agreed that we would daily leave the dinner-table whenever the signal was given that a pint of wine for each had been drunk. I happened one day to sit next to Captain Sparrow at the table and Captain Law (the son of Archdeacon Law of Rochester), of another regiment, sat on the other side. When, at the agreed signal, the whole of the officers of General De Burgh's regiment stood up to depart, Sparrow, in the most good-humoured manner, insisted that Captain Nicolson, an officer of the Rangers, and I should not go; and consequently put his hands upon my shoulder. When all the officers of De Burgh were leaving the room, a jocular hissing was heard to proceed from one or two of the sitters. On going out, and when the officers of my corps saw Sparrow's arm on my shoulder while he was entreating me not to go, Captain Blake and others shouted to me from outside the window not to allow myself to be detained; and accordingly, when I had determined to go, I parted with Sparrow and the others in the best humour. On joining my brother officers, however, on the pavement in front of the mess-house, I was surprised to find them in an agitated state and an angry feeling generally prevailing. There was immediately a meeting of the officers, at which it was decided that an insult had been offered to the officers of General De Burgh's regiment by the officers of the detachment mess in the persons of two of our officers – the Surgeon and Captain Nicolson – who, I ought to have added, was detained at the same time with me, or rather, supposed to be detained. It was quite in vain that Captain Nicolson and I declared that no offence had really been committed against us, that the show of constraining us to stay after the other officers got up was a mere jocular business; that everything was done in kindness and that, in fact, when at length determined to go, they instantly permitted us, with sentiments of regret that we left their society. All this availed nothing: it was the unanimous opinion of all the officers, Nicolson and myself excepted, that an insult had been offered in our persons to the corps and the next resolution was that this insult to the corps must be atoned for. The resolution, which followed close upon this, not a little astonished Nicolson and myself. It was that Nicolson and I should demand satisfaction for the corps from the officers of the detachment mess, and that we were to call out Captain Sparrow and Captain Law. Captain Nicolson was not less astonished than myself at this hasty demand for he had as little taken offence at the antagonist whom it was determined in our safe council he should call out.

Our respective messages to the two gentlemen whom we were ordered to fight having been sent, they, after expressing extreme astonishment, requested to see us. This being thought informal, they readily offered to apologise in any way to the officers of De Burgh's regiment, as they had not the most distant intention of offering insult or offence to a corps of officers whom they respected and esteemed collectively and individually. On this offer being laid before the meeting of officers, it was deemed insufficient and it was decided, as the insult had been public, that the apology must be made publicly, on the parade of the garrison and in the hearing of the whole officers of the garrison who might be present on parade. This was assented to by our two antagonists and proved satisfactory to those who had ordered us to meet them. We shook hands and parted, to my no small delight, and I determined in my own mind that by no possibility would I ever again be brought into a a similar situation.

After the conclusion of this business, Captain Sparrow called upon Captain Nicolson and myself and asked us to dine with him on the following day at the Mitre Tavern, Rochester, and told us that he would, if agreeable to us, ask Captain Nicolson's opponent to be of the party. To this Nicolson and I readily assented. Nicolson was an extremely good-humoured fellow and an Irishman. He was withal a very clever fellow and had much more experience in the world, and of military affairs, than any other officer in the corps. He had passed his fortieth year and for the last few years, and during the revolution, had served in the French army. He had imbibed a good deal of the feelings of Frenchmen of that day but he was a man of high honour and when he found his own country engaged in war with France, he immediately left the French army and returned to his own where he had previously attained the rank of captain. In a new levy such a man as Nicolson, with the experience he had gained, was a great acquisition to us for, with two or three exceptions, all the rest of the officers were what was called raw hands.

At the Mitre Tavern, Sparrow had prepared a magnificent banquet for us. We sat long, and indulged most liberally in the juice of the grape. On the following day, Colonel Keppel sent for me to his quarters. After I was seated, he spoke ironically of the entertainment of the preceding evening, which was by this time the subject of conversation throughout the garrison. He said that there was an extraordinary report of my exploits as a hard drinker and that, after disposing of all my friends at the Mitre Tavern, I had quietly gone home, not the least affected by the immense potations I had shared in. He said that he gave not the least credit to this extraordinary rumour as it could not be true that I, a professional man, should be distinguished in such a manner. After quietly hearing him out, I replied that I was very sorry to say the report he had heard was to a certain extent true and that he might rely upon it I would never again be a partaker in such a scene as that which he now alluded to. He replied most kindly: 'I give you the fullest credit for your candid acknowledgement, and from your countenance and manner I am fully assured you have not been accustomed to such scenes and that you will never give cause again for the report which has made such a noise in the garrison.' This business made a deep impression on my mind and during the eleven years I remained in the 88th Regiment, as well as afterwards, I was noted as one of the most temperate members of the mess.

By this time, 1794, we had collected a considerable number of men and we got our Colours and Number, to wit, the 88th or Connaught Rangers. Orders then arrived from the Horse Guards for our embarkation at Gravesend for the island of Jersey where, upon our arrival, we were placed in the barracks at St Helier's, at headquarters.

Lord Balcarras was then the Governor of Jersey; Major-General Gordon and Brigadier-General Monson serving under him. The garrison of Jersey consisted of the Buffs or 3rd Foot, the 63rd, a regiment of Fencibles and another regiment, the name of which I forget.

I here first had the pleasure of meeting with Dr Robert Jackson, surgeon of the Buffs; a very able man and celebrated as the writer of many of the best works on military surgery, and on the constitution and organisation of armies. Dr Cormac, of the 63rd Regiment, was likewise an old and experienced officer.

When we arrived in Jersey it was in the heat of the most bloody part of the French revolution, when Robespierre was in full sway and the island teemed with French exiles: boats coming over daily from the opposite coast with fugitives, male and female, and no boat arrived without bringing accounts of fresh victims to the guillotine – frequently the husbands, brothers, fathers or sisters of some of the unfortunate refugees who watched the arrivals from France.

I remember a pretty, engaging Frenchwoman, one of the numerous female refugees whom we had in the island at that time, a Marquise, who was in the society of the officers' ladies of the Connaught Rangers or 88th Regiment. One of the boats which arrived from Granville, among other accounts of a deplorable nature, brought that of the death of this lady's husband, who had fallen by the guillotine. On first hearing the sad tidings, the grief of the Marquise was excessive; she was inconsolable. The ladies of our officers, uninvited, went to her lodging and some of them remained constantly with her. At this time the Lieut. Governor was about to give a grand ball to all the fashionables of the island, to the military and to the chief of the French refugees. Some time before receiving the account of her husband having been guillotined, the Marquise had received a card of invitation from the Governor and had accepted the invitation. She not a little astonished the ladies who visited her for consolation by asking them on the third day after she had received accounts of the Marquise being guillotined, 'if it would be proper for her to go to the Governor's ball in mourning.'

At this time typhus fever prevailed to some extent in the 88th Regiment. It may be said to have been a prevalent disease in the army, more especially in all the new levies. We carried much of this formidable disease with us from Chatham, where it was prevalent and fatal in a high degree. The 88th Regiment soon became overwhelmed with it in Jersey.

The loss to the British army from this disease during the first year of the war must have amounted to some thousands. The treatment of it at that time differed much from that now pursued. At length, I was attacked with the disease myself and had it in its severest form. I had abundance of medical attendance, for my friend Dr Jackson, with all the medical officers in Jersey, visited me. I was for several days insensible and the earliest thing I recollected was great soreness from blisters which had been applied to my head, neck and legs, together with great prostration of strength. I was on the most friendly terms with every officer in the corps and a great favourite with the soldiers, which was evinced by one incident that strongly affected me. My extreme state of debility continuing and convalescence being slow, it was determined by my medical friends who attended me that I should be removed from my lodgings at St Helier's into the country. Quarters were accordingly engaged for me about a mile out of town. A difficulty, however, arose as to how I should be removed for my debility was extreme. I was not only still confined to my bed but unable to move in bed without the assistance of my servant and an orderly, who both slept in the room where I lay, one of them sitting up in turn. At length, it was determined that I should be placed at my length in a kind of case, with a framework made to hold my bedding. The soldiers, however, hearing of this, said they could carry me in the framework much more easily than I could be drawn and they expressed as much solicitude to carry 'the doctor' that their plan was acceded to and I was carried by them to my new abode in the country; the poor fellows exerting themselves to do so with the most ease to me.

In my country residence I was daily gaining strength, and had begun to sit up in an armchair, when an order arrived from England for the corps to embark for Ostend.

I was anything but fit to proceed on service and it was decided that I should remain in Jersey with some sick officers and, I believe, upwards of one hundred men unable to proceed and unfit for duty. This occasioned me much distress, my desire to accompany the regiment being unconquerable and, at length, by entreaty, and feeling assured that if left behind I should die, Colonel Keppel was prevailed upon to permit my embarkation with the regiment although, from the state I was in, it was plain I could be of no service as a medical officer for a long time to come. However, I was carried on board one of the transports and from that day, what from sea air and the excitement of going on actual service, I daily gained strength in an extraordinary degree; so much so that one day, when all the transports of our little fleet were becalmed and when the officers in the different small vessels were visiting each other, I accompanied three of the officers in our transport on their visit to another transport. During this visit an occurrence took place that made us repent paying it and determined me for ever after to confine my visiting to terra firma. It was no other than while we were at dinner with our friends in their cabin the alarm was given that the ship was on fire. We all jumped up from table and ran upon deck where everything was confusion. About 150 soldiers, who were on board with their wives and children, ran upon deck, the latter all screaming. A volume of smoke was seen issuing from the steerage, in the place where the sailors slept. Our captain, who was not gifted with much presence of mind, exclaimed we should all be in eternity in less than five minutes for his powder was immediately under the place whence the smoke came. This intelligence startled us all. The soldiers instantly ran to the sides of the ship, many of them to cling on outside, and not a few went to the rigging. While the utmost state of confusion prevailed on board, the mate of the vessel, an undaunted and rough, though a most shrewd fellow, threw himself down the place whence the smoke issued. In an instant after, he threw up blankets, pillows and flock mattresses, all smoking; indeed, some of them ignited. He then shouted for buckets of water to be handed down to him as speedily as possible, which was done by the sailors. He then led up a sailor in a state of stupefaction. It appeared that this man, after coming off his watch, had lain over his berth, taken a pipe with him and smoked till he fell asleep. The lighted pipe, as it would appear, had fallen out of his mouth upon some straw when he fell asleep, which, when lighted, had set the blankets and all the furniture of the bed in a state of combustion. No doubt, when the whole got into this state, the volume of smoke in his confined berth brought on a state of stupor and would in no long time have proved fatal to him. On examination, we found the lower wooden part of the berth quite warm underneath and at no great distance was the small magazine of powder of the vessel. This evinced the awful situation every soul on board would have been in, if they had not been rescued by the mate's timely presence of mind. While this was going on a cry ran through the soldiers that every one should save himself by going overboard and all those who could swim were casting off their clothes for that purpose, but the officers went among the men and by their exertions prevented them from leaping overboard. The confusion on board was seen by all the vessels of our convoy, which were pretty close together and we hoisted signals of distress, but as those in the vessels saw the ship was on fire, they thought it possible she would blow up. Therefore, instead of sending boats to our assistance, all the transports sheered off from us, fearful of the effects of our blowing up upon themselves.

We were in the situation of the hunted stag, deserted by his friends when he was closely pursued by the hounds. A considerable time elapsed before order could be restored on board. We then prepared to return to our own vessel, all of us resolved never again to pay visits at sea. Before our departure, along with our brother officers on board, we agreed to make a handsome present to the intrepid mate of the vessel.

This story, while amusing, also illustrates the fact that, amazing as it now may seem, some soldiers' wives and children followed their men even to battlefields abroad. The women were apparently so valuable, as unpaid nurses and cooks, that if widowed they were likely to re-marry sometimes within twenty-four hours.

After rather a long passage, we went up the Schelde, passing Flushing, to Bergen op Zoom, where we landed. I had perfectly recovered from the very debilitated state in which I embarked. At the time of our landing, there was a strong garrison in Bergen op Zoom for, from the rapid progress of the French under Pichegru, it was expected they would soon besiege the place. The garrison consisted of Dutch and Nassan troops, French emigrant corps, Germans and two British regiments – the 87th and 88th. Indeed the 87th, or Irish heroes as they termed themselves, came in from the army soon after our landing and a curious spectacle they presented. They were a fine body of men, but most unsoldier-like to behold, for although the majority of them had muskets, they were without accoutrements and the usual kit of soldiers, and so soiled and dirtied were their coats, that it was difficult to discover they had ever been of a scarlet colour. The fact was, this unformed corps was hurried from Dublin, where they were raised, to the scene of action and their irregularities rendered them more formidable to their friends than to their enemies. They were sent from the army into garrison.

At this time, the headquarters of the British army were near Breda, which was then besieged by the enemy, and we could daily distinctly hear the roar of the cannon at the siege.

The typhus fever, which raged in the 88th both at Chatham and Jersey, had become extinct before we embarked, but here it again broke out with increased violence. In a short time I had no less than ten cases of it in hospital, and the sick of the regiment amounting altogether to not less than two hundred, Mr Nicol, my assistant, and I were overwhelmed with work.

The other British regiment in garrison at Bergen op Zoom suffered not less severely than the Connaught Rangers from the fatal fever which committed so great havoc. After occupying every place that could be obtained through the magistrates, for the accommodation of our daily overwhelming increase of sick, we were obliged to seize on every vacant place that could be discovered. One day, I espied a Calvinistic chapel; I then got a sergeant's guard and, while the congregation were engaged in the afternoon service, made the sergeant place two sentries at each door. When the congregation dispersed, we took possession of the church. The minister, a very aged man, with his elders first remonstrated with me, then entreated and at length in great wrath denounced my proceedings. After this, our sickness increased; our mortality was frightful and both myself and my only assistant Mr Nicol became severely ill. And when ill, I could not get the aged clergyman, with his snow-white locks and imploring attitude, from before my eyes.

The enemy now seemed in earnest in their attempts against Bergen op Zoom. The army which environed us was greatly increased in force and our foraging parties were frequently attacked and driven in. One morning, when we were exercising on our regimental parade ground in one of the bastions, a strong party of French cavalry followed our foragers to the gates of the fortress, but we opened a fire upon them from the batteries, which made them scamper off in fine style. About this time, Lieutenant Popham of the navy, afterwards the renowned Sir Home Popham, appeared in Bergen op Zoom and, in a very dark night, conveyed the 88th Regiment from Bergen op Zoom to transports in the Schelde, where on the following morning we found ourselves opposite to Willemstad. We were afterwards landed at Bommel and marched to Nijmegen, then about to be besieged by the enemy. On our arrival opposite the town and on the banks of the Waal, a branch of the Rhine, we were met by our first Lieut. Colonel, Brownrigge, with His Royal Highness the Duke of York, to whom Brownrigge was then military secretary. The regiment was drawn up and the Duke reviewed us. Along with the other officers of the corps, I had the honour of being presented to him. He held some conversation with me and it is remarkable that, when I was at his levee at the Horse Guards, upwards of twenty years afterwards, with the extraordinary memory characteristic of every member of his family, he referred to that conversation.

Frederick, Duke of York, the second son of George III, commanded the British army during the Flanders campaign. Lampooned as 'The grand old Duke of York who had ten thousand men', he was, nonetheless, most genuinely concerned for the welfare of the soldiers, as McGrigor's testimony confirms.

Nijmegen was, at this time, invested by the enemy and the Connaught Rangers were marched into town to form a part of the garrison which was composed mostly of English troops, although we had some Dutch and Austrian corps with us. The scene was now a most enlivening one from the recontres which parties of our cavalry had with the enemy and which we witnessed with much interest from the walls. Day after day, and as the enemy advanced their approaches, the interest increased. At length the place was completely invested by the enemy, from one side of the river to the other, in the form of a crescent, the two extremities of which ended at the flying bridge. The surgeon of the 78th Highlanders being ill, I had to take care of the wounded of the 78th, as well as those of the 88th Regiment. When it was nearly dark, the sortie parties from each corps were collected together and formed with their officers. At this time a heavy cannonade was opened on the working parties of the enemy, in their first parallel, now nearly completed. Under the cover of our cannonade, a party of our cavalry sallied out, advanced at a quick trot and I could see them in a few minutes in the midst of the enemy's working parties, many of whom fled, but the greater part continued a fire. Our storming party of infantry was but a short time getting there and now commenced a heavy fire, which appeared in a little time to be general. It soon became quite dark, but although the fire of musketry was mostly in the quarter where our storming party attacked, we heard a general firing from every part of the crescent coming, it was said, from 60,000 muskets, and the cannonade came from every part of the line, arising, as I suppose, from their ignorance in the dark that we had only attacked on one point. In a dark night, the whole horizon was lighted up by the firing. I ought to have stated that after our infantry with the cavalry had followed the enemy out of their entrenchments, we could see a party of our pioneers, who accompanied them, busy with shovels and other tools levelling the works the enemy had constructed.

By and by, at my hospital (a church) where I was in readiness to receive the wounded of the 78th and 88th, many poor fellows were led or carried in to me, some of them mortally wounded, and several officers – among them a Captain Monro of the 78th. I went to his billet to visit him; his vision was destroyed by a wound in the head. By eleven o'clock, the sortie party returned, but a very heavy fire was kept up throughout the night. The injury we had done to the advanced works of the enemy did not appear to have been considerable for we could see from the walls that it was soon repaired and they were at another parallel. The scene now became a most animated one. An immense French force hemmed us in daily closer and closer. The cannonade from the walls became constantly heavier as we endeavoured to annoy them in advancing their second parallel. Their shot at length took effect on many parts of the town and in some streets the houses were seen completely riddled. The large church, in which my sick and wounded with those of other corps were placed, was not spared; although a hospital flag was displayed on the steeple. While engaged in dressing the wounded, I saw several cannon shots go through the walls, and some shells burst into the church. I had, therefore, to remove the men from the gable end of the large church which was most exposed to shot to another part of the building.

At last matters approached a crisis and one night (a very dark one) the 88th Regiment took the duty outside the wall. We went out very softly by one of the gates and relieved another corps. While we quickly lay down, we could hear the enemy hard at their works, at no great distance from us. It was whispered about that we were that night to evacuate Nijmegen and we soon heard different corps filing off and passing the bridge. A communication was sent to our colonel to hold us in readiness to leave our post quietly and march off by the bridge, but not to move till we got a second communication. After waiting a considerable time, and until it appeared to us that most of the corps must have left the town, Colonel Keppel sent in an officer to report our situation and to receive orders. Although this officer could have been at the general's house in a few minutes, I believe an hour and a half elapsed, and he returned not. As we did not now hear any more of our troops passing the bridge, our situation appeared to us critical. We thought that we had either been forgotten or that the officer sent had been killed on his way to the town for all night long a heavy cannonade of shot and shell was kept up against the walls and buildings in the town. Most of the shot and shell went over our heads, although occasionally they fell close to us. In this situation Colonel Keppel called all the officers together for consultation. It was observed that, being half-past two o'clock in the morning, the moon would rise in half an hour, discover our situation to the enemy and render an escape by the bridge impracticable. It was therefore decided that another officer should be sent to the general in command in the town and it was agreed that, if he did not return, in order that our colours might not fall into the hands of the enemy, they should be burned on the spot, for which purpose we immediately removed them from the staff. While this was doing, the officer last sent returned with orders for Colonel Keppel to file off his men immediately and to get off by the bridge with all possible expedition, but with the utmost silence, for we were so near the enemy that any extraordinary noise would discover us to them. Off, therefore, we immediately moved and the officers exerted themselves to make all as still as possible, for on this depended our safety. When I came to the Nijmegen extremity of the bridge of boats, I found an officer who ordered me to leave my horse as the tramp of horses would make a noise to discover us. I had travelled much with mine and entreated I might be permitted to retain him, for he had been my companion on many a wearisome journey. This was strongly objected to by the officer who told me I should bring a fire on the battalion. While I was considering what I should do, a drummer came up to me and whispered that if I left the matter to him, he could bring my horse over quietly, after the battalion crossed the bridge as other horses were then coming over. I readily assented to this. All had hitherto been darkness, but as we were crossing the bridge, the moon began to rise. By the time the animals and batt-horses and baggage which followed us had passed, the moon shone bright. The noise of their passing was considerable and a very heavy fire from several batteries was opened on the bridge by the enemy. On the other side of the bridge, we were anxious lookers on. At length, one of the centre boats which formed the bridge was detached and swung round. Measures were taken by the engineers to repair this and continue the communication, but the enemy's fire redoubled. By the time daylight broke in upon us, the centre of the bridge was demolished. We were marched off towards Arnhem, where we halted for several days.

The allies had for some time been losing ground daily. After this, our pursuit by the French became rather a hot one. Our troops, raw and composed in a great measure of new levies, gave way under the harassing marches, bad quarters and the toil to which they were exposed. They not unfrequently committed excesses and outrage on the inhabitants, and no small animosity existed between them. The Dutch, wishing for the advance of our pursuers, afforded them, as it was said, frequent aid. Disease, particularly typhus fever, became general. Our hospitals were filled to overflowing and the mortality among the medical officers in particular was great. At length, I myself was attacked by fever and as our retreat was now rapid, I was hurried to some distance, to Emden.

The want of system in our hospitals and the inexperience of medical officers in the duties, in which in after years they became so expert, were at this time very striking.

Captain Maconnochie of the 88th Regiment who, like myself, was very ill, got a spring wagon for our accommodation and in the middle of a severe winter we journeyed through North Holland. By the time Captain Maconnochie and I reached Emden, we had greatly revived. At Emden, a Prussian town, we found several British officers, who like ourselves had been sent there sick from the army. The 40th Regiment was there, I believe, for the protection of a small hospital establishment. Having recovered our health, Maconnochie and I returned to the army and found the headquarters of General Abercromby, then in command, at Bentheim. The army had a halt here, but it was a short one. Our march through North Holland was a rapid one, closely pursued by the enemy and disease continued to make great ravages. The strongest, worn down by harassing fatigues, succumbed daily and thinned our ranks. In the extreme cold the soldiers lay down in the snow by the roadside, over-powered with drowsiness, and all the entreaties of the officers could not make them move on.

The winter of 1794–95 in the Netherlands was one of the worst on record.

One night we had a farmhouse allotted to us as the quarters of some companies of the regiment. We arrived wet and fatigued, having travelled through a country flooded with water. The farmhouse and out-houses could barely contain the diminished number to which we were now reduced; space for lying down horizontally was out of the question. There were two officers besides myself. We wanted a separate apartment; one was locked, the other we found occupied by a numerous family, of which several were females. We demanded the key of the locked apartment; the people were obstinately silent, but we insisted on having it; and all of them, the women in particular, evincing the utmost grief, entreated the soldiers to desist from breaking it open, which our men were about to do with their muskets. At last the door flew open and we found cause for their grief and entreaties. The mother of the farmer, and grandmother of the numerous family which surrounded us, lay a corpse in a bed in the wall. In a short time, the corpse was removed, we took possession of the apartment and soon after partook of our scanty meal. I felt excessively fatigued and soon, without undressing, got into the bed from which the corpse of the old woman had been taken, for it was the only bed in the room. It was nevertheless a very capacious one and two more of the officers got into it afterwards, likewise with their clothes on. The order in the army had been for some time that all should go to rest in this manner, with their arms beside them, to obviate surprise as we were often called upon to get up suddenly by alarms. When the drum beat to arms at a very early hour in the morning, I felt very ill, my limbs benumbed and with a deadly faintness. I was sensible at once that I had got the deadly typhus which had so thinned our ranks. When all were preparing to march, I found myself unable to move. The officers entreated me to get up and stated that the enemy were close upon us. I begged they would leave me with my servant to become prisoners. By this time my friend Maconnochie had learned my situation; he came to me and implored me to endeavour to get up. He told me that in revenge for burning so many of their houses and outhouses, which in the very inclement weather we were obliged to pull to pieces for firewood, the country people had cut the throats of many officers and men the moment the troops had set out from their quarters and before the French could come in to take possession of prisoners. This had an effect on me. I raised myself in bed and with the assistance of Captain Maconnochie and my servant, I got up; but when placed in a chair, I felt deadly sick and faint, and again entreated they would leave me to my fate for, feeling much giddiness, I thought I should soon be insensible to everything and that all would soon be over. My kind friend did not heed my entreaties but carried me out and placed me on my horse. It was immediately found that I could not keep my seat. Captain Maconnochie then placed me across my horse, with one soldier supporting my head, another my feet and several of the poor fellows voluntarily came forward to relieve each other. Awful as my position was, I found that after remaining in the open air I had revived a good deal since starting.

In the course of the day, passing a farmhouse, they took possession of a cart, filled it with straw, placed me on it and in this way I was moved on for two days by a draught horse; but of what passed in that time I soon lost all recollection. I afterwards learned that I had been delirious. My first return of consciousness was several days after when, on awaking, I looked round for some time and found myself lying in a mud-walled apartment, upon a truckle bedstead. I felt my shirt very wet about the neck and breast and saw that it was clotted with something brown, like mud. While I was straining my recollection and endeavouring to distinguish where I was, my servant entered and, without noticing me, raised my head and forcibly emptied into my mouth (for I had no strength for resistance) a cup of something brown, which was very distasteful. I cried much, spoke to the man and asked where I was. He told me that I had been carried forward in a cart, that two other officers had been brought to the same house where I was, and were at the same time ill of the fever and delirious, like myself; that he had been left with me and provided with a quantity of bark and port wine, which he had been directed to thrust down my throat from time to time. This then was the brown plastered stuff which made me so wet and uncomfortable about the chest. I felt hungry and demanded something to eat which was brought to me by the kind old farmer and his wife, in whose house I was, who were delighted to see me sensible and calling for food. In a little time I inquired who the two officers were who had been brought to the house at the same time with myself and found they were two of my friends – one a captain of artillery and the other a medical officer. On my inquiring after them, my servant made me no answer but walked out. On his return I repeated my question and was anxiously curious to know their fate, which I began by this time to suspect. My servant pointed to an apartment opposite and then told me they were there, corpses since two days, and that they would have buried them but that the ground was too hard from the severe frost to be broken up.

The quarter I was in was a miserable and cold hovel, but my aged host and hostess were most kindly attentive to me, as was my warm-hearted Irish servant. I learned that the army had nearly all embarked at Brielle, a port near at hand; so near, that if I could be got out, I might see the masts of the transports from a hillock near the farmhouse. My desire to see these, and to get off with the embarking army, was excessive. They told me that if on the following day I had strength for it, I should be carried out and see the masts of the vessels.

On the following day, my ancient host brought a wheelbarrow into my apartment, stuffed with straw and blankets. On this I was placed by my host, hostess and servant, and wheeled out in front of the house to a small eminence, where they told me if I could be made to stand up I would see the masts of the ships. I found it, however, impossible to be lifted up in an erect posture. Any attempt they made induced sickness and faintness, although they repeatedly gave me wine. I endeavoured to get on my knees, but all would not do and I was re-wheeled into the house, got to bed, and had a long and sound sleep from which I awoke refreshed, and gave orders for my movement to the vessels on the following day.

On the following day my kind old host provided a cart and horse for me. It was well stuffed with straw and blankets, on which I was placed, and conveyed to the port where the shipping lay. On the way, I saw my horses, which I was obliged to leave behind me, grazing in a field by the road-side.

When we got the cart to the place of embarkation, my servant found out the name of the vessel in which the headquarters of the 88th Regiment were embarked and which was to sail on the following day. The transport lay at a long distance from the shore and several boatmen thronged round us, offering to carry me on board, but their demands were most exorbitant, indeed, beyond the money I had about me. I was much fretted at this when a Naval officer, observing me in a very helpless state in the cart and inquiring about me from my servant, ordered those ruthless fellows off and went and brought a man-of war's boat crew to me. When the boatmen saw this, they abated at first one half, then to a fourth of their original demand, but the officer beat them off with his sword. The seamen carried me very gently on their arms from the cart into a boat, where I was laid flat on my back upon straw and blankets which were spread gently under me. When we reached the vessel, which was a long way from the shore, I was placed in a chair and hauled upon deck by pulleys. Arrived on the deck of the vessel where my regiment was embarked, I was instantly surrounded by my friends, who were much shocked to observe my miserable and, as they afterwards told me, my death-like appearance. Indeed, they never expected to have seen me again. I know not from whom I received the kindest attention on my getting on board – from the officers or the men. They carried me below to a bed in the cabin which was speedily prepared for me. At sea, I gained appetite and strength wonderfully and by the time we cast anchor at Yarmouth, I was able to come on deck where we now enjoyed what had for some time been unknown to us – English wheaten bread, butter and milk, with tea and sugar.

EDITOR'S INTRODUCTION TO CHAPTER 3

James McGrigor returned to England to find the country in a state of unrest. William Pitt the Younger, now Prime Minister for over ten years, was committed to continuing the war with France while his adversary, Charles James Fox, was strongly in favour of a treaty of peace. Fox was strongly supported, not only by his followers among the nobility, but also by a growing section of the populace inflamed by revolutionary ideas.

So great was the fear of rebellion that the armed forces were increased. The Connaught Rangers, together with other regiments, was reinforced with more men. In May 1795 they marched to Norwich, a well-known centre of dissidents, to support the existing military force.

McGrigor describes their reception in the town where the very real fear of an uprising kept everyone on the alert.

Pitt was determined to subdue the French by gaining control of their interests in the West Indies, then a source of enormous wealth. The West Indian plantations produced more revenue than Canada and Ireland combined. To this purpose, at least half of the British army was sent to the West Indies to conduct a war that cost at least 80,000 lives.

Today these islands have become what travel agents call 'a tropical paradise' and it is hard to imagine the misery of men, wearing full uniform, who succumbed almost as they landed to usually fatal disease. The now mostly ruined stone forts, fronted by cannon, which are normally trained upon a harbour, give some clue as to how the soldiers lived. And cemeteries, often much neglected with rudely cut, leaning stones, indicate how many died.

Pitt sent an army to defend British commerce in the West Indies, where there was increasing unrest amongst the slaves. Negro slaves, excited by the Revolutionists' promises of freedom and equality, had risen in the French islands. The revolt began in Haiti and spread quickly throughout the French and British islands of the Archipelago. Death and the destruction of their property threatened the entire white population. Few French troops manned the islands and the terrified French planters deserted their allegiance to the Republic and begged the British government to save them. Their wealth is revealed in James's awful description of the hanging of a Negro slave. Pitt was forced to take action to save both French and British settlers in the islands but it was disease, rather than warfare, which caused such appalling loss of life. He and his ministers were censured by the historian Fortescue for causing this now near-forgotten tragedy. 'They poured their troops into these pestilent islands, in the expectation that thereby they would destroy the power of France, only to discover, when it was too late, that they had practically destroyed the British army.' [1]

Malaria, known as 'intermittent fever', was, of course, carried by the parasites of the anopheles mosquitoes. James McGrigor, although as ignorant of this as the other medical men of his day, did realise that swampy ground, particularly in hot weather, was a factor in causing the disease. For this reason he kept a diary of weather conditions, noting the temperature of the air, throughout his campaigns. In the light of our present knowledge, it seems strange that the connection between insect life and human illness did not become apparent to his perceptive mind. While increasingly aware of contagion from one person to another, the discovery that lice and other insects actually carried infection was not to be made for almost a hundred years.

McGrigor became convinced that Yellow Fever, greatest of all scourges in the West Indian islands, had a strong connection with Bubonic plague. Later, he was to compare the near identical symptoms in his *Medical Sketch of the Expedition to Egypt from India*, which includes a description of his first-hand experience in dealing with the plague. The fact that he studied both diseases in such detail proves a growing obsession with the cause of illness, as opposed to its treatment and cure. The terrible loss of life in the West Indies, so nearly forgotten today, would seem to have fired his interest in trying to understand its cause. Ironically, only ten years later, in 1807, the Slave Trade was abolished throughout the British colonies by law. Had Pitt only yielded earlier to the suggestions of William Wilberforce, the enslaved people of the West Indies would have supported Britain rather than the French and the appalling loss of life might have been largely averted if not entirely saved.

CHAPTER 3

The Connaught Rangers at Norwich − French revolutionary sympathies − Appointed superintendent surgeon of the hospitals − Connaught Rangers at Chelmsford − At Southampton − First interview with Colonel Beresford − Altercation − Reconciliation − Expedition to the West Indies − Disasters to Admiral Christian's fleet − Arrival at Barbados − Insurrection at Grenada − Shipwrecked − Capture of Fort in Grenada − Personal illness − Re-capture of Grenada − Executions − Yellow fever

The regiment disembarked at Harwich. I proceeded in a post-chaise with my old friend Maconnochie, the first stage, to Ipswich, and in the evening after the arrival of the regiment we dined at the Head Inn.

By the time the regiment reached Norwich, I had nearly recovered from my extremely debilitated state and it was well I got into health for a very heavy press of duty soon devolved upon me. Several of the other regiments returned also from the continent, and of these, the 53rd, the 2nd Dragoon Guards and others, were sent to Norwich, which had a very strong garrison (on account, I believe, of the very turbulent state of the population). At this period, the revolutionary feeling had found its way from France to England and in no place was the admiration of what had been effected in France, together with the spirit of republicanism, greater than in Norwich.

On our first arrival the officers could hardly appear in the streets without insult from the populace. At night, if they went out, they were knocked down and attempts were even made to show disaffection among the soldiers. Desertions became frequent and at length so numerous that it was no unusual occurrence for twenty or thirty men of the garrison to desert in a night. We found that there was a society in Norwich for the encouragement of desertion. It was amply supplied with funds and the members of this society secreted the soldiers, provided them with coloured clothes and money, and then despatched them to their respective homes. In the meantime, typhus fever broke out in every regiment in the garrison and committed dreadful havoc. A large building was hired for the reception of the worst cases which were sent thither from each corps and, as senior surgeon, I received the order of the Medical Board to assume the superintendence of the whole and to take orders from General Johnstone, who commanded the troops in garrison at Norwich.

At this time my esteemed friend, the late Sir John Webb, who was then assistant surgeon of the 53rd Regiment, officiated under me on my first appointment as action on the staff. Some time after, Sir Joseph Gilpin, Physician to the Forces, with two hospital mates (one of them the late Dr McNeal) arrived, and Sir Joseph retained me in the superintendence. In course of time, and after the soldiers had had many encounters with the townspeople, we got the mastery of the democrats and levellers, as they were then called, and an association of respectable tradesmen was formed against republicanism.

The regiment having attained some degree of health, and our numbers having been recruited from Ireland, we got an order to march to Chelmsford. On the order for the march of the Connaught Rangers reaching us, my acting appointment on the staff for the superintendence of the hospitals in Norwich, eased and I was succeeded in it by the late Sir John Webb as senior regimental surgeon of the garrison. I can now bring to my recollection that it was with no small degree of mortification I felt the loss of my brief authority although, when appointed, I knew that my command was but temporary. Arrived at Chelmsford, where we found two other regiments, we learned that an expedition was to be formed for the West Indies and for the capture of the French West India Islands, under General Abercromby, of which we were to form a part. After a short interval, we were marched to the neighbourhood of Southampton, where we found a large army encamped, preparing for embarkation.

The 88th was under a new commanding officer – Lieut. Colonel Beresford, afterwards Field-Marshal Beresford, who became one of the ablest and most distinguished officers of the British army.

With the constant arrival of recruits, not in the cleanest state, accompanied with numerous families, I saw the probability of the reappearance of an old enemy – the typhus – from the habitual drunkenness and other irregularities of the men. There was much fever prevalent, which I foresaw would degenerate into typhus, and I did everything to keep the hospital sweet and well ventilated. I think that I succeeded, for its clean and cheerful appearance attracted the notice of all the officers.

From the hour the new colonel arrived to take the command of the regiment, his temper appeared bitter and his conduct harsh: he was perhaps dissatisfied with the state in which he found the regiment. On his arrival, he found the hospital full and many sick in barracks. By his order, I waited upon him every morning with a report of the sick of the corps. He was always discontented with it. One morning, when I found the adjutant and quartermaster of the regiment with him, he appeared unusually out of humour. He neither noticed the bow I made on my entrance, nor desired me to be seated. After remaining standing for a few minutes, I helped myself to a chair and sat down. Soon after, he took the sick report out of my hand and perusing it said, 'This state of things must not continue; I will not have such a number of sick in my regiment, and I am sure the greater part of them are not sick.' I felt strongly at that moment the contrast between him and my former commanding officer. I was much moved and said in reply that it was not my fault there were so many sick in the 88th Regiment; all I could do was to cure them as fast as I could and, as to not one half of them being sick, I affirmed that everyone in the report in his hand was sick. In the sharpest manner, and with an oath, he said they could not be and that malingerers deceived me. I, as positively and in warm terms, denied this and I added that, so long as the regiment continued in its present state, the sick would increase and they would soon be doubled. He asked what I meant. I said that the irregularities which prevailed would occasion an increase and from the filthy state of the temporary barracks, which at the same time were not weather proof, they were a nursery for disease. He desired me to make good my words and, hurrying out with the quartermaster and adjutant, he went through all the barracks, cooking-houses, &c., making a minute survey of each, loudly and angrily calling as he passed through each for the officers of each company and giving no small portion of abuse to most of them for not having strictly reported the state of things. When, after two hours of this unpleasant duty, he had gone through the whole, I begged that he would now accompany me and see the only place over which I had jurisdiction – the hospital. He passed in silence through the different wards, but this I felt I could not permit; I called upon him to say if he found fault with the condition of things here. He confessed he could not. He did more for, when he went out, he desired the officers commanding companies to go in, as he had done, and view the comfort men could be placed in and mark the contrast. Still he did not express himself satisfied and I fancy he felt my discontented, cool manner towards him and on the following day, when the regiment was on parade, he sent a sergeant for me. I was at the hospital and proceeded to him immediately. In the front of the regiment, he demanded the reason why I chose to absent myself from parade. I told him there was an assistant surgeon present and that I was employed in what I considered more important duty, viz., attending the sick in hospital, which duty occupied me some hours morning and evening and, further, that the rest of the day was occupied in visiting the numerous sick in barracks, viz., the women, children and officers. He told me it was his order that the surgeon should always be present at parade. I bowed obedience.

Seeing the different kind of life I was likely to lead under such a man, I determined in my own mind to quit the regiment and with this view I wrote to Mr Macdonald, our agent, to procure an exchange for me into any other corps, and that to accomplish this I was ready to pay a moderate sum of money to any officer who would exchange with me.

About this time, my brother, then a lieutenant in the 90th Regiment, who had just landed at Portsmouth from America, came to visit me. He was most kindly received by my friends, the officers and was my guest at the mess. To him, as well as to some officers of the corps, I had communicated my determination to leave the regiment. The officers all warmly regretted the decision I had come to but as the circumstances which led to it were generally known, they could say little to dissuade me. At any rate, my resolution was taken. A few days after my brother had joined me, when the officers were walking and talking together before parade, the colonel called me to him and I joined him in his walk. He observed: 'Your brother is a very fine young man and I should much like to have him in the regiment. I am sure that will gratify you and I shall be happy to do anything to afford you pleasure.' I thanked him but said that would not gratify me, for I was about to quit the regiment. He appeared struck and with surprise said he 'hoped not'. I told him that I was now in negotiation, through the agent, to exchange into another corps. He asked what regiment? I replied I did not know and did not care – any regiment – for I was sure my exertions would be better appreciated in any other and that I was sure he must know I could not but feel what had passed since he had

Colonel Charles McGrigor, C.B.,
(1774–1841), younger brother of
Sir James McGrigor
(McGrigor family portrait,
photographed by Roy Summers)

assumed the command of the 88th. Nothing further passed but in an hour or two after he sent for me to his quarters, took me by the hand on entering and expressed his sorrow if, in the dissatisfaction he felt at the state in which he found the corps on his joining, he had spoken warmly to me, for that really my department of it was the only one of which he could say anything favourable and that he had so reported to the Horse Guards. In short we became friends, warm friends, and continued so ever after.

At length, the embarkation of the army commenced. The 88th was marched to Portsmouth and went on board the *Jamaica*, a fine West-Indiaman. We were daily receiving recruits, a portion of them from some of the young levies which were drafted into the embarking corps. It had been determined that one of these (which I forget) should be drafted into the 88th and into two other regiments, and one morning after breakfast, as I was writing on board the *Jamaica* – then lying at the Motherbank amidst a crowd of transports – an order arrived from headquarters to the colonel to send the surgeon of the 88th Regiment on board a transport to inspect the men and that he was to return on board with those approved for the 88th Regiment. The commanding officer of this levy brought this order with him and I had to accompany him and his adjutant to the transport, which was at anchor in the harbour near the shore. I merely exchanged the slippers I had on for a pair of boots, put a boat cloak over my shoulders and jumped into the boat alongside, intending to have got back in the evening and, therefore, without taking leave of my brother (then an officer in the 88th) or of any officer on board, little thinking that so long a time would elapse before I should again see my friends. After a long and heavy pull, the boat came alongside the transport with the new levy which I found to be composed of very indifferent materials. It was very late in the day and nearly dark before I concluded this duty. There being a heavy sea on, and the wind against me, the commanding officer of the levy represented the impossibility of my being able to regain my own ship that night and kindly invited me to dine with him and take a shake down at his lodgings, where his lady and family were for, so crowded was Portsmouth then, with the great fleet and the army embarking, that a bed was not to be had for money. I readily assented to this, accompanied him ashore and dined and spent the evening pleasantly with him and his lady.

I got a shake-down in the dining-room of my kind host, but by daybreak in the morning was awakened by a firing of great guns in several directions. It signalised the sailing of the fleet. I should have said that at this time there were two large fleets of transports and men-of-war at Portsmouth – one of upwards of two hundred to sail for the Mediterranean and the other of five hundred for the West Indies. The signals now made were for the former but, this not being generally understood, much confusion ensued so that a great many of the transports for the West Indies got under way in the belief also that the signal was for us. Accompanied by the adjutant and a subaltern of the drafted levy, I proceeded in a sloop we hired to the transport for the drafted men for the 88th, but I found that, during the night, all had deserted, with the exception of a few lame men who were unable to effect their escape. Nevertheless, I then decided to proceed to the *Jamaica* and the two officers kindly accompanied me. On setting sail, amidst much confusion we observed, as we thought, the whole fleet getting under way. On proceeding further, we saw many sail ahead of us. We hailed several to know if it was the *Jamaica* and if it had the 88th on board. Failing in our inquiries and nearly at the Needles, the extremity of the Isle of Wight, on hailing a vessel I found it was the *Betsey*, with the headquarters of the 48th Regiment, proceeding to Barbados. I therefore went on board and requested they would let me remain till I found out my own ship, the *Jamaica*.

On my getting on board, being a stranger to all the officers, I told my tale and, I fancy, I made an odd figure without a particle of baggage and in the clothes I had slept in the night before. I was kindly received and most hospitably treated by the 48th in the *Betsey*, but on the following day no *Jamaica* was to be seen. Indeed, very few ships were in sight and they were much ahead of us. We crowded sail but, although the *Betsey* was a fast sailer, we did not come up with any of them. I became at length reconciled to remain where I was, although without clothes; for one officer supplied me with some of his shirts, another with stockings and so on, with all the articles of dress in so much that, from all together, I had a small kit made up for me. It happened moreover that, by the sudden sailing of the *Betsey*, two field officers and two captains were left behind. I thus got the cabin of Colonel Malcolm and was most comfortably lodged during the voyage. It was a very short one – the wind and everything proving favourable – while the society was very pleasant as it included the late Lieut. General Sir George Airey, then Captain Airey; Colonel Toneyn, then Captain Toneyn, 48th; and my friend Mr Holland, surgeon 48th; and several other officers. I believe we effected our passage in about six weeks but our surprise was great when we came in sight of Carlisle Bay, Barbados, not to see, as we expected, the whole of the fleet there before us. We now thought they had proceeded on the object of the expedition against the different French islands for hardly a mast was to be seen in the harbour. The truth was, the *Betsey* was the only transport of the West India expedition that had arrived and, as was afterwards ascertained, the signal on the morning of our departure was meant for the two hundred vessels and convoy of men-of-war of the fleet proceeding to the Mediterranean, and when the general confusion from the signal firing occurred, and almost every vessel was getting under way, all the frigates of the fleet were sent after the West Indiamen which had sailed and brought back every one of them, but the *Betsey*. Fortunate it had been, if all the West India armament had sailed at the same time for then they would have had, as we had, fine weather and a short voyage, and would have been speedily enabled to reduce the French islands. As is well known, the West India armament did not put to sea for some time after we sailed when the weather became most boisterous and the wind unfavourable, and Admiral Christian's fleet was dispersed and many vessels wrecked off the Isle of Portland soon after sailing. Not a vessel of the West India fleet came in for a fortnight after our arrival. Then, ship after ship came in and with surprise found us at Barbados till at length the whole fleet arrived. We then learned that one of the transports with the 88th had been obliged to put in at Gibraltar and that the headquarter ship, the *Jamaica*, in which I was to have sailed and in which I left all my baggage and clothes, had been captured a few days after sailing by the *Tribune*, French frigate, and carried into Brest.

I subsequently learned from the officers of the 88th who arrived in the only transport which reached the West Indies, with a part of the corps, that on my not returning with the draft for the 88th on the evening I left her at the Motherbank, nor on the following day, that it blew tremendously hard and consequently all the officers, particularly my brother who was on board, became alarmed for my safety. On the third day my brother went on shore to inquire after me but could obtain no tidings – the officers of the drafted corps having left Portsmouth. It appears that on the day of great confusion, when the whole fleet at Portsmouth was getting under way, an officer, in attempting to pass from one transport to another, had been crushed to death and that his body at once sunk. From the description, I was supposed to have been the officer and on this information reaching my brother, he sent all my clothes and baggage on shore. There was so little doubt of my death that another officer-surgeon (Hamilton), from the Glasgow regiment, was put in my place and soon gazetted.

What strange events occur and how wonderful are the dispensations of an all-wise and gracious Providence! By what was thought my great misfortune and death, and although I proceeded without clothes or any preparation to a tropical region – pregnant with disease of a most fatal character – I escaped capture by the French and the loss of all my baggage, besides being thrown into a French prison, like my brother officers, who were most harshly treated and received but a scanty portion of bad provisions. As I have said, the *Jamaica* was captured in the channel by the *Tribune*, French frigate. This was at the hottest period of the French revolution when Robespierre reigned triumphant in massacre and in blood.

The composition of the French army, and still more of their navy, was of the worst description. The captain of the *Tribune* was one of these worthies. When the *Jamaica* transport was captured and the officers brought to the quarter-deck of the *Tribune*, their pockets were publicly rifled and their purses, watches and everything of value removed *sans ceremonie*. They were scoffed at, insulted and even buffeted by the French officers and men, and were lodged in a damp cellar as their jail. Many of the men sickened and died of disease and bad treatment. But in time the officers were exchanged as prisoners of war and sent to England; my brother among them.

Although separated from my corps at Barbados, I did not pass my time unpleasantly. Corps after corps duly arrived. I had hospital duty appointed to me by Mr Young – the Inspector-General of Hospitals – whom I found a rigid officer and a strict disciplinarian. Some of the corps, particularly the 56th, intended for St Domingo, arrived overwhelmed with typhus and a great mortality ensued. At the sale of the effects of some of the officers, who died of the prevailing fever, I got an equipment of clothes, in addition to what I had obtained from my kind friends of the 48th.

Accounts having reached Barbados of the frightful devastation committed by the brigands at Grenada (where, some time before, the Governor and twenty of the principal inhabitants had been shot in cold blood) and that now the blacks were in complete possession of the whole island, except Georgetown and Richmond Hill, it was determined immediately to send a force to that island.

Grenada belonged to the French until ceded to Britain in 1763. Retaken by the French during the American War of Independence it was returned to Britain in 1783, but the French settlers, led by Julien Fedon, a mulatto planter, shortly rose in rebellion. The rebels captured most of the island except for the town of St George's where the garrison was besieged. In March 1796, McGrigor sailed from Carlisle Bay in Barbados with a force of 400 men to relieve the defenders. They did not succeed, but in April a larger force, commanded by Brigadier-General Oliver Nicolls, arrived and drove Fedon from his fortress in the hills. A still larger British army finally completed the victory and the rebels were hunted down and killed without mercy in a way that horrified McGrigor. [2]

It was speedily embarked in a man-of-war and I was sent by Mr Young with it as principal medical officer. The man-of-war was choke-full of us. We were sadly crowded; there was not room for all of us to lie down at one time at night to sleep, every floor and deck of the ship being crowded. However, the wind was favourable and we had a short passage, and were all of us safely landed at St George's. The greater part immediately marched to Richmond Hill, two miles distant, that being the only post in the island left in our possession. Our piquets were but a short distance from Richmond Hill and frequently exchanged shots with the enemy. On Richmond Hill we were sadly crowded. I was one of five officers, shut up in a bomb proof which, at night when we slept in our cots, was intolerably hot. At length, more troops arriving, we took possession of a post on the other side of the island, whither troops were sent from Barbados.

In the meantime, I got dysentery, which then prevailed among the troops. However, I was sent round with a part of the 25th Regiment, under the command of Colonel Dyott, afterwards General Dyott. It was in a small schooner in which the master of the vessel was the only white man, all the sailors being blacks. Towards the evening we came to anchor at one of the Grenadines, and all the officers landed and got refreshments at the hospitable house of a planter. We then went on board and set sail for Madam Hook's Bay. While I kept watch, Colonel Dyott and some officers were fast asleep on the deck. Suddenly we received a terrible shock which removed them all from their sleeping places on the deck. They had not recovered their legs when we had another shock; in short, the vessel had struck upon a reef of rocks. All was confusion: the captain lost all presence of mind and cried out, 'we shall be in eternity in a few minutes.' The black sailors attempted to get out the only boat we had – which was a small one. In cutting it away from amidships, where it was slung, one of them had his arm broken and they desisted. Colonel Dyott, however, remonstrated with the captain and brought him to his senses; he then ordered the few soldiers on board to lend their assistance and to obey the captain's orders. It was now full daylight and the vessel from time to time was thumping on the rock. We could now plainly see the shore about two leagues distant. The Colonel made the soldiers fire their muskets from time to time as signals of distress. At last we had the great delight to see that our situation was observed on the shore and that several boats were pushing off from the vessels near the shore to our aid. The doubt was whether the schooner would hold together till the boats could reach her, for she was now making much water rapidly. In the meantime, the sailors and soldiers together launched the boat over the side of the vessel and instantly everyone rushed into the boat. So many were in that we were afraid she would sink, and certainly never could make the shore. Still others were jumping in at this time and the swords of several were drawn to prevent any more entering. A poor woman hung by the side of the vessel and implored us to take her in, but our common safety steeled our hearts and we pushed off without her. Indeed, we thought that the chance of life was fully equal for those we had left on board to what it was for those in our boat, which was literally crammed; the sides and gunwales being quite level with the water. It required the utmost caution in steering to keep the boat alive and free of the surf, which beat on several rocks near us. Had not the weather been most favourable and the sea perfectly calm, it would have been hopeless to have attempted rowing the distance we had to go. As we slowly and cautiously rowed on our joy was great to see several boats coming up fast to us from the shore for they saw the imminent danger the vessel was in and feared, as they afterwards told us, that she would go down before they could reach us. One of the boats came up to us and, observing the dangerous crowded state our boat was in, took out the half of us. We soon made the shore and afterwards the several boats which put off to our rescue succeeded in landing every soul safely; but without a particle of our baggage. Before night, not a plank of the schooner was to be seen.

Our brother-officers of the detachment on shore received us most hospitably. I shared the tent of an old friend, who offered me likewise a share of his wardrobe. When we were at breakfast in the morning, and while I was recounting the circumstances of our escape, a sergeant came to me with my portmanteau, which I never expected to have seen again. Indeed, I never cast away a thought on it. It had been taken ashore by his wife, the identical woman whom with others we cut at to prevent their coming into the boat. The honesty of this couple was great for in my small trunk I had between one and two hundred dollars, which from their weight must have betrayed part of the contents of the portmanteau.

At length, one of the transports with the 88th Regiment which had been driven into Gibraltar reached Barbados, and was immediately after sent down to Grenada, to land the troops at a quarter of the island where it was intended military operations should be carried on against the insurgents. I immediately set off to join them and the meeting with my old friends was most joyous. The detachment was commanded by Captain Vandeleur and the surgeon who had been appointed when it was supposed that I was lost was with them. When I entered the encampment I was first recognised by the soldiers, who shouted and came out of their tents, and in an extraordinary manner I was carried forward in triumph. The officers, aroused by the shouts of the men, also came out and greeted me most warmly. I was, I believe, beloved by the soldiers but I attribute the enthusiastic reception with which I was received by the men quite as much to their dislike of my successor as to their love to me. He came out with the officers, but nothing could suppress the expression of their disapprobation of him and I heard many of the men and women exclaim, 'Now your master has come, go home as soon as you can.'

As troops were successively sent out from Barbados and two general officers – General Nicolls and Brigadier-General Campbell of the 29th – with them, preparations were made for commencing hostilities against the enemy. A staff was likewise appointed. Mr Horn, the garrison-surgeon of Grenada, ought to have been the head of this but, although an old and estimable officer, he was at too advanced a period of life to take the field and to perform the operations which were to be looked for. In consequence of this, as the senior regimental surgeon (after comparing dates with my friend Mr Reynolds), I was put in orders as head of the medical staff; all reports from the medical officers were ordered to be made to me and I was directed to appoint an acting apothecary and an acting purveyor to the army in the field.

In the morning after parade, the officers of the 88th were assembled and we were informed that an attack was intended against a strong post of the enemy, and that the force intended for it was to be assembled at sunset and march off as soon as it was dark so as to surprise them, if possible. The effect of this intelligence on the officers I can never forget. The announcement was received with unbounded joy by all but one. He was at first silent, and then much depressed. Walking, by himself, he came into the mess-room where I sat with my legs dangling from the table and, in the joyous mood all were in, humming a tune. He said to me, 'I would give the world to be in your mood.' On my inquiring why he was cast down, he said, 'If you had a wife and nine children dependent on the fate of tomorrow's dawn, you would be cast down at this time.'

At sunset we were paraded, marched off and by daylight exchanged some shots with the enemy, who retreated to a strong position on a hill. However, they left a strong party in a position below, which I suppose we did not discover till close upon them when they opened a volley on us, which immediately brought down many and thinned our ranks. We found that we were in an awkward position for, undiscovered by us, we had pushed beyond a body of the enemy, which now fired on us from our rear and we were now actually almost surrounded. Major Houston endeavoured to bring off our men and retreat in order; but this was impossible. As the men fell, or were wounded, the latter were brought to me under a tree. While employed in dressing their wounds, the situation being rather an exposed one, a gun was opened on it and one shot killed two of the wounded close to where I stood. I felt something moist on my face. At the same time that I observed the two poor fellows dead, and terribly mangled close to me, a sergeant came up to me and, taking me by the arm, told me I was wounded and he would assist in placing me on the grass. I said I believed I was not wounded but, as he insisted, I was placed on the ground where on rubbing my face, I found it covered with the blood and part of the brains of one of the poor fellows near me, and getting up I convinced the sergeant that I was not wounded. In a very little time after this, I found the men and officers in rapid retreat and passing me. I lost no time in joining them and, I confess, I never made better use of my legs. At one part of the road which we had to pass at an angle, the enemy poured in several volleys upon us and many men fell. I was then close to Lieutenant Mc. – now Major-General Mc. – and I never saw a hotter fire. The bullets absolutely tore up the ground close to us on either side and even between our legs; how we escaped was to me a miracle. At length, another corps, I believe the 29th, came to our support and checked the pursuit of the enemy. We then re-formed and finally our little army, commanded by General Nicolls, beat back the enemy and dispossessed them of all the ground they had gained from us, bringing them back to their own position.

On the following day, after much skirmishing, we pursued the enemy, who took post on a hill where they had a fort mounted with small guns. There was a small village on the opposite side and a haven for ships, and we could discover the masts of small craft. We found that it was determined to take this strong fort by storm and the duty was assigned to the **** regiment. The regiment was paraded for this purpose at the same time as the 9th, 29th, 63rd and 88th. The **** regiment advanced and we could see a strong party of the enemy drawn up, about one third up the hill, determined to resist its advance. Very few shots were fired until the **** regiment had got to a belt of brushwood which seemed in this part to encircle the hill. As the regiment was preparing to get through this belt, the enemy from above opened a very heavy fire. Betwixt its being galled by this fire and the difficulty of scrambling over and through the thick brushwood we could see some hesitation, and then disorder, in the ranks of the regiment. A few had got over and the whole on both sides, instead of reserving their fire till all were over, began firing in a very irregular manner. In a moment we saw them turn round and take to flight in the greatest disorder; their officers endeavouring to restrain them, beating them with their swords in their efforts to bring them back. But all would not do and they ultimately fled in confusion, pursued closely by the enemy, several falling as they fled. At this time the other troops were drawn up and I distinctly heard the exclamation of the soldiers from one end of the line to the other, 'Ah, old boys of the **** regiment at your old tricks! Run away! Run away!' When order was restored, Brigadier-General Campbell offered to carry the fort with the 29th Regiment. No time was lost. He instantly put himself at their head and while we were all anxiously looking on we saw the 29th Regiment advance steadily, and in perfect order, to the belt of brushwood which they passed through in the most gallant manner under a very sharp fire from the enemy, who advanced down the hill close upon them. The 29th formed on the other side of the thicket in great order and gave a few volleys to the enemy, who retreated slowly up the hill. In the meantime, parties were detached right and left to threaten the rear of the enemy. While this was going on, we observed signals repeatedly made from the top of the hill and, as the 29th advanced towards the summit, we saw two large schooners making their escape from the harbour. We had no doubt they contained valuables and perhaps fugitives from the fort. As the schooners proceeded with all sail set out of the harbour, we could observe an English frigate give chase to them. The sight was a most cheering one. We saw the corvettes take opposite courses. At length we saw the frigate nearing one of them but before the conclusion we were ourselves called upon to act. As the 29th with a reserve neared the top of the hill, we were ordered round to take the enemy in flank. On marching forward, we saw the enemy in retreat. He had abandoned the hill and the fort. The light troops which followed them cut off and killed a great number. I saw a French drummer overtaken by a soldier of the 68th. When very near him, the Frenchman fell on his knees, appearing to entreat him to spare his life, which the gallant fellow did, leaving him behind and preparing to pursue others who were flying. When our soldiers had moved a few yards, the Frenchman, crawling on the ground, clutched at his own firelock and fired it at the man of the 68th who had spared his life. The small party I was with, who were not observed by him, then ran up and the drummer, who had missed the man of the 68th, was carried a prisoner to a negro village a little way off. While we were speaking to the drummer and remonstrating with him on his dastardly treachery in attempting to shoot the man who had spared his life, a soldier came into the circle and, deliberately placing his loaded musket to the Frenchman's ear, discharged the contents into his head. The poor wretch died instantly. I was much horrified at this act, perpetrated almost in cold blood; however, at the time, it was prudent to be silent for the soldiers had been irritated by many of their comrades having been treacherously butchered in cold blood when made prisoners.

After I had made all the arrangements for the wounded, as principal medical officer, sending some to headquarters at Grenada and the worst cases in a transport to Barbados, I was myself severely attacked with dysentery and I found it necessary to go round to St George's. The General took the opportunity to give me charge of the despatches for England, which were to be forwarded by the officer in command at St George's. I embarked in a small schooner and suffered much from the complaint I was afflicted with, as well as from sea-sickness during the passage, so that when we came to a port, which I was told was only four miles distant from Richmond Hill, rather than continue the voyage to St George's, I landed. I had, however, been but a short time ashore when I found I was in a state of debility of which I had previously no idea. The morning was warm and I could proceed but a short distance when I was obliged to lie down for rest. In this way great part of the day was spent. I became alarmed and made little progress. Observing a house at a little distance off, I made for it and, on entering one of the rooms, found all in darkness from the verandahs being shut to keep out the rays of a scorching sun. I scrambled to a settee and lay down upon it in great pain, and extremely exhausted. After remaining thus a few minutes, I found there was someone in the apartment and from the sound I heard, I concluded it proceeded from someone smoking. I called out for assistance, saying I was extremely ill. The person in the room approached and upon his opening a jalousie to discover who I was, I saw a face leaning over me which I thought was familiar to me. A very few minutes afterwards I recognised, with surprise and delight, in the gentleman who had returned with some wine that he was my old friend and fellow student, Mr Pemberton, a West Indian, who had come to King's College, Aberdeen, and subsequently studied medicine there and at Edinburgh. My old friend's kind attentions were unbounded. He entreated me to go to bed in his house and to remain there till I recovered, telling me that I was labouring under a disease the most fatal to Europeans of any they met with in that climate. Having the despatches in my charge, and being likewise anxious to get to Richmond Hill where my little baggage was in the care of some officers of my regiment, I resisted all his entreaties. He then got a horse for me but, when placed in the saddle, I was so feeble as to be unable to sit upright. However, he got two servants, one on each side, to support me and, mounting his own horse, accompanied me to Richmond Hill, which proved to be three miles distant; to me, as I thought, the longest miles I had ever ridden.

On my arrival, I found the barracks at Richmond Hill crowded with troops sent down by Sir Ralph Abercromby from Barbados for the subjugation of the island, and I had assigned to me as my quarters, with five other officers, a small dark bomb-proof with one port-embrasure, extremely ill-ventilated. There being no bedsteads, we slung in hammocks. The heat at night was suffocating and my sufferings from so loathsome a complaint as dysentery were great. Nothing, however, could equal the kindness of the officers with whom I was thus crammed up; indeed, of all the officers on the Hill, particularly of Colonel Hope, then deputy adjutant-general (afterwards Lord Hopetoun), whom I first met there. In the course of a few weeks, by the kind attention of friends and the support of a good Highland constitution, I weathered it and regained my health. The force sent to Grenada was such as to speedily enable us to regain the whole of the island. All the jails were now crowded with such of the rebels as had been made prisoners. Among them were most of the principal French proprietors who were taken with arms in their hands. Having often before sworn allegiance to the British crown, there was no excuse for them. Again, some of these gentlemen were said to have been accessory to the murder in cold blood of Governor Hume and of several of his council some time after they had been treacherously made prisoners. In one day about twenty of these French proprietors were executed on a large gibbet in the market place of St George's, leaving wives and families. It was said that the greater part of them possessed incomes of upwards of 1,500*l*. sterling per annum.

For some time, an execution was a daily occurrence and, the court sitting daily, the trial was a speedy one. When the blacks were taken, their being captured with arms in their hands was to the attorney-general sufficient evidence for conviction, and if they were of the brigand class – of those especially who had committed murder and devastation upon their master's property – they were led directly from the bar of the court to the gallows. I witnessed one extraordinary instance of this kind.

I went one morning down to St George's to call upon a gentleman universally respected throughout the army in the West Indies – the chaplain to Sir Ralph Abercromby – who, I learned, had just arrived. I found him at breakfast at the hotel in the square or market place and while we stood conversing a black man, having his hands tied together with a rope and accompanied by half a dozen people, passed quickly by. My reverend friend asked who they were. I replied that I believed the black man was going to be executed; of the others, one was the hangman and one a sheriff's officer. He appeared shocked and asked if executions were so frequent as to attract no more notice for at this time not less than two or three hundred people were in and about the stalls in the market place, yet scarcely any of them moved. The clergyman took his hat and requested me to accompany him. On going out, we found the party under the gallows which was always standing. My reverend friend was shocked at seeing blackie unaccompanied by any minister of religion and offered his services, the answer to which was a laugh from the only white man of the party, the sheriff's officer, who, on being questioned as to the man's crime, informed us he was a brigand who had fired his master's house. The poor black man, who by this time was on the platform, the executioner adjusting the rope, understood what he was charged with and, addressing us in French, earnestly denied it; moreover, he said that he had most important disclosures to make in regard to the murders committed and the combination in the island. My reverend friend immediately ascended the scaffold, requesting me to accompany him. I addressed the officer of justice – the sheriff's officer – requesting him to delay the execution as important discoveries might be made. He told me he would not and could not. I begged him to delay the execution for ten minutes till I could see the attorney-general then, as I knew, in court. The ruffian would not but desired me instantly to come down, saying if we did not, he would immediately withdraw the bolt and leave us where we were, and blackie dangling round us. As I felt assured he would be as good as his word and as I feared that on being cast off the black might get hold of our clothes, I quickly ran down the steps, my friend following me, and immediately we heard the belt drawn. In another instant the poor black was swinging in the air. It would appear that, just as he was being cast off, the poor man was in the act of speaking, perhaps of imploring us, for when we looked up at him swinging, we could see blood flowing from his mouth as though he had bitten his tongue in the act of speaking when the belt was drawn. With glazed eyes he appeared to stare wildly upon us and the horrible sight haunted me for many days. I do not recollect ever to have seen anything so shocking. In the haste of the ruffian sheriff's officer, the executioner had not time to pull the cap over the poor man's face. My reverend friend was moved beyond measure and he declared that never, till then, could he have believed such a monster in human form had existed. I went with a strong statement of his conduct to the attorney-general but got no redress; I was told the times did not allow scrutiny into such matters.

A considerable force having been sent to Grenada, the rebellion there was at length quelled. One after another, every post in the island fell into our hands and the whole island was subjected to the British rule. But when quiet was restored and inaction of the troops in quarters succeeded to the active operations in the field where all was excitement, then, as I believe has ever happened in similar situations, much disease appeared. It now presented itself also with overwhelming force and with hideous mortality, being more fatal to the army by far than the enemy. The number that died of yellow fever was four times that of those who fell by the bullet and bayonet. By reference of the comprehensive work of my friend the late Dr Chisholm, who gave a complete history of the bulam, or yellow fever, from its origin, and which for many years after devastated the whole of the West India Islands, it appeared that the fever had proved very fatal to the troops at Grenada before our little army came to it from Barbados. As I learned also from the officers of the 9th and 68th Regiments on my arrival at Grenada, those two corps had become skeletons from the effects of it and we found them such on our arrival. The disease, however, appeared in a more aggravated or hideous form among the troops when the rebellion was checked. They were numerous, too much so for the accommodation for them in the island, and consequently they were much crowded in many places; and I feel a conviction that, in many cases, the disease was communicated by contagion, although not in its origin a contagious disease. At length the mortality, particularly of the officers, became frightful. Of the officers quartered at Richmond Hill, many of them came down every morning to St George's to see their friends of other corps and to read the newspapers in the coffee house. The first question put on an officer entering the coffee room was: 'Who died since yesterday?' and almost always several well-known names of officers were announced.

NOTES

1   Fortescue, IV, p. 385.

2   Blanco, R.L., *Wellington's Surgeon-General – Sir James McGrigor*, pp. 49–51.

McGrigor's description of his voyages brings the hardship and danger of the old sailing ships most vividly to mind. Vessels were entirely at the mercy of the elements and those crossing the Atlantic went in peril of their lives.

In the early years of the nineteenth century the ships were still the same 'wooden walls' that had made old England famous and yet hid so much misery for the sick and wounded below decks. The conditions described by Smollett in *Roderick Random* were reproduced fairly closely: 'But when I followed him into the Side-Berth or hospital and observed the conditions of the patients I was much less surprised that people should die on board than that any sick should recover . . . deprived of the light of day as well as of the fresh air, breathing nothing but the noisome atmosphere of the morbid steams exhaled from their own excrement and diseased bodies.' [1]

McGrigor's increasing insistence on cleanliness reveals an ever-growing awareness that dirt was a cause of illness. Although uncertain of the realities of contagion, he did realise – as subsequent chapters prove – that space, fresh air and bathing were essential in the treatment of disease.

CHAPTER 4

Orders to return to England − Escapade of Dr Bruce − Scarcity of provisions − Tempestuous weather − Captain Vandeleur takes command of the ship − Reaches Cork − Quarantine at Portsmouth

Orders arrived for the detachment of the 88th Regiment to prepare to embark, to join their regiment in England. On this occasion Dr Reynolds, surgeon of a regiment the number of which I forget, sent a communication to me through a friend requesting to know if I would exchange with him, on his giving me a sum of money for the exchange. As I felt no objection to remain in the West Indies, where it appeared to me I had as good a chance of promotion as anywhere else, I expressed a readiness to enter into negotiation and invited Reynolds to come the following day to dine with me at the mess of the officers of the 88th. He came and dined with me, saying we would settle the articles of exchange after dinner. But, as my friend drank so much wine, I could not enter on business with him and the late Brigadier-General Kenneth Mackenzie, then a member of our mess, suggested to me that I ought not to permit my friend to return to St George's that night and kindly offered him a bed at his quarters. However, I found Reynolds obstinately determined upon going, and having a servant with a second horse, he departed with another officer who was returning to St George's. In the morning I proceeded to St George's to see Reynolds and to settle the business of our exchange. On entering his quarter about 2 or 3 o'clock in the afternoon, I found the house in some confusion and no one to answer my inquiries. At length I was excessively shocked to learn that poor Reynolds had just expired. It appears that soon after coming home, he was seized with violent diarrhoea and about daylight in the morning, a black servant, not finding him in his bed, went to the closet, where he found him sitting in great debility, his whole skin of a yellow colour, when he himself exclaimed, 'I have got the fever.'

After this, as may readily be believed, I had no desire to exchange into another regiment and remain in Grenada. But my able assistant, the late surgeon of the military college Mr Bruce, was at this time in negotiation and had nearly closed an engagement to enter as assistant, and subsequently as a partner, with one of the civil practitioners on the island. In no long time after this and when our numbers had been greatly diminished by the fatal fever, the remains of the three companies of the 88th Regiment were embarked for England. On our way to the rendezvous to proceed under convoy from the Virgin Islands, Bruce had finally concluded a contract and he parted with all of us on the day of our embarkation, rather in a melancholy mood. On the following day, as the vessels were getting under way, a boat was seen making from the shore to our vessel and, by the aid of glasses, the officers discerned that Dr Bruce was on board. As the boat came near, we could observe that he had trunks and baggage with him. On coming upon deck, he told me that he had spent the most horrible night he ever passed in his life and that no consideration in the world, not the wealth of the Indies, would induce him to remain in such a Golgotha and part from his friends. In fact, Bruce ran for it and acknowledged that he had made no communication to the other contracting party of his resolve to start for England. We were all delighted to have Bruce with us because, although a very silent man, he was most kind-hearted and a man of sterling worth, withal of an independent spirit, of profound learning and great professional reading.

The hurricane season approaching, we were hurried off with other transports, particularly those with the 10th Regiment on board, to the island of Tortola – the place of rendezvous – from which the convoy for England hastened our departure nor gave us time to take in provisions for the voyage. The frigate sent us on board a few bags of biscuit and rice, with some barrels of salt pork. We purchased with difficulty a dozen of fowls, the only stock of fresh provisions we could obtain for seven officers and about one hundred men.

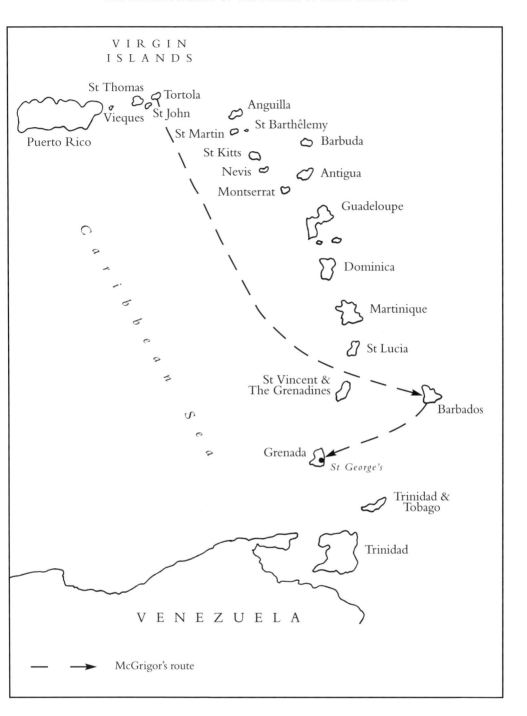

The Expedition to the West Indies, although the exact route
McGrigor took from Tortola to Barbados is
not given in his Autobiography

I went on shore at Tortola with the officers, but saw little of the island, though we saw a very great number of turtle, both as the vessel approached and left the place. The inn at the little island of Tortola was excessively crowded, officers of every corps at the rendezvous seeking refreshments, and nothing to be had. On the following morning we got under way, as indeed did the whole fleet, on their voyage to England. It was anything but a prosperous one to the whole fleet and in an especial degree to us.

The hurricane season was just setting in – that was the reason why we were hurried off without taking in any stock of provisions for the ship, and without any for the officers except the dozen of fowls for seven of us. There were, moreover, no comforts laid in for what sickness might occur during the voyage. All this was done to save the insurance of the vessel which, in case any accident befell her, would have been forfeited if we did not take our departure before a certain day, which was now at hand.

At Grenada we did not take a sick man on board; I minutely inspected the whole detachment before a man was allowed to enter the boats and objected to every man who had the least appearance of disease or debility. I was scrupulously careful in this, the yellow fever having prevailed in the detachment of the 88th, as well as in every corps in Grenada, at the time of our embarkation. However, in the few days occupied in sailing from Barbados to Tortola, some cases of fever made their appearance, but they at first seemed to me so slight as not to occasion any alarm. The vessel in which we embarked was an old crank transport of the worst description and, as afterwards appeared, ought never to have been taken up for the service. Sometime before we had embarked, I learned that the captain had died of yellow fever. The vessel was then commanded by the mate who had been promoted to be captain. But, a few days after we sailed from Tortola, he also was seized with yellow fever and speedily died of it. To the best of my recollection, two or three of the seamen also succumbed to it. It then made its appearance among the troops and committed great havoc. Nearly one fourth were attacked by it and the mortality was very high. At length we had some cause to regret the death of the acting captain, with whom we had embarked, for his successor – a man from before the mast – was, we found, not only grossly ignorant of navigation, but likewise grossly intemperate. We found him not infrequently lying dead drunk opposite the companion door. We had not been at sea above ten days when we experienced the most tempestuous weather. This proved fatal to several transports which foundered at sea. The dead lights were constantly in.

Our tub of a vessel rolled about fearfully and appeared quite unmanageable. Indeed, we had no one on board to handle her properly. At this time our situation was anything but enviable: the billows running mountains high, our cabin in total darkness and occasionally admitting water, our acting captain almost always drunk, some men dying daily and thrown overboard, and I endeavouring to read the service over them. There was neither bread nor biscuit on board. A little rice only in lieu of it was sparingly distributed to us, our only food salt and fresh pork alternately; our vessel very crank and the crew and soldiers dispirited. I ought to have mentioned that, when our captain died, it was thought decent that the carpenter should make a coffin for him. He put some planks together but, as it appeared, so loosely that when the sailors threw it overboard, as I pronounced the words in the burial service 'we therefore commit his body to the deep,' &c., the slender coffin fell to pieces upon striking the water and the corpse of our poor captain floated on the surface of the sea, to the horror of the sailors. From this circumstance, that superstitious race boded that something bad would befall us, and ascribed to it the subsequent great mortality on board and the terrible weather we suffered. The acting captain was so constantly drunk and the vessel left so entirely to the mercy of the waves, that all, seeing the very perilous situation we were in, became alarmed. One remedy alone appeared left to us. Among the seven officers on board was a Captain Vandeleur, who, before he entered the army, had been for several years a midshipman in the navy. We determined to depose our drunken captain and conferred the command of the vessel on honest Jack Vandeleur, who still retained more the appearance, as well as the blunt humour and manner of a sailor than a soldier, although, as will appear, he did not display profound nautical skill in the command of the *Betsey* transport. Captain Vandeleur immediately set to work and, with all the externals of a skipper, he began to take observations. The weather somewhat moderating, one day at noon, after taking his observation, he told us we were approaching the British Channel. Next day he told us we were in it. The third day, he told us we were in the Downs but we were enveloped in a thick fog so that he could not go through the form of taking an observation and, indeed, no one on board could see the distance of the length of the ship. At length we heard a ship's bell tolling which, continuing for some time, the attention of all was directed to it. We judged from the sound that the vessel must be very near to us. We hailed and Vandeleur inquired through the trumpet, 'What ship?' 'The *Mary of New York*' was the reply. Vandeleur then inquired, 'How near Dover are we?' 'Dover!' replied the Yankee, 'You are in the St George's Channel, the mouth of the Mersey not far off!' We instantly put the ship about, not much impressed with the correctness of the details of reckoning which Vandeleur daily told us he had kept. For some time we held on a course which Vandeleur thought would bring us into the mouth of the Channel when, early in the morning, there was a cry of 'Breakers ahead!' The ship's course was instantly changed and we put about; but on the mist clearing away, we discovered rocks and land on each side of us. On consulting the chart, we found we had got among the Scilly Islands and were in a narrow strait among them, which was considered dangerous and never attempted by vessel. However, situated as we were, Captain Vandeleur thought it prudent to thread it through and as the weather was most favourable, we accomplished it. At this time, we had a very calm sea and little or no wind, but what was favourable to our getting up the Channel. However, in the night, the wind got up and by the morning it blew a hurricane, quite in our teeth. After some time Vandeleur told us he must put about ship and make for any port in Ireland. He did so; we almost flew before the wind, but the vessel made so much water, that we, sailors and all, became uneasy. However, we all cheered up when we saw land ahead and we were told it was the coast somewhere about Cork, which harbour we safely anchored in and in the afternoon the crazy vessel was brought up to Cove. The officers instantly went ashore and to a small inn on the quay, and seldom perhaps was the situation of any seven officers more happily changed from our crank unsafe vessel, where everything was dirty and wet, without provisions or water (for even that had been dealt out at short allowance), to the comforts of an inn, however small. The constant feeding on pork alone, the only change being that it was one day salt and next day fresh, had induced a distaste for it amounting almost to nausea. Indeed several, myself included, had a horror of the sight of the pork, but fortunate it was for me, as a Scotchman, there was a considerable quantity of oatmeal and some porter belonging to the officers' stock on board so that I had dined for several weeks on bourgoun or, as it is called in Scotland, 'pottage'. Mr Bruce was at first my only mess-mate in this dinner fare, but at length all became accustomed to it and even liked it. Our Captain Vandeleur, reporting our arrival to the officer in command at Cork, General Massey (afterwards Lord Clarina), politely gave us an invitation to dine with him, but then a great difficulty occurred: our wardrobes were all in so miserable a state as not to afford sufficient to make a decent appearance at the General's table and, what was worse, we were penniless, for we had been so hurried off, first from Grenada and then from Tortola, that no time was given us to get money from the Deputy Paymaster General. Furthermore, money was absolutely required to procure necessaries and supply the wants of the troops on board, but unknown as every individual was at the Cork banks, they would not advance any. On this occasion, old General Massey handsomely came forward and gave his security at the principal bank for any demands we might make. We certainly were in a pitiable plight and made a most miserable appearance.

An examination and survey of our transport was ordered by the Admiral on the Cork station. When this survey was effected, the very damaged state of the old *Betsey* was discovered and the surveyor said it was a miracle that she had ever been brought into port. She was condemned and a report made accordingly to the Admiralty. There being no transport, however, to convey us to England, an order having been received to send us thither as quickly as possible, they set about repairing the *Betsey* to make her seaworthy.

In the meantime we removed from Cove to Cork. We lived and messed in an excellent inn, where the good cheer tempted us to make up for our late sufferings and starvation on ship-board. While we were here, as our vessel was the first arrival from the West Indies, many came to make inquiry after their relations in the corps in the West Indies; many of whom were mothers, sisters, brothers or other relatives of officers of the army of Sir Ralph Abercromby. But to many of these we regretted our inability to render any information of their relatives.

The irregularities of the men were considerable and they brought me rather a heavy sick list in proportion to our numbers. But this was not surprising, considering that they had just broken loose from a melancholy confinement and privation on board a vessel where during the voyage they had seen so many of their comrades consigned to the deep.

NOTES

1   From 'Echoes from the Past' by Colonel S. Lyle Cummins in *The Lancet*, 1850, Vol. II.

EDITOR'S INTRODUCTION TO CHAPTER 5

The state of unrest in England resulting from the French Revolution is here very well described. By 1797, The First Coalition against France had dissolved. Prussia, determined to annexe Poland, had been the first to abandon a struggle that she had actually begun. Spain was the next to make peace before becoming an ally of France. Then, when Austria also deserted the coalition, Switzerland and Holland succumbed to Napoleon's influence to leave Britain standing alone against Europe.

Sea power was paramount to the nation's safety and at this time of crisis sailors mutinied first at Spithead and then the Nore. The demonstration at Spithead was a perfectly justified strike by men whose very real grievances had been for too long ignored. Resentment against cruelty and the abuse of authority led the mutineers to put ashore no less than 114 of their officers, including four captains and Vice-Admiral Colpoys. [1] Conditions in most of the old wooden warships were atrocious. Rations were often minimal and discipline incredibly harsh – flogging was a common form of punishment. Pay was also below what men who faced atrocious weather conditions, at constant risk to their lives, were entitled to expect. While the wages of the merchant service had risen steadily for the last thirty years, those of the navy had remained largely unchanged. The government, faced with a coup, granted most of what was asked by men who, if disgruntled, were still basically loyal.

The second mutiny, however, had a more sinister tone in that the insurgents were 'rabble rousers' imbued with revolutionary ideas. These rebels, who were deeply resented by most people, including many of the sailors themselves, were eventually routed out and punished severely for their crimes. It is testament to his skill that, during the mutiny, Admiral Duncan, with only two loyal ships, contained the whole of the Dutch fleet in the Texel. Then, with the mutiny ended, he achieved the brilliant sea victory of Camperdown. British naval supremacy had begun.

CHAPTER 5

After the bustle of the first week of our arrival at Cork had been got over, I had leisure for reading and study and as usual became a purchaser of books at booksellers, shops and stalls. Paine's works were then the rage; I read them, with replies from various quarters, and I was particularly taken with that of Dr Watson, 'The Bishop of Llandaff's Apology for the Bible,' as he termed it. I was likewise able to get some of the recent professional works, as well as the cheap Irish editions of some standard works.

At length, the *Betsey* having undergone a repair, been surveyed by the navy and declared seaworthy, the detachment of the 88th Regiment was embarked. We sailed with a fair wind and had a quick passage to Portsmouth. For what reason I never heard distinctly, but about twelve hours after we came to anchor, we were ordered to the Motherbank and to hoist the yellow flag, as being in quarantine. I understood that the horrible mortality at this time in the West Indies had spread consternation and when it was fully ascertained that we came thence, we were ordered into quarantine, the authorities ridiculously forgetting that we had been several weeks at Cork and ignorant of the fact that several of the officers had been on shore during the night at Portsmouth. However, so it was, and the officers hurried on board the *Betsey* at the Motherbank, where she hoisted an old blanket, having no yellow flag on board.

After a short quarantine, the remains of the three companies of the 88th Regiment were landed and sent on a long march to join the headquarters at Halifax, in Yorkshire, where the clothiers had been turbulent. With some other officers, I obtained leave of absence and went to London, intending to join at Halifax soon after the detachment should have terminated their long march.

One hazy November day in London, when coming up from the Horse Guards towards the Northumberland Coffee House, where I usually lodged, I suddenly met my old and esteemed friend Captain Maconnochie, formerly of the 88th, now of a regiment which had served in St Domingo. When I met my old friend and laid hold of his hand, I found him in great perturbation, mixed with apparent surprise. He breathed hard but a few words, which were almost inarticulate. I ascribed this to his wonted disease, asthma, with which he was frequently afflicted, but he long grasped my hands, without saying anything, looking remarkably pale. Thinking he had been suddenly taken ill, I laid hold of his arm, saying he must go in somewhere, as I was sure he was very ill. He allowed me to lead him to the Northumberland Coffee House, which was hard by, and sometime after he had been seated, and that I had given him a glass of wine, while grasping my hands, he told me the cause of his great surprise. It was that for many months he firmly believed I was numbered with the dead and he recounted circumstances as follows.

When an account of the operations in Grenada reached the headquarters at Barbados, Captain Maconnochie had just arrived at that island; a mail had just come in from England, the bags were sent to the post office and my old friend with a crowd of people were besieging the post office, waiting for their letters. My friend Dr Robertson, of the naval hospital at Barbados, was among the crowd at the post office. After getting his own letters, he inquired of the post master if he had any letter for Mr McGrigor, surgeon of the 88th Regiment. Maconnochie, who was close to Dr Robertson, immediately inquired if he could tell him where I was. Robertson told him I had been unfortunately killed 'in that action the other day at Grenada' and that he was now collecting all my letters and papers, as well as my baggage, to send to my father at Aberdeen; and Dr Robertson actually wrote to Dr Livingstone at Aberdeen an account of the circumstances of my death, desiring him to communicate it in the best manner and in proper terms to my father. But to return to my old friend Maconnochie: it appeared he had embarked for St Domingo two days after meeting Dr Robertson. He was subsequently made prisoner and never heard any contradiction of the report of my death until he met me near Charing Cross, shortly after his arrival in London. The extreme surprise and the apparent sudden illness of my friend were thus at once accounted for. We dined and spent the evening together at the Northumberland Coffee House, and we each recounted our travels and adventures since we had last parted. Having visited all my friends in town and entirely recovered my health, I laid in a fresh stock of books, as I always did whenever I visited the metropolis, and determined to set off to join my regiment in Yorkshire. Captain Maconnochie agreed to accompany me, provided I would afterwards journey with him to Scotland. This I readily agreed to do, provided I could obtain leave form the commanding officer, Lieut. Colonel Beresford. Our arrival at Halifax in Yorkshire, where the whole of the 88th Regiment was stationed, was warmly greeted by our brother officers there, among whom I found my brother, then a lieutenant.

After visiting my friends in Scotland, and staying some time with them, I set off to rejoin my regiment and found all my brother officers enjoying much hospitality and entertainment at Halifax in Yorkshire. At this place, the corps received orders to march for Portsmouth, to be there embarked for the island of Jersey. I well remember that long march, which was a very pleasant one.

As we proceeded on the route, we learned the very serious mutiny of the fleet at Portsmouth and hurried thither by forced marches. At Petersfield, however, we were halted for three days. This place was one of the principal depots for French officers – prisoners of war – and an extraordinary occurrence befell us there. After marching into Petersfield and when the officers had refreshed and dressed themselves after a fatiguing march in the morning, they sauntered in parties about the town. Several of us were in the apartment allotted for our mess-room at the principal inn, when Lieutenant Blake entered and told us that in his walk he had met that infamous scoundrel of a Frenchman, the Commodore who had commanded the *Tribune*, when they were made prisoners, who stood on his quarter-deck while the French sailors and sub-officers rifled their pockets, robbed them of their watches and even took their buckles and epaulettes from them. Blake said the fellow saluted him and was coming up with another Frenchman when he turned on his heel from them. Some of the young officers present spoke in terms of indignation and said they would insult and be revenged on the Frenchmen for all the ill-treatment they had gone through while prisoners. Colonel Beresford, who was in the room, desired them to leave the matter entirely to him and he would settle the business. He told them they should see the French Commodore their guest at the mess-table and under the severest penalty, and utmost displeasure, forbade any gentleman there to act otherwise than most courteously to the Commodore, or any French officer who might accompany him. He desired, furthermore, that extreme courtesy, respect and attention might be shown to the Frenchmen in the most minute particulars. Accordingly, the Colonel went to pay his respects to the French Commodore, accompanied by the two other field officers, and not only invited him to dine with him that day, but told him it was the request of the officers of the 88th Regiment that he would be their guest daily at their mess while they remained at Petersfield and, further, that he was to bring along with him such of the officers of the *Tribune* as were at Petersfield. The Commodore, with a profusion of thanks and French compliments, refused the dinner invitation, feeling, as he must have done, how little he was entitled to kindness or attention from gentlemen to whom he had behaved in so scandalous a manner. However, Beresford, who had been educated in France and who knew Frenchmen well was peremptory, repeated again and again his invitation that the Commodore and all his friends should make our headquarters their home and dine with us daily. The Frenchman was very painfully desirous to get off, but could not; Beresford stuck to him and with a French overflow of compliment, he with one of his officers agreed to dine with us.

Well, the dinner hour came; the French arrived in due time, the drums beat 'The Roast Beef of Old England' and Colonel Beresford, taking the chair, seated the Frenchmen, one on his right the other on his left. On entering the room, Colonel Beresford introduced the officers one by one to the Commodore and as he passed those he had taken prisoners in the *Tribune*, he greeted each. Having their cue, they behaved most courteously to him. At first he was evidently ill at ease but as the dinner went on, and as several officers asked him to drink wine, this wore off. In a little time no one in the room appeared more at ease than the French Commodore. The cloth being removed, and *vin de Bordeaux* placed on the table, the usual toasts were given by Colonel Beresford; first the king, then the navy and army; the third toast was the navy and army of the French Republic. This toast seemed to stagger him for a moment. However, he got up, made a French speech in which, instead of lauding French sailors, he abused them as compared to English and ended by dwelling on their inferiority and insubordination, concluding finally by stating that their officers had no control over them.

We all at once saw through the meaning of this; it was intended as an apology and excuse for the rifling and robbing of the English officers when they came on board the *Tribune*. After resuming his seat for a moment, the Commodore got again on his legs and proposed the health of Le Roi George, lauding him and our government in extravagant terms. During the two more days that we remained at Petersfield, the Commodore was our daily guest and appeared to be quite at his ease.

Late on the evening of the third day from that on which we marched into Petersfield, an order arrived for our settling out on the march to Portsmouth by daylight of the following morning. On our arrival at Portsmouth, we found a great body of troops and everything in the most critical state on board the fleet, the officers having been sent on shore and the crews' delegates ruling everything at Spithead. Great numbers of the sailors were on shore, roaming the streets and the neighbouring country in a mutinous and drunken state, their language and conduct most insubordinate and treasonable. At this time it was not thought prudent to interrupt them much; in fact, a great part of the inhabitants of Portsmouth and its neighbourhood, and all the owners of public houses and of slop shops, with the dissolute females of the town, appeared to be of their party. Still, troops were pouring daily into Portsmouth and we foresaw that the season for action was approaching.

At first, a military officer dared not go to the theatre in uniform. 'God save the King' was not allowed to be sung. If a soldier went to the theatre he was sent out of it or insulted. As the soldiers increased in number, the friends of the sailors, who profited by them, appeared daily to diminish. At length the soldiers in strong parties dared to go to the theatre and officers ventured to appear there in uniform. At this time, the corps of officers of the 88th – about thirty in number – took places and went to the theatre together. A great body of the soldiers, all Irishmen, got tickets for the gallery, where there were many disorderly sailors with their dissolute female companions. We called for 'God save the King'. This was the commencement of a trial between the parties: the sailors and several of the inhabitants resisting the loyal song being sung. However, we carried it and the soldiers turned out all the malcontents. After this, the song was sung, I believe, half a dozen times in the course of the evening, every individual standing up and joining in the chorus. After this struggle it was never omitted in the Patent Theatre.

About this time, or soon after, the conciliatory measures of government took effect on board the fleet and they gave up their delegates.

NOTES

1   Gill, *The Naval Mutinies*, pp. 269–76.

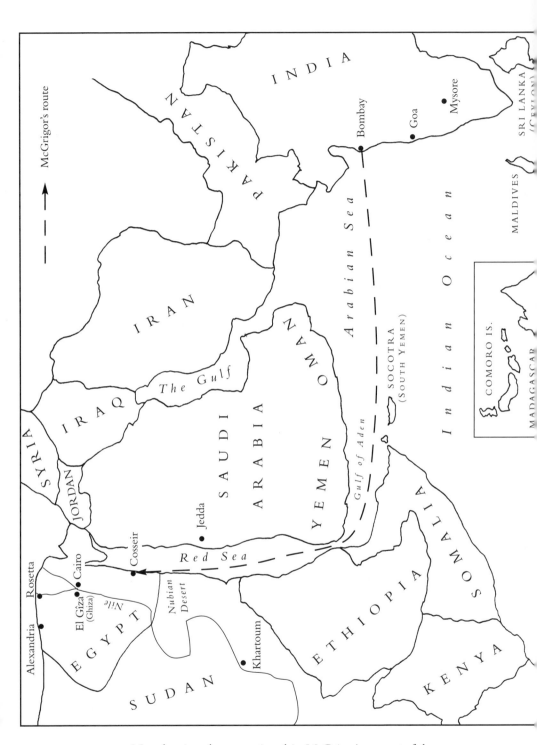

*Map showing places mentioned in McGrigor's account of the
Indian/Egyptian Campaign, 1798–1801*

EDITOR'S INTRODUCTION TO CHAPTER 6

The fact of it taking five months to reach India in 1799 seems incredible in the modern day. James McGrigor obviously enjoyed the voyage and recorded all that he saw. The Comoro islands (which he calls the 'Comorins') lie off the coast of Mozambique in East Africa, to the north-west of the island of Madagascar. In his day, they were a well-known stopping place for ships on a voyage to India to replenish their stores. However, they were also a haunt of pirates and McGrigor's testimony of the natives being carried off by slave traders from Madagascar indicates the enormous extent of the slave trade at that time.

The Presbyterian side of McGrigor's character emerges in Ceylon (now Sri Lanka); here he disapproves of his fellow officers behaving with 'too much joviality for me', although his morals in no way prevented him from appreciating the funny side of life. The shooting of monkeys which so distressed him indicates his love of animals – his great concern for his horses is told elsewhere. He was in every sense a kind man, dedicated to prevent suffering in any living thing.

CHAPTER 6

Regiment embarks for India – Contrast of the military medical officers at the time and subsequently – Bombay – Ceylon – Disease of the Guinea-worm – Counter-orders to the Red Sea

On Christmas Day, 1798, we embarked at Portsmouth for India, and arrived in Bombay about the middle of the following May. Two companies, under Colonel Callender, followed us some months after and by some mischance were landed at Madras. A year nearly elapsed before they joined headquarters at Bombay. On our arrival, we found two king's regiments in quarters in the garrison of Bombay - the 84th and 86th - and we experienced the usual hospitalities which regiments meeting on foreign stations receive from each other. The 88th had the small island of Colabah assigned to them as their quarters. Unless at low water, Colabah is surrounded by the sea, but at the time of low water it is accessible to the natives, who scramble over the rocks which connect it to the fortress.

On approaching Bombay and on landing, we were struck with the dress and manners of the various castes and tribes of the natives. The mode of conveyance – the palanquin – surprised us no less than the bustle of the different castes of native attendants.

I found, as I was led to expect, that when the regiment was collected together my situation in point of emolument would be a very comfortable one and, in truth, considering the drudgery to be undergone and the excessive labour which falls on the medical officer who thoroughly does his duty, he ought to have a high reward to look to.

The advantages of medical officers in the service during the last forty years have, it is true, been greatly increased, but government was compelled to increase them because, soon after the commencement of the revolutionary war with France, the greatest difficulty was found in obtaining those who were qualified for the duties. It was at one time found absolutely necessary to advertise for them and, in fact, to beat up for them, offering present pay and good quarters. Placards were posted on the college gates of Dublin, Edinburgh and Glasgow, offering commissions to such as could pass some kind of examination which, if passed, immediately entitled them, under a warrant from the army medical board, to pay and quarters. They had, moreover, all their travelling charges defrayed from the place whence they came. This was continued for many years, indeed, till nearly the close of the war and it was the occasion of many uneducated and unqualified persons being introduced to the service not a few of whom, in quarters where the promotion was rapid, found means to pass through different grades to the rank of regimental and staff surgeon. Not a few apothecaries, and even drugists' apprentices, found their way into the service in this manner.

I ought not to omit stating that, whilst a number of most deserving, although ill-educated, young men thus gained admission into the service, from the increase of pay and half-pay and other advantages which government found it necessary to concede from time to time and to increase, the encouragement then held out induced likewise many men of finished education and great endowments to enter, who redeemed the character of the medical officer with the army in general.

It is not only in the sense of humanity, but in that of a sound policy and real economy, that the state should provide able medical and surgical advice for the soldier when sick or wounded. I look upon it to be an implied part of the compact of citizens with the state that, whoever enters the service of his country as a soldier to fight its battles should be provided with the same quality of medical aid when sick or wounded which he enjoyed when a citizen. In every large town, whence the great bulk of recruits is drawn, there are public hospitals and dispensaries, which, supported by the subscriptions of the rich, are always open to the sick and poor and to persons of the middle classes; in fact, to those ranks in life from which the soldier comes. The physicians and surgeons of these public institutions are always the ablest men in the profession of medicine. After the enjoyment of such medical aid the soldier should not therefore, be consigned to the ignorant and uneducated of the profession; he is clearly entitled to the same quality of medical advice as when he was a citizen and is not to be put off with a cheap article of a doctor and with one who could not afford the expense of a regular medical education.

With a full knowledge of the subject, and strongly impressed with the circumstance which I have stated, and which I have witnessed hundreds of times when I came into office as head of the department at the conclusion of the war, my first object was to find a remedy for this great evil. I gradually collected full statements of the education and services of every individual medical officer in the army which were drawn up and duly signed by each. Having thus come to the full knowledge of the education and qualification of each individual, I intimated to everyone who was deficient that he was not to expect any further promotion in the service until he had completed his medical education according to a scale which, in conjunction with my colleagues at the Board, I had established. At the end of the war there was, of course, a great reduction of medical officers and a very great number were placed on the half-pay list. I earnestly recommended these to betake themselves to colleges and schools of medicine, either at home or abroad. Accordingly, a great number, and not a few of those who had previously a tolerably good medical education, betook themselves to Edinburgh, Glasgow, Dublin, Paris and the German schools. Several went to those schools to perfect their studies and to pass the time till they should be recalled to full pay; it being intimated to all that the higher the qualifications any individual possessed the better chance he would have of promotion. Further, not a few of the officers on full pay, at home or abroad, obtained six or twelve months leave of absence and proceeded to some of the schools to add to their qualifications. The effect of this measure really exceeded the most sanguine expectations I had formed of it. There appeared a new spirit of emulation in the service which gained for the department much credit with our brethren in civil life, and the effect of the measure in the advantage gained to the public service has been incalculable, for I can fearlessly assert that in the ranks of the medical officers of the army men are to be found upon a level at least with those of the colleges of physicians and surgeons of London, Edinburgh and Dublin, and the soldier now well knows that he has as able advice, and is quite as kindly treated, as when he was a patient of the first hospital or dispensary in the kingdom previous to his enlistment.

But to return from this digression to Bombay, where we landed in a tolerably healthy state, although we were not without sickness on board during a voyage of little less than half a year. I kept a regular journal of the cases which occurred on board and therefrom drew out a statement which, at the desire of Dr Gregory, the Professor of Medicine in the University of Edinburgh, I transmitted to him. He wrote me word that from this statement he had read extracts to his class, particularly on dysentery and hepatitis, of which we had several cases after we had entered the tropics.

We stopped a few days at the Cape, but did not revictual there, taking on board some casks of water and fresh provisions only for the officers' table. One of the ships, being a slow sailer, delayed us much and annoyed our convoy; my friend the Hon. Captain Elphinstone, not forgetting his promise to his brother, Lord Elphinstone, gave me a feed occasionally at sea. As we proceeded and rather out of our course, we made for the island of Johanna, one of the Comorin islands, where we remained a few days and as the scurvy began to make its appearance, I recommended that parties of the men should be daily landed and walked about while we took in a stock of cocoa-nuts, and such vegetables and fruits for them as the island afforded.

Soon after we dropped anchor, his Majesty the King of Johanna came on board, attended by some of his sable ministers. I remember that the black fellow, whom we understood to be his prime minister, was called Mr Pitt, but the others had names corresponding to our distinguished characters at home, such as the Duke of Richmond, Marquis of Huntley, Duke of York, &c. The ladies had likewise their names and the black lady who washed for me said she was the Duchess of Devonshire. We visited a fort and a mosque in Johanna. The inhabitants are Mussulmen and they complained much of their neighbours in Madagascar, who frequently land and carry them off as slaves. His Majesty begged hard for a few guns from the captain, then for two swivels to defend himself. Not obtaining either, it was made known to the officers that an old uniform coat, with the epaulettes, would be acceptable to his Majesty. Of these he obtained two, I believe, from the officers; indeed, we soon found His Majesty habited in a full dress British uniform all of which, particularly the pantaloons, were much the worse for wear.

Having taken on board what vegetables and fruit we could obtain, we weighed anchor and, as already stated, made for Bombay. Our stock taken on board at Johanna had the effect of arresting scurvy.

We found General James Stuart – an old officer of the King's service – in command of the troops at Bombay. Commencing at his table, we received a round of hospitalities on our landing. Besides these invitations to the corps of officers, I was much indebted to my brothers in the Company's service, particularly to Dr Moir, first member of the Medical Board; to Dr Sandwith; to Dr Stuart; and of all others to the very able and ingenious Dr Helenus Scott, whose acquaintance I first made at Bombay, and with whom I continued on terms of friendship for twenty years, till the termination of his life. Dr Scott was no common man and his life, had he written it, would have been replete with adventure and interest.

I gradually slid into the acquaintance and friendship of Mr Jonathan Duncan, then Governor of Bombay, who, with many peculiarities, was likewise an able man and of much and varied information on most subjects. On everything relating to India, its history, the manners of the inhabitants, &c., he was perhaps without a rival in his time. He much admired the character of the natives, mixed much with them and spoke most of the languages, or dialects of language, of Hindustan.

The kind hospitality which is shown to strangers, more, I believe, at Bombay than at the larger presidencies of Madras and Calcutta, procured for me for a short time the acquaintance and subsequently the friendship of nearly all my brethren, the medical officers of the Company's service; and long after I left Bombay, and had returned to Europe, I enjoyed the friendship and correspondence of all the superior medical officers.

We had hardly been a month at Bombay when, partly from the irregularities of the men, the heat of the climate and the thirst for toddy and arrack, I accumulated an hospital full of sick; the prevailing diseases being dysentery and hepatitis.

At length, when quietly settled in our bungalows on the esplanade of the fort, where I had built a very commodious one, the 88th Regiment was ordered, by an overland despatch, to proceed to Ceylon and it was understood a force was to rendezvous there for a particular service from all presidencies of India. The note of preparation was sounded and all was bustle.

I had to leave my bungalow at the disposal of Colonel Grant of the 77th, afterwards Major-General Grant of the 82nd Regiment, an invalid friend who was my guest and ill when I had to embark. I left my furniture, horses, palanquin and library with the Colonel and others of my kind friends, who, after my departure, disposed of all but the last.

We were hastily embarked in a large vessel which Government took up for us, but the officers were much crowded and the weather excessively warm. The wind was very scant, though favourable, on our passage. As we kept close to the coast we were enabled to see almost every place on the Malabar shore. On St Patrick's day we were opposite Goa where the 84th Regiment was stationed and Sir William Clark sent off to us a basket of vegetables, fruits and especially the fine Goa mango. Colonel Beresford contributed some champagne from his private stock to drink to the health of the patron saint of the day and I presented six bottles of fine old hock from my stock. We passed the day in the most good-humoured conviviality and there was a dance on deck in the evening for the soldiers and their wives.

Approaching the island of Ceylon we plainly smelt the perfume of the cinnamon tree. On landing, we found the 19th and 51st Foot at Point de Galle, the 80th at Trincomalee while, soon after our landing, both European and native corps daily joined us from Calcutta, Madras and Bombay. It now transpired that the object of the expedition was Batavia, and ultimately the Isle of France. This raised the spirits of all, for everyone expected to be enriched by the plunder to be found there. Before it was known who was appointed Commander of the expedition, or what staff had been appointed by Government, the officers met and appointed the prize agents for the expedition. It was even calculated what amount of prize money was to come to each rank, and strange and extraordinary as it may seem, some of the shares were played for and lost at cards!

The army assembled at Ceylon passed the time in much, too much, joviality for me. Having no hospital on shore and treating my sick on shipboard, where I had the whole vessel almost entirely to myself, I took up my abode on board. In addition to the captain and two of his officers, I had there the society of my friend the late Colonel Robert MacGregor who, being in delicate health, took up his abode on board with me. After doing the duties of my hospital, I had much leisure for reading and, the weather being fine, I generally took the boat and went on shore daily, although my assistant was there to attend to the officers and to casual cases which did not require hospital confinement on board. The officers of the different corps in the island made numerous excursions into the country in the neighbourhood of Galle. I joined in one of these with a party which went to a lake nearly ten miles distant. We set off in the morning, taking our provision with us. Starting at a very early hour, we had got nearly to the destined spot before the flaming heat of the sun burst upon us. Arrived at the spot, it excited the admiration of all the party; it was most delightful. After breakfast we went on the lake in two canoes, which we lashed together, making a canopy of the boughs of trees to shelter us from the sun. The sinuosities of this beautiful lake were numerous and we did not proceed far up. Those who had guns amused themselves with firing at birds, wild turkey and at the monkeys which were very numerous. The cries of one of them, which was wounded, were so woefully mournful, so like the human female voice, that to me it was distressing in the extreme and I succeeded in preventing my friends from further shooting them. Indeed, the pointing of a gun at any of them had the effect of bringing from them this painfully mournful cry. The plumage of the birds was superb and the vegetation most luxuriant, both on several small islands and on each side of this beautiful lake which, we were informed, stretched a distance of fifty miles into the interior of the island.

After a delightful, although rather a fatiguing day, we returned to Point de Galle in the evening.

While my time was occupied with the sick on board, my friend Mr Bruce had medical charge on shore. He did not occupy his time, as did most of the officers, in constant card-playing or at billiards. I have already mentioned his turn for music and also for languages, and the amazing facility with which he acquired them. He found that there was neither a grammar nor dictionary of the Cingalese, the language of the natives of Ceylon. He therefore set about compiling both and had he remained sufficiently long at Ceylon, I am confident, from his general knowledge of the construction of various languages, from his habits of industry and extraordinary perseverance, and particularly from his acutely fine musical ear, he would have accomplished both. From morning till night, sitting on the stone steps which led to an upper apartment of a house where he lodged, Bruce was to be seen with paper, pen, and ink surrounded by a number of the natives whom he questioned as to the names of various things. While at Ceylon he had taken down much in writing and was constructing what he had into the radicals of the language.

Of the cases which came under my care, in my hospital on board ship, a large proportion was what is called guinea-worm, which continued to infect the legs of the men after we left Bombay and I think first appeared one or two days before we made Ceylon.

The arrival of a beautiful vessel, one of the Company's cruisers, arrested one morning the attention of all: she came with despatches, which everyone thought were to hasten the embarkation of the army for the baneful climate of Manilla, from which many expected they never would return, yet all were apparently in high spirits. But the news brought by the cruiser astonished all. Our destination was changed from Batavia to the Red Sea and now all was joy – for fighting and promotion were considered the certain result of an expedition to that quarter.[1]

The following anecdote is highly interesting and characteristic:

When the attack upon Seringapatam was contemplated, the authorities found that the gunpowder was not to be depended upon. It became necessary to examine the gunpowder, to detect the cause. The authorities advertised for some persons to analyse the powder and Sir James undertook the task: he soon discovered that the fault lay in a deficiency of charcoal in the manufacture. Of course the mistake was soon rectified, without which the storming of Seringapatam would have been less successful. This important circumstance, which occurred soon after his arrival, was, no doubt, one of the first things which brought him into notice, and led to his being looked upon as a rising officer by the authorities in the East. [2]

Notes

1   See Appendix 1.

2   Extract from 'Biographical Sketch of Sir James McGrigor', in *The Lancet* (MDCCCL), Vol. II.

*E*DITOR'S INTRODUCTION TO CHAPTER 7

The zeal, attention and perseverance displayed, particularly by those employed in the plague-establishments, deserve every praise. Nothing can so powerfully excite the exertions of medical men, in such circumstances of danger, as the consciousness of co-operating with the best and most enlightened of mankind for the alleviation of human misery. Intrepidity is more a military than a medical virtue, but seldom, I believe, has there been a greater display of it than among the medical officers in Egypt, whose duty it became to reside in the pest-houses. [1]

McGrigor's claim that the biography of Sir David Baird was 'so full of adventure, that it is more like romance than history' is no exaggeration. General Sir David Baird (1757–1829) was a fellow Scot who survived vicissitudes that would have killed most other men. The fifth son of an Edinburgh merchant, who died leaving his widow to bring up fourteen children, he inherited the commission, purchased for his dead elder brother, when he was only fourteen. Serving in India, he was taken prisoner by Tipu Sultan, Rajah of Mysore and held, near starving and with wounds full of maggots, in the stinking jail of Seringapatam for four years. Told that he was shackled to another officer, his mother, tight-lipped to contain her sorrow, merely said, 'Lord help the chiel that is chained to our Davy.'

James McGrigor wrote of Baird that 'he was at all times firm and influenced less by alarm than any man I ever met.' Nowhere was this better proved than when Baird, seven years after his imprisonment, returned to become 'the hero of Seringapatam'. A prime target at the height of six foot three, he calmly led his soldiers across a ford of the River Cavery, drawing the enemy's fire. The town was taken and yet, in the moment of triumph, Baird was superseded by Arthur Wellesley (later the Duke of Wellington) in his command.

Rivalry continued between the two. Rumours were rife that Wellesley feigned illness when Baird (who was senior in rank) was given command of the expedition intended for Batavia by the Governor-General Lord Mornington (Wellesley brother). However, McGrigor's statement that, 'I was sorry to find him [Wellesley] in greatly impaired health in Bombay' suggests Wellesley's illness was genuine and not a display of petulance induced by his brother's choice.

Wellesley's claim that 'Baird was a gallant hard-headed officer but that he had no talent, no tact, an unpredictable temper and by past experience was unfitted to govern the natives' is, in this chapter, most strongly disproved by McGrigor. Instead, he describes Baird's great attention to the welfare of the soldiers, most particularly those of the Indian Army, in defiance of Wellesley's claims (see Appendix 9).

Baird's flair for administration is proved by his march across the Egyptian desert from Cosseir to the Nile, a distance of about one hundred miles. The route was unknown to the British and water was essential to survival. Wells were dug wherever possible, but most water was carried in the skin bags called 'musacks', which McGrigor says were brought from

General Sir David Baird
(1757–1829)

India, The musacks, when coated with a compound invented by a transport officer, proved to be fairly watertight and were carried by camels back and forth between the leading divisions and the rear. The heat of the day was appalling, far worse than in India, and yet Baird led 7,886 men, over half of them Indians, over the desert with the loss of only three men.[2]

The orders of the march demonstrate Baird's understanding of what was then a novel concept of teamwork, with the chain of command extending from the top down to each individual soldier who had to assume personal responsibility for his own safety.'[3]

After this tremendous achievement Baird reached Ghiza, on 8 August, 1801, only to be met with the news that the French commander was about to surrender. Orders were received that most of the British soldiers would be sent to Malta. The Indian Army, however, was to remain in Egypt on garrison duty and Baird placed McGrigor in charge of the medical department.'[4] The choice was fortunate. McGrigor . . . probably did more than any single man to improve the health of the common soldier.'

Knighted in 1804 and created a baronet, Baird led the force which took the Cape from the Dutch in 1805–6. He was also at the siege of Copenhagen in 1807. Wounded at Corunna, his arm was amputated, as McGrigor describes, on the terrible voyage home. Amazingly, he survived and lived to enjoy old age.[5]

Later, when Baird returned wounded from Corunna, McGrigor described him as 'my old friend' (see page 145) and, following his retirement, he remained his doctor until the end of his life.

CHAPTER 7

An overland despatch from England had ordered that the expedition intended against Batavia should be sent to Eygpt to assist in expelling the French from the dominions of the Grand Signor, and thus avert the possibility of their invading the Company's territories in India. Both Sepoys and European troops were to compose the force sent for this object. There was, however, some difficulty in obtaining the consent of the different castes of Sepoys to be applied to such distant service. Their officers, nevertheless, succeeded at length in reconciling them to it.

All embarked and set sail for Bombay, where we were to take in water in mussacks, or water-bags, for its transport over the desert; various stores for the service in Egypt; and, above all things, money for the army. But the greatest difficulty was found in obtaining this latter most important requisite.

At Bombay we found Colonel Wellesley, who was to command the expedition, and I, having been appointed head of the medical staff by my liberal friends of the Medical Board of Bombay, with a Company's commission or appointment in that character (the first King's medical officer, I believe, who was ever so employed), was presented to Colonel Wellesley by my excellent friend Dr Helenus Scott.

In my subsequent life I saw much of that illustrious man, under whom I was then to serve for the first time, and I was sorry to find him in greatly impaired health at Bombay. But, as will hereafter be seen, we did not proceed under Colonel Wellesley, but under Brigadier-General Baird. The circumstances which led to this change in the command are fully detailed in the *Life of Sir David Baird*,[6] a biographical narrative so full of adventure that it is more like romance than history; yet I can testify to the fidelity of a great part thereof.

In consequence of an overland despatch from England we hurried off from Bombay without having completed our water and some corps left behind them their mussacks for its conveyance.

The guinea-worm still raged on board and I found that, in the vessel in which was Mr Bruce, it had spread to a greater extent than in that in which I was, having run through most of the soldiers, several of the ship's crew and attacked Mr Bruce himself, who suffered much torture from one in each leg. The disease is a very extraordinary one and was new to me when I first met with it, although I was very well stocked with books, having had, I have reason to believe, a larger stock than most surgeons when we went to India. I looked in vain for an account of this loathsome and painful disease: I found mention merely of its name and antiquity, and that the only treatment was to pull it out daily.

A steady wind brought us past the opening of the Persian Gulf and in a little time into the Straits of Babelmandel. We were then becalmed opposite the island of Socotra, which appeared a mere barren rock.

Most travellers have some object, something predominant, which they keep in view when visiting foreign countries. The interest of some is engrossed by the antiquities of the places they visit; some direct attention to their national, and some to their natural history; but the absorbing and only object with all those in our two transports was the capability of fortifying this island and how far it might command the straits and the two opposite coasts so as to exclude an enemy from entering the Red Sea.

We touched both at Jedda and Mocha. In going into the former place we struck on a sandbank and got off with some difficulty. In the same place we found the *La Forte* frigate aground; she was subsequently lost in the Red Sea.

At Mocha we took on board a stock of its far-famed honey which was most rich and delicious. From Jedda to Cosseir the weather was bad; it blew fresh and some accidents happened to the shipping before we anchored opposite Cosseir.

As the different vessels of the fleet anchored here the troops and stores were disembarked under the orders of Colonel Murray, afterwards Sir John Murray, who so much distinguished himself by his military exploits on the east coast of Spain. Admiral Blankett, who had been previously detached with a naval force to the Red Sea by Admiral Rainier, then in command on the Indian station, had made what arrangements he could for us before our coming. The arrival of transport after transport, numbering not less than one hundred, with troops, provisions cattle, &c., &c., occasioned no small bustle at the miserable little mud village of Cosseir. The situation of this place is altogether remarkable.

Acting on the commission which I had the honour to receive from the Company, bestowed upon me through the very liberal representations of the Medical Board at Bombay, I entered regularly on the duties of Superintendent of the medical concerns of the army and made the best arrangements I could for the sick and the care of the stores, appointing an acting apothecary to the army, and Mr Small of the 8th Light Dragoons as purveyor to take the management of the accounts and to be responsible for the money issued by him with my sanction from the paymaster-general of the Bengal service.

Following the return of the army to England, a Military Enquiry was held concerning the accusations of extravagance in the use of the wine and other stores sent to Egypt from The Cape of Good Hope. McGrigor, accused of exaggerating the number of his medical officers, was exonerated. The Commissioners found that 'the alleged excess of the officers of the Medical Staff . . . has been amply refuted.'

On landing, we found the weather excessively warm, encamped as we were on arid sand and I got a smart attack of fever occasioned, I believe, not more by the weather than by the fatiguing duty I had to perform. Having no assistant with me, I myself assiduously attended the sick of the 88th Regiment, whom I got most comfortably accommodated on shipboard where I visited them daily. But then I had the organisation of the hospital concerns of our daily increasing army – a duty which was toilsome and harassing, and I regret to say, the toils were much increased by some of my brethren, who did not fail to throw difficulties in the way. I could make allowance for some feelings of jealousy in the medical officers of the Company on seeing, I believe for the first time, an officer of the King's service placed over them in the superintendence of the medical concerns of a company's army. This was felt perhaps more by the medical officers from the Bengal and Madras Presidencies than by those of Bombay, to most of whom I was known. However, I had the happiness to find that, in no long time, all of them became reconciled to the new order of things, with the exception of two from Bengal, who obstinately persevered in a kind of opposition to the very last. With regard to all the rest, it is but justice to those most respectable officers to say that they yielded most readily a perfect obedience on all occasions and gave me the most firm support, and with several of them I continued on terms of friendship to the close of their lives.

At length, the part of the expedition sent from the Cape began to arrive, viz., the 8th Dragoons and 61st Regiment, and with them came a medical staff sent out from England. Dr Shapter, Inspector of Hospitals, arrived at the head of this staff and I immediately gave over the charge of superintending the medical department to this gentleman, one of the most amiable men that ever lived. Having gone so far with the arrangements, and having with much labour brought things to the state I had got them, I confess I felt nevertheless not a little mortified at being thus superseded, but no one could have conducted himself with more delicacy than did Dr Shapter. He offered to recommend me for promotion to the rank of staff surgeon and that I should act in the superintendence immediately under him. This, however, although pressed upon me by Sir David Baird, I refused, at the same time offering the aid and assistance which my experience of the Indian service enabled me to give to Dr

Shapter. It was therefore decided that I should conduct the duties and superintend till the army crossed the desert and had joined the English army in Lower Egypt.

It is in anomalous positions of this kind that McGrigor seems to have shone in his younger days; his innate courtesy and ready tact disarming opposition and reconciling even those who thought themselves aggrieved by his advancement. His devotion to duty and high professional attainments helped to consolidate a position that was not altogether based in the claims of seniority. [7]

I went down the Nile in the first of the djerms destined for the conveyance of the troops and landed at Ghiza where some part of the English army had already arrived.

At Ghiza I met Dr Frank, Inspector of Hospitals, the next officer of the English staff under Mr Young, the Inspector-General of the hospitals of the English army. Dr Frank demanded returns of the sick of the Indian army to be sent to him. Considering the Indian army to be a separate command and as I was acting on the system of the service of the Indian Company, I thought it right not to accede to Dr Frank's order, at least till I had communicated with Sir David Baird, who, by this time, had taken the command of the expedition from India. On communicating with General Baird, he told me I was quite right in not sending returns to Dr Frank and this communication I made to Dr Frank in terms of civility.

At Ghiza, I suffered an attack of fever which proved to be remittent, but which at first was feared would prove to be the plague. The attack was a severe one, and followed by long and protracted debility. When it could be done, I was removed to an airy situation in Cairo, near the Nile, and here soon after I received as my guest Dr Shapter in very bad health. He had just crossed the desert and was extremely debilitated.

Although still extremely weak, I embarked in a boat for Rosetta with a party of the 88th. The djerm provided for me was a large and commodious boat on which there was a kind of cabin for me, and I was carried on board by some of the soldiers. These poor fellows, seeing me so feeble and so greatly reduced, vied with each other in their attentions, which were truly affectionate; yet I knew that some of the most forward of them in endearing acts of kindness were the worst subjects and wildest characters in the regiment. Some of them were men towards whom for previous conduct I had found it necessary to act with great severity; yet all was forgotten when they saw 'the doctor' in such a state.

In going down the river we came to anchor every evening when the victuals were cooked and all partook of the meal of the day. On the morning of the second day, about the time the Arabs were getting the vessel under way, while I was taking breakfast, I saw about a dozen of the soldiers running towards it and found that they carried a sheep with them. On inquiring how they came by it, an orator among them said, 'Your honour, how could we see you so weak and without mutton to make a little broth?' On my saying, 'You rascals, have you stolen the sheep?' I saw a grin on their faces; and the sheep was not the only article of plunder they had possessed themselves of for another fellow had two fowls under his arm. In a little time a party of the natives appeared in pursuit. These were the owners of the sheep and fowls to whom I paid their value, although all this seemed to be a very unnecessary proceeding to my Connaught Ranger friends.

In coming down the Nile, although on embarking I was in a state of extreme debility, I was happy to find that I daily gained strength. My appetite became good, I felt returning health, and I enjoyed the merriment and jokes of the soldiers, my companions in the djerm. On arriving at Rosetta, I found the 88th and other regiments of the Indian army encamped at El Hamed, within two miles of Rosetta and but a little distance from the Nile. In a few days after my arrival on the ground of encampment, my servants, horses and camels reached the ground, and likewise the whole of my stock which I now began to add to, for sheep, fowls, rabbits, &c., were to be had cheap and in abundance.

Much had been said by our brethren of the King's army from England, whom we here met, of the luxury in which the Indian army had traversed the desert, and not without reason. They jeered us much and called us the army of Darius for, besides many articles of apparel and other things which were unknown in the English army, several officers carried with them a stock of wine, such as hock, claret, &c., besides various luxuries for the table.

I had not been long encamped at El Hamed before I made myself very comfortable. I had upwards of a dozen Indian servants with their wives, besides my English soldier servant, and for my stock, three camels, two horses, twenty-four sheep, three goats, several dozen of fowls, with a good many pigeons, rabbits, &c. My own large Indian marquee was in the centre and around were the small Arab tents, which my Indian servants had raised for themselves. In another quarter were found all my animals and a store tent in which some of the servants nightly kept watch and made rounds to see that no marauders made incursion upon us, which, however, they did occasionally, carrying off fowls, sheep, &c. Outside the whole I had a high mound thrown up, made from the vegetation on the bank of the river, having only one large gate to my premises. El Hamed was on the border of the desert and a sandy plain, but my animals were fed with the grass from the bank of the river and the grain which my blacks, with two Arab servants, could collect.

I can never forget the astonishment of some officers of the English army, old friends who had visited me, on my showing them the extent of my premises. They told me that I brought to their mind the age of the patriarchs of old, with their herds and their flocks, their man-servants and their maid-servants.

At Cairo, having initiated my excellent friend Dr Shapter and Mr Moss, the purveyor, in the superintending duties of the Indian army, and made them acquainted with the mustering and paying of the doolie train of the army, and in all particulars of the Indian service, I resigned the medical superintendence of it and returned to my duty as surgeon of the 88th Regiment. To Dr Shapter, to whom all the Indian duties were new and strange, the succession to my office was by no means agreeable and, further, I think he felt uncomfortable in superseding me. Soon after our arrival at El Hamed, the greater part of the English army received orders to return from Egypt, and Dr Young, the Inspector-General of Hospitals, with them. This brought Dr Shapter to the superintendence of the medical department of the English army upon which General Baird expressed a desire that I might be re-appointed to the separate charge of the Indian army, refusing the request of an old officer of high medical rank at Malta, who had served several years in India, for the appointment.

In a little time I left the encampment at El Hamed and moved into Rosetta where my friend Mr James, purveyor of hospitals, gave up to me a commodious quarter which he had occupied, in a delightful situation close to the river.

On my resuming the medical superintendence of the army of India, my first measure was to take steps to meet the appearance of the plague for although no case actually existed, I thought it right to make the necessary preparations. I made the proper representation to General Baird and, with his sanction, make immediate arrangements for pest-houses, houses of observation, quarantine, &c., as well as for the formation of a board of health.

After the embarkation of the greater part of the English army, the Indian army was moved to Alexandria, being quartered in Rosetta, Damietta and other places, and I was stationed at headquarters in Alexandria.

At length, and as stated in my sketch of the campaign of the army from India to Egypt,[8] the plague made its appearance in Alexandria. During the illness of my assistant, Mr Tonnere of the 88th Regiment, when there was a numerous sick list, I did all the duties of the regimental hospital myself and in that corps, to the great alarm of the whole army, the plague made its first appearance.

The predominant disease in hospital at this time was fever, which in many instances ran its course rapidly and terminated fatally with the appearance of typhus. Within the last three days the deaths had been very numerous so as to occasion me much uneasiness. The hospital which the 88th occupied consisted of two adjoining houses, each of them having a court at the entrance. The rooms were small and extremely ill-ventilated. However, in these small, dirty old apartments I was obliged to huddle together eighty men of the 88th Regiment. I appropriated one room, which I believe had been the apartment of a porter, to be the receiving room and therein I had three large portable baths where every man on admission was well washed previous to his being placed in a ward and receiving the hospital dress.

One morning, as I was leaving the hospital where I had been sedulously employed with the sick for three hours, from five o'clock in the morning, I passed the receiving room and observed that one man who was coming out of the bath had buboes both in the groin and about the neck. On my noticing this to the hospital steward he told me that several of the last admissions were similarly affected and added that every one of the three corpses then in the dead-house, of men who had died the previous day and night, had those swellings. On my visiting the dead-house and examining the three bodies, to my horror I found this to be the case and, returning to the wards, found that several of the severe cases had buboes. Having no doubt that I had the plague in my hospital, on returning to my quarters it may readily be believed that I went with little appetite to breakfast as, from the intercourse which I had with the sick and spending daily at least four hours with them, I felt I could hardly escape the disease. However, after changing my clothes, I took my horse and immediately proceeded to the camp to Sir David Baird, to whom I communicated the unwelcome news. At all times firm and influenced less by alarm at danger than any man I ever met, after the recital (made to him in private), he was even less moved than I expected – perhaps on account of Dr Whyte's opinion, who inculcated that plague was not a contagious disease and who of late had had several interviews with Sir David on the subject. He enjoined the strictest silence on me, but at the same time he issued the necessary means which I had suggested to him on our entering Lower Egypt, viz., those relating to the formation of pest-houses, quarantines, observation grounds, &c.

The whole of the sick of the 88th Regiment were removed from their hospital in Rosetta into the pest establishment there, while the regiment was removed from the general encampment and took up ground separately from the rest of the army, being kept in a state of observation and any febrile case, as it appeared, being instantly sent either into the pest establishment or into the observation ground in tents attached to it. However, the measures taken occasioned no small alarm, more especially when, on the day following that on which I reported the 88th Regiment, I found that some more than suspicious cases had presented themselves in the 61st Regiment, where the same measures were introduced which had been adopted in regard to the 88th. Subsequently, as stated in the *Medical Sketch*, cases appeared in other corps of the Indian army and many officers as well as men were placed in quarantine, but it was not till three weeks after that it was observed that Dr McGrigor ought to be sent thither.

By this time I had had many interviews not only with the commander-in-chief and all the heads of departments, but with almost every individual medical officer of the army in Egypt. By the blessing of Providence alone it was that I escaped and I believe that after I made report to Sir David Baird I had not the least alarm or fear. At any rate, it was evident, after what had happened during the three weeks, it was useless to place me in quarantine and the intention was, I believe, never entertained.

The late Mr George McGrigor, grandson of Sir James, who remembered him well, wrote as follows:

> The expedition to Egypt was made to 'assist in expelling the French from the dominions of the grand Signor (sic) and thus avert the possibility of their invading the [East India] Company's territories in India'. Colonel Wellesley [later the Duke of Wellington] was ill, so Sir David Baird was placed in command. Under him my grandfather had, in 1801, to deal with an outbreak of plague.
>
> On this subject the following words from the *Royal Army Medical Journal* are notable: 'Only by the strong impression of his individuality on the General commanding was such intelligent appreciation of coming events made fruitful. McGrigor deserves the credit of getting done what others under the circumstances only got talked about.'
>
> Captain and Surgeon McGrigor (as he then was) received the medal of the Crescent of the Grand Seigneur, Selim the Third, for his gallant work in the Indian Army.

NOTES

1 James McGrigor in the introduction to his *Medical Sketch of the Expedition to Egypt from India*. (An abridged version of this work is found in Appendix 9.)

2 Haley, A.H., *Our Davy*, pp. 98–103.

3 Haley, A.H., *Our Davy*, .p. 100.

4 Ibid, p. 106.

5 From Collins' *Encyclopaedia of Scotland*, edited by John and Julia Keay, p. 52.

6 *Life of Sir David Baird*, Vol. I. p. 291.

7 From an article on Sir James McGrigor by Lieutenant-Colonel M.W. Russell as it appeared in the *Journal* of the R.A.M.C., Vol. XIII, August, 1909.

8 *Medical Sketch of the Expedition to Egypt from India* by Sir James McGrigor.

Chapter 8

Orders to return from Egypt to India — Re-crosses the desert — Jealous ferocity of Mussulmen towards women and abhorrence of Christians in general — Project of visiting the Holy Land defeated — Perilous fording of the Red Sea — Renewed appearance of the plague — Quarantine at Butcher's Island, off Bombay — Appointment by the East India Company — Orders for return to England — Voyage — Successful stratagem against privateers — Arrival at Bantry Bay — London

At length, intelligence reached us from Europe that hostilities with France had ceased, that negotiations were being carried on and that peace might with certainty be looked for. In no long time after this, orders were received by Lord Cavan, then in Command in Egypt, from General Fox at Malta — who had the general command in the Mediterranean — that we were to evacuate Egypt and that the greater part of the English troops composing the Egyptian expedition, from India, were not to return thither. My regiment, the 88th, was specified as one of those which were to return to England. This was no pleasant intelligence to me.

At length the order was given for the portion of the Indian army which was to return to Europe to join the English army under Lord Cavan. Among them, that part of my corps, the 88th, which had come from India, the 10th, 84th and 86th, with the 8th Dragoons, were ordered to return to India under Sir David Baird. As superintending surgeon, I was ordered to return and as head of the department to remain in India until the final audit of the public accounts, agreeably to the usage of the Company's service. The place of my residence ought to have been for that period the seat of the supreme government, Calcutta, but by the interposition of my excellent friend Sir David Baird, I was permitted to reside at Bombay. This was a great accommodation to me, not only on account of my having left the principal part of my baggage at Bombay, on the regiment being suddenly ordered from thence, but because at Bombay there were two companies of my regiment and among the officers the paymaster, Mr Duncan Campbell, my assistant, Mr Bruce, and some others of my old and esteemed friends.

Having taken leave of my friends in Alexandria, I embarked in a djerm which I had hired, got well over the bar of Rosetta, halted a day opposite that

Baird's advance into Egypt

place and from thence sailed up the Nile to Cairo, near which I found that most of the army ordered to return to India had arrived and were encamped in the neighbourhood, near the road which passes the Desert to Suez. After organising the medical department of the remainder of the Indian-Egyptian army, we prepared for our journey across the Desert and such precautions were taken for our march by our vigilant commander, Baird, that its success was ensured.

At this time an extraordinary incident occurred. I believe, on the day before we commenced our march, all the troops mustered for inspection by the General and a few only who were sick, or the servants of the officers, and some females who followed the army remained in their tents. My ears were suddenly assailed by female cries and violent lamentation, and when I came out of my tent I saw three females Greeks or Circassians pursued by Turks on horseback. They had got close to the women, at whom one of them made a cut with his scimitar, while the others presented pistols at them. Without hesitation I and my servant interfered, and the servant putting a loaded pistol into my hand, I presented it at the nearest Turkish horseman. He then pulled up and finally galloped off when I and my servant, who quickly brought our horses, chased these ruffians out of the camp, but somewhat inconsiderately, for being more than a match for us two, when near the confines of the camp and far from further assistance, they might have turned back and have overpowered us. They were all of them young and powerful men, and most fully armed, but they rode off, swift as the wind.

On returning to the camp, where a crowd was collected about the three females, we found the cause of the attack of the Turks to be this: these females, like many others the wives and mistresses of Turks, had been taken from the Turks by the French or had attached themselves to them on their taking possession of the country. When the English overthrew the French, these ladies were part of the booty or chose to follow the fortunes of the English conquerors. The three females in question had lived as the *cheres amies* of three English officers who had been ordered to England.

The Turks near Alexandria and Rosetta, as well as in other places where they could find them, had seized a great number of females similarly situated and the punishment which they mercilessly inflicted upon every female they found was to place her in a sack, the mouth of which they tied up, and then throw her into the Nile. The corpses of numbers of these poor wretches were cast on the shore on the banks of the river. The reason assigned by the Turks was that they had lived with infidel dogs. The three ladies in question were youthful and had no small share of personal beauty. An officer carried one of them to Bengal and another gentleman, by no means of young or tender years, took not only one but both the others with him to India and I was delighted to be thus readily relieved of a charge which I had brought unwittingly upon myself.

Soon after this, I met with an instance which showed that, however much the Turks and Egyptians at this time valued our assistance in ridding them of the French yet, as Mohammedans, they viewed us and our religion with abhorrence. When I was about to leave the 88th Regiment at Alexandria and return to India by Cairo, Major Vandeleur requested me to take with me on the djerm, along with my servants, to Cairo, a fine lad, his servant, whom he had engaged there. As the major was returning to England, he wished Mahomet to go back to his friends.

Several days after embarkation from Suez, and when we were many leagues on the Red Sea on our route to Bombay, the captain of the transport reproached me one day on the deck with not having given a correct account of all the servants I had embarked with me. He stated that he had one more to provision than appeared in the statement which I had given in. I assured him with confidence that my account of the number of servants was correct, upon which he desired the sailors to bring forward a man, when to my astonishment I saw standing before me Mahomet, the lad whom Major Vandeleur had sent up with me from Alexandria. He told his story before the captain of the ship and all the officers on board, which was as follows. When on landing at Cairo I paid him the wages dues to him by Major Vandeleur, he went to his father's house where he met with the worst reception from his father, mother and all his kindred. They beat him unmercifully and treated him most harshly for having lived with the Christian dogs, upon which he ran off to my servants in camp, who secreted him carefully till our arrival at Suez when they smuggled him on board of ship, stowing him away in the hold where he was discovered on their clearing away to get at some water casks. Mahomet continued in my service while I remained at Bombay and when I was about to embark for England, I offered either to get him a good master at Bombay or to be at the expense of conveying him to Egypt, but he entreated so hard to be permitted to accompany me to England, that I assented. He there continued for several years, when he married a Portuguese woman. They afterwards kept a public house at Lisbon, where they perhaps are while I am writing this.

Many other instances came to my knowledge of the tenacity of the Mussulmen to their religion and of their abhorrence of Christians.

Till the period of our embarkation we were encamped close to the place known by the name of 'the Wells of Moses', of which the natives have a tradition that it is the spot opposite to that by which the Israelites crossed the Red Sea when pursued by Pharaoh and his host. The country near us on every side was a complete desert. We were within distinct view of Mount Horeb and Mount Sinai.

Two other officers formed with me a plan to visit Mount Sinai. The distinctness with which we saw it every morning and its apparently short distance were tantalising, and after much discussion, day after day, we decided on setting out on our expedition. On making inquiry of some Arabs, who we found had been there, they informed us that the distance was considerably greater than we imagined, and that it was by no means free from danger for our journey would come to the knowledge of a predatory tribe which would certainly attack us. We decided that we would go well prepared for this, but while we were making our preparations orders arrived for the army to embark in a few days. This much disconcerted us all; we thought we could accomplish the journey and return before the embarkation if no obstacles occurred. However, the chance of these, and the situation we should have been in if the fleet should sail and leave us behind, alarmed us all and deterred us from making the attempt. As it afterwards happened, we might have easily got to the top of Mount Sinai and returned before the sailing of the fleet. This was afterwards the source of bitter reflection to me, as I had lost a chance such as I could never hope to have again of visiting Mounts Sinai and Horeb; I lost a similar chance of visiting other parts of the Holy Land which I had proposed to visit with two other officers when in Egypt. This journey had been suggested to me by a friend, an officer of artillery, with whom I passed many evenings talking of it while in Egypt. He afterwards published an account of his travels in that country.

A day or two after the Mount Sinai party had been abandoned, I projected with my friend, Dr Dick of the 80th Regiment, to go round the extremity of the Red Sea and visit Suez, once a place of celebrity, and which from its situation may become so again.

Dr Dick and I set off in the morning after an early breakfast, thinking we could get something for luncheon at Suez and then return to a dinner ordered for both of us at my tent at the Wells of Moses. We set off accordingly, had a pleasant ride along the beach and, when we observed it muddy, struck off across the sands till we came nearly opposite Suez. We went on for some time and, being engaged in conversation, observed nothing to the right or left and never looked to the rear, but at length Dr Dick cried out in alarm to me that the tide was fast gaining upon us. We turned towards the rear and to the route by which we had advanced, but found that in that direction our retreat was cut off by a large body of water. We saw the tide advancing fast and galloped on to a rising ground which we discerned at some distance before us, and which appeared to us to be connected with the town of Suez. We soon gained the highest point and to our dismay and horror, when we had attained the top of this high sandbank, we found that a body of water intervened between us and Suez, so high that we saw the masts of two or three small vessels at anchor in it, and the tide advancing with velocity through this channel. For a moment our spirits forsook us and we gave ourselves up to despair, but an over-ruling Providence decided that we should be spared when no help seemed at hand and when our condition appeared to be without hope.

We had not been on the top of the sandbank on horseback but a few minutes when we could see that we were observed and that many Arabs ran out from Suez, seeing our desperate situation. They called loudly to us, but we could understand nothing by their cries. They pointed to the water and we immediately rode down the bank, plunged our horses (which were powerful English horses) into the stream and the noble animals, although carried downwards some way by the strong tide, gained the opposite bank. On feeling that he was getting a footing, my very powerful horse, John Bull, which had been the charger of an officer of the 23rd Dragoons, made a leap for the land. Unfortunately, the shore being very muddy, he sunk deep into the mud, made several unsuccessful struggles to extricate himself and appeared to sink deeper still. I now felt my situation was more perilous than ever and was astounded by the cries of a number of the Arabs from Suez who advised something which I could not understand. I essayed to get upon the saddle and attempted to jump from thence to the shore, but before I could effect this, and before I had quitted the saddle, John Bull made one more furious exertion, extricated himself and reached terra firma in a state of great exhaustion.[1]

We got a little refreshment at Suez and would have remained for the night but certain appearances, and a report that some very ill-disposed people were there, made us determine, when we had fed our horses, to return to the Wells of Moses. We therefore set out, going quite round the extremity of the Red Sea. The journey proved altogether a very long and toilsome one, and one very hard upon our horses, although two of the best in the army, certainly of the best mettle. Not long after we had turned the extremity of the Red Sea, to which we now gave a very wide berth, my companion complained much of fatigue and faintness. We sat down and rested, when we took a small portion of brandy, which we carried with us, but seeing at a little distance two Arabs of a very suspicious appearance lurking about us, and fearing they might be supported by others who knew our condition, we got up, mounted our jaded animals and spurred them on at a quick pace.

In no long time, however, Dr Dick told me he was so faint that he must rest. He was extremely thirsty, but our canteen of cold tea, which we carried with us, was now exhausted. On my representing to him that we had not much of our journey to accomplish, and that I feared that the suspicious looking Arabs whom we had seen were probably at no great distance, he again re-mounted and we rode off. However, after this, I was repeatedly obliged to stop and rest with Dr Dick. He was so much exhausted that I became alarmed, and at length I determined to leave him with the little remains of our flask of brandy and ride to the camp to procure assistance to bring him in. I found that John Bull, when smartly spurred, could carry me well. I set off at a very quick pace and very soon reached the camp. As it became dark, I first sent out a party on horseback with a little food and cordials, directing them to be very sparing in their use, and then I sent six men with a doolie to bring in my friend. When he arrived, I had the satisfaction to see him well cared for and on the following day complaining of nothing but sore bones.

Just as the whole army was about to go on board and the last corps, the 7th Bombay Native Infantry, which formed the rear guard of the army and had remained behind to bring up all stragglers, had reached the last stage, the one next to our encampment after crossing the desert, Colonel Holmes, who commanded, sent in a report that a case of plague had appeared in one of the followers. This was very annoying and distressing to Sir David Baird, as no case had appeared of this horrible disease for a long time and I had assured him the army might be said to have embarked with a clean bill of health, free from the disease and ready to join the army at each of the Presidencies on their arrival in India, without the very troublesome process of undergoing quarantine. I met the adjutant-general at Sir David's tent and, after some consultation, I offered to go a stage back in the desert to Colonel Holmes's camp and inspect the state of health there.

As the weather was fine and I knew the way, I set off alone, without making much preparation for the journey. I started at a very early hour in the morning, while it was almost cold with the damp night air and got to Colonel Holmes's (afterwards Sir George Holmes) encampment to a late breakfast. The middle of the day had passed before I had executed my duty of a health inspection and the Colonel remonstrated against my setting off with a meridian sun striking on my head, urging me to delay my return till about sunset when he would send an escort with me and himself ride part of the way with me. However, being eager to return in the least possible time, as I knew the anxiety Sir David would feel to see me and that on the opinion I should give he would shape the measures he would take with the army, I set off. I soon began to feel the effect of the sun and John Bull showed symptoms of fatigue, although I had him well fed at the camp. We both soon felt thirst and in an extreme degree. At length we got to the only well in this desert, but there was merely a little brackish water therein and it was thick with mud and the dung of camels. At the well, I found some Arabs, with their camels spouting some of the mixture of mud and water from their mouths. It was altogether so filthy that in England a thirsty beggar would have turned away with disgust from it. However, so extreme was the thirst of poor John Bull and myself that we both eagerly stooped to get at some of it, mixed with mud and filth as it was. I stooped on my hands and knees, endeavouring to separate a little of it from the mud in the hollow of my hand.

Having obtained as much as I could for myself and steed, I set off, but soon found my thirst again excessive; I think it was rather increased by the brackish water which I had drunk. The heat of the sun was overpowering. I had recourse to a pebble in my mouth, which I think rather allayed my thirst, but my horse could scarcely struggle on from fatigue; in fact, he at last appeared to be worn out, when at sunset I saw the tents at a distance. I made for that of my friend Colonel Macquarrie, threw myself on a sofa and demanded a cup of tea.

When a little recovered, I was about to go to Sir David when he entered the tent accompanied by Colonel (afterwards Sir John) Murray, the quartermaster-general. I related to him the condition of the Sepoy regiment and gave my opinion that even should no other case of the plague appear in their camp, it was proper that they should remain six weeks in quarantine and that no communication should be held with them. Much inconvenience was felt at this state of things. However, Sir David determined on immediately embarking the rest of the army and forwarding them to their respective Presidencies, leaving the 7th Bombay Regiment with a portion of the commissariat behind.

Embarkation accordingly commenced and in no long time we were all under way. In the transport in which I sailed, I had the company of my friends Colonel Sir John Murray, Macquarrie and Torrens, and we had also embarked with us a large body of volunteers from the German Legion for various corps in India.

Nothing worthy of remark occurred till we reached Mocha, the place appointed for our rendezvous, where we found the whole of the fleet at anchor. I went ashore the day after we had dropped anchor, in company with Colonels Murray, Macquarrie and Torrens. We met Major (afterwards Sir Henry) Torrens of the 86th and we made a party to dine together on shore after walking about the town. The day was the most intolerably hot one I ever experienced during my life. On returning on board we were all fatigued and exhausted in an extraordinary degree, but as I learned a few days afterwards, Colonel Torrens was alarmingly so: fever, affecting the brain, was the consequence and he did not recover from its effects for nearly a year.

Intelligence of the state of the 1st Bombay Native Regiment having reached India, notice was sent to Sir David Baird that, Butcher's Island near Bombay having been appointed a quarantine station, every corps was to rendezvous there. At the same time, a notification came to Sir David Baird that at the recommendation of the Medical Board of Bombay, I had been appointed superintendent of quarantine; that I was to be stationed on the island to make all arrangements for encamping the troops if necessary and that a commander of the Company's marine was to be stationed, with a sloop-of-war, off the island to enforce the quarantine regulation. This intelligence was most gratifying to me and to my friend. It was the second liberal act to me of the Bombay Medical Board and both were without a precedent towards a King's medical officer. Indeed, considering that they were departing from the established regulation and conferring on me appointments which might be said to belong of right to their own service only, the acts were generous in the extreme. But the board had heard of my regiment having been ordered from Egypt to England. They knew this would be a great loss to me and, as my appointment of superintending surgeon must cease on my arrival in India, they took this means of retaining me in the country until I should be able to effect an exchange with the surgeon of some of the King's regiments in India. This was not all. Colonel Carr, the auditor-general to the army in the Bombay Presidency, gave me an order to remain at Bombay for twelve months till all the hospital accounts of the Egyptian army should be finally audited.

After watering and taking in coffee for breakfast, a stock of honey and some fruit at Mocha, the fleet again got under way and our voyage through the Straits of Babelmandel to our destination was a prosperous one. The weather was uncommonly fine and the time passed merrily on board our transport. The one hundred German volunteers on board for the Company's service did much to cheer us in our passage. A few of them performed on musical instruments and I believe all of them without exception were vocal performers so that we were never without a concert. Every evening they sang in parts, and their native German airs extremely well.

On casting anchor off Butcher's Island, the instructions of Government were sent to me through the Medical Board of Bombay. I was directed to take up my residence on the island, being the only inhabitant there, to take upon me the quarantine duties and to act in concert with the captain of the Company's marine, whose sloop-of-war was at anchor close to the shore.

As the different vessels of our fleet came to anchor off the island, I had to go on board and inspect the health of troops. At first, most of the vessels remained a few days at anchor off the island, but latterly they got under way as soon as inspected for Ceylon, Madras or Calcutta. I had to disembark only a few companies of one regiment of which I entertained suspicions, but after encamping a few days on the island, no disease appearing, they were re-embarked and proceeded to their destination. I made daily reports to the secretary of the medical board. My communications were forwarded with due precautions through a small vessel which was sent to the captain of the sloop-of-war, and through him to me, every morning. By this means I daily received my letters and what stores I required with my victuals. My friend Mr Duncan Campbell, paymaster of the 88th Regiment, kindly acted as my agent on shore and let me want for nothing, and although I had no person on the island but my servants, I felt nothing like desolation during the several weeks that I remained on Butcher's Island. I had my books (very numerous) sent to me by Mr Campbell. My friend the captain of the sloop-of-war came daily on shore for a walk on the island, when the weather would permit, and he and I lived in a kind of mess together, if alternately dining with each other every day in the week could be so termed.

So passed several weeks by no means unpleasantly for I read much and in my naval friend had a pleasant well-informed companion in our dinners and walks.

At length, orders came to break up the quarantine establishment and I went to Bombay where I took charge of the hospital of the 88th Regiment in the island of Colabah from my assistant the late Mr Bruce of the military college, and joined in a mess with my old and respected friend Mr Duncan Campbell, paymaster of the 88th Regiment. After my return to Bombay I was received by many of my friends with warm hospitality, particularly by my professional brethren, and especially by my much esteemed friend Dr Helenus Scott. We instituted together many experiments with his favourite remedy then in vogue – the nitro-muriatic-acid bath.[2]

At length, orders arrived for the return of the companies of the 88th

Regiment to join headquarters in England. Our voyage went on prosperously till we began to approach the latitude of the Cape, to the southward of which we steered considerably, and there met with one of the terrible typhoons which happen in that latitude. Off the Malabar coast we had taken in a stock of vegetables and fruits, which lasted us till we landed off Simons Town in safety and health. From thence we travelled in waggons to Cape Town. At Simons Town, I met the captain of a Danish Indiaman, a pleasant and well-informed gentleman, and with him I proceeded to Constantia and viewed the manufacture of the famed Constantia wine, the whole of which was explained to us by the proprietors of the so famed Kleine (little) Constantia farms. We sojourned with our Danish friend a day.

At Cape Town, we found Admiral Lenois, with the French troops, sent out at the conclusion of the war to re-occupy the French possessions, which on the peace had been restored to them. Captain Gordon of the navy and myself, attired in our uniforms, paid our respects to the French General in command and likewise to Admiral Lenois on board his ship, and were received by them and their staff with the courtesy peculiar to their nation. Understanding that I had been with the British army in Egypt, the questions he put to me were numerous.

On learning that we were about to return to England, the Admiral and General requested I would take charge of some public despatches, and leave them at the house of the French ambassador in London, who would forward them to his own government at Paris. I readily assented and some officers of the staff who were with us in the Admiral's cabin begged me to take letters from them for their friends in Paris. I agreed thereto, adding that I would have much pleasure in being the bearer of letters from any of the French officers of their navy or army who were desirous to write to their friends in Europe, requesting that they would send them to my lodgings in Cape Town. Accordingly, I found a box directed to the address of the French ambassador, of no small magnitude, sent to my care, with polite notes from the Admiral and General.

Having refitted the vessel with some repairs, which the severe gales off the Cape had rendered necessary, and taken in an ample supply of provisions of every kind, with a stock of Constantia wine, we again put to sea, steering for the island of Ascension, where we took on board a stock of turtle.

Hitherto our voyage had been a peaceful one for we had sailed in what we imagined a period of profound peace, but in no long time we found this was not the case. We met with an American vessel bound for India, the master of which informed us that the peace had been broken and that a fierce war was raging between France and England. Knowing that the Americans were too prone to what they called hoaxing, we paid little attention to this unpleasant information. In two days afterwards, however, we met another American privateer outward bound, which we hailed and came close under her quarters.

She repeated the same intelligence, giving particulars, so that we could no longer doubt the unpleasant intelligence. Indeed, they gave us a close description of some of the privateers which were directly in our course and which had been sent out from several of the ports of France to cruise in the tracks of ships from India.

Our situation was now a serious one and Captain Gordon gave it all the consideration which it demanded. He had with him, as passengers in the *Cambrian*, upwards of fifty sailors sent home from India as invalids from the fleet. Although invalids, most of these tars were equal to some duty and everyone was anxious to be employed, and have a blow at the 'Mounseers', as they called them. The few guns (we had only six) were brought forward, imperfect as they were. However, Captain Gordon set the carpenters to work to make wooden guns, called quakers, and in no long time they were painted, with the sides of the ship, so as to make us appear like a frigate. The sailors were daily exercised at the guns and to go aloft with rapidity. Some alteration was also made in the rigging to make us look man-of-war-like.

A night or two after these warlike preparations had been commenced and before they were finished, towards dusk, a very suspicious-looking vessel was observed keeping in our wake, and nearly as it became dark, a gun, one of our six, was brought to the stern, shotted and fired at our pursuer, who was supposed to have sheered off. In the morning, however, the same dark suspicious-looking vessel was observed at a considerable distance, and some time after it was discovered that she had a consort of nearly the same size as ourselves. This made Captain Gordon hasten all his preparations for defence, which he did very completely and in a very seamanlike style.

The quakers on our little deck, as we observed on going out in a boat, made us look very frigate-like and well armed. Captain Gordon had the sailors of the Royal Navy dressed and in trim, and knowing that our two neighbours, which we could not doubt were enemies, had all their glasses out viewing the *Cambrian*, he made the sailors, lascars and all, amounting to upwards of one hundred, frequently go up and down the rigging. This made our force appear formidable while, from the rapidity with which every order was executed, the enemy could not doubt that our strong crew were men-of-war's men. Captain Gordon paraded the deck in his captain's full naval uniform, the invalid lieutenant of the navy in his, while Mr Fawcett came on deck dressed in his uniform of a Bombay Light Horse Volunteer, and I paraded in my uniform of the 88th. We joked much together on the appearance we made. Captain Gordon and the navy Lieutenant frequently went aloft, so as to be well seen by our enemies, while three of us in scarlet placed ourselves in various conspicuous situations upon deck, so as to be taken for three marine officers.

Our enemies after approaching us from different quarters, nearing us and then going off, and having most narrowly examined us, made off in the afternoon in full sail on the course we had come, hoping no doubt to be more successful with other vessels of smaller force than they calculated we were.

During the remainder of our voyage, particularly as we approached the chops of the Channel, many smaller vessels neared us, but none of them remained any time as our frigate-like appearance no doubt deterred them. Much merriment did this excite among the King's sailors, who were daily practised under Captain Gordon and the lieutenant at boarding, clearing for action and exercise at our harmless quarter guns.

The adverse winds and boisterous state of the weather obliged us to seek shelter on the Irish coast and we put into Bantry Bay. It would seem that Indiamen had rarely appeared here for, thinly peopled as the neighbouring country was, the ship and everything about her, and more particularly the lascars we had on board, were as great objects of curiosity to the Irish of this quarter as Captain Cook and his white sailors were when he first visited the Society Isles.

Daily, while we remained at anchor in Bantry Bay, boats full of the natives crowded on board; their curiosity appeared insatiable. My Egyptian servant, Mahomet, appeared to engage more of their attention than any other individual on board. When we came to anchor, thinking he was at last arrived in England, he dressed himself in his best and, as at St Helena, wore his superb turban. From his slender make, effeminate appearance and his Muslim dress, he was taken by all for a female, much to the amusement of our sailors. The females who came on board seemed the most impressed with this opinion and, believing him to be of their own sex, the Irish ladies were constantly taking him apart, and treating him as a female, taking no small liberty in examining every part of his dress, much to the annoyance of Mahomet, and greatly to our amusement.

Our passenger, Mrs Pyne, by our coming unexpectedly into Bantry Bay, was brought close to her home and Captain Gordon and I conveyed her with her two granddaughters in the launch ten or fifteen miles up by the bar, or rather loch, to the town of Bantry, where her two maiden sisters resided. At Bantry we found an Irish militia regiment, the officers of which dissuaded me from taking a journey which I intended across the country to Cork. Those gentlemen reported the country in my route to be in so unsettled a state that without a strong escort I could not proceed with safety. So, with Captain Gordon, I returned in the boat and we reached the *Cambrian* early in the following morning. We soon after sailed for Cork, when I reported myself to the general officer in command, as did Captain Gordon to the admiral on that station. On the following day, an officer came to me from the admiral with an order that I should deliver up the French despatches in my possession from the Cape of Good Hope and the letters of the French officers to their friends. On my remonstrating on the impropriety of my giving up the private letters of the officers to their friends which had been confided to me, and which now perhaps might be published, he told me the admiral's order was peremptory and that the whole must be given up as the admiral had determined to send them immediately to his Majesty's ministers.

After taking on board a variety of refreshments, we set sail and with a favourable wind soon got into the British Channel. A small sloop met us and on coming on board the master told us he was from the Downs – Deal – if I recollect, and had come to look out for homeward bound Indiamen.

Mr Fawcett, on finding that we were about fifteen leagues from Weymouth, asked him how much he would take to land himself, his family and a little of his baggage at Weymouth, while the ship would proceed to London with all the heavy baggage and some of his servants. He at once demanded one hundred guineas. Mr Fawcett immediately refused this. After talking some time, he requested us to see his little vessel that we might know how he could accommodate us. Captain Gordon and I accompanied Mr Fawcett. We found the vessel nothing but a large decked boat. What he called the cabin had room only for three people to sit in and the hold must have been our habitation, lying upon the shingle with which it was covered as ballast. Before we left the little vessel, the master agreed to take thirty guineas to carry us to Weymouth and to include me in the conveyance, with Mahomet my servant. We got everything we meant to take with us into the little vessel and about sunset set sail for Weymouth, which we reached next day about noon. Besides the valuable trinkets, shawls, &c., which Mr Fawcett's family carried with them from India to England, everyone on board, I believe, went charged by friends in Bombay with presents for their friends in England. I had a great number of such remembrances from numerous families in Bombay to friends in England and Scotland, and before I succeeded in delivering them all, I experienced a world of trouble and expense by my engagement to take charge of them.

When we were coming on shore at the landing place at Weymouth, our appearance, and particularly that of the black servants, collected a large crowd. In the afternoon we set off for London, which I reached in good health after so long an absence.

NOTES

1   An incident somewhat similar to the above is described by Alison as occurring to Napoleon I: 'Meanwhile, Napoleon made an expedition in person to Suez, in order to inspect the line of the Roman Canal, which united the Mediterranean and the Red Sea. At Suez he visited the harbour, gave orders for the construction of new works, and the formation of an infant marine; and

passed the Red Sea, in a dry channel, when the tide was out, on the identical passage which had been traversed three thousand years before by the children of Israel. Having refreshed himself at the fountains which still bear the name of the Wells of Moses, at the foot of Mount Sinai, and visited a great reservoir, constructed by the Venetians in the sixteenth century, he returned to recross to the African side. It was dark when he reached the shore; and in crossing the sands, as the tide was flowing, they wandered from the right path, and were for some time exposed to the most imminent danger. Already the water was up to their middle, and still rapidly flowing, when the presence of mind of Napoleon extricated them from their perilous situation. He caused one of his escorts to go in every direction, and shout when he found the depth of water increasing, and that he had lost his footing; by this means it was discovered in what quarter the slope of the shore descended, and the party at length gained the coast of Egypt. "Had I perished in that manner like Pharaoh," said Napoleon, "it would have furnished all the preachers of Christendom with a magnificent text against me." (Alison, vol. iii., p. 464.)

2   Of the resort to this specific at that time in Bombay, adverted to by Sir James McGrigor, mention is made in the 'Wellington Despatches' in the following words: 'I have had no fever since I saw you, but I am sorry to say that the breaking out of which I complained is worse than it was; and has become so bad, as to induce Mr Scott to order me to begin a course of nitrous baths.' (From 'The Duke of Wellington's Despatches', No. 29.)

EDITOR'S INTRODUCTION TO CHAPTER 9

Following his return to London, James McGrigor became involved in a violent dispute concerning position of rank amongst doctors serving as surgeons in the army. 'The medical arrangements for the Home Contingent on shore were on what was then known as the general hospital system as opposed to the regimental system favoured by the East India Company. In this system, general hospitals, if formed, had to be staffed almost entirely by regimental officers. The general medical staff attached to the British forces included, besides the inspector or deputy inspector, physicians, staff-surgeons, purveyors, apothecaries and hospital mates, though the subordinate staff had to be found by the combatant units . . . '

Among other physicians to the forces was E.N. Bancroft, 'a man of considerable note. He took his Cambridge degree in 1794 and entered the army as physician the following year, becoming F.R.C.P. in 1806 . . . he engaged in the violent controversy over the relative claims of the physician and the regimental officer to high army rank, and wrote several pamphlets to prove the inferiority of the latter. On the other side McGrigor and Robert Jackson were his main opponents.' [1]

McGrigor was furious to the point of challenging Bancroft to meet him, possibly in a duel. In a letter to the Commissioners of Military Enquiry in reply to some Animadversions of Dr Nathaniel Bancroft on their fifth report by James McGrigor M.D., F.R.S.E., F.R.C.P. Edinburgh, Deputy Inspector General of Hospitals, etc., 8vo, 1808, he thunders, 'Away with such dark and assassin-like insinuations. Speak out like a man: I am fully prepared to meet you. I challenge you to state any one circumstance which can occasion me the least pain on recollection. And to compel you, if possible, to accept this challenge, I thus publicly declare that, unless you do speak out, I shall regard you in no less better light than that of the malignant and dastardly assassin.' [2]

CHAPTER 9

Publication of 'Medical Sketch of the Expedition to Egypt from India' – Joins the Connaught Rangers at Helsham on their return from the Mediterranean – Appointed to the Royal Regiment of Horse Guards Blue – Takes leave of the Connaught Rangers – Popularity of a medical officer in a regiment – Its conditions – Outbreak of gangrene – Orders for Windsor – Anecdotes of his late Majesty George III

Having called upon and visited most of my old friends, I waited upon the Colonel of the 88th Regiment – General Reid – to report myself and obtain some leave of absence, for I had now to return to my rank of regimental surgeon. I was most kindly received by that fine old gentleman [see Appendix 2], who told me that the 88th Regiment would return in a few months to this country from the Mediterranean and that I might spend the intervening time with my friends in Scotland or as I pleased. General Reid was famed in his day as a musician of no mean ability; he was ardently fond of music, particularly of military music, and was the author and composer of the fine old song 'In the Garb of Old Gaul.'

I have said that after my return from Egypt to Bombay, having but a small charge of sick, I had much leisure time on my hands. At Bombay, as well as on my passage homewards, I employed some of that time in compiling from my notes, and from public documents to which I had access, an account of the medical transactions of the army from India to Egypt. This I did for my amusement and to pass away time. On mentioning to my friend Sir Walter Farquhar, in London, what I had done, he expressed a desire to see the manuscript. Sir Walter showed it to the late Sir Gilbert Blane, who strongly urged me to publish it as the public had no account of it from any quarter and he said it was particularly desirable they should know what had been done at the time of the plague. I hesitated, because I thought it was understood that my friend the late Dr Buchan, then physician to the forces, who had nobly volunteered his services in the pest hospital at a time of general consternation, and when several medical officers died of plague, would give a full account of it. I felt assured that if Dr Buchan undertook the task, it would be in much better hands than mine. From his very extensive reading, from his thorough acquaintance with every author, ancient or modern, who had written on the subject and from his habits of study and reflection, he was of all men the fittest for the task. He was a man of close observation, cautious in induction and he had a store of facts derived from reading and observation, which he brought to bear on any subject that came before him. It was said by some that Dr Buchan, from too much reading, was over cautious in practice, sceptical in his opinion of remedies and that his practice was sometimes inert. But Dr Buchan was a first-rate practitioner, a most honourable man and was possessed of some of the highest qualities of the head and heart. I immediately communicated with Dr Buchan, informed him of the nature of my papers and the recommendations with which I was pressed to publish them, but apprised him that, if he intended to publish on the same subject, I would abandon my intention. Dr Buchan informed me that he had a mass of papers on plague and on the other diseases he had met with in Egypt and the Mediterranean which he might at a future period give to the world. He said that he had not yet entirely made up his mind upon the subject, but that, at any rate, some years would elapse before such a work could be completed. He added that, as my plan was different from his, and as I did not appear to contemplate giving a complete history of the plague or of any other disease, he trusted I would go on with my work.

I joined my regiment at Helsham in Sussex. Our quarter was a miserable one, at least to my eyes. The country was bleak, cold and uncomfortable, but we passed a winter in it.

At this time, when Napoleon threatened invasion, the Sussex, Kent and Hampshire coasts were crowded with troops. I, however, soon got abundance of occupation for the 88th Regiment became unhealthy, particularly the many new recruits which we received from Ireland, and I found the duty irksome and heavy without an assistant, for my friend Bruce was still in India. I believe I further felt the descent in position, from having been a commanding officer in Egypt. It was suggested to me that I would have an easier life in a heavy dragoon regiment, the men of which were generally healthy and in no long time after I found myself gazetted to the Royal Regiment of Horse Guards Blue, the successor of Dr Hussey, who had rather unusually been promoted from the surgeoncy of the Blues to be Deputy Inspector of hospitals, without having passed through the immediate ranks. In February 1804, with the most profound regret, I took leave of my old friends the Connaught Rangers and joined the Blues, then quartered in Canterbury.

I had been eleven years with the Connaught Rangers and, as I have said, on entering the corps, I was the only Scotch officer in it. The commanding officer, Colonel Keppel, and the paymaster were the only Englishmen; all the other officers were Irish, almost all of them from the county of Galway, and a more pleasant and gentleman-like corps was not to be found in the British army. They were everywhere noted as a particularly fine and well-conducted set of officers. The soldiers of the corps, like their countrymen in general, were giddy and, I confess, they committed many irregularities, I might say a few serious crimes, but they were an affectionate, kind-hearted body of men, and attached and submissive to their officers in a degree which I never saw in an English or Scottish regiment. During the eleven years that I had served with these poor fellows, I had travelled over much ground with them and served in a variety of climates. I had seen them march in the face of an enemy, and admired their gallantry and undaunted courage. There were few of them, as also of their wives and children, who had not been sick and under my care during the eleven years, and I ever found them not only grateful and respectful in the highest degree, but truly affectionate towards me. They were ever ready to serve me and of their attachment I had many convincing proofs.

From ample experience and what I have seen in a very long service in the army I am enabled to say that it is greatly the fault of a medical officer if he become not the favourite of both the men and officers of a regiment. He has a thousand opportunities of ingratiating himself by a kind and humane manner in the discharge of his duties, and when he does so, they never fail to prove grateful to him.

At the same time, I never found that gratitude was ensured by conduct such as I have seen pursued, though by a very few medical officers only. I allude especially to instances where their attentions are excessive to the military officers, by taking upon themselves all the duties of the orderlies and the nurse, as well as those of the physician and surgeon. This conduct I never observed to be highly appreciated. It begets loss of respect and always demeans the medical officer. As far as my observation goes, the gratitude of the soldier to the doctor lasts longer than that of the military officer.

Soon after my arrival in Canterbury, Colonel Dorrien, a rigid disciplinarian, made me appear accoutred as an officer of the corps; and when I presented myself in the ancient costume of that distinguished old corps – the Royal Regiment of Horse Guards Blue – I burst into a laugh at my own appearance, equipped as I was with a broad buff belt, jack boots that came high up my thigh and stout leather gloves which reached nearly to my elbows, with a large, fierce-looking cocked hat and a sword of great weight as well as length.

Among the officers of this regiment were the sons of the nobility and also of the most opulent men in the kingdom. All of them were men of polished manners and several of great information, and with a university education. But I found that the officers of this corps were not so much imbued with the military sentiment as were those of many other cavalry regiments. Several of them had no intention to follow the military profession. Heirs to large properties, they had been placed in the Blues for a few years to learn life and see a little of the world, then to retire and take charge of their own estates.

A little before I joined the Blues, my *Medical Sketch on the Expedition to Egypt from India* made its appearance. It was my first and last work [see Appendices 3

*Dr James McGrigor wearing the uniform of the Royal Regiment of Horse Guards Blue
(photographed by Gordon Ross Thomson)*

and 9]. It is true that before and after that time, I sent papers to the periodical journals and always with my name for I had ever a dislike to anonymous writing which I had associated with something discreditable to open dealing, and that sense of honour which I found so highly regarded in the army.

My hospital in the Blues was a small one and the fine body of men which composed the corps was in general very healthy. However, a few months after I joined the corps, gangrene made its appearance in the hospital and ran rapidly through most of the patients in hospital. Every, even the slightest surgical case or contusion, where venesection had been performed or a blister applied, developed hospital gangrene. The hospital was too small and ill-ventilated for the number of such cases as were sent to it, and I had applied for another building when a route arrived for the regiment to march to Windsor to do duty near the king and royal family.

At Windsor we got rid of both typhus fever and hospital gangrene, not a case of the former having appeared after we left Canterbury. Gangrene, however, lingered with us for some time after we got to Windsor. The hospital was large and roomy, and by moving the men from one ward to another, changing the atmosphere, and destroying all the sponges used in dressing, together with other precautions, we finally got rid of the disease.

McGrigor had all the latest medical publications sent to him whether at home or abroad. In 1897, he had been much struck by an article written by Dr Carmichael Smyth, a famous London physician who advocated fumigating the clothes and quarters of fever-stricken men with fumes of nitrous acid. McGrigor had already written to Smyth, on 8 October 1797, to tell him that, 'On my return from the West Indies . . . I determined to take the earliest opportunity of giving a trial to the mode which you recommended, of weakening and destroying contagion . . . The effect of the nitrous fumigation is evident, not only in the diminished number of cases, but also in their degree of virulence . . .' [3]

We had not been long at Windsor before the corps was honoured by royal notice. The king had the regiment inspected on Winkfield Plain, once and again, and expressed his greatest satisfaction with the men to Colonel Dorrien. He even came to our morning parades at the barracks and at length signified his desire to have a troop in the corps, of which he would be the captain and which should be denominated the King's Troop. He made various changes of men and horses in this troop, according to his fancy, and he came not unfrequently to the barracks to inspect his own troop as their captain and, by questioning the men, he had by heart the name not only of every man, his country and history, but I believe also that of all the women and children in his troop. One morning after the regiment had returned from a field day on Winkfield Plain and when the officers were at breakfast in the mess-room, the trumpet sounded and immediately the king with a train of attendants was seen on horseback in the barrack square. The officers ran hastily out of the mess-room, and men and officers were formed in the square. At this moment, I was at breakfast in my own apartment, which was immediately over the mess-room. I had disengaged myself from the huge heavy regimental jack boots and had my feet in a pair of Morocco slippers. Finding the officers and regiment not yet all assembled in the square with his majesty, I came down to the mess-room and took up the *Gazette* to look at it.

While looking over it, his majesty, accompanied by the late General Gordon, entered the mess-room, unobserved by me, by one of the doors which communicated with the riding school and the first notice I had of the king's presence was his passing the well-furnished sidetable, and the various articles on it, with the remark, 'Look, Gordon, abundant breakfast! Excellent breakfast! Cold beef, venison pasty, ham, and game!' and turning to the table; 'tea, coffee, eggs, beef-steaks, hi, hi, excellent breakfast, Gordon!' My astonishment may be imagined when I took my eyes off the *Gazette* and found that by his majesty's advance my retreat was cut off from the door by which I had entered the mess-room. When the king came up to me, I could only bow profoundly, in my slippers; the king only said, 'Reading the *Gazette*!' and walking round the other side of the table went out at the same door by which he entered. I ran upstairs to my apartment and saw the king inspect the whole regiment, which by this time was drawn up for his inspection.

Some days after this, his majesty was present at one of our field-days on Winkfield Plain, when I was honoured with his majesty's notice and, on the regiment returning to Windsor, I had the honour of conversing with him all the way homeward until he turned off with his suite to the castle. In this and on other occasions when I was honoured with his notice, I found him fully acquainted with all my services. I was questioned by him about the continent when I served under the Duke of York. He asked me about the state of slavery in the West Indies, about India and made many inquiries about Egypt. About this latter country I likewise found the Duke of Kent inquisitive and well informed. His royal highness was on a visit to the castle and accompanied his majesty in several of his visits to the barracks of the Blues.

During the time the regiment was at Windsor, the grand installation of Knights of the Garter took place at St George's Chapel, and after a preparation of several weeks grand entertainments were given in the castle to the principals of the nobility. After the installations, I had the honour, with several officers of the Blues, to dine at the royal table and surely nothing was ever more splendid than the assemblage.

After this, the queen gave a series of balls, two of them at the castle and one of them at Frogmore, and I was honoured by invitations to all of them; but military etiquette interfered to annoy me not a little.

In the first ball at the castle, I appeared in what seemed to me the proper dress for me - the uniform appointed for me by His Royal Highness the Duke of York, commander-in-chief of the army. In the course of the evening, I observed that his majesty had eyed my dress much. On the following morning, Colonel Dorrien, who had acted as silver stick, informed me that his majesty had noticed that I had appeared at the ball not in the full dress of the corps. When I stated to the colonel that the dress I had appeared in was that appointed by the regulations for the surgeon of the corps, Colonel Dorrien expressed his satisfaction. Thinking I was quite correct, I appeared at the second court ball in my uniform as surgeon, which was without lace and without a sash. Colonel Dorrien sent for me on the following morning to express to me his majesty's dissatisfaction that I should have appeared at the ball in any other than in a full dress suit of the uniform of the regiment, and the colonel said that, if invited again, he recommended that I should either go in a full dress suit or not go at all. For the third time I received, through the vice-chamberlain, his majesty's command to a ball at the castle when I determined to appear dressed according to the desire of this majesty. The full dress of the officers of the Blues was a splendid, I may say, a gorgeous one and very expensive; the coat alone, I believe, cost twenty-eight guineas. I therefore borrowed the coat and sash of my friend Captain Kingsby, and my appearance seemed to be to the satisfaction of the King, but not so of the Duke of York. I happened to stand opposite to him for some time, looking on at a dance, and he appeared to eye my dress so curiously that I felt as if he had said: 'How came you here not dressed according to the regulations?' On mentioning this to Sir Henry Torrens, who was present, he promised to explain to the commander-in-chief why I appeared as I did and that it was by express desire of the king.

At these royal balls, as well as at the installation, I saw the late Queen Caroline – then Princess of Wales. At the balls, she did not dance, although I believe all the other princesses did, but she sat by herself, retired in one part of the ballroom, much the picture of discontent. At the time, I observed that not many of the nobility went up to speak to her. At the installation, she sat with the other female branches of the royal family and with some of the female nobility in seats near and over the altar. In the imposing ceremonial, when three of the Knights of the Garter advance to the music of a march from under the organ gallery to the altar, making their obeisance as they advance at different stages, the king's graceful manner was much admired and almost applauded. The old Duke of Gloucester was likewise much admired, as were the Dukes of York, Cumberland and Beaufort; but when the Prince of Wales advanced, the admiration, particularly of the ladies, was extreme and it was feared this would burst forth into something like applause. Those who watched the countenance of the Princess of Wales said they saw tears in her eyes.

Not long after this period, his majesty began to suffer much from inflammation of the eyes and his medical attendants ordered his removal from Windsor to Weymouth for sea air. On the Sunday afternoon, before the departure of the Court, the king, with all the royal family, promenaded, as was usual on Sundays, upon the terrace - the military band playing to crowds of fashionables who in those days came in numbers from town to this loyal sight. On that afternoon, the whole of the officers of the Blues made a point of attending and the majority of them were at one part of the terrace when the king, followed by the queen and princesses, passed. His majesty graciously noticed us all. I stood last, at the extremity of our line, and the king looked me full in the face. I expressed my regret to see his majesty suffering in his eyes. 'Aye, aye,' replied he, 'this is one of the fruits of the expedition to Egypt.' After this time I never again saw George III. Not one of his subjects had a more benevolent disposition or a kinder heart and he possessed greater talents than the world attributed to him. I believe that not long after this the symptoms of his mental malady reappeared.

I must mention another incident about his majesty. My friend the late Mr Fawcett, the head of an eminent mercantile house in Bombay, being desirous to see the Sunday promenade of the royal family on the terrace at Windsor, I accompanied him, leading his son, a boy of six years of age, by the hand. When we came up to the spot where his majesty was standing, he noticed the boy as a fine child and asked if he was the son of the gentleman who stood next to me, and was born in India. The king immediately called the attention of the queen to him, saying, 'Look at this fine boy; he is a native of India.' The boy immediately called out, 'Are you the king?' 'Yes,' replied his majesty, 'look at me, look at me.' This boy subsequently entered the Bombay army and is, at the time of my writing these lines, Colonel Fawcett, on the retired list of the Bombay army.

A few months before this time, I had whooping cough and in a very severe degree. My having it at my period of life and my being frequently seized with attacks of it in the street became a subject of conversation in so small a town as Windsor, and I was surprised one morning by my friend Dr Lind, librarian to the queen, calling upon me. He told me he came, by desire of her majesty, to recommend my using oil of amber for my whooping cough, to be rubbed on the spine. I confess I had no faith in the remedy and did not use it, but my cough continuing inveterate and inducing much determination of blood to the head, I took my friend Dr Lind's advice of change of air, and moved to the close confined air of a narrow street in the Strand where, in the course of ten days, my cough entirely left me.

NOTES

1 From an article by G.A. Kempthorne in the *Journal* of the R.A.M.C., September 1930, p. 229.

2 From pamphlet amongst the 'Additional MSS' in the British Museum. This extract is copied from *The Gentleman's Magazine*, 1809, Vol. 79, p. 59. An editor's note affirms that 'with every wish to act impartially in matters of controversy, we consider this as one of those unfortunate disputes which belong to another tribunal.'

3 Blanco, R.L. *Wellington's Surgeon-General – Sir James McGrigor*, p. 63.

EDITOR'S INTRODUCTION TO CHAPTER 10

In this chapter McGrigor gives a carefully worded description of the professional jealousy between the heads of the factions of the Army Medical Board. This consisted of a triumvirate: firstly, Sir Lucas Pepys, the Physician General; secondly, Thomas Keate, the Surgeon General; and thirdly Francis Knight, the Inspector General of Hospitals. Of the three, only Knight had seen service abroad. Keate had served as a surgeon in one of the regiments of Foot Guards but Sir Lucas Pepys, a fashionable London doctor, had never been a soldier at all.

McGrigor's friend Robert Jackson, had criticised the Board through a series of books and letters for its corruption and inefficiency and also for its neglect of the soldiers themselves. Jackson exposed the fact that Pepys, since appointed to his office, had only once visited a military hospital. [1] Not surprisingly, when he himself applied for a post in Spain, both Pepys and Keate turned him down. Jackson, furious, met Pepys in a London street and set about him with his cane. Subsequently, he served six months in prison, a sentence no doubt imposed by a judge biased towards those Jackson exposed.

Francis Knight, realising that McGrigor was educated and had a flair for administration, arranged his promotion, moving him up 'three steps in the service'. The resulting resentment amongst long-serving hospital staff was natural and the fact that McGrigor, as he says, 'surmounted it' to the point where many of his adversaries later became some of his closest friends, gives further proof of the diplomacy which singled him out for high office.

Now as an inspector of hospitals, he began to inaugurate at least some of the reforms that were so greatly overdue. The woeful inadequacy of many of the hospital doctors became increasingly plain. One whom he found drunk when making his morning round was summarily dismissed. Incensed as he then was by such incidents, he nonetheless writes, 'At this distance of time, and when the heat of animosity has given place to cool reflection . . . it appears to me . . . that the ranks of the medical officers of the army furnished but very few indeed who, from education and talent, were fit for the appointment of physicians to large hospitals.'

Thus, it is plain that, now holding some authority, the plans for the reforms that he would make if attaining greater power were already clear in his mind.

CHAPTER 10

Promotion to Head of Medical Board in India — Political Partisanship — Declines Promotion — Strange incident respecting the loss of Mrs Dundas — Gazetted as Deputy Inspector of Hospitals — Mr Francis Knight, his character, &c. — Office of Inspector-General — Regimental and general hospitals — Improvement in the army medical officers — Views on army medical reform — Deputy Inspector of Northern District — Headquarters at Beverley, Yorkshire — Introduces many reforms in the military hospitals — Treatment of typhus fever and ulcerated legs — Sir Everard Home, and Drs Currie, Jackson and Baynton — Excitement in York on the death of a soldier from typhus — Bad feeling in York against the government — Promotion from York to the South-West District — Low state of the army medical profession — Comparative advantages of the civil and military practitioner — Progress in the army medical profession during the last forty years — Temptation of the young medical officer at mess — Studious habits

At Windsor the Blues became very healthy and my duty with an assistant, Dr Laing, now Professor of Surgery at Aberdeen, was very light. I had a good collection of books and had much leisure for study while, at the same time, I visited in my daily rides every remarkable place near Windsor, and also rode to Oxford where I saw everything of note in that classical place.

I was quartered at Windsor, when I received proposals from my kind friend, Mr William Dundas, to accompany him to the East.

At that period, when Harry Dundas, afterwards Lord Melville, was at the head of the Board of Control, an idea was entertained of establishing, in addition to Bengal, Madras and Bombay, a fourth presidency for our dominion in the East; one which would include all the eastern islands - the seat of government to be at Pulo Penang, or Prince of Wales Island. My friend Mr W. Dundas was to be at the head of the fourth presidency. It was intended that the fourth government should have the same boards and establishments as the other three presidencies and, of course, a medical board at the head of which Mr Dundas was desirous to have me placed. For this purpose it was necessary that I should quit the king's service and enter that of the Hon. East India Company. I came to London on the invitation of Mr Dundas and obtained what I requested - a few days to consult my friends - but the proposal was so advantageous and it held out prospects so much better than I could ever look for in the king's service that I soon gave my assent. I even intimated my intentions to my kind friend Mr Knight, at that time inspector-general at the army medical board.

When the establishment of the new presidency was determined on, the applications for appointments were considerable. Several were made, but many were the disappointments. When the intention of appointing me to the head of the medical department got wind, there was a great outcry and not without reason. It was thought unjust that the whole body of the Company's medical officers should be overlooked and that I, a stranger to their service, should be put over them. Harry Dundas (who was high in office) had by this time become unpopular and one party – that which subsequently brought him to trial – had ever since been vociferous against any measure of his and pursued him with the utmost virulence of party feelings. The opposition papers teemed daily with what they termed the infamous job of a new Indian presidency and of the number of hungry Scotsmen appointed by Mr Dundas. One of the most witty of their writers – himself a Scotchman – my friend the late Mr Perry, who conducted the *Morning Chronicle*, termed the new presidency 'Nova Scotia', which name the whole party immediately took up in full cry and this keynote was daily resounded.

The directors of the East India Company, who did not at first object to Mr Dundas's proposition to have me appointed to the head of the medical department, now took a different view of the subject. Nevertheless, his earnest representations induced several of them to assent. But two of them, and those two of the most influential – the late Mr Charles Grant and the Hon. Mr Elphinstone – put themselves at the head of an opposition to Mr Dundas's appointment of me and strongly represented the injustice which such appointments would be to their own servants. I learned from Mr Dundas this state of affairs, and further, his determination to overcome this opposition, and that he had that morning communicated in a note to the chairman his resolution to resign his appointment, unless I was permitted to accompany him in the line chalked out. I also ascertained that Mr Dundas's warmth and decision on this point were displeasing to his family and friends.

All this information occasioned me much uneasiness. The loss of an appointment, which in a few years would have led me to independence, if not opulence, was certainly a severe disappointment. But I came to an immediate decision. Before leaving town, I waited on Mr Knight, informed him of the circumstances and that I had now determined not to quit the king's service, at which he expressed satisfaction in a kind and flattering manner.

On my return to Windsor I wrote to Mr Dundas and, after due acknowledgements for his warm friendship, informed him of my firm and final decision not to leave the king's service and not to go to India. In reply, Mr Dundas begged to see me in town where, when he found me firm, he made the warmest acknowledgements and did full justice to the principle on which I acted.

In a few weeks afterwards, my poor friend with his family and staff embarked for his government. He did not live long to enjoy it for both himself and Mrs Dundas died at Prince of Wales Island within a year after he left England. The same might have been my fate (as it often struck me) had I accompanied him and all my ambitious prospects would have been thwarted by the All-wise Providence, who directs all things for the best, and on whom, through life, I have placed my trust.

A curious and very extraordinary circumstance occurred in India, relative to the first wife of my much lamented friend Mr Dundas which, at the time it occurred, excited a great sensation in Bombay and throughout India. Although here somewhat out of place, I cannot help adverting to it.

Mrs Dundas, a native of Ireland, one of the most accomplished women I ever met, had for a long time suffered from ill health in India and it was, at length, the opinion of Dr Helenus Scott and my own, that it was necessary she should return to Europe. A passage was accordingly taken for her in an Indiaman. Captain Dempster and Miss Anderson, sister of Captain Anderson of the Bombay Marine, took a passage in the same ship with their friend Mrs Dundas. The vessel, one of the finest in the service with superb accommodation, took the China voyage and was to stop at Canton. She sailed under the most auspicious circumstances. However, about two months after her sailing, a report was prevalent in Bombay that some country vessel from China to Bombay had found near some of the islands beyond the Straits of Malacca parts of the wreck of a large Indiaman floating on the water. I had received a letter from Mrs Dundas after her sailing, by a vessel they met at sea near Prince of Wales Island; a few lines merely, giving me an account of her health from the time she left Bombay. On looking at my letter, I had reason to fear that the accounts of the shipwrecked vessel's remains having been seen were posterior to the date of her letter. Indeed, putting all things together, I could have no doubts on the subject. The prevalent report at length reached Mr Dundas, who came to me in the greatest of agitation about it and to inquire respecting the date of Mrs. Dundas's letter to me. On seeing my letter and comparing dates with the reports his agitation was greatly increased. In this juncture, Mr Duncan, the governor, at once ordered one of the stoutest and best of the Company's cruisers to be got ready – a sloop-of-war commanded by an able officer and an excellent crew. She was despatched with all speed and had orders to cruise in the latitude described in the reports, and to minutely examine every quarter in the neighbourhood.

Month after month passed since the vessel was despatched and various were the reports and rumours which reached Bombay. One in general circulation was that two white females had been seen on a naked rock in the ocean. The distress of Mr Dundas may be imagined. Half a year having elapsed since the cruiser was despatched and no accounts of her having been received, another armed vessel, the best in the Company's service, was fitted out with an able and very intelligent officer to command her. He was despatched with orders to make the most narrow search for the two missing vessels but, strange to say, to this hour no account of either of the three vessels has been received. Various were the ways in which it was attempted to account for the disappearance of the three ships.

I ought to have mentioned that, after all negotiations for my Indian appointment had ceased and after my firm and decisive letter to Mr Dundas had been written, one morning, while I was at breakfast, the adjutant of the Blues came into my room and surprised me with a most unlooked-for piece of intelligence. By the desire of the king, instead of a commissioned officer to attend his majesty as orderly officer daily at the castle, a corporal of the regiment had been substituted for that duty. This non-commissioned officer was daily relieved about breakfast time and after his majesty had dressed. The corporal, who had come off duty, had just arrived and reported himself to the adjutant. The news he brought was that the king, while he was being shaved, addressed the corporal (a very respectable and intelligent man, as all the non-commissioned officers of the corps were) and among other things said, 'You are about to lose your surgeon of the Blues, I have this morning signed a new commission for him on his promotion.' As this intelligence greatly surprised me, the adjutant sent for the corporal, who related to me what had passed between him and the king. I had now no longer any doubt that my promotion was forthcoming and that I owed it to Mr Knight, the inspector-general of the army medical board, who had given me many flattering marks of approbation in public letters and who had expressed very great regret when I communicated to him my views and intention to leave the king's service.

In due time my promotion appeared in the *Gazette* and I proceeded to town to tender my thanks to Mr Knight.

I ought not to omit mentioning that about the time my promotion appeared in the *Gazette* I was honoured by his majesty's notice on the terrace, who asked me how I could leave the Blues? I made my acknowledgements for the gracious favour conferred upon me in making me a deputy-inspector of hospitals. The king continued, 'But don't you think it a greater honour to be surgeon of such a corps as the Blues?' I rejoined, 'Every officer is naturally desirous of moving forward in your majesty's service.' He added, 'Aye, aye, all you Scotsmen are ambitious.' It was not long after this that I met his majesty for the last time on the terrace of Windsor with a green shade over his eyes, as already stated.

The promotion which I gained was a very considerable one for looking to the various grades of medical rank as they then stood, of staff-surgeon and physicians to the forces as they were then considered, I had at once got three steps in the service and my appearance in the *Gazette* excited no small commotion in the department. The obtaining of the highest rank but one in the service was to me most important. However, my promotion from regimental-surgeon to deputy-inspector was not quite unprecedented for my predecessor in the Blues had in like manner been promoted from the surgeoncy of that distinguished corps to be deputy-inspector. As it afterwards turned out, the clamour, which at first was loud, ended in an unpleasant feeling towards me from what is denominated the hospital staff. This was evinced in various unpleasant shapes, but by conciliatory conduct I, in the end, surmounted this and had ultimately to number amongst my warmest and most attached friends some of those who at one period entertained that feeling. I am not sure of the precise origin of the rank of inspecting officer among the medical officers of the army, but if any such existed before the time of Mr Knight, he, in his official reign, brought the system into operation.

Mr Francis Knight, who had been educated in the London school – the best for a surgeon – had been, as well as Mr Thomas Keate, surgeon of one of the regiments of foot guards, when, by his very polished manner and professional talents as a surgeon, he attracted the notice of the late Duke of York. Mr Knight had established a very perfect system of economy and arrangement in his hospital. He had a talent for finance. Mr Knight's system was, I believe, extended to all the regiments of Guards and a very good one it was, with perfect checks on all undue expenditure. Shortly after Mr Keate had been removed from the Guards and appointed surgeon-general to the army, Mr Knight was appointed inspector-general of hospitals and the late Sir Lucas Pepys, Bart. was appointed physician-general of regimental hospitals. It was the desire of the Duke of York that, with the capacity for clear arrangement which Mr Knight had evinced in the Guards, he should extend the system pursued in the Guards to the regimental hospitals of the whole army.

In order to carry this system into effect and to render it uniform, a class of inspectorial officers was established, viz., inspectors of hospitals and deputy-inspectors – the former for large and very extended districts (as for Scotland), or for an army in the field, or for large districts of colonies (as the West Indies); and the latter for the small, various military districts into which England was at that time divided. There can be no doubt but that, both on account of the economical concerns of hospitals as well as the inspection of the practice pursued in them, the institution of these appointments was most beneficial to the service. But it struck me how very easily these appointments might be turned to beneficial account professionally and for the advancement of medical science in general which, as it appeared, had never been thought of. However, the institution of inspectorial officers proved the cause of much dissatisfaction in the army medical board, which spread into discreditable controversy among the officers serving under the board, the officers of the hospital staff and the regimental medical officers.

By an absurd and unnatural division of that patronage of which the members of the medical profession are not less ambitious and jealous than the members of the law and those of the priesthood, the appointment to office of the hospital staff rested with the physician-general and surgeon-general, while the regimental medical rank rested with the inspector-general of regimental infirmaries. The most important and valuable from their income rested with the two first-named members of the board, while the inspector-general had by far the greatest patronage in the number of appointments. Sir Lucas Pepys had the appointment of all the physicians in the army, whom he chose from the ranks of civil life without regard to previous service in the army. The same rule, in some degree, guided Mr Keate in his selection of surgeons to the forces or, as they are usually called, staff-surgeons to the forces. Sir Lucas Pepys, stating as his principle that the physician should have the most extensive acquirements and the most complete education, made it a rule that all candidates for the office should be Fellows or Licentiates of the College of Physicians of London, of which he himself was at the time the president, and he made his selection without any regard to the candidate having any previous service in the inferior grades of medical rank in the army. Mr Keate followed at first the same rule in appointing staff-surgeons. Desiring that they should be the most perfect operating surgeons, he appointed them from among the pupils of the London hospitals and, in some cases, the surgeons of those hospitals, and there is no doubt, had the performance of capital operations been the only requirement for a staff-surgeon, he went to the best source for ability.

On the other hand, Mr Knight entertained very opposite views on the subject. In selecting inspectors and deputy-inspectors of hospitals, he held it indispensable that they themselves should have seen service in the army. He deemed it necessary that, for the correct execution of his duties, the inspector ought himself to be acquainted with the duties required of the subordinate officers; should be well acquainted from experience with the habits of soldiers; with the diseases incidental to them; with the many tricks practised by the soldier in assuming disease or what is termed malingering, &c.; and with many other points: information on which can only be obtained by the lengthened experience of a medical officer.

Both parties were in error. At this distance of time and when the heat of animosity has given place to cool reflection it appears to me, from what I recollect of the medical officers about the beginning of the French revolutionary war, that the ranks of the medical officers of the army furnished but very few indeed who, from education and talent, were fit for the appointment of physicians to large hospitals. In the progress of the war, therefore, it was found expedient to establish general hospitals at home and abroad to which the sick and wounded of regimental hospitals were removed whenever their numbers became considerable. A physician was appointed to each general hospital, who was assisted by a proportion of staff assistant surgeons and others of an inferior grade – denominated 'hospital mates'. The regimental surgeons, although a respectable body of men from their being appointed by the colonels of regiments of whom they frequently purchased their surgeoncies, were by no means possessed of high professional knowledge, much less of general scientific acquirements or university education.

During the long peace which followed the American war, the duties were light, the sick few and the classes of diseases which came before them were very limited. From such a class, it would be difficult to select men adequate to the charge of the very large hospitals filled with diseases of a complicated nature which occurred and, if confined to this class, their employment must sometimes have been much to the detriment of the service. Again, of the several able physicians as well as inspectors and deputy-inspectors who were appointed at the commencement of the war, most of them found that they practised with great disadvantage in a military hospital, in total ignorance of the usage of the service and of the diseases peculiar to soldiers. Of these not a few malingered, as it is called, played all manner of tricks in feigning diseases which they had not and exposed the physician to the ridicule of the commanding officer of a regiment, as well as of its surgeon. This could gain no respect for the new physician appointed and, in consequence, complaints came from the officers commanding regiments which were ultimately brought before the Duke of York.

Mr Knight, on this, intimated that he would appoint no physician or staff-surgeon to the rank of inspector or deputy-inspector of hospitals who had not attained what he thought the requisite experience by previous service as assistant surgeon and surgeon of a regiment. The war between these contending parties lasted long and not without acrimony on both sides, but while they were contending, the evil silently cured itself. Gentlemen entering the service, finding that they could not hope to attain the highest rank in the medical department of the army without acquirements not hitherto considered requisite, accomplished themselves accordingly and several of the candidates for assistant surgeoncies and hospital mateships appeared with the degree of M.D. from the Universities of Edinburgh, Dublin and Glasgow. In due time also, these, with their qualifications, moved into the higher ranks of physicians to the forces, of deputy-inspectors and of inspector, and with great advantage to the service.

The number at first was not great, but among them were some of the oldest and best officers who subsequently ably filled the highest rank in the department, viz., deputy-inspector and inspector-general of hospitals.

I have been led into a digression, but to proceed with my story: my new appointment was, independently of its being a promotion, from the nature of the duties which it imposed upon me, one which was particularly congenial to my mind and habits. From my first entrance into the service I had some turn for statistical statements, for collecting medical facts and generalising upon them, and I made, for my own satisfaction, monthly, quarterly and annual statements of the diseases which had come under my notice, both in the 88th Regiment and the Blues. I further extended them, in various diseases, to five and seven years, marking the proportional occurrence of disease and mortality, and I communicated some remarks deduced from them to some of the public journals of the day. I now rejoiced to have a wider field before me for these researches and for the co-operation of others in whom I could confide, by which, either to correct any errors into which I might have fallen or to extend my deductions and have them confirmed.

Further, it had for a long time struck me that the medical board, in demanding reports and returns from the medical officers of the army, as in all their correspondence, seemed to look solely to the fiscal concerns to the neglect of all that was professional. The most minute and scrupulous attention was not only exacted in the number of ounces of soap, salt, oatmeal, &c., given to each patient, but an error even in the fractional parts brought down the animadversion of the board and was frequently the subject of protracted correspondence while no notice was taken of any new or extraordinary feature of prevailing diseases, no proposition made for the trial of new remedies and for the return of reports thereon, nor any injunctions issued to notice post mortem appearances. In short, nothing with regard to professional duty in the interests of science was noticed unless there happened to be an extraordinary mortality in a corps. At this time, and for some time afterwards, the duties of regimental surgeon and assistant surgeon were chiefly those of clerks, as accountants to the public for their expenditure on each sick man. With these ideas strongly impressed upon me, I had not long been an inspectorial officer when I acted upon them as soon as I had a district assigned to me.

I took leave of the Blues, but not with the strong feelings of affection with which I left the Connaught Rangers. With the first, I had many arduous duties to perform and suffered not a few privations in the execution of them. Although the society of the Blues was the more polished and the life I led a much easier one, it was not of the same interesting character as that which I enjoyed with the Connaught Rangers. Besides, that with the Blues was all on home service.

My new appointment was to the superintendence of the health concerns of the troops stationed in the northern district, including the whole of the troops, militia and line, distributed through the extensive county of York, in Lincolnshire, and part of Northumberland. Before proceeding to my charge, Mr Knight kept me some time in town for instruction, to read over the

Captain Duncan Grant of the 78th Highlanders (1777–1803), brother of Sir James Grant and Colonel Colquhoun Grant. Killed when leading 'The Forlorn Hope' at the Siege of Armednagar, 1803 (McGrigor family portrait, photographed by Roy Summers)

correspondence and examine the returns of sick from my district for some time previously.

At length, with my man Mahomet I set off for Beverley – the headquarters of the district. I stopped at Hull to see my old friend Grant (afterwards my brother-in-law, Sir James Grant). At this time he was a staff surgeon, next in rank to the deputy inspector, and from the time of the departure of Dr Baillie – my predecessor in the York district – he remained in charge of the medical duties of the district.

I had learned in London that Grant was the candidate for the step in promotion which I got, who was thought most likely to obtain it, being a staff surgeon and my senior in the service. When calling upon him, therefore, I could hardly expect a cordial reception, but that he would look upon me as an intruder. It was otherwise; for after mentioning his just disappointment, he shook me cordially by the hand and said, as he did not himself get the step, I was the individual in the service of all others whom he most desired should get it. Mr Grant's liberal and generous conduct left an indelible impression on my mind. I felt the injustice done to him by my promotion over his head, being senior to me in the service and I never lost an opportunity of bringing his merits before Mr Knight. In about a year afterwards, I had the great pleasure to go to him at Maidstone, where he was then stationed, to inform him that he was soon to appear in the *Gazette* as deputy inspector of hospitals.

After spending the day with Grant at Hull, and getting from him an account of the state of all the corps in the York district, he accompanied me on the following day to headquarters, at Beverley, where he presented me to General

Vyse who commanded the district. The general was quite of the old school; a gentleman of very polished manners, who received me with much formality and cold politeness. He frankly said that he would have rather seen Mr Grant, whom he had strongly recommended for it, in the situation than any stranger and thought his merits had not been sufficiently attended to by the head of his department. He concluded by saying he had no doubt from what he had heard that I should discharge the duties with credit to myself and advantage to the public service, and asked me with Mr Grant to dine with him that day. Afterwards, I got on very cordially with General Vyse, who was extremely hospitable. His staff was composed of very agreeable men – Colonel Delaney, Deputy Quartermaster-General, afterwards killed at Waterloo; Major Pritzler, Deputy Adjutant-General, afterwards Sir Theophilus Pritzler; Major Hart; and the general's son, Captain Vyse, aides-de-camp. We formed a small mess and had agreeable society for the society in and about Beverley was very pleasant and I received the greatest attentions from the families there, particularly from my professional brethren in civil life whose society I ever made it my business to cultivate.

I had been but a few days at Beverley, the headquarters of the district, when I decided on visiting each station where troops were quartered, beginning with the garrison of Hull where four or five regiments were garrisoned under the command of General McKenzie of Fairburn. I bore steadily in mind my views of turning the reports and returns made by the surgeons and assistant surgeons of each regiment to the purposes of professional and scientific information and improvement, instead of confining them to accounts and money matters only. In fact, at this time, the chief duty of a regimental surgeon appeared to be that of an accountant, and he was the most applauded who was the most correct in accounts and the greatest economist in oatmeal, salt, barley, &c.

After an inspection of the hospitals of the corps in Hull, as well as in all quarters of the district, I clearly ascertained the actual state of each, but did not immediately adopt any measure of remedy till I had fully weighed the whole in my mind. I went no further than, in conversation with each medical officer, to impress upon him a minute attention to the professional parts of his duties and to indicate to him the fine field for experience and observation which lay before him. I urged in every disease, where one mode of practice was not successful, to have recourse to another and a full detail of the effects of the remedies resorted to. I referred him to the opinion of different authors and recommended a perusal of their works, and furthermore, I showed that a military hospital was the best for trying the effects of all new remedies or modes of treatment because there the patient was more under control and observation than in any other. Above all, I exerted myself to gain the confidence of each medical officer and, while by every means I showed myself their friend and used the utmost courtesy to the good officer, I was severe and unrelenting to the bad, the negligent and the ignorant, who were averse to learn. It must also be acknowledged that, at this time, we had many officers, particularly in the militia, who, if not extremely ignorant, had a very imperfect professional education.

In the York district I commenced a practice which I ever after persevered in and found it of the greatest advantage. In my inspection of the hospital of each corps, accompanied by its medical officers, I examined each patient's history, the medical officer reading the particulars of the case at the patient's bedside and the treatment hitherto pursued; I then questioned the patient, generally approving of what had been done but suggesting what might occur to me as to further treatment. On the evening of the day on which I inspected an hospital, all the hospital books were sent to my inn where I examined them, making note of my remarks. These remarks I subsequently embodied in a letter to the surgeon, when I did not fail to advert to whatever I had indicated on former instructions if it appeared to have been unattended to, and in this letter I referred to different authors on the diseases which were prevalent, or in which diseases the surgeon appeared not to have been successful. These letters, marked private, and always couched in friendly terms had, but with few exceptions, the best effects; where they had not, I at first threatened, once or twice, to report to the general in command of the district and finally to the board, in order that ultimate steps might be taken. It rarely happened, however, that friendly exhortation to the officer, aided sometimes by a notice or recommendation from the commanding officer of the regiment, failed to effect the best results.

I confidentially reported my inspections to Mr Knight, the inspector general, with the state of the medical officers and the steps which I was taking. He approved much of this and his letters were ever couched in the most flattering terms, as well as those of his deputy Dr Borland. But still I found I had not satisfactorily accomplished all that was expected of me, for I had not scrutinised so minutely as was desired the expenditure in each article of hospital consumption.

At this period, as for a long time before, even from the very commencement of the war, typhus was more or less prevalent in every corps in the district. It prevailed likewise in civil life. At the beginning of the war, so great were its ravages that half of the sickness of every regiment consisted of low fever and ulcers of the legs. This may be accounted for by the manner in which regiments were hastily raised, when little or no attention was paid to the description of recruits received into the service. In some quarters, the mortality from typhus was dreadful and the loss of men to the service from ulcerated legs, which proved intractable in the cure, was very great. The report got wind that if the sores on the legs were not readily cured, the man would get his discharge and hence there was a general manufacture of ulcerated legs. A system of malingering prevailed in the service and the attention of the medical officers was directed thereto. Many treatises appeared on ulcers, some of them by medical officers of the army; that by the late Sir Everard Home obtained most attention. At this time, Baynton published his excellent treatise on adhesive straps and bandaging. Soon afterwards, Dr Currie of Liverpool and Dr Jackson gave to the public their works on fever and on the use of cold water in its treatment. From this period may be dated a great change in medical practice with the most demonstrative proof of improvement. I look upon the change of practice in fever, with the use of cold water, and Baynton's method of treating ulcers, to be the two greatest improvements which medicine and surgery received in the age in which those three distinguished men – Currie, Jackson and Baynton – lived.

Among other points to which I directed the attention of the medical officers under me was fever, also the works which treated upon it – Baynton's system and Homes's classification of ulcers. Eventually, I may say, we completely mastered both fevers and ulcers, and by showing to our brethren in civil life what was done in military hospitals, we hastened the introduction of this great improvement into civil hospitals, dispensaries and poorhouses.

A work of Jackson's which appeared soon after this period excited much notice, viz., that on the *Organisation and Inspection of Armies*. The military authorities took up the subject and thence I date much of the improvement which subsequently took place in the class of men introduced into the army on recruiting and the great immunity from disease which followed. While I believe no corps in my district could be said to be at this time free from typhus, it prevailed most in the 1st or Royal Dragoons, quartered at York.

The constituents of this corps were good, like all the old regiments of heavy cavalry: the men of a certain height, of strong frame and generally of good character, enlisted from agricultural pursuits and not from the manufacturing population. Typhus, however, appeared in this corps and, as it gained ground considerably and was attended with much mortality, I rode over from Beverley to York, every Saturday, to make a narrow inspection and to follow with my own eyes the measures which I recommended to be carried into execution. The commanding officer, the Hon. Colonel De Grey, was most attentive to the men of his well-disciplined corps and Dr Irwin, the surgeon, was an able and well-informed practitioner. Both the commanding officer and surgeon entered into my views and fully supported me in everything, yet the disease continued to gain ground and the mortality to keep pace with the increase of disease. It struck me that the relapses were unusually frequent and I could not discover that this was owing to a very common cause – error in diet, that is, putting a convalescent too soon upon animal food and wine. However, it occurred to me in one of my Saturday inspections that the convalescents were discharged too soon to the barracks and that this was a cause of the very frequent relapses. I therefore decided that I would see every man in hospital before he was discharged and I directed that this should take place only on Saturdays. On one of these Saturdays, when examining the men proposed for discharge, drawn up for that purpose in front of the hospital, I noted one man from the peculiar aspect and appearance which he presented, and it struck me greatly that he was diseased. On questioning him, however, with Dr Irwin, we could not discover that he had any symptoms of fever and the hospital sergeant reminded us that this man had been in hospital, not on account of fever, but on account of punishment which had been inflicted on him. I then ordered the man to strip but, on examining his back, found it perfectly healed. Still, however, on looking at the man I was struck with his appearance and directed that he should remain in hospital, under observation, until I returned to inspect the regiment. In about ten days after this – in consequence of an express from Colonel De Grey to General Vyse that the radicals in York had excited a great commotion there on account of a man having died on whom punishment had been inflicted; that they had insisted on the disinterment of the body and threatened vengeance on the commanding officer and surgeon – I proceeded to York. On going to the barracks, to my surprise I found that a coroner's inquest was sitting in the hospital on the body of the man in question, and I was indeed much surprised to learn from Dr Irwin that he was the identical man whom, on my last inspection, I had remanded to hospital after carefully examining his back. The fact was that, in the evening of the day on which I examined the man, the symptoms of typhus, which no doubt were lurking about him and affected his appearance, broke out with violence, exhibiting one of the most unfavourable of the cases that had appeared and ran its career very rapidly. The body was buried after the usual interval, but the report got abroad that the man had died of the punishment. The radicals insisted on the body being disinterred and a jury was assembled. I found them examining evidence when I hastily made my appearance among them. After announcing myself, my office and rank, I offered myself for their examination; their answer was, 'You are one of the party concerned; you want to get the doctor and colonel off, but they shall go to the castle.' On examining the face of the corpse and the largely sloughing ulcerated state of the loins and sacrum, I in vain assured them that the appearances were those common in fatal cases of low fever; that punishment was never inflicted in that quarter and that I myself could swear to the man's being perfectly cured of his punishment before he was seized with the prevailing fever. But all would not do. Several vociferated, 'You are a party concerned; you are not a proper witness; we will not take your testimony.' In this state of affairs I was quite at a loss what to do. I learned that the members of this inquest were determined to bring in a charge of murder against Colonel De Grey and Dr Irwin, and to commit them to the castle of York. I rode to Colonel De Grey's lodgings in York, where I found him and his wife in the utmost agony at the proceedings – he wringing his hands and pacing the apartment in agitation. On leaving, quite at a loss what to do, I fortunately met Mr Atkinson, the celebrated surgeon of York, in his carriage. I related the circumstances to him and he hastily took me into his carriage, and drove to the barracks. I could have found no individual in York so fit and so able as my friend Atkinson to extricate us all from this terrible dilemma. He was a hearty, honest fellow, with much blandness of manner, of unbounded kindness and humanity, held in great estimation for his professional talents, very hospitable and of very liberal principles – a feature in his character which made him regarded by the radical party of York as one of their chief men. I shall never forget his entry into the room where the inquest was sitting. They all stood up on his appearance and he forthwith began to rate one and all of them in set terms. 'You rascals! Do you know what you are doing? You a jury! Pretending to investigate the cause of the poor man's death and refuse the evidence of the only competent witness that you could have! You deserve, everyone of you, to be sent to the castle.' Then addressing a humble looking person there, whom they had been examining and who proved to be a little druggist in York, he continued, 'And you, you rascal! What know you of wounds and punishments? Go back to your counter.' Upon inquiry, we found that the druggist, upon looking at the sloughing ulcer on the sacrum, had deposed that to be the evident cause of death and that the man had died of excessive punishment. Mr Atkinson desired them instantly to go on with my examination, which they did in the most respectful manner while he stood by, and my detail clearly exonerated the colonel and the doctor.

On my calling sometime after this upon Colonel De Grey, he told me with horror that two of the jurymen had called on him for something to drink his health upon his escape from being lodged in York Castle! At this time, in no quarter did the current of public opinion run more strongly against government than in York, where the lower classes were loud in their abuse.

About this time also, in a flattering letter from the inspector-general wherein he expressed his approbation of the manner in which I conducted the superintending duties of the York district, he was pleased to inform me that the Duke of York had told him that I must not be confined to so narrow a sphere and that he had decided on confiding to me the south-west district, one of the largest in England, and that I was to be relieved in the north district by Dr Whitelock – a very able officer, but whose health suffered from foreign service and who was to be removed from the district of which Lichfield was the headquarters.

The announcement of my intended removal occasioned me some regret. I had met with the utmost hospitality in Beverley and its neighbourhood. I had formed friendships there and in other parts of the district.

During the time I was on the York district, I had gained much information, and by frequent and minute inspection of the hospital concerns ascertained their precise state, their advantages and their defects; and in consequence, after mature deliberation, I introduced by degrees that system which to my mind was requisite to ameliorate them professionally. As well by personal intercourse and much conversation on professional subjects on the new works and on the discoveries and improvements made, as by constant correspondence respecting them, I endeavoured to awaken the attention of the medical officers and excite emulation in the professional part of their duties. I am also enabled to say that I hardly ever met with a rebuff, but parted with all of them as personal friends.

The inspectorial office is a difficult and delicate one, and much discretion is required in the discharge of the inspector's duties. In common with the whole class of literary men, medical men are jealous of their attainments, skill and experience. The charge of deficiency in either, or the expression even of a doubt of them, gives more or less of offence or uneasiness to the individual, according to his temperament; but the abrupt expression of censure, or doubt of qualification, is sure to do mischief.

At this time, as I have more than once said, the medical department of the army was not composed of the most perfect materials. I believe that, in general, the surgeons and assistant surgeons of regiments – more particularly those of the militia corps – had little more than the education of a country apothecary. No doubt there were numerous exceptions and I recollect several who had received an education and attended the lectures at the London hospitals, then considered the best school for a surgeon. A few, and they were but few, of the surgeons had in addition to this a degree from the university of Edinburgh, considered the best school for a physician. In the army, at this period, with a very extensive field of experience, medical officers were not taught to take advantage of and to treasure up facts. They kept no regular registers or records, but the great evil with the regimental officer was that his professional duty was not considered the most important of his duties or that which recommended him to his superiors.

For collecting facts, for obtaining authentic and correct histories of disease, for observing with exactness the effects of every remedy and mode of treatment, the medical officers of the army possess singular advantages. In a military hospital, the medical officer can depend on the regimen which he prescribes being the only one which the patient can obtain. The prescribing officer has not only the patient but all the nurses and servants under military control, and they have punishment staring them in the face if they disobey the doctor. For obtaining a correct knowledge of the effects of any new remedy, or mode of treatment, the military hospital is certainly the best place. Doubtless, the military practitioner has his prejudices as well as others and may inordinately extol a remedy which he has been the first to use and bring into notice, but usually there is more than one officer attending the hospital at the same time. Should that not be the case, the inspector visits the hospital and examines the patient, and is likely to correct any error into which the medical officer may have been led. When first in his annual reports a medical officer states his great success with a remedy, this is examined into and not only entered at the army medical board, but those reports being open to the after inspection, and for the information of his brother officers, the conclusions he has come to are further scrutinised; or his brother officers give his treatment a trial in their hospitals and, should they fail, he is required to review his conclusion, and to correct it according to a further experience. The reports made and the facts stated by medical officers of the army are thus so much canvassed and sifted, and their opportunities of ascertaining facts so great, that an error in treatment is soon discovered and corrected.

In the army, nevertheless, a professional man labours under one disadvantage of no mean importance. No man leaving the university or school of medicine in which he is brought up can conceive that he has finished his studies on leaving it. Perhaps the preferable time for study is the period when a gentleman enters his profession in civil life. For several years, alas, the physician, or what is termed the pure surgeon, is not so over burdened with patients as to prevent his prosecution of his studies. The few patients he may obtain, or his occasional attendance at a public hospital, are singularly useful while continuing his studies. They are, if I may use the expression, a kind of demonstration, in the same manner as practical anatomy or dissection is to anatomy, or the manipulation of chemistry to the lectures in that science. This is the road to eminence for the physician or surgeon, if he then industriously employs the first years of his entrance upon his profession and until he succeeds to the appointment of physician or surgeon to some hospital or dispensary, and becomes a teacher in some branch of medicine or of the collateral sciences.

But on entering upon his profession in the army, the medical officer is by no means so advantageously placed as his brother in civil life. The army is officered by gentlemen of anything but a studious turn of mind. There is more of gaiety and perhaps of giddiness or thoughtlessness among them than among any other class. Unless in time of war, their duties on entering the service are slight and amusement is too often their principal occupation. A great many of them being well born and all of them gentlemen, they do not look with much respect to a profession which requires study and close attention, or what they term 'plodding and drudgery'. In fact, not a small portion of them have betaken themselves to the army from their distaste to study and some of them from unsteadiness. Their parents have intended them for the church, the law or some other profession in which they had the fairest prospects of success, but after their failures in either of these, they have viewed with envy the seemingly easy, gentlemanly life of some officer in the army who happened to have no other object than riding out after the morning parade or sauntering about a town ogling and coquetting with the fair, who admired his dress and equipments, and who was an object of notice at concerts, theatre and evening parties. Unless the medical man, just come from the schools, possesses a good share of steadiness, he is very apt, on joining a corps, to be captivated with all this and to fall into the idle habits and pursuits of those around him, and if he be of good figure and engaging manner, the danger is greatly increased. He reads less and less every day, makes his hospital duty as light as he can, stops but a short time with his patients and is in haste to join his brother officers in their plans of amusement for passing the day. In this position the medical officers of the army are placed very disadvantageously compared with their brethren just entering the profession in civil life, particularly with those of narrow means, who are in a great measure dependent on the practice they can obtain for their subsistence. I fear that, but a few years back, the picture which I have endeavoured to give of a medical officer's entering the army was one which applied to no small portion of them. I believe that in civil life it was supposed to be universal in its application. In fact, although no small portion of the military officers of the army were those who, having tried the study of divinity or other professions, had not steadiness to prosecute the studies requisite thereto, perhaps a portion of the medical officers were those who, having studied medicine, were deterred from practising it in civil life from dread of the drudgery and difficulties which beset all on their first entering into practice.

But, whatever may formerly have been the condition of those who entered the medical department of the army, it is now, and has been, far otherwise for the last thirty or forty years at least. Moral character is investigated in every candidate and the qualifications required of each are of a very high order; indeed, more is now required of each candidate for the army than is required for civil life by either of the colleges of physicians or surgeons of London, Edinburgh and Dublin. I may add, indeed, that taking the profession in civil life generally, that is, including physicians, surgeons and apothecaries or, as the more genteel appellation has it, the general practitioner, there are comprised in the body of the medical officers of the army not fewer men of literary attainments and university education than in the ranks of civil life.

The state in which I found the medical officers in the York district made a strong impression upon me, particularly that they appeared to have made no progress in study from the time they entered the army, trusting merely to the loose manner in which they acquired experience in the few most prevailing diseases which occurred in their regiments, viz., fever, venereal complaints, ulcers, &c. Each officer was possessed of a very scanty stock of books and those were not of the highest authorities. Of this I am sure, that while the medical officer has a taste for his profession and for the study of it, and prefers that to the daily trivial conversation of the officers, the reflecting part of these respect him in a degree they never would were he their constant companion in all their frivolous pursuits. Still more will they respect him if he abstains from their lengthened conviviality at the mess-table and if he is moderate in the use of wine. Of this I have seen much and had an instance of it in my own case. When I entered the army, and for several years afterwards, the custom with all was to drink much wine. A bottle of port, the wine chiefly drunk, was a very common dose for each and when there were guests, particularly when two corps of officers dined together on the arrival of a corps at a station where the other had been established, the dose was doubled, and with a proportion of sherry, claret and champagne besides. Every young man soon after joining became habituated to this. It was fortunate for me that a weakness of stomach, indicated by frequent attacks of violent headache, from which I suffered from my earliest years, prevented my indulging in the quantity of wine drunk by those around me. I had, further, always a strong sense of the impropriety of this pernicious habit in a professional man and had constantly recurrence to one expedient or other to avoid it. I had ever been very fond of tea and much preferred it to sitting at the mess-table. As I have always been most punctual in visiting my patients in the hospital in the evening, I made this the excuse on ordinary days for leaving the table early, but on gala days, and when we were all expected to support the credit of the corps by making their guests drunk, I found it more difficult to get away, more especially when I happened to be the president or vice-president for the week. On these occasions I gave orders to one of the orderly attendants of the hospital to come and say, 'A man is ill in hospital'. At length, however, this excuse became stale and whenever the announcement was made to me of a man being very ill, there was a general exclamation, 'Oh! Oh! Is the doctor's tea ready?' But among the majority of the officers my motive was understood and, as I found, greatly respected by them.

When we were at Alexandria, I met there a countryman, who was on the staff; a most agreeable man of some talents and attainments, but notorious even among those who were late sitters at the mess-table. I invited him several times to our mess-table, where he was one of our most agreeable guests. But once seated, there was no getting him up and he never took his departure till one or two in the morning. This annoyed me for I could not decently desert and leave my guest at table. However, at last I found that if I produced a substitute my friend would not take offence. I therefore got a hard-headed substitute, a subaltern in the 88th Regiment, who would sit with my friend Major M. till daylight and he actually did so on many occasions. After this, by an understanding between us, I got my hard-headed friend to take my duty as president of the mess whenever the turn came round to me.

For this and for various other things of the kind, which became generally known to the men as well as to the officers of the corps, I never lost caste with them. On the contrary, I found that I had gained general respect. Instead of joining them in several of the amusements, by which they tried to while time away, I had my regular hours of study which were known and respected and not intruded upon. I laid down to myself a course of study in which I persevered throughout the whole period of my service. In every quarter where I was stationed, I was regularly supplied with the medical journals by a bookseller in London, and the accounts which Duncan's *Edinburgh Commentaries* and *Journal*, with the *Medical and Chirurgical Reviews* published in London, furnished me of professional works, led me to purchase all the most approved, which were regularly sent out to me. I further read some works in *Natural Philosophy*, and a good many in *Natural History* and *Belles Lettres*. Whenever my library became cumbrous, I sent the works which I had read to Mr Stewart, bookseller, London, who hired a room for me where they were kept. By accumulation, the number had become considerable by the end of the Peninsular war, which terminated my peregrinations in 1814, at which time I purchased a house and settled in London. The upholsterer who fitted up the house, fitted up one room with shelving for what he thought a decent number of books, but when mine were unpacked, it would not contain half of them. Many of my old friends, those books which had accompanied me to one quarter or other of the globe, were in a miserably ragged condition, and Lady McGrigor insisted that the tattered, half-bound volumes should appear in full dress. Accordingly, all my old friends were made to appear very fine, and I felt a regard for those old friends which had been my companions in Europe, Asia, Africa and America. Besides the room fitted up as a library, they occupied much of three other apartments in my house and, from the weight of them in the upper room, I felt somewhat uneasy for the stability of that part of the house.

NOTES

1   Robert Jackson in 'A Letter to the Commissioners of Military Enquiry;
     Explaining the Constitution of a Medical Staff, the Best Form of Economy for
     Hospitals' (London, 1808), p. 12.

CHAPTER 11

Appointed Inspector at Portsmouth in addition to the South-Western District — Duke of Cumberland, Commander-in-Chief of the South-Western District — Inspectorial duties at Portsmouth — Sphere of inspection increased with part of Sussex — Sir George Prevost — General Whetham — Treatment of hydrothorax — Superintendence of transports — Sick and wounded from Corunna — Arrival of Sir David Baird: his wounds — Haslar Hospital & character of its governor — Spread of disease: a mixture of typhus and pneumonia — The Prince of Wales and the Duke of Clarence at Portsmouth

Having paid farewell visits to all my most kind and hospitable friends in and about Beverley, I set off for London. The better to see the country, I had determined to make the journey on horseback, my servant Mahomet carrying a valise with him containing some clothes and a few books.

I went the first day to Lincoln, having sent on my horse across the Humber. I took Cambridge by the way, having a letter to a Fellow there, of Trinity, who showed me everything important during the few days I sojourned there.

When in London, I received much hospitality and kindness from Mr Knight, the inspector-general of hospitals and, as I was desirous of every information I could gain relative to the medical department in every other district, to the prevalent diseases and the proportions of sick and mortality, Mr Knight gave me access to the office books and the returns and correspondence from abroad as well as at home from which I took some notes.

At length I took leave of my friends in the metropolis, and of those at the Board, fraught with all the information I could get and with a stock of new publications. Arrived at Winchester, the headquarters of the south-west district, of which His Royal Highness the Duke of Cumberland was in command, I immediately reported myself to him, having been introduced to his royal highness by Mr Knight in London. I had learned that, like his brother the Duke of Kent, he was a most strict disciplinarian; but the Duke of Kent, with all his rigid Prussian ideas of military discipline, was possessed of many of the kinder feelings and qualities of heart which were not readily discoverable in his brother of Cumberland who, in austerity and rigor, was observed to bear no slight resemblance to his ancestor of the same title — Duke William of Cumberland. The duke's staff at Winchester was composed of very pleasant, gentlemanlike men. His adjutant, Major (afterwards General) Foster, entered the army as a medical officer and had attained the rank of apothecary to the forces when he entered the military service. Sir Thomas Dyer was the quartermaster-general. He afterwards served in Spain as one of the British officers attached to the Spanish army and undoubtedly he was one of the ablest of them, as well as one of the most honourable and upright. Mr Lindsay, of the Balcarras family, was the commissary-general; Mr Mapother was purveyor of hospitals; and Dr Whelmar, apothecary.

My predecessor, Mr Whitelock (brother of the general of that name), had left Winchester when I joined there. From him, however, I had gained previously much information of the localities of this extensive district, of the prevailing diseases and the characters of the medical officers, &c. The south-west district included the troops in Hampshire (excepting Portsmouth and the Isle of Wight), Dorset, Wiltshire, Somersetshire and South Wales; so that I had a wide range to travel over. This I could not complain of, for from my boyhood I ever delighted in travelling and I found an inspection tour a great relaxation after much writing duty and my regular course of reading at headquarters.

Before setting out on an inspection tour of the district, I remained a month at headquarters for general arrangements and to make a close inspection of the garrison, which consisted of four German corps and one British. After thoroughly inspecting the hospital concerns of the four battalions of the German Legion and Militia Regiment at Winchester, I proceeded to Southampton to inspect the second, or Queen's, regimental hospital, under the care of a respectable old surgeon, Dr Maxton.

As had been intimated to me by Mr Knight in London, I found the hospital concerns of the south-west district 'not in the highest order', my predecessor having been rather lax in his discipline. However, when the medical officers and I had had some intercourse and knew each other, I found all willing to conform to any regulation I might lay down. I framed some district instructions of the duties from the experience which I had had of the York district and circulated them to each medical officer in the south-west district, communicating my views to the officers commanding corps when I saw them; all of whom gave me the readiest support.

I was soon informed that the royal commander of the district was a most rigid disciplinarian and the anecdotes related at headquarters of the rigor with which he exacted observance of certain orders were numerous and some of them very laughable. I will relate one or two of those which occurred to myself.

On either the first or second day, being Sunday, after I came to Winchester, I had occasion to be engaged in writing at my lodging when a sergeant came in and said that his royal highness desired I would attend divine service in the cathedral with the other officers of the staff and the troops in garrison. I told the sergeant that I would not fail to attend. Perhaps in about seven or eight minutes afterwards, when I was engaged in sealing my letters and putting up my papers, another sergeant appeared and told me that the duke desired I would instantly attend at the cathedral. I buckled on my sword accordingly and immediately followed the sergeant to the cathedral. I was directed to the pew where his royal highness was with the whole of his staff, viz., the adjutant-general, quartermaster-general, commissary-general, brigadier-major and *aides-de-camp*. On my entering the pew, the duke addressed me, raising very loud his squeaking voice, 'Dr McGrigor, it is very strange that you take upon yourself to disobey orders, and so soon after you have joined the district.' I pleaded ignorance of the order, but he silenced me by telling me that it was my duty to have made myself acquainted with all his orders upon joining the district. All this passed before the assembled congregation, consisting of five regiments and not a few citizens, who had followed the bands of the five regiments into the cathedral. When I sat down, I observed the duke holding his watch in his hand and I soon discovered that I was not the only delinquent. Addressing Major Foster, he inquired if he had again sent for Captain Shandy, who was the deputy barrack-master general, then considered as a civil officer for which reason he, a half-pay officer as a civilian, was without uniform, which indeed he was not entitled to wear. In addition, Captain Shandy, a very gentlemanlike man, was very defective in his vision and was in delicate health. At length, he appeared in the pew, a sergeant following him. The duke instantly addressed him and, looking at his watch, informed the barrack master that he had kept him, the clergyman and the whole congregation a quarter of an hour waiting his arrival, and desired him immediately to give an account of himself, and further, to explain his presuming to come there out of uniform. To the first of these categorical questions the captain respectfully pleaded the state of his health and to the second that, his majesty not having appointed an uniform for the barrack department, he could not presume to wear that of any other department. The duke, rather foiled, said, 'There is an uniform.' The captain bowed most submissively, but to me and others it appeared a kind of mock humility and as though he were playing the part of Corporal Trim to Captain Shandy. Immediately after the bow of Captain Shandy, the duke nodded to the clergyman, saying, 'Go on now,' when he proceeded with the service.

After what had occurred to myself it will be readily believed that I was not long in making myself master of all the district orders of the duke and I found that one of them was: if any officer of the staff went on leave of absence, for whatever purpose, to London, he was invariably to present himself at the duke's apartments in St James's Palace. I thought it lucky I had read the orderly book for I was about proceeding to London on three days' leave. I presented myself accordingly; the porter gave me a list on which I placed my name and I was desired to return at one o'clock at which hour his royal highness would see all the gentlemen who came to wait upon him. At one o'clock there were several gentlemen in the room and their number gradually increased until half-past one, at which time the names were called in turn. As soon as I was admitted, the duke merely asked me what leave I had, when I came to town, and on what business I came. I was then given to understand by his manner that he required nothing further from me. I made my bow and departed.

At this time, many troops were congregated in England, chiefly in the south-west district, and a good deal of sickness prevailed.

It was intimated to me by the Board that my duties were to be extended, and that Portsmouth and the Isle of Wight were to be added to them. Hitherto, these had formed a separate district. Although there was no great extent of ground, the duties were of a peculiar kind and very important. All the great embarkations took place at Portsmouth – almost all the great expeditions were equipped at that port; there was a very large depot of prisoners of war afloat, as well as ashore, and in Portsmouth and its neighbourhood was a garrison of nine or ten regiments.

At the Isle of Wight was the depot of the recruiting for all the regiments in the service and the only large general hospital in the country. On receiving charge from my predecessor, Mr Jobson, he gave me a formidable account of the duties expected of me, adding that much of my time would be spent afloat, inspecting every transport which arrived and every vessel of a fleet about to sail from Portsmouth with troops. I was not dismayed, however, by the extent and formidable nature of the duties now about to be imposed upon me. At this time I courted such a charge. I was full of activity and zeal, and full of confidence that I should well acquit myself of my duties. Above all, I liked them and felt assured I could do good, having always in view my original plan, which I wanted to execute on an extended scale. If I grasped at much, my appetite was soon gratified. The Sussex district being reduced about this time, one part of it was added to my two other districts, the Portsmouth and south-west, and the remainder was added to the Kent district, under a very able officer, Dr Fergusson. My portion of it included Chichester, where there was a regiment of cavalry and one of infantry, and Bognor, Aldwicke and Silsea, which three stations constituted the ophthalmic depot, then recently established for the reception of all cases of ocular disease from every part of the kingdom. Some time after this, Dr Fergusson complaining of the great extent of his riding duties, a further slice of Sussex was added to my district, viz., Horsham, Arundel, Brighton, Lewes and a large military station adjoining. In the last addition made, I got the medical superintendence of upwards of 5,000 more troops.

My charge was now the greatest in the country for, besides the great number of troops, I had the harassing duties of the embarkations and disembarkations at Portsmouth; the fitting out of all expeditions with their medical requisites; the payment of the medical officers proceeding on service; and furthermore, the large general hospital at the Isle of Wight, with the great depot for ophthalmia and other ocular diseases, often containing 1,000 cases of diseases of the eye.

The field for my observation was now as complete as my heart could wish, and I entered warmly and zealously upon it. It included the counties of Hants, Sussex, Dorset, Wilts, Somerset, Gloucester and Worcester, along with South Wales – in which, at this time, a large body of troops with much disease prevailing among them was stationed. I had to travel from Portsmouth to Haverfordwest, and from Brighton to Dorchester and Weymouth. In these various districts, I served under several general officers, all of whom, seeing me zealous, uniformly supported me.

At Portsmouth I found the late Sir George Prevost in command, a worthy man and an officer of reputation in the service, but frigid in his manner. I did not succeed in interesting him so warmly in the hospital concerns as I did some other of the general officers; but on one occasion his rigidity of manner, for it was manner only, somewhat relaxed. I was desirous that he should see the old general hospital at Gosport where I had the sick of several regiments. One morning he agreed to accompany me to it. When we had got nearly in sight of this large building, at the door of a little public house which we passed, there stood a plain deal coffin. The circumstance struck us both, for no person was near it, and I said, 'I fancy that coffin is not empty,' and to assure myself, I put my hand on it. I told Sir George I was quite sure it contained the body of one of the patients in the hospital and that I fancied I should find the funeral party inside the public house. This proved to be the case for on entering I found the whole party carousing, sergeant and all, drinking and singing in full chorus. With my cane I drove the whole of them out of the public house when, to their astonishment, they met the governor face to face, but he lectured them only in a gentle manner on their unfeeling behaviour, in getting drunk while conveying the remains of a comrade to his grave.

Shortly afterwards, the services of Sir George Prevost were called for in North America and he was succeeded in the command at Portsmouth by Major-General Whetham, a gentleman with whom I ultimately enjoyed a close friendship. In the composition of General Whetham's character there entered some contrary and opposite features, such as are not often met with in the same person. After returning from the memorable siege of Gibraltar, being a young man of high connections in the country, he continued in the Guards. In his carriage and demeanour he had the high polish of the gentleman and with this exterior I was not prepared to meet with the frequent sallies of sterling humour with which he enlivened every society he came into. Above all things, he was very charitable; he indulged in warm hospitality to his friends, had the highest principles of honour, with the most scrupulous integrity of conduct and possessed a warmth of heart for his friends beyond most of those whom it has been my fortune to meet with in life.

General Whetham was a well-read man and had studied his profession as a science in Germany and France. A few years before I met him, he received a wound in a duel, from which he occasionally suffered much, as well as from hydrothorax, under which formidable disease he lived longer (I believe for thirteen or fourteen years) than any individual I ever heard of. The digitalis in infusion was of the greatest service to him, and I believe prolonged his life for that number of years. He took the digitalis according to the prescription of his friend, the late Sir Everard Home, and it never failed for that long period to afford him relief. Indeed, after using it, he had no sensation of the symptoms for a long time. But when, after a while, a swelling of the legs and oppression at the chest manifested the accumulation going on, and that at last respiration was performed with the utmost difficulty, and only when sitting in an erect position, he would then recommence his course of the digitalis and by the third day afterwards he was in his usual health and spirits.

From several years' experience, he was so well assured of the state of things, that he would make Colonel Nicolson, his *aide-de-camp*, issue invitation cards for dinner parties to the number of fifteen or twenty gentlemen for the fourth day after he intended to enter on the digitalis course.

The state of health of the troops in the district under my medical superintendence was generally bad and the sick list high.

In addition to the extensive duties of the districts which I now superintended, I had many important duties committed to me whenever an expedition was started from Portsmouth, the medical concerns of which were entirely in my hands. I had to examine each of the transports appointed for the reception of troops, the quantity and quality of the provisions, and particularly the water, on board; also the accommodation for any sick that might accrue during the voyage and the supplies of medical comforts as well as of medicine, together with the stock of chirurgical materials and instruments supplied and embarked for the expedition. I had, furthermore, to examine and inspect each corps as to its health when it arrived; to receive each of the medical officers of the staff; to warrant the advance of their pay, travelling charges and lodging-money at Portsmouth; and finally, to survey each transport and inspect each corps after embarkation, as also to report to the Board the state in which each regiment had embarked. In fact, I placed the medical concerns of every expedition in an efficient state in the hands of the inspector, or principal medical officer of the expedition, before he sailed from Portsmouth, leaving him little to do while there.

At length, an overwhelming duty fell upon me. Successful and glorious as the battle of Corunna had been, in which the gallant chief Sir John Moore, one of the ablest officers the country ever possessed, fell, the army was hastily embarked for England. In their retreat, the troops had suffered extremely from hunger, fatigue, and all the privations incident to war, while the seeds of contagious fever had made their appearance; and by the time they disembarked, typhus fever had spread widely among them. With the exception of some transports and men-of-war, which had made for Plymouth, the whole fleet landed their troops at Portsmouth. Never was situation more favourable for the propagation of contagion than the mode of return of the British army from Corunna. The men were huddled on board with little attention to order. Men of different corps were mixed together in men-of-war or transports and, in the latter particularly, they were exceedingly crowded. The sick and healthy being mixed together indiscriminately, it was no matter of wonder that the number of cases of fever landed in the last stage of typhus was great; in fact, it was enormous and it excited great alarm at Portsmouth and in the neighbouring country when an account of the mortality came to be noised abroad.

I was in London with General Whetham and his staff when by telegraph it was notified to the admiralty that the remains of Sir John Moore's army were at Spithead, with an overwhelming number of sick and wounded. With the general, I was ordered to proceed instantly to Portsmouth. On arrival there I found an *aide-de-camp* of my old friend Sir David Baird waiting for me. Sir David, as is well known from the many published accounts, had his arm amputated at the shoulder joint on board the ship which conveyed him to Plymouth, but on his arrival there, at his request, he was sent round in the *Ville de Paris* to be near me, whom he knew to be at Portsmouth. I immediately went on board to see my old friend and arranged for his being brought on shore. His landing excited much attention, mutilated as he was by the loss of nearly a fourth part of his frame. The lower class of people, of whom there was a great assemblage from the landing place to the lodgings taken for him, showed the greatest respect towards him, mixed with strong remarks of feeling; all admiring his manly, soldier-like bearing, although his face was wan.

In the following extract from his biography, *Our Davy* (pages 164–6), Arthur Haley describes the almost superhuman powers of endurance of this extraordinary man.

Baird was struck by a charge of grapeshot on his left arm within an inch of his shoulder. Another blast tore a hole in his side. Although stunned he managed to dismount. As his mind slowly cleared he tried to remount. Finding it impossible, he was persuaded by an aide to retire from the field. His arm supported by his sash, he walked the two miles back to his quarters in the town, his face and manner so normal that several officers he passed had no idea that he was wounded.

He was taken on board his ship where the surgeon, finding him composed, said cheerfully that he would 'soon have him to rights'.

His self-control momentarily lost, Baird asked the man angrily if he thought he would have left the field for a trifle. Investigation showed the bone of his arm smashed to pieces with splinters so near the shoulder that the usual form of amputation was impossible. Told his arm would have to be removed from its socket, Baird expressed doubts but was assured, if his life was to be saved, it had to be done. At the suggestion that he must be exhausted and the operation deferred to the next day, he replied he was ready for it to be carried out at once.

The amputation, an unusual one at that time, was performed with Baird seated with his right arm resting on the table. He remained impassive until the final separation of the arm from the joint, when a single exclamation of pain escaped his lips . . .

The voyage home proved a fitting epilogue to the campaign. The transports with their cargoes of wounded, ragged, emaciated, lice-ridden men were struck by storms. Two foundered on the Cornish coast with the loss of 270 men. In the ceaseless tossing and clamour of the ship, Baird suffered dreadfully from his wounds and the delayed shock of the operation. The faithful Sorell [his military secretary] tells of how his mind constantly dwelt on the events of the campaign and how, at times, he had to be restrained from attempting to get up to perform his duties to his men.

When the ship berthed at Plymouth, hearing that his old friend Dr McGrigor was based at Portsmouth, Baird requested to be taken there by sea. He arrived on 25th January, his fever abated and in good spirits though the boisterous weather prevented him from being brought ashore.

On 27th, his brother Joseph went on board with Dr McGrigor to see him and at noon he was lifted ashore in a large cot normally used for swinging ladies on to the ship. He was carried by several members of the crew to a house in the High Street.

The number of sick and wounded was overwhelming for the accommodation which Portsmouth could afford. I had all my energies at work in framing arrangements. In order to provide the medical attendance, Mr Knight sent down the medical officers of the household troops and those of the militia who were disposable, and I was further empowered to engage the services of such of the civil practitioners as I could obtain in and about Portsmouth, and the whole of these found ample employment. After occupying all the ordinary hospital accommodation in and about Portsmouth, and converting some barracks into hospitals, on application to the admiralty, the large naval hospital at Haslar, calculated to accommodate 4,000 sick and wounded seamen, was given up to us – I mean the unoccupied part of it, which was the largest share of the building. Still the number of typhus fever cases continued to accumulate and we were obliged to have recourse to floating hospitals, such as transports, prison ships, &c., and these were the very worst description of hospital. Two deputy

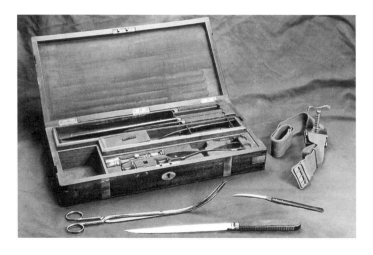

An amputation set, including a 'trephine' – a surgical saw-like instrument for removing sections of bone, especially from the skull (by kind permission of Aberdeen Medico-Chirurgical Society, photographed by the Medical Illustrations Department, Aberdeen University)

inspectors of hospitals were sent to Portsmouth to act under my orders. I appointed one of them for the inspection afloat, the other for those on shore, especially the naval hospital at Haslar, which we had obtained possession of only on condition that we should strictly conform to all the rules of naval discipline (and it was intimated to us in such a way, as though they feared a breach of it), and that the naval captain at the head of the hospital, who was styled 'Governor.' I inculcated on Mr Hogg, the deputy inspector at Haslar, that he should impress on all the young medical officers the utmost respect towards this personage and that he would see that the externals of respect, which I knew the 'Governor' rigidly looked for, were most ceremoniously paid to him. In no long time I found that the young medical officers, having become acquainted with the character of 'His excellency the Governor' of the hospital, rather exceeded in the externals of respect towards the old gentleman and received him with much mock state, which, however, he for some reason received most graciously until he found out that this marked respectful demeanour was shown in derision. He then complained to General Whetham and said that, by the introduction of these young army doctors, the discipline of the hospital would be destroyed and that he would never again be able to bring the medical officers of the navy to a due sense of the respect they owed him.

One of the standing orders of this dignified personage was, that on entering the gates of the hospital, every military as well as naval officer should have his name taken down by the porter in a book, with the precise hour and minute of his entry, so that his excellency should be acquainted with all the movements of each individual. Another of his orders was to the effect – that every medical officer should touch his hat to him every time he saw his excellency, however often that might be. Two very young Irish assistant surgeons had somehow been wanting in this mark of respect for the governor of which he made a formal complaint to General Whetham, and the complaint was conveyed in such terms that I was sent, with General Porter, second-in-command of the garrison, to explain and to pacify the governor. We had some difficulty in keeping our countenance during the time we executed our mission to his excellency. I called the medical officers together and explained to them that, while we were indulged with the use of the naval hospital for the soldiers, we must conform to all its regulations and that the utmost courtesy must be paid to the governor. This was caught up immediately and carried into execution in its most literal meaning.

On the following day, and for many days afterwards, the medical officers assembled in the courtyard of the hospital and awaited the appearance of the governor, when they formed a line on each side the path through which he was to pass and as he passed through the line he smiled the most complacently, bowing on each side very graciously. On another occasion, he called for higher honours than the military guard at the hospital paid to him and he insisted that, besides the guard turning out to him when he passed, he was entitled to a march by beat of drum. The sergeant came up to the young Irish officer who commanded the guard for instructions and he instantly told him to beat the 'Rogues March' which quite satisfied and delighted his excellency, he not knowing the kind of air which was played to him, although every man of the guard was almost suffocated with laughter. But the beating a march was never repeated.

The number of sick landed at Portsmouth was great and that number was increased considerably. Typhus fever spread to all the militia and other corps in and near Portsmouth, and the militia suffered most. These corps furnished orderlies and attendants for the sick, and further, all their medical officers gave their professional attendance to the sick and wounded at Portsmouth. But in no long time, disease spread far beyond Portsmouth and its neighbourhood. Throughout the districts under my superintendence, particularly Sussex, a very formidable disease, a mixture of typhus and pneumonia, prevailed among the troops. It committed great havoc in six militia regiments stationed at Horsham and the mortality, both in the line and the militia, was very considerable.

Not long after the arrival of the troops at Portsmouth from Corunna and after I had made general arrangements for the care and disposal of their sick and wounded, which entirely met the approbation not only of General Whetham, but of General Brownrigge the quartermaster-general and others of the Horse Guards staff, who came down from London, Mr Knight arrived, intending himself to direct all the medical arrangements. I received him, as was my duty, and as all his kindnesses to me demanded. He sojourned with me and I had daily some of the principal officers to meet him. But Mr Knight, after a few days' stay, returned to London to make his report to his royal highness with what he had seen.

Some time elapsed before the hospitals at Portsmouth were cleared of the sick of the different corps and of the contagion left behind, and before they could be brought back to their pristine state of order and regularity. It was at the period while tranquillity and some degree of repose existed at Portsmouth, that the Prince of Wales paid a visit to General Whetham, who was a special favourite of the prince's, as he was indeed of the king and of every branch of the royal family. At Portsmouth the Prince of Wales was received with every demonstration of joy and loyalty, and I was honoured by General Whethan's invitation to meet him at dinner, when he graciously recognised me and brought to my recollection my having been honoured by an invitation to dine with him on the occasion of his regiment, the 10th Light Dragoons, embarking for service at Portsmouth.

The day before he left Portsmouth, he invited General Whetham and several of the officers whom he had seen at the General's table to dine with him and I had the honour to be of the party. I had often heard of the highly polished manners of the prince, the most perfect gentleman, as it was said in the kingdom, but his appearance that day and the manner in which he received his guests exceeded all the ideas I had formed of him. In the evening, a few of the gentlemen who dined with the prince met him again at supper, when, being in a flow of spirits, he volunteered to sing a song in which he showed considerable vocal powers and, indeed, during the whole day everyone was charmed with his elegant manners, kindness, dignity and condescension.

Some time afterwards, the Duke of Clarence volunteered a visit to the Lieutenant-Governor and remained a week as his guest, at the government house. During his stay, I had the honour of twice meeting him at General Whetham's table when he mixed very freely and with much good humour with the company he met there, chiefly with the commanding officers of corps in garrison at Portsmouth. On one of these days, his royal highness jocularly ridiculed Scotsmen, their nationality, their rigid economy, &c., when Sir David Rae, Colonel of the Middlesex regiment of militia, and I were the only Scotsmen in the company. Sir David, an old man, did not know how to take this, but seriously expatiated on the virtues of our countrymen and referred much to history on the subject, greatly to the entertainment of the company. It happened that his royal highness took a fancy to a horse of mine, which he daily rode, my groom bringing the horse every morning to the government house at the hour the duke usually rode out. Before I went out in the mornings, I had directed Charles to lead down the horse to the government house for his royal highness. But on the morning in question, viz., that after the day when I dined with the Duke of Clarence at government house, I had forgotten to give any orders about the horse, although I could not doubt that my groom would lead him down as on former days for the Duke of Clarence. Charles, who was an honest blunt John Bull and a soldier to boot, would do nothing without orders from his master. The cortege to attend the duke was assembled at the usual hour, the horses were all out and several of the riders mounted. His royal highness called for his horse, but no horse was there. General Whetham despatched a sergeant to my lodgings, who saw Charles and his reply was that, as his master had given no orders that morning about the horse, he had not led him down. During the delay which this occasioned and when the duke expressed surprise that his horse had not appeared, General Whetham, with that ready humour which he possessed, said to the duke, 'I know the cause of delay; your royal highness last night abused Scotsmen,' and in allusion to what the sergeant had said, that I had given no orders to my groom, added, 'McGrigor says, he will be d–d if the duke shall ride a horse of his.' With the greatest good humour the duke replied, 'I did not say they had no good doctors in Scotland; I only spoke of some officers generally. I know they have ever been famed for their doctors; witness Baillie,' &c. The horse at length appeared and all went off well.

An incident occurred many years afterwards which showed that the Duke of Clarence was also possessed of the extraordinary memory for which every other member of the royal family was remarkable. Some time after he ascended the throne, I had the honour of dining with him at the Pavilion at Brighton. The late Sir Herbert Taylor who sat next to me said, 'His majesty is addressing you.' I instantly stood up and the king, who had the late Duke of Argyll next to him, called out, 'Sir James McGrigor, Sir James McGrigor, your countryman the Duke of Argyll desires to drink wine with you,' which I accordingly did, but the manner in which the king spoke was singular and pointed. He leaned his head upon his hand, laughing slightly, which soon brought to my mind the allusion he was making to the accidental delay of my horse at Portsmouth, after his pretended abuse of Scotchmen.

Mr George McGrigor (Sir James McGrigor's grandson) writes: 'Sir James while in charge of the medical supervision of the South-Western District, had to deal with the troopers returning from Corunna, carrying fever with them wherever they went. So appalling was the state of affairs that he declared it insurmountable, yet he did surmount it.'

Moreover, the Royal Army Medical Journal reported that 'McGrigor's powers shone out when coping with an emergency which would have daunted many another man, and his reputation grew as the foundation on which it was based became better known.'

CHAPTER 12

*Appointment to the Head of the Medical Staff of the Portuguese army cancelled –
Commissioned to succeed Sir John Webb at Walcheren – Shipwreck of the 'Venerable' off
Flushing – Reception by Sir Eyre Coote – Appalling disease and mortality at
Walcheren – Sad want of Peruvian bark – Fortunate relief by an American
adventurer – Disordered condition of the purveying department – Increased sickness in
the army and consequent recall of it to England – Sir Eyre Coote relieved in command by
Sir George Don – Conflagration at Flushing – Sail homeward – Terrible confusion
among the transports – Arrival in England – Illness at Canterbury – Excitement in
Parliament respecting the Walcheren Expedition – Summoned to the Bar of the House of
Commons – Scenes in the Speaker's Chamber – Sir Richard Strachan – Examination
before the Bar of the House of Commons – Evidence*

At this time the war was being carried on in the Peninsula on a large scale. We
had made a stand there, which, after frustrating the attempts of the French
army, presented a mark for our allies in Europe and showed them what could
be done.

Lord Beresford, in taking charge of the Portuguese army, obtained the
authority to appoint British officers to regimental and staff commissions and, as
a field marshal commanding, his staff of that army was almost entirely
composed of them. Desirous to organise the medical department after the
British fashion, he asked and obtained from the Duke of York and the Horse
Guards that I should be sent to Portugal as chief of the Portuguese medical staff,
with the rank of inspector of hospitals. But before this could be carried
through, the parliamentary investigation of the charges of the celebrated Mrs
Mary Ann Clarke and of Colonel Wardle made it necessary that his royal
highness should retire from the Horse Guards and give up the command in
chief of the British army. Sir David Dundas was placed as chief at the Horse
Guards and, after some difficulty, he agreed to my appointment as one which
the Duke of York had approved before he went out of office.

Before I could take measures to proceed to Lisbon as chief of the medical
department of the Portuguese army, accounts arrived of the most disastrous
state of the health of the army in Walcheren and of the death of Sir John Webb,
head of the medical department of that army. It subsequently appeared that,

although Sir John Webb had been put on board ship in a hopeless state at Flushing, the accounts of his death were premature.

My friend the late Sir John Webb, who had so efficiently superintended the medical department in that service, under the most arduous circumstances and with an increasing sickness and mortality among troops (unknown I believe either in our fleets or armies since the unfortunate expedition under Hosier to Carthegena), had himself been attacked with the prevailing fever, and when the despatches were sent off from Walcheren by Sir Eyre Coote (who had succeeded Lord Chatham in the command), he was not expected to be alive when the latter left Flushing. In this emergency, the army medical board fixed upon me to embark with all possible speed to Deal, where I should find a vessel in readiness for me. I accordingly left Portsmouth on the evening of the day on which I received my orders and, as directed, went to London in my way for instructions. I stopped only a few hours in town to receive my orders when I was told there was every reason to believe my predecessor was then no more.

I set off in a chaise and reached Deal at a very early hour on a Sunday morning. After looking to my baggage, I ordered breakfast, walked out and found that there were four transports ready to sail for Walcheren, and that the agent of transports had received orders to send to sea any one of them which I might select, with me and some other medical officers expected to arrive to fill up vacancies in Walcheren. On my way to the inn, I observed two sentries at a door and, on inquiring who resided there, I was informed the Hon. Admiral Campbell – port admiral. Thinking it a proper mark of courtesy and respect, I left a card for the admiral. I had proceeded but a short way from the door, when a servant overtook me and informed me the admiral desired to see me. On entering, I found him at breakfast in which, at his invitation, I joined him. He told me I was the very person he was in search of, for that he had a telegraph communication from the admiralty regarding me and had orders to send me to the opposite coast the moment I arrived, for I was much wanted at Walcheren, where it was supposed the head of the medical department of the army had died; and that he was instructed to send with me several medical officers who were expected. At this time his secretary entered, of whom he inquired, 'What king's ship is quite ready for sea?' and added, 'This is Dr McGrigor whom I am ordered to send over with the utmost despatch the moment he arrives here.' The secretary replied that there was no small vessel perfectly ready and that the only ship quite ready to put to sea was Sir Home Popham's – the *Venerable*. I here joined in the conversation and informed the admiral that in my morning's walk I had found several transports in readiness, and that the agent had informed me I might select any one of them and he would immediately order it to sea. The admiral did not heed this but, addressing the secretary, said, 'Go to Captain King,' who in the absence of Sir Home Popham commanded the *Venerable*, 'with Dr McGrigor and desire him to proceed instantly with the doctor to Walcheren, and take with him any medical officers who may have come in by the coaches this morning.' Knowing from former experience that the conveying of military officers was not always the most acceptable duty to captains in his majesty's navy, I said, 'Admiral, I beg you will allow me first to call and pay my respects to Captain King as I know what is expected and due to the commanders of ships in the king's service.' The admiral said, 'Hoot! Hoot! I must do my duty, and instantly, by conveying my orders to Captain King and not be mealy-mouthed. Do your courtesies as you please hereafter.' From what afterwards happened, I am minute in this detail and have a perfect recollection of every syllable that passed, having very frequently recited the whole since the occurrence.

As the admiral objected to my having a previous courteous interview with Captain King before his orders were conveyed to the captain, nothing remained to me but to accompany the secretary in his visit to Captain King at his lodgings. We had not to go thither for we met Captain King, with another captain, in the street. The secretary addressing him said, 'Captain King, this is Dr McGrigor, head of the medical department of the army in Walcheren. I am to convey to you the admiral's orders that you put the *Venerable* to sea immediately and convey him and some medical officers to Walcheren.' The instant reply of Captain King was, ' Is the *Venerable* to be made a transport of? His majesty's ship will be lost.' On hearing this very discourteous speech, I addressed Captain King saying, 'I was on my way to call upon you and pay my respects to you but, after what I have just heard, I think there is an end of further ceremony.' He immediately replied, 'When will you be ready to go on board?' I replied, 'I am quite ready and I shall be on board the *Venerable* in half an hour.' Bidding him good morning, I went for my baggage to the inn where I found several medical officers arrived from London waiting for me. Having ordered them to proceed on board the *Venerable* with the utmost expedition, I myself immediately proceeded on board, but so rapid were my movements that Captain King had not had time to announce me or the other medical officers as passengers, so that, on going on board, although I saw bustle and preparation for getting under weigh, I was unacknowledged till the captain came on board.

On board I learned that there existed other causes of discontent, besides that of making a transport of his majesty's ship *Venerable* by carrying out medical officers of the army for the service in Walcheren where, nevertheless, no service could at the moment be more important and where these officers were extremely wanted for duty, by reason of the terrible mortality which had especially stricken the medical officers. After the vessel was under weigh and had stood out to sea, and after repeated signals from the admiral on shore, she made no way on her passage and intended, as it appeared, to make little till a lady came on board. That lady was the wife of an officer at Walcheren, Captain Codrington, afterwards Sir Edward Codrington. She was at Canterbury, whither I was informed an express had been sent for her. When Captain King came on board, he had not only recovered his temper but appeared to feel ashamed of what had so suddenly burst from him in the street in Deal. He told me that he regretted he could not give me the aftercabin, having promised it to the lady of Captain Codrington, whom he expected with a friend on board, but that I should have half of his cabin; that in everything he would endeavour to make me as comfortable as possible and that the medical officers who came with me would mess in the ward room with the lieutenants, who would do everything for their comfort. There were Dr Adolphus, staff surgeon, afterwards Sir Jacob Adolphus, and six hospital assistants, with two of my clerks as purveyor's clerks. Although we got under weigh, and so far as to get beyond reach of the admiral's glasses, I soon found that we were not making our passage. In reality, Captain King was waiting for Mrs Codrington and it was not till late at night, or perhaps the following morning, that she, with a lady her companion, came on board. In the afternoon of that day, when Mrs Codrington and the lady her companion, with Captain King and myself, were sitting at table at dinner, the vessel gave a tremendous lurch. Captain King cleared the end of the table at a bound and was on deck in an instant. Mrs Codrington exclaimed, 'What is the matter?' I was quite sure what the matter was for I had instantly brought to mind my first shipwreck at Grenada when the schooner I was in was lost and also the same sensation I experienced when our transport struck the bottom on entering Mocha in the Red Sea. I replied to Mrs Codrington, 'I fancy nothing of consequence. But Captain King has gone to put all to rights.' She replied, 'I know by your features there is something of awful consequence. I entreat you to see and tell me.' On my reaching the deck, I found Captain King questioning the two Deal pilots, whose faces were the colour of ashes. We had struck on a sandbank and the vessel, on swinging round from this, struck upon another. An anchor was let go, which we lost. Another was thrown out and with consternation it was found we had got into a quarter where we ought not to have been. We were in fact surrounded by sandbanks.

As night advanced, the scene became terrific. The ship was constantly thumping at a terrible rate and I could hear the sailors say, 'Her bottom will not bear this long.' The night was very dark and about ten o'clock, after a violent thump, her rudder was carried away and we heard a gush of water rush in. She was found to admit water very fast, although all hands were at the pumps. At this time, Captain King, taking me aside, begged I would take the ladies below into the wardroom for he was about to cut away the mainmast and in its fall it might injure the cabin and the persons in it. On this, I conveyed the ladies below where we could distinctly hear the heavy blows of the carpenters at the main mast, which at length fell with a tremendous crash and, getting entangled with the foremast, carried it overboard with it in its fall. The water was still continuing to gain in the leaks. A great deal of stowage was thrown overboard and all the guns, six only excepted, which were retained for signals. The water increasing much, and the men and officers being exhausted, a last expedient was had recourse to – that of thrumming a tarred sail under her bottom at the place where the leaks were. But, after a long trial, the men were found to be so much exhausted as not to be able to accomplish this, and we gained little upon the leaks. At this awful time, I surveyed part of the ship. In the wardroom were several casks of brandy with two marine sentries over them. The brandy was being served out from time to time to the exhausted crew, all the rest of the stock of spirits having been thrown overboard, to prevent intoxication and those horrible scenes which have sometimes occurred in shipwrecks. A great many bags of biscuits were stored in the wardroom for exigencies. Over these, in deep sleep, were the midshipmen, who, poor little fellows, had been quite exhausted. In their sleep I observed the fine countenance of young gentlemen or noblemen, some brought up in the lap of luxury and whose parents no doubt never dreamed of their dear boys being in such a situation as I then saw them. From this, I went again on deck where everything wore a most gloomy aspect. Feeling excessively fatigued, and somewhat faint, I went into the captain's cabin; I called for the steward, requesting him to get me a glass of wine or a little brandy and water. But the man told me with an ironical expression that I must know every glass, bottle and tumbler in the ship was shattered to atoms. Having nothing else for it, and in order to be in readiness for the worst, I wrapt myself in my cloak and lay down on the floor of the cabin. I had lain there but a short time when Captain King came in. He paced the cabin several times to and fro, apparently in great agony of mind, speaking to himself and unconscious that anyone was in the cabin. In the awkwardness of this situation, and not wishing that he should say anything in ignorance of my hearing him, I got up and, with a view of comforting him, said 'Captain King, I trust the worst is now over and that, when morning comes in, you will be able to get off this fine ship. Flushing is but four leagues off.' He instantly exclaimed, 'Sir, you fortunately are ignorant of the state the ship is in. I wish I could save the lives of a part of those on board.' Although I was by no means free from apprehension, this, as may be believed, was no pleasant communication to me from the captain. At this time our situation became truly awful; the vessel appeared at every thump to take in more water and I witnessed more than one instance of the rather ridiculous effects which our fearful situation had upon some. One gentleman was on his knees, praying fervently and so loudly imploring Providence that he was quite unconscious of all about him and of some young men, who were much tickled by the figure he made. Even when, by shaking him, I endeavoured to recall him to himself, I could not with the aid of others raise him on his feet. But, in truth, the situation was very appalling. As day broke upon us, the spectacle of the wreck was frightful. The whole deck was a mass of ruin and the sides were all out, torn away in part by the guns in throwing them overboard; on mast, the mizen only was standing. We were at this time firing signal guns of distress every five minutes. We had about eighty women on board, mostly Irish, the wives of soldiers going to their husbands at Walcheren. After every signal from the guns, a general screech and yell followed from the women, who were most troublesome, running about

Map showing McGrigor's involvement in the Walcheren Campaign
and those of 1794–95

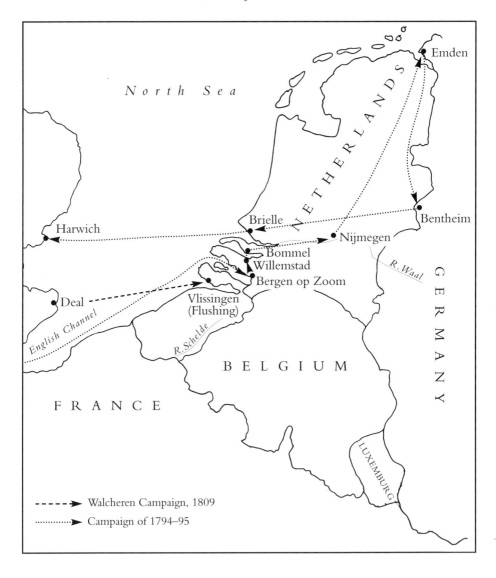

below and above. At length, we had more light and every eye was at a glass, where one could be procured, to see if any succour was coming to us. A vessel was descried. We made her out to be an American. But to our utter dismay it was observed that, although she must have seen us in our distressed situation and heard our guns, she bore away from us and made for Flushing. It was then that an officer of the ship unfortunately was heard to day. 'We are doomed to destruction. The *Venerable* will not hold out till other vessels can near us.' I had never been actually depressed till I heard this. In the meantime I observed that the boats were getting in readiness and all looked with some anxiety to them. It was now broad daylight and the weather was mild and warm. There had been little wind during the night. The sailors observed at this time that, had it not been calm weather, the ship must have gone to pieces before morn.

We were constantly firing guns of distress and every volley from them was followed by a general screech from the soldiers' wives. The two ladies, however, behaved well: Mrs Codrington, who showed an extraordinary degree of fortitude, was always collected and prepared to meet the worst. At length, another sail was described from the top of our remaining mast. Every eye was applied to the nearest accessible glass. It was discovered that she was a small vessel; a brig. The utmost anxiety prevailed. To our infinite joy it was discovered that she had observed our signal of distress and heard our guns, and finally that she made for us. She came not very close, but kept rather at a respectful distance, fearing, I believe, that we might go down and carry her with us in our vortex.

In the meantime our signal guns had been heard at Walcheren and our distressed situation observed, but it was immediately determined to take advantage of the small brig, as far as her means would go, and all the women were sent on board of her, as likewise the papers and plate of Sir Home Popham. This had hardly been accomplished when we observed assistance coming to us from Flushing. All the boats of the fleet were manned and on their way to us; we watched their progress with anxious eyes. But the tide turning and the wind being against them, they made at last so little way that an officer exclaimed, 'We are doomed to destruction; the ship will not hold together till the boats can reach us.' This unwise exclamation, so incautiously uttered in public, caused a look of dismay in the faces of all. At length, one after another, the boats reached us and took us, with the exhausted crew, on shore; the *Venerable* was then manned by the crews of the fleet lying off Flushing, who brought her next day into harbour under jury masts.

When I reached the shore, I found my old and esteemed friend Dr Forbes on the lookout for me; he brought me to his billet, made me comfortable and put me to bed for I had got soaked in seawater from working with others at the pumps. I well remember my disturbed dream when I fell asleep; it was that of being at the bottom of the sea where I was attacked by all sorts of horrible fishes which were about to devour me. I next day proceeded to Middelburg where I was received in the kindest manner by the commander-in-chief, Sir Eyre Coote, who had lately succeeded Lord Chatham in the command. Sir Eyre had kindly ordered for me one of the best quarters in Middelburg and I found my apartments not only commodious, but splendid, being billeted on a director of the Dutch East India Company. I was soon visited by many old friends, military as well as medical, among the latter Sir James Grant, afterwards my brother-in-law. From the reports which prevailed at Deal when I left it, I expected on my arrival to have found my predecessor, Sir John Webb, no more. I found that he had been carried on board ship, but in such a hopeless phase of the prevailing fever, that it was not expected he could reach England alive. This happily turned out otherwise. Sir John's constitution carried him through. He landed in England amended by the voyage, but I believe years passed before his health was firmly re-established. He was subsequently appointed director-general of the ordnance medical department, an office which none of his predecessors filled with more ability. That situation has been filled by some very able men, as Dr Rollo, Sir John Macnamara, Hayes, &c.

From the time I left Beverley and the northern district, the sphere of my observation had, as I wished it, been greatly increased. At Walcheren it attained to the height of my wishes. The number of sick was immense; that of the wounded officers and men who could not be conveyed thither was considerable, and both together, most unhappily, nearly equalled that of the men in health. In the Portsmouth and south-west districts, by the greatly extended sphere of action in which I was there placed, I had added much to my plan of organisation. But the amount of sickness at Walcheren was great beyond all comparison with that which I had hitherto witnessed.

My first object after my arrival at Walcheren was to make an inspection of each of the numerous hospitals spread over the country. I could not expect to find them in perfect order after such an overwhelming influx of sick, with imperfect means.

On examining the stores, both of apothecaries and purveyors, I found them drained of many articles of the most essential description. There had been a great increase in the consumption of bark and I found little in store. I therefore wrote repeatedly to the surgeon-general, Mr Keate, entreating him to send a supply as expeditiously as possible. Before it could reach us, however, we were nearly quite destitute of that powerful remedy. But about the same time, I learned that an American vessel, which came with a large supply of champagne and claret for the sutlers, had brought some chests of bark on a venture, having most probably heard of the deficient state of the stores of all the belligerents in that article. I immediately ordered the purveyor to make a purchase of whatever stock of bark the Americans might have, and the supply we obtained lasted till the quantities forwarded by the mail coaches to Deal, and thence by the packets to Walcheren, arrived. I give this little detail at present for a reason which will be seen in the sequel, when a public inquiry was made into this, one of the largest expeditions ever sent out by the country from which so much was expected and which ended in disappointment, after an immense expenditure of lives and money.

In taking a survey of the position of the medical department in Walcheren, after I came to the charge of it, the purveyor's branch, which included all the money concerns, gave me no small uneasiness. Mr Stewart, who was at the head of this branch, was a man of business, of the greatest probity and honour, and with much experience of the service. But, in succession, many of his clerks had been attacked with the prevailing fever and those who supplied their places were so inexperienced that the accumulation of the business of his office quite overwhelmed him and he came quite to a standstill, fearful of the confusion his accounts had got into. I immediately wrote to England and requested that Mr Moss, one of the ablest as well as most upright purveyors in the service, might be sent out to me so that he might conduct the purveyor's duties, while Mr Stewart would have leisure to bring up his accounts and put them into some order before they got into irretrievable confusion. My request was granted. Mr Moss arrived and by his activity, business-like habits and exertions brought everything into order, besides arranging our accounts in connection with the commissary-general, Sir R. Robertson, likewise one of the ablest officers of his department.

At length, government came to the decision that, from the overwhelming sickness and from the mortality which had occurred at Walcheren, one of the members of the medical board should be ordered to proceed thither to investigate and report to his majesty's government. Accordingly, the physician-general, Sir Lucas Pepys, was ordered to proceed thither. But in an evil hour he declined, and what was his excuse? That he was not acquainted with the diseases of the soldier in camp or in quarters. Equally unfortunate it was that neither of the other two members volunteered their services. This unfortunate constitution of the army medical board excited at the time not only ridicule and contempt, but great indignation was expressed threat in parliament. In this very awkward state of affairs, none of the members of the board feeling inclined to adventure a voyage to Walcheren, they ordered two of the oldest medical officers to go out – Dr Borland, inspector-general of hospitals, and Dr Lempriere, physician to the forces, with whom was associated Sir Gilbert Blane, an eminent physician in London, who had been in the navy and who volunteered his services. These three gentlemen went out as commissioners to see with their own eyes and report the state of matters at Walcheren. They remained a few days, saw the miserable plight the army was in and the immense mass of sickness and mortality, but I believe they could recommend nothing further than the removal of the remainder of the army to England from the pestiferous region in which it was located.

The French force, which now nearly surrounded us, was by degrees much increased and, without great reinforcements, amounting almost to a renewal of our exhausted army, it was very apparent we could not hold our ground. Orders therefore came from England and preparations were commenced for our departure.

Soon after this, Sir Eyre Coote was relieved in the command of the British army at Walcheren by Sir George Don, an old and experienced commander.

The preparations for embarkation were now hastened. With several officers of the hospital staff, with the remains of two companies of the hospital corps who acted as orderlies in the hospital, and with Captain Walker, one of their officers, I embarked in the Asia hospital ship. Among those on board with me were the present Sir James Grant; Dr McLeod, physician; Mr Moss, purveyor; and others who formed a good mess and afforded pleasant society.

On the night of the day on which we embarked, while riding at anchor in the road of Flushing, everything having been previously arranged, the dockyard of Flushing was set on fire and from our anchorage we had full view of an awfully grand sight. From the numerous explosions and the violence of the fire, fed by barrels of tar and every kind of combustible, not only everything in the dockyard was doomed to destruction, but several men-of-war on the stocks.

The transports moved out so as to be beyond the reach of the explosions, but we were rather crowded. It began to blow excessively hard – almost a hurricane – and the night was tremendous. The place allotted for the fleet of transports was small and they were of course much crowded together. Not a few of them ran foul of each other, but we were excessively alarmed, a little before daylight, by a terrible concussion. This proceeded from a man-of-war – the *Gorgon* – a forty-four, which, having broken loose from her anchorage and swinging down among the transports, came across us, her bowsprit driving in through our side at a place where staff-surgeon Liddesdale was in his berth, from which, however, he sprang up in an instant and ran upon deck. Fortunate was it that he did so for the bowsprit passed quite across his bedplace and ran on till, pointing upwards, it tore up all the deck in that quarter. Never was there a more providential escape than that of surgeon Liddesdale.

Nothing remarkable occurred till we reached Deal, which was on the morning of Christmas day. I set off post thence and slept at Canterbury that night where I was taken ill, having carried with me the seeds of the prevailing fever from Walcheren. I had reason to be thankful that my seizure took place in England and not in the pestiferous spot where it ran its course so rapidly.

On my arrival in London, I met with the kindest reception from each of the members of the board. My reception by Sir Lucas Pepys and Mr Keate was not externally warmer than that of my kind friend Mr Knight. Each acknowledged that I had executed the superintendence of the medical department at

Walcheren to their credit, as well as to my own. But it required little observation to discern that the most bitter feuds existed among themselves. These were by this time so notorious that government had determined to break up the board.

In the meantime, it had been carried in the House of Commons, against the ministers, that a parliamentary inquiry should be instituted regarding the expedition to Walcheren, and it was understood that the shafts of the opposition were in a particular manner directed against Lord Chatham, who commanded it, as well as against the planner of that ill-fated expedition. I had not been many days in town when I was visited by Lord Radnor and two of his friends, who, after some discussion on the subject of the sickness and mortality of the army, intimated to me that I should receive the Speaker's warrant to attend as a witness at the bar of the House of Commons. I did receive the Speaker's order and Lord Radnor with his friends repeatedly called upon me. I found that caution was necessary and that I ought to have recourse to my notes before I gave replies which required the utmost accuracy. Not long after this, I got notice from Lord Radnor, then Lord Folkestone, that my evidence would not be required and my attendance would be dispensed with.

In a day or two afterwards, I received a note from Lord Ripon, then Mr Robinson, requesting, by desire of Lord Castlereagh, that I would wait upon his lordship on the following morning in St James's Square at eleven o'clock. I was punctual to the appointment and found his lordship and Mr Robinson together. After noticing that Lord Radnor and others had sought information from me on the subject of the Walcheren expedition, they put a few questions to me and informed me that they would require me to attend as a witness at the bar of the House of Commons for which I must be prepared to receive the Speaker's warrant. Having just learned that my excellent friend General Whetham was ill at Portsmouth, I stated that I had just heard of the illness of a friend there, whom I was desirous to see, and begged that, if possible, the warrant might not be sent to me for a week so that I might be enabled to go to Portsmouth for that purpose. This was immediately conceded and I took my leave, the two ministers having been most courteous and kind to me.

On my arrival at Portsmouth, I found my truly kind-hearted friend recovered from one of those attacks of hydrothorax from which he had suffered for many years. He welcomed my return to Portsmouth in the kindest and most cordial manner, saying that my visit revived him. I passed a few days most pleasantly with him and some other kind friends.

Having announced my return to town, I soon received the Speaker's warrant to attend as a witness before a committee of the whole house on the Walcheren expedition, which had been in progress for some time. I went to the Speaker's chamber at four o'clock where I found several other witnesses. Among them was the late Sir John Webb, who had received a similar warrant.

I did this daily for upwards of a fortnight, being every day at the Speaker's chamber by four o'clock, the warrant being renewed and sent to me every day. At length my turn came and I was in some agitation, which the appearance of the witness cited immediately before me did not tend to diminish. This was no other than Sir Richard Strachan, as brave a man as ever trod a quarter-deck. Yet, when a messenger came to the Speaker's chamber, and two members, his friends, appeared to conduct him to the bar of the house, his appearance was anything but that of a man of courage. When his name was called, his face was as white as a sheet. He was agitated and his friends immediately sent for a glass of wine for him, after which he proceeded between them to the bar of the house. His examination was a long one and on his coming out, I was called in. Sir Eyre Coote followed the messenger into the Speaker's room with two of his friends, to whom he introduced me. They counselled me to be calm and collected, and not to widen my replies to questions, but to give affirmation and negation merely, whenever I could properly do so. Between them I marched in and soon found myself at the bar of a crowded house.

My examination by both sides of the house was a very long one. I kept fully possession of myself for a considerable time. But at last, from the extreme heat of the house, my position and the length of my examination, I became somewhat confused, and I completely stuck at one place relative to the supply of medicine to the sick. Mr Whitbread had pressed me much upon this. I had admitted that at one time our stores were nearly empty and that little or no Peruvian bark – one of our most essential medicines – remained. Reverting to my former replies (that our sick did not suffer from the want of medicine), he desired me to reconcile that apparent inconsistency. My reply was that I had given orders to the purveyor to purchase all the bark he could get. His next question was, 'Where was a quantity of bark to be purchased in Walcheren?' My reply was, 'From adventurers.' He rejoined, 'What adventurers?' For the life of me I could not explain my meaning of the word adventurer. He several times repeated the question, but I could not go on and felt most confused. At length, Mr Perceval got up and in a kind voice, addressing me said, 'I suppose you mean by adventurers, those who might have come to the British army to sell their wares, such as wines, provisions and so forth.' This immediately brought me to myself and I replied, 'Precisely so,' and addressing Mr Whitbread, who smiled, I told him that some American vessels came in and, among other merchandise, we found that they had some cases of bark; all of which I directed the purveyor or commissary of hospitals to purchase and that the stock lasted till the supplies arrived from England, which I had so pressingly written for. This was satisfactory, and after having been questioned and cross-questioned by both sides of the house during what appeared to me a very long time, I had permission to retire from the little gentleman with the black wig – as Mr Abbott, the Speaker of the day, was termed [see Appendix 4].

The Walcheren Expedition was one of the worst disasters in British Military History. The 'Walcheren fever' was a form of malaria that recurred over many years. Some victims never recovered. In his memoirs, Rifleman Harris said that he suffered from uncontrollable bouts of trembling. [1] On one occasion when on board a coach he suffered a sudden attack to the horror of his fellow passengers who, terrified of contagion, ordered him to get out. [2]

The campaign is one of the classical examples of an army being devastated by disease through want of knowledge and a consequent neglect of sanitary precautions. As the result of the ensuing Parliamentary Enquiry, the old Medical Board was broken up. It was, at last, realised that gentlemen, however eminent, engaged in private practice in London with little or no knowledge of the army, and none of foreign service with troops, could not satisfactorily manage the affairs of a military department . . . It was therefore decided that the members of the new Board should be persons of extensive first-hand knowledge of the service and who had served abroad with troops.' [3]

Notes

1   *Recollections of Rifleman Harris* edited & introduced by Christopher Hibbert, p. 120.

2   Ibid.

3   From an article on Sir James McGrigor by Lieutenant-Colonel M.W. Russell as it appeared in the *Journal* of the R.A.M.C., Vol. XIII, August, 1909.

Chapter 13

Marriage – Proceeds to the Peninsula

On inquiry, I found I had not permission to leave town and therefore passed much time with many old and kind friends. Among others, I spent much time in company with my dear friend and distant relation Dr – now Sir James – Grant, through whom I was introduced to his sister, whom I had afterwards the good fortune to marry and who, without the slightest exaggeration, brought me the greatest happiness of my life by uniting her lot to mine.

I returned to Portsmouth and resumed the superintendence of my districts, which my friend General Whetham had arranged with the Horse Guards, and which during my absence had been held by Dr Fergusson.

In June 1810, I was united in marriage to Miss Grant. Arrived at Portsmouth, General Whetham did everything in his power to make our abode comfortable and being a bachelor, he sent for his sister, the wife of a clergyman, who, with her husband, came to Portsmouth; and thus he made the Government House a comfortable place for us to visit.

It will be in the recollection of the reader that before I was sent to Walcheren to succeed Sir John Webb in the superintendence, I had been requested by government, through Marshal Beresford, to superintend the medical department of the Portuguese army and to organise a system of medical regulation and discipline. On my proceeding to Walcheren, the rank of inspector of hospitals, which would have been local had I joined the Portuguese army, was made permanent by my services as chief at Walcheren. However, on my return from Walcheren, Marshal Beresford was anxious for my services with him, but my recent marriage had rendered the situation of chief of the medical department of the Portuguese army less desirable than it would have been when I was a bachelor and, after some exertion, I was mainly instrumental in getting my friend Dr Fergusson appointed inspector of hospitals with the Portuguese army, which obtained him a step in promotion and he proceeded forthwith to Portugal.

Before I had proceeded to Walcheren, the medical concerns of the southern and south-west districts appeared to me to be very considerable, but the mass of sick which I had to deal with in Walcheren made those of my old districts

Jean Grant (1743–1825), daughter of Thomas Grant of Kylvemore (of the Grants of Arndilly); wife of Duncan Grant (6th and last of Mullochard, Provost of Forres 1785–88); and mother of Mary (wife of Sir James McGrigor), Sir James Grant, Colonel Colquhoun Grant and Captain Duncan Grant (McGrigor family portrait, photographed by Roy Summers)

appear small. I, however, followed up in those districts the plan of observation which I had commenced in the York district and, as I had reason to believe, I proceeded in their superintendence much to the satisfaction of the generals who commanded therein.

I ought to have mentioned that, on the conclusion of the parliamentary inquiry into the Walcheren expedition, a new board for the medical department of the army was constituted and, as it appeared at the parliamentary investigation that the members of the last board had no extensive knowledge of the service, nor had ever served abroad, the members of the new board were to be free from that disadvantage [see Appendix 4]. They were Dr Weir, a gentleman of very advanced age, who had served much abroad; the late Sir Charles Kerr, who had long served in the East as well as in the West Indies; and Dr Gordon, who, in addition to a long and varied service, was looked up to as one of the most judicious and talented officers in the medical department of the army. Unfortunately, the defective vision of Dr Gordon obliged him to retire at an early period. However, he was replaced by the late Sir William Franklin, who enjoyed the esteem and confidence of the whole army, and whom I subsequently had the happiness to have as acting colleague for upwards of twenty years.

The Sussex district was commanded by Lord Charles Somerset; the south-west, as before stated, by the Duke of Cumberland; and Portsmouth by my attached friend General Whetham.

On the 2nd of May, 1811, my beloved wife presented me with a son,[1] who was not six months old, when one morning the London post suddenly and unexpectedly brought me orders to prepare for embarkation for the Peninsula, there to replace Dr Frank as chief of the medical staff under Lord Wellington.

In a dispatch dated 3 October, 1811, Grenada, the Duke of Wellington asked that, to replace Dr Franks who was ill, he should have 'the most active and intelligent person that can be found to fill his place.' [2]

At any other time this appointment would have gratified me to the full extent of my ambition, but the happiness I had enjoyed in the married state made it now a sad and painful change to me. The announcement was a sad blow to my beloved wife, who at once determined to be my companion. I had, however seen enough of ladies on service in the field to decide me against that step, and I knew well that with the care of my wife and child, I could not do my duty in the way in which I had determined it should be done while I remained in the service. I went to the secretary of the board for instructions to examine old and recent sick reports, and returns of sick and wounded from the Peninsular army, in order to make myself master of the actual state of the health and hospital concerns, and to be prepared for my duties. I found that a transport had been provided for me and Dr Forbes, then a staff surgeon and one of the ablest medical officers I ever met with in the service, who desired to accompany me, and I also took out with me my four clerks.

I left my house with my brother, the late Colonel McGrigor, and went to take leave of General Whetham, who accompanied me to the place of embarkation. I embarked with Dr Forbes and my clerks in a small brig. The accommodations were certainly small, but we had the consolation of having the whole of the vessel to ourselves. We put to sea on the following day, and on that and for several succeeding days it blew exceedingly hard; but we finally reached Lisbon on the 10th day of January, 1812.

We came to anchor at Belem late in the day. I proceeded to the hotel and went to bed. On waking in the morning, my surprise was great to see from the windows of my bedroom, which opened upon the garden, the orange trees bearing fruit, while but a few days before I had found the streets of Falmouth covered with black ice and the surrounding mountainous country white with snow.

McGrigor kept a *Journal* of all that occurred during his time in the Peninsula. Some of it is in his own handwriting, which is difficult to read, but much was transcribed by his secretary, Dr Charles Forbes (later Inspector-General of Hospitals), and the four clerks who accompanied him to Portugal and Spain.

Arriving in Lisbon, McGrigor at once heard the joyful news that, only ten days before, Wellington had captured Ciudad Rodrigo, one of the most important forts on the frontier between Spain and Portugal. The victory, however, had been achieved with great loss of life – nearly 5,000 men of the British army having been killed or wounded. Many others were ill on account of the privations they endured.

> The army was sickly and the greater part of the sick were crowded into the general hospitals, particularly to Lisbon, in most of which there was a high proportion of mortality particularly at Coimbra, Celerico, Castaniera and Abrantes.

Once settled in a billet at Lisbon, I had abundance of duties on my hands. I made a most minute inspection of the stores and accounts of the purveyor and apothecary. A variety of reports had reached England very condemnatory of both these departments, some of which reports were very scandalous and unfounded. But I determined to show that I would look into them narrowly and, on inspection, I certainly found great irregularities in both. There was an immense number of sick and of medical officers at Lisbon, and also a very great number of either sick or reported sick or wounded officers. In England I had heard much that was unfavourable respecting them and after I had narrowly examined the whole, I made up my mind to make a report and a proposition thereupon to Lord Wellington when I had joined headquarters. The report related to the very great accumulation of sick and to the still greater exceptional accumulation of officers, their ladies and the wives of soldiers at Lisbon, which detained at the capital of the country a disproportionate part of the medical officers of the army. My repeated inspection of all the hospitals, and of a great many of the officers, convinced me that Lisbon was so very agreeable a residence that many officers and soldiers would be slow to resume their duties in the field, and that it was a much more attractive station for the medical officers themselves than the divisions of the army about Ciudad Rodrigo in an inclement season of the year.

After I had fully satisfied my own mind by repeated inspection of every establishment at Lisbon and much conversation with General Peacock the commandant there, I communicated my ideas to Lord Wellington; and after giving a full report of the existing state of things, I submitted to his lordship three distinct propositions.

1. As to the large proportion of the army in the hospitals, particularly at Lisbon, I proposed that, in future, only special cases of either wounds or sickness should be sent to the rear and such only as should be approved by me. In order to effect this, I submitted that each corps should have a temporary hospital of its own where all slight cases of

disease and wounds should be treated by the regimental medical officers, under the superintendence of the principal medical officer of the division.

2. That all sick and wounded officers of the same description, instead of being sent to Lisbon, as heretofore, should be treated in the same manner.

3. That, as in future no sick or wounded would be at Lisbon, except those that would ultimately be embarked for England, all the medical officers should be ordered up to the army, excepting the small establishment which I indicated for the Lisbon duties. Finally, I gave a statement of the sick I found at Lisbon, proposing that one part of them, officers and men, should be sent as inefficient to England and the remainder ordered to join their regiments in the field, for duty, or to be under the care of the medical officers of their regiments.

I made further propositions for the prevention of the accumulation of the stores of every kind which I found at Lisbon.

I received a cordial letter of thanks from Lord Wellington, who requested me to join the army in order that he might talk over the subject of my report with me, desiring me, however, to inspect narrowly the large hospital stations of Coimbra and Celerico, and others on my route. I subsequently received two more letters from him when he expressed his desire that I would join him with all speed.

With Dr Forbes and my four clerks, we set off from Lisbon to Villa Franca, our first stage. Thence we hurried on to Coimbra. The weather was bad and tempestuous for it rained throughout the journey and we reached Coimbra much fatigued, and with our baggage animals quite exhausted.

―――――――――

McGrigor's *Journal* reads:

'On the [ ] of January with Dr Forbes, Messers Croft and Biggs, set off from Lisbon for Coimbra. We traversed a fine country and with much wood, particularly the olive, and having the Tagus on our right. Passing through the famous lines of Torres Vaddras, we soon reached Villa Franca or first stage.

'On the [ ] set out from Villa Franca and continued throughout a day that rained incessantly, and through a bleak country which everywhere bore the marks of its having been ravaged by the French, till eventually we reached the miserable village of Rio Major [sic]. Our mules could, with difficulty, reach Rio Major and we were obliged to halt in it during the following day to recruit them and dry our own clothes. I was hospitably received by the Apothecaries of the village.

'On the [ ] set out from Rio Major and reached [ ], here we were all lodged in the caravans, the roofs of which everywhere admitted the rain on us which poured in, in torrents.

'On the [ ] of January arrived at Coimbra, where I remained some time, narrowly inspecting the hospitals under that energetic officer, Mr Tagart . . . We occupied the best buildings in it as hospitals; their situation was good and they were large and airy with lofty roofs, and abundantly ventilated. They were the College of Arts in the upper part of the town, the Franciscan Convent on the opposite side of the town and the St Jose Convent used as a surgical hospital . . .

'The principal, if not the greatest, means of preserving health in an army, is the treating of every case when it can be done in the corps at first and as long as it can be done. In acute disease everything depends on active treatment being pursued at the very commencement. With this in view, every corps was amply provided, not only with every means of having an hospital of its own at all times, but with additional medical officers available to the regimental [hospitals] frequently.

'In this manner . . . when it was found necessary to send men to the rear, the first plan had not been neglected: they were met with officers who knew their care and also brought with them a detailed statement of the care and of the treatment which had been pursued.

'I cannot pass over the College of Arts of which Dr Tier had the correspondence. No hospital, civil or military, in this kingdom could be any cleaner, sweeter or in higher order. There were present some wants which, as he could not supply, did not rest with him:

1. The floors were all of brick, and the sick were laid on them with nothing intervening between them and the floor but some straw and their bedding. This was not a favourable situation for the recovery of debilitated men, or of the sick, particularly those ill of pulmonary disease, dysentery or rheumatism.

2. There were nowhere any fireplaces but in the kitchens, and the wards were everywhere cold in the mornings and evenings. On the lower floors they were damp and moist both on the walls and floors.

3. I found disease of every kind – medical and surgical – and I suspected that some of them were contagious, mixed, fevers, wounds, dystenteries, pulmonary diseases.

4. There was no convalescent hospital . . .

'I established at Coimbra a regulation which I subsequently found of the greatest service in all our hospitals – separate hospitals for care of continued fever, for dysentery, for wounds and ulcers, and for convalescents.

'At Coimbra, I found that relapse from disease was extremely frequent . . . Men sent from hospitals as recovered, generally returned from the depot in a few days and with severe disease, and it was observed that a large part of the mortality was from the relapses.

'The recovered men went from the warmer hospitals to the depot which was a dreadfully cold place where they had only one blanket, and where the duty they had to perform was rather severe. I therefore established a convalescent hospital in a convent, and to this place every convalescent was sent from all the hospitals and remained for two or three weeks ... It was decided that no man should be sent to the depot who was not fit for all duties of a soldier and fit to be marched off for his corps.

'A medical officer was likewise appointed to the depot acting therein under the orders of the principal medical officer in charge of the convalescent hospital. The medical officer was directed twice a day minutely to examine every man in the depot, to send immediately those having any symptom of disease to the proper hospital and to clear the weakly men to the convalescent hospital. A code of regulations was further presented to the military commandant and recommended for adoption in the depot. A special attention was requested in the diet and temperance of these men, and that they should be completed in necessaries and clothing before they were exposed to any duty. The necessity of these injunctions was most obvious because the neglect of any of them never failed speedily to induce disease and bring back the patient to the hospital ...

'The general hospitals at this time were: Lisbon, Santares, Abrantes, Castelo Branco, Coimbra, Celerico and Castaniera. The field hospitals were at, or near, Ciudad Rodrigo. The wounded and sick of the army were carried to Castaniera and Celerico where I saw them in a sufficiently miserable and deplorable state, many of them with frost-bitten limbs, some tetanic, and typhus prevalent among them. They were eventually carried from Celerico to Coimbra ...

'The suffering of the sick and wounded on this route were very great ... [they] were conveyed ... almost always only on bullock carts ... often without the means of having any victuals cooked and not unfrequently without comforts; their distress and misery may easily be imagined ... They suffered so much by the transport, the weather and by privations that many particularly of the wounded and those ill of dysentery arrived in so bad a state as only to survive a few days of hours after their reception into the hospitals at either Celerico or Coimbra. In truth, the medical officers ... had not fair play with them. They received their patients at that stage when it was impossible to do anything with them.

'I have said that the mortality at Coimbra had been very high and I saw that there was much severe and untreatable disease there. Many of the cases arrived in the last stages of fever or dysentery and many of the wounds were in a gangrenous state. To remedy this I established two intermediate or, as they were called, 'relay' stations between Celerico and Coimbra. I placed there some medical officers with mattresses, bedding and medical comforts. Notice being sent to these medical officers whenever sick were sent off from Celerico to have beds, warm [ ] and comforts in readiness for them by the time of their arrival.

[An obvious later addition] 'In my letter to the Board of 11th February, I noted that the mortality from diseases exceeded 500 during the preceding months. Sixteen medical officers were attacked with low fever at Coimbra during this period.'

Next to Lisbon, our largest hospital establishment was at Coimbra, where we occupied the numerous convents, churches and monasteries of the place as hospitals, and it took me nearly a week to examine the whole of them minutely. Coimbra is the seat of the principal Portuguese university where George Buchanan, after he fled from his country, was elected to a chair, and was interesting to me for many reasons.

I had hardly finished my inspection at Coimbra, when I received a letter from Lord Wellington, pressing me to join him at headquarters. I set off for Busaco, in the monastery of which place we halted for the night, the monks entertaining us.

Again, McGrigor's *Journal* provides some further details:

'While our dinner was preparing I walked out and surveyed the field of battle, the Friar pointing out the principal spots. There was everywhere sufficient marks and remains of clothing – French and English – plumes, shoes, heaps of bones. The pious monk, pulling me by the sleeve to one spot, said this was a place where he found a wounded Frenchman whom he put out of pain by knocking his brains out with a stone.

'It was here that the Portuguese troops first fought in the ranks with the British and with them made a successful stand against the French; to be seen the situation in which our army was most formidable, the ascent by which the French advanced bold and steep in the extreme.'

On reaching Celerico, I found the hospital establishment in that miserable dilapidated place anything but comfortable for the sick and wounded, which was chiefly owing to its locality and to the great deficiency of means to afford comfort. The circumstances of the campaign, and the situation, rendered it nevertheless necessary to have an hospital establishment there.

His *Journal* expands:

'It was at this place, when I arrived on the 16th, that I first saw more of miserable disease than I had hitherto seen. The place was so very badly calculated for an hospital station: a village in rugged mountain and bare country. The dilapidated houses were our only hospitals. However there was no choice ...

'So unfavourable were reports in the army regarding Celerico that Lord Wellington himself visited it himself in December 1811 and ordered 380 men from it to Coimbra.

'Castaniera: which I reached on the 19th. If the accommodations for the hospitals at Celerico were bad they were infinitely worse at this place, the most wretched, dilapidated

McGrigor's route through Spain and Portugal during January to April, 1812

village I have ever seen in Portugal, Tabrigal not excepted …

'On the 19th February I arrived at Castelo Bom and immediately proceeded to Headquarters at Freineda to wait upon Viscount Wellington, Commander of the Forces.'

At length, I reached headquarters and, on inquiring for the commander-in-chief, found that Lord Wellington was out hunting. Sir Ulysses Burgh, now Lord Downes, received me and said he was sure Lord Wellington would expect me to dine with him. I accordingly awaited the return of his lordship from the chase. He received me most kindly, recollected immediately our having met in Bombay and thereupon, in the midst of a large party assembled in the dining-room, for drawing-room there was none, asked me if I had met my old regiment the 88th, or Connaught Rangers, on my route. On my replying that I had not, he laughingly said, 'I hope from your long living with them, you have not contracted any of their leading propensities for I hang and shoot more of your old friends for murders, robberies, &c., than I do of all the rest of the army.' The laughter of the whole party was loud. At this I felt somewhat abashed which, Lord Wellington observing, he continued, 'One thing I will tell you, however. Whenever anything very gallant, very desperate is to be done, there is no corps in the army I would sooner employ than your old friends in the Connaught Rangers.' Before I took my departure, his lordship said he would be glad to see me on business in the morning. I went home to a small fort about a mile distant, Castelo Bom, which had been appropriated for my quarters and those of my staff, viz., Mr Gunning, the surgeon of headquarters, my clerks, the servants, muleteers, &c.

Castelo Bom was a very dilapidated town, the population of which consisted of the priest, the chief magistrate – or *juez de foro* – and from fifty to sixty miserable, poor, starved-looking creatures. Indeed, but a few months before we became its inmates, famine and disease had nearly depopulated Castelo Bom and our habitations were of the poorest description; not even in the chief magistrate's house, which was assigned to me (as being the best in the place), was there a pane of glass in any of the windows.

From his *Journal*:

'Immediately on my joining headquarters, a number of things crossed my mind which I had thought would be improvements in the medical departments of the army; several of them were suggestions from inspections at Lisbon, Coimbra, Celerico, Vizen and Castaniera.

'In fact, I had visited most of the hospitals before I had seen Lord Wellington. I had examined the depots, some regimental hospitals and I had witnessed the mode of sending the recovered from the hospitals to the army and I saw much of what appeared exceptionable to me.

'Nothing seemed worse than the mode of transporting the sick, this was oftenest done on the backs of mules or in the carts of the country. There was besides a better provision to a certain extent: viz., by spring wagons. These I found under the charge of the Commissariat and they served them as well as the medical departments . . .

'None of the hospital stations, unless Lisbon, was supplied with boards and trestles, and bedsteads. Another great evil always complained of was the difficulty of transporting stores to the hospital stations and to the army. For transport of any kind we are at all times dependent on the commissariat . . .

'At an early period in my letters from Lisbon and Coimbra addressed to the Adjutant General for the information of Lord Wellington, I recommended that as few hospitals as possible, far in the rear should be kept up and that those at Lisbon should be immediately reduced to the lowest degree, and that there should not be at Lisbon a depot for sick and wounded officers, but that all cases should continue to be treated either within the divisions of the army and by their own surgeons or be sent only to the nearest hospital stations . . .

'I early determined that there should be no permanent or fixed situation but that my medical officers of whatever rank in the army should be moveable and hold himself in readiness to take all duties.'

When I came to take possession of the office I found it denuded of all papers, excepting a few very uninteresting returns, my predecessor having carried with him to England almost all the office books and papers, even the letter books and the orderly book, and those containing Lord Wellington's standing orders to the army. Without these I could not proceed a step, as in fact I was to be guided by them in everything, and I was obliged to report the want of these to Lord Wellington, who was very wroth. He desired I would immediately write to the army medical board, while he wrote to the Duke of York, requesting that all these might be immediately returned to the army as public property and necessary for my guidance.

On examination of the returns rendered to me, I found that they contained very imperfect or, indeed, scarcely any information upon the sick and wounded; reports of sickness having never been regularly required. I therefore immediately set about establishing certain returns and reports, nearly on the plan that I had commenced with the York district, but greatly improved by my subsequent experience at Portsmouth and Walcheren.

On my first interview with Lord Wellington, after dining with him on the day of my joining, I found him much pleased with what I had done at the hospitals in Lisbon and Coimbra.

'I explained fully my views to his Lordship of the medical department and had the satisfaction to find a coincidence. As the basis of all, I did not fail to recommend the system of regimental hospitals whenever it could be pursued.'

He said he much wanted such an officer as me, who thoroughly understood the duties, who was acquainted with the habits of soldiers and who would prevent the malingering propensities of both officers and men at the hospital stations, where all sorts of irregularities prevailed; and he promised me his utmost support, which from that moment I fully experienced. His lordship dwelt on the little support he received from some of the heads of departments, whom he freely named, saying he had to do their duties as well as command the army. I replied that it would be my endeavour to prevent his having that trouble with the medical department of the army. We parted on the best terms and he desired me to come to him every morning at the same hour, with the other heads of departments, the adjutant-general, quartermaster-general and commissary-general.

On my appearing the second morning, I found in the outer department the commissary-general, Sir Robert Kennedy, and the adjutant-general Brigadier-General Stewart (the late Lord Londonderry), with his book under his arm, who, coming up to me, said it was unnecessary for me to come to Lord Wellington, that I might come to his office and he would transact my business for me with his lordship, whom it was unnecessary for me to trouble. I replied I preferred doing business directly with Lord Wellington and that it was by his lordship's desire I came there. At this moment, the door of his little inner apartment was opened by Lord Wellington who, nodding to me, desired me to come in. After this I daily made my appearance to take his orders and to make my reports on the number of sick and wounded with all the details of their movements. These reports I made to his lordship ever afterwards, whether in the field or in quarters, immediately after his breakfast, which was the time he fixed for seeing the adjutant-general and quartermaster-general; the commissary-general; myself and occasionally the paymaster-general; and the head of the intelligence department when at headquarters, my brother-in-law, the late Colonel Colquhoun Grant. At this time he gave me notice of movements and, after my giving him a statement of the total sick and wounded of the army, I gave him the total in each hospital station in Portugal, Spain and afterwards in France and the total number of dead; the number of fit to be marched to their regiments or convalescent; the cases or diseases, with the causes of these; and, in fine, everything relating to the health department of the army.

'On the 21st [February] I assumed the direction of the medical department of the army and, in consequence of a communication with Lord Wellington, found orders for the campaign in the Alentjo to the Medical and Purveying officers, requiring the Commissary General to give orders to the officers of his department to supply such stores as the Commissariat furnished, as well as to supply transport to the new hospital stations which I pitched on. The new hospitals: Alta da Chao, Esternoz, Elvas . . . '

At first, it was my custom to wait upon Lord Wellington with a paper in my hand, on which I had entered the heads of the business about which I wished to receive his orders, or to lay before him. But I shortly discovered that he disliked my coming with a written paper; he was fidgety and evidently displeased when I referred to my notes. I therefore discontinued this and came to him daily, having the heads of business arranged in my mind and discussed them after I had presented the state of the hospitals. When money was required for hospital purposes, I brought with me the purveyor's estimates, under different heads, such as purchases of provisions, wine, building repairs, &c.

A few days after I had joined at headquarters, in my morning interview and discussion with his lordship, I broached the subject of my written communication to him from Lisbon and Coimbra. He entirely approved of my plan of breaking up the great depot of sick officers, particularly at Lisbon, and of a code of regulations which I submitted to him on the subject and, further, of that regarding the sending sick or wounded soldiers as well as officers to the rear. By these regulations, neither sick nor wounded officers or men were to be sent to the rear, except on the proceedings of boards of medical officers, which proceedings were to be submitted for my approval. But regard was had, of course, for exceptional cases, such as during retrograde movements of the army or after action. It was further directed that, after the arrival of officers or men at Lisbon, they were immediately to appear before another board of medical officers, and, if recovery was not effected in a limited time at Lisbon, all were to be embarked for England. This at once cut at the root of the great abuses which had existed at Lisbon where, besides the great number of malingering soldiers, there were generally many officers congregated, as well as their wives. General Peacock, as commandant at Lisbon, told me that the ladies were the most insubordinate and troublesome part of his charge. Lord Wellington at once saw the great advantage that would accrue to the army from this part of my plan, in the considerable addition which it would give to his force in the field, and he immediately gave his unqualified assent to the regulations which I laid before him, ordering General Stewart, the adjutant-general, to issue them in orders to the whole army. When, however, I proposed, with the still further view of preventing the accumulation of sick and wounded in the rear (which existed in all the hospital stations), that each regiment and brigade should have its own hospital, where all slight cases of disease and wounds should in the first instance be accommodated, and that conveyance for the hospital establishment should be provided for each corps and brigade, he at once exclaimed against it and said he would have no interruption to the movements of the army, which my plans would clog. On my further explaining, he warmly said he would have no vehicles with the army but for the conveyance of the guns so that, for the time, I was obliged to give up my plan. I saw he was very strongly opposed to it. I found, however, that he had not entirely dismissed it from his mind for some days afterwards he said to me that my views were excellent, if they had been practicable, because it was lamentable to see so many men slightly ill or wounded sent constantly to the rear, and thus diminishing the force of the army in a greater proportion than the reinforcements from England were adding to it; but he said, 'I cannot risk encumbering the army and impeding its movements, either in advancing or retiring,' and for the time the matter dropped.

Notes

1   Charles McGrigor, his eldest son.

2   *Journal* of the Royal Army Medical Corps, January, 1951.

EDITOR'S INTRODUCTION TO CHAPTER 14

'On my joining the army, as stated in my letter to the Board of 26 February, there were 18,000 men on the sick list. I had 111 effective medical officers of the general staff and 10 sick of 67 Corps, of the line and foreign, whose establishment is not 201 medical officers, only 109 are present effective and doing duty. The effective medical staff were surely too weak for the number of sick, particularly dispersed as they were in a great part of Portugal and part of Spain.' [1]

CHAPTER 14

The siege and capture of Badajoz

From appearances it was evident that the army was about to move and I received some general instructions respecting the hospitals. Ever since my arrival in Portugal I had been taking measures to introduce my own plan of reports and returns, which I had kept steadily in view since I entered upon my inspectorial duties in the York district. My objects were to have a check on the expenditure of stores for the public and to elicit as much information as possible from the reports and returns rendered to me. The stores are of two descriptions: viz., apothecary and purveyor's stores. The stores of the apothecary include medicine, surgical materials and surgical instruments, while those of the purveyor or hospital commissary include hospital clothing and bedding, wines, articles of comfort for the sick, materials for repair, hospital tents, marquees, &c. Various reports were prevalent on my arrival of the immense and improvident expenditure of these stores, particularly of the purveyor's, and it was whispered that some of the departmental clerks of the purveyor had been carrying on a system of peculation.

On this subject I had several communications with Lord Wellington, who desired me to keep a vigilant eye on those gentlemen and put some anonymous letters, addressed to him, into my hand. When Lord Wellington announced to me the object of the march of the army, viz., the siege of Badajoz, I issued orders to the purveyor and to the apothecary to have depots of their respective stores, and at the same time I issued orders to the superintending medical officers of divisions of the army to see that each corps in their divisions sent in requisitions for such medicines, surgical materials and instruments as they were in want of. By the time the movements commenced towards Badajoz, every division and every corps had received the supply of medicine and materials which they required, while the apothecary and purveyor established at Elvas a depot of their respective stores, from which the several corps could obtain what they stood in need of. When I moved with my office establishment, passing the different divisions of the army, and saw the description of sick they were depositing at the appointed stations on the route, I entered into conversation with the regimental surgeons all of whom agreed with me that if they had only some kind of conveyance, such as the common carts of the country, it would be necessary to send but few men to the rear. Their commanding officers were of the same opinion, being very unwilling to part with a man in moments of emergency but, having no authority, they feared to incur censure by carrying slight cases with them. This practice however gradually crept in: few corps were to be seen without a cart to carry their slight cases with them when they marched and the commanding officers, wishing to have as many effective men as possible with their regiments, were anxiously desirous to carry with them men who, in a few days, could carry their firelock and appear in the ranks. The medical officers, knowing that the plan was one which I especially advocated, entered readily into it.

Early in March, 1812, headquarters broke up and, with my office establishment, I left our miserable quarters at Castelo Bom and crossed the Tagus. We continued our march through Estremadura till I reached Elvas where I was stationed. On the following day, crossing the Guadiana by a bridge of boats, I found Lord Wellington with part of the army encamped before Badajoz.

I established my office at Elvas, where in two days of letters and returns forwarded to me from the hospital stations and divisions of the army, I found as many as filled a large corn-sack. However, with my four very efficient clerks, and my friend Dr James Forbes, whom I retained with me at headquarters to conduct the professional part of the correspondence, we soon mastered the formidable sack.

Sir James McGrigor records in the first volume of his *Journal*:

> On my arrival, I found an inundation of complaints of the inadequacy of the means which the medical department had for opening the campaign.
> 14 March
> To this day the Commissariat had not found conveyance for the purveyor for any bedding, stores or even medicines to Elvas or any of the new stations, so that we were everywhere absolutely without any provision whatever for sick and wounded in this part of the country. I was further mortified to find that the medical and

purveying officers arrived very slowly at their destination, as all alleged that time was required to fit them out for active service. I directed that, in future, every officer was always to hold himself in readiness to move on the shortest notice and that I might know that no unnecessary delay was made upon the road, movement returns were directed.

To this date there was not a single spring wagon in the Alentejo.

By a letter from Dr Tier at Celerico, I have the melancholy report of the deaths of not less than sixteen cases on the road from Carteniers to Celerico.

Neither were there any panniers for the mules which carried hospital stores. McGrigor, no doubt fuming with impatience, received a letter from Colonel Sir William Delancey, on Wellington's Staff, on 29 April, telling that, 'the application for these articles should be forwarded to this office by the commanding officers of the regiments through the assistant quartermaster-general of the division to whom it belongs.' [2]

McGrigor's *Journal* continues:

The ground was broken before Badajoz and casualties commenced. A field hospital was, therefore, directed to be established.

[Later in March] At this point Dr James writes to me that he is sending up hospital marquees from Abrantes.

30 March
This day Staff Surgeon Cook with assistants was stationed at the flying bridge, having with him medicines, instruments, surgical materials with some provisions and hospital comforts for the wounded.

April, 1812
The siege was pushed on briskly and our daily casualties became numerous . . . In addition to the buildings appropriated as a receiving field hospital . . . hospital marquees were erected.

During the time I was in camp, a sortie was made by the enemy, which, however, effected little more than throwing more wounded into the hospitals.

This day the rains commenced and it rained for several days most heavily, so as to render the duties of the siege harassing and fatiguing in no ordinary degree.

As I rode over daily to see and report to Lord Wellington, he kindly ordered a tent to be pitched for me contiguous to his own, furnished with some straw and two blankets, where I could repose at night if anything detained me. I established a small field hospital to which such accidents and wounds as now daily occurred were sent in the first instance and got some spring wagons appointed for the daily conveyance of the cases from the field hospitals to those established in Elvas. Further, by application to Lord Wellington, I got an order for Colonel Digby, of the wagon corps, to attach two spring wagons to each corps employed in the siege.

Two days after my arrival from Elvas, soon after I had passed the Guadiana on my way over to Badajoz, I suddenly heard a sharp fire of musketry, while at the same time some cannon-shot passed over my head. The musketry fire became very sharp and I hesitated about entering our encampment. Lucky it was, also, that I did not, for the enemy had penetrated into it, having made a sortie; all the circumstances of which I heard in a very short time when, on finding the fire had ceased, I cautiously approached the tents and, seeing red coats, entered.

Having ascertained the number wounded and that the nature of the cases was in general slight, I set off on my return to Elvas and, when nearly halfway, met Lord Wellington and Marshal Beresford galloping very hard. They inquired most anxiously about the result of the sortie of which, when I had fully informed them, they proceeded more leisurely to our encampment.

McGrigor's *Journal* notes: 'The first of April found us engaged in the siege of Badajoz.'

It is unnecessary for me to detail the particulars of the siege; they have been duly described by many military writers. I will advert therefore only to one or two incidents.

Composing part of the corps employed in the siege of Badajoz, and encamped near the headquarter tents, was the 88th or Connaught Rangers, in the 5th division of the army – Sir Thomas Picton's column – and it may be readily supposed, when I had a moment of leisure, that I called to see the few officers who remained of my acquaintance in the Connaught Rangers. The first night that I remained out of Elvas, at the encampment, and before Lord Wellington had ordered a tent to be pitched for me at the headquarters, I took refuge with my old friends the Connaught Rangers and got a spare tent with some straw in it and a blanket for the night, throughout which it rained incessantly, inundating the tent round which I continued to shift my straw in search of the driest spot. In the morning I breakfasted with Captain Thomson, who afterwards, as I wished to see what was doing and as the men of the 88th had that morning the duty in the trenches, took me into them to show me that part of the soldier's duty. We were very soon obliged to creep on all fours as we advanced for there were sharp-shooters on the lookout, who popped at every head that appeared, and who, as it seems, were good marksmen for they had killed many of our men in this way. Under the care of my friend Thomson, we returned in safety, but what was my horror when, in less than two hours after this, an officer of the 88th came to me with the information that our poor friend Thomson had been shot through the head while engaged with a friend in the same manner as he had but so lately been with me. An officer of another regiment had called upon him immediately after his return from the trenches with me and had also expressed a wish to see the state of the trenches. Thomson offered to accompany him and they had proceeded but a short way when Thomson, in bravado, stood up, looking directly at the spot from whence the shot came every now and then, believing he was out of reach, when he was struck on the head by a bullet and fell dead.

The other incident has been a memorable one with me, for at the time it happened it made a strong impression upon me, and I have so often related it since its occurrence that I am still able to give a faithful account of it.

On the 6th of April, the engineers having reported the main breach practicable, it was known to those about Lord Wellington that an assault would be given that evening. I dined that day with Marshal Beresford in his tent, contiguous to that of Lord Wellington; the company consisted chiefly of the marshal's staff. There was little conversation at table, but a young man inconsiderately said, 'Of the number now present, how many will be alive and with their limbs whole this time tomorrow, or even four hours hence?' A dead silence of some continuance followed this observation and the marshal gave the officer a look of displeasure. After dinner, all sallied out. I had determined to post myself near Lord Wellington, to receive any orders he might give to me, and I desired Dr Forbes, afterwards Sir Charles Forbes, to accompany me, taking with him what I deemed necessary in the event of Lord Wellington being wounded, and likewise intending to send him to any quarter it might be necessary to communicate with. By the time we reached Lord Wellington, who was on a hillock not far from the main breach, the storming party had advanced; the firing of shot, shells and grenades had commenced, and blue lights were thrown out which illuminated occasionally everything around us. I found myself in a situation similar to one I had been in years before, at an assault, but with this difference, that there we were the besieged and here we were the besiegers.

Lord Wellington was attended only by two of his aides-de-camp: the Prince of Orange and the Duke of Richmond, then Lord March, both young men. His lordship, on our coming up, was so intent on what was going on that I believe he did not at first observe that Dr Forbes and I had joined him. Soon after our arrival, an officer came up with an unfavourable report of the assault, announcing that Colonel McLeod and several officers were killed, with heaps of men, who choked the approach to the breach. At the place where we stood, we were within hearing of the voices of the assailants and of the assailed; and it was now painful to notice that the voices of our countrymen had become fainter while the French cry of 'Avancez, étrillons ces Anglais!' became stronger.

Another officer came up with a still more unfavourable report that no progress was being made and that he feared none could be made for almost all the officers were killed, and none left to lead on the men of whom a great many had fallen. At this moment I cast my eyes on the countenance of Lord Wellington, lit up by the glare of the torch held by Lord March; I never shall forget it to the last moment of my existence and I could even now sketch it. The jaw had fallen and the face was of unusual length, while the torchlight gave his countenance a lurid aspect, but still, the expression of the face was firm. Suddenly, turning to me and putting his hand on my arm, he said, 'Go over immediately to Picton and tell him he must try if he cannot succeed on the castle.' I replied, 'My Lord, I have not my horse, but I will walk as fast as I can and I think I can find the way. I know part of the road is swampy.' 'No, no,' he replied, 'I beg your pardon. I thought it was Delancey.' I repeated my offer, saying I was sure I could find the way, but he said 'No.' In this very uncomfortable state of mind Lord Wellington had remained but a few minutes when we heard a noise and we all instantly said it was a horseman approaching. Immediately after this, a voice called out harshly and loudly, 'Where is Lord Wellington?' We all five exclaimed, 'Here! here!' 'My Lord,' continued the officer, 'the castle is your own,' and on being further questioned he said he believed that Sir Thomas Picton and the whole division were in possession. Lord Wellington conveyed some orders by this officer and, if I recollect correctly, the purport of them was for Picton to push down into the town. After the departure of this officer, Lord Wellington sent information to the main breach of our being in possession of the castle with orders to push in, for the castle was in our possession and they would now find little, if any, opposition. Then, calling for his own horse and for those of the Prince of Orange and Lord March to be sent to them, he proceeded to the main breach, which was immediately entered and, as is well known from the many published accounts, the town of Badajoz was forthwith in our possession.

McGrigor does not describe how the French fired the mines in the ditch before the fortress, perhaps because, even in retrospect, it was too horrible to recall. Sir Charles Oman describes how many men of the Light Division were in the ditch when the French engineers fired the series of fougasses, mines and powder-barrels which they had laid.

'They worked perfectly and the result was appalling – the 500 volunteers who formed the advance of each division were almost all slain, scorched or disabled'.

McGrigor does say, however, that Brigadier-General Kempt was the hero of the day. Kempt took command of the 3rd Division when General Picton was wounded and backed up by Portuguese, and by the rear brigades, succeeded in taking the Castle of Badajoz and thereby entering the town. [3]

Accompanied by Dr Forbes, I immediately followed. It was grey dawn of day, but I shall never forget the horrible sights that met our eyes on every side as we entered by the breach and after we had passed it. We had even then great difficulty in entering and in picking our steps to pass the still formidable obstacles which met us on every side, at the sight of which we no longer wondered at the protracted assault and at the difficulty the bravest soldiers – of what we considered the best army in the world – had met with in their attempts to storm it. The obstacles appeared to me insurmountable. On every side were to be seen half barrels of powder, with here and there a burning or smoking fuse among them, threatening explosion every instant. I need not dwell on the formidable nature of the defenses, which have been over and over again described by military authorities.

In a little time the whole of the soldiers appeared to be in a state of mad drunkenness. In every corner we met them forcing their way like furies into houses, firing through the keyholes of the doors so as to force the locks, or at any person they saw at a window imploring mercy. In passing some houses which they had entered, we heard the shrieks of females, and sometimes the groans of those whom they were no doubt butchering. All was disorder and dire confusion. Three soldiers, whom we met in the streets, having lost all respect for the uniform of an officer, looked at him with a threatening aspect if addressed; and if threatened, they would sometimes point their muskets at him.

In one street, I met General Philippon, the governor, with his two daughters, holding each by the hand; all three with their hair dishevelled, and with them were two British officers, each holding one of the ladies by the arm, and with their drawn swords making thrusts occasionally at soldiers who attempted to drag the ladies away. I am glad to say that these two British officers succeeded in conveying the governor and his daughters safely through the breach to the camp. With the exception of these ladies, I was told that very few females, old or young, escaped violation by our brutal soldiery, mad with brandy and with passion. At any other time, the rank and age of General Philippon, bare-headed, with his grey hairs streaming in the wind, would have protected him from any soldiers. When I saw them pulling at these two ladies and endeavouring to drag them away from their father, and the two young officers who so gallantly defended them at the peril of their lives, I could not forbear going up and endeavouring with threats to bring to the recollection of two soldiers of my old regiment the 88th, how much they tarnished the glory which the Connaught Rangers had ever earned in the field by such cowardly conduct. But it was only by my reminding them that I was an old Connaught Ranger, who felt for the glory of the corps, that I disarmed their rage towards me and that their raised muskets were lowered. Going towards the cathedral and castle, or wherever I went, I encountered nothing but a scene of savage riot and wild drunkenness in which, at length, some of the wives even of the soldiers were active participators. It was said that Lord Wellington was met by a party of these drunken men, who desired to fire what they called a *feu de joie* in honour of him, and that they placed him in no small danger by their manner of evincing their admiration of him as they loaded and re-loaded their pieces, firing them off in all directions and from drunkenness unable to comprehend the direction they fired in.

My principal object in entering the fortress was to ascertain, in some degree, the number of wounded, particularly of the officers, and the description of their wounds. I could accomplish this but very imperfectly and from what I witnessed I had no doubt that the number killed and wounded, both officers and men, had been increased since we got possession of the place from the horrible and brutal state of drunkenness the soldiery were in. I succeeded better outside the walls and from the staff surgeons of the brigades engaged, as well as from the regimental surgeons, I collected a tolerably good account of their wounded and the description of their wounds. I visited a good many of the officers and returned to camp not a little exhausted. I immediately made my way to Lord Wellington and found him in his tent, writing the despatches. He received me most cordially and, after I had given him my detail, thanked me much. He was in excellent spirits. I therefore said, 'I trust, my lord, you are satisfied that the medical officers during last night did their duty as well as the military officers and that you will receive my testimony that they discharged their arduous and laborious duties most zealously, and often under circumstances of personal danger of which they were regardless.' He replied that he himself had witnessed it. I then added, 'Nothing could more gratify those officers, nothing could be a greater incentive to their exertions on future occasions than his noticing them in his public despatches.' He asked, 'Is that usual?' My reply was, 'It would be of the most essential service,' and, I ventured to add, that 'really their extraordinary exertions gave them in justice a claim in this.' He rejoined, 'I have finished my despatch, but, very well, I will add something about the doctors.' When the *Gazette* appeared the medical officers of the army in England saw with delight that the merits of their brethren had been publicly acknowledged in the same manner as those of the military officers. This was the *first time* that their merits had been thus publicly acknowledged and the example of Lord Wellington has been followed after every great action that has since been fought, and some time afterwards the navy followed the example [see Appendix 5].

From the great number of wounded the labours of the medical officers after the fall of Badajoz were immense. Their duties before and during the siege were heavy upon them. But it is after a siege or general engagement, when the military officer is in comparative ease and with very light duties, that the toil of the medical officer is arduous in the extreme, and the fatigue of the mind is not less that that of the body. While laboriously employed from morning to night, the anxiety he feels frequently prevents the refreshment of sleep at night when, wrapt in thought, and drawing constantly on his professional resources, he becomes care-worn and exhausted. It is at these times that his value is felt by the army at large and that by the officers in particular he is caressed, flattered and almost idolised. He nearly everywhere alleviates pain; in many instances he gets credit for saving life; and on all sides expressions of gratitude and eternal obligation are made to him. From what one sees and hears at such times, one might be led to fancy that the doctor would be cherished ever afterwards. But, alas, those feelings are but too often the feelings of the moment only; they grow fainter and fainter with the lapse of time and I have but too frequently observed that the doctor and his doings have, in a few years, been quite forgotten and when these have become the subject of conversation it has been too often said, 'Well, what more did he do than his duty? Was it not the doctor's duty to have done all this?' I do not say that this is the cold transitory feelings of all military officers for I know bright examples of the contrary in the highest ranks in the army and of civil life who, to their dying day, have honoured as a cherished friend the medical officer, who in battle, or in dangerous illness, was their surgeon or physician. Yet, as the result of close personal observation, during a period of upwards of fifty years, I must affirm that too frequently the feeling of gratitude has subsided in time, and even in instances where the attention has been extreme and much beyond what the strict line of duty required of the medical officer. I have indeed known more than one instance where the surgeon, besides visiting the officer three or four times a day, when great pressure of fatiguing duty devolved upon him, after expending all the bandages he could get from the stores, has torn up his own shirts for bandages and dressings for his patients; while he has furthermore supplied not only all the wine required, but the very eatables from his own stock, and nothing but that constant kind attention saved life.

'A terrible price had been paid for the victory of Badajoz in the loss of nearly 5,000 officers and men killed and wounded. Wellington, describing the deficiencies in the engineering department in a letter to Lord Liverpool, added, 'The capture of Badajoz affords as strong an instance of the gallantry of our troops as has ever been displayed. But I greatly hope that I shall never again be the instrument of putting them to such a test as they were put to last night.' [4]

Despite their state of exhaustion, no rest was allowed or indeed possible for the allies. To the south was Soult, with nearly 25,000 men, whose advance, however, upon hearing of the fall of Badajoz, was checked; his attention was thus, by the movements of Spanish forces in Andalusia and the necessity of saving Seville, diverted from the Allied army. To the east was Napoleon's brother, Joseph, whom he had made King of Spain, with 20,000 men protecting Madrid. From this quarter, however, there was, for the moment, not much to fear. But to the north was Marmont with nearly 70,000 men threatening Ciudad Rodrigo. As usual, the movements of the French armies were hampered by the impossibility of finding subsistence in regions already desolated and exhausted by warfare, in addition, 'The Emperor himself was now far away and fully occupied with his designs upon Russia.' [5]

NOTES

1 From Sir James McGrigor's *Journal*, Vol. I.

2 National Library of Scotland, MSS number 46. 3.16.82.

3 Sir Charles Oman, *History of the Peninsular War*, Vol. V, p. 248.

4 Ibid, p. 255.

5 From 'Letters from the Peninsula, 1808-1812' by Lieut-General Sir William Warre C.B., K.T.S., edited by his nephew the Rev. Edmond Warre D.D., C,B., M.V.O., with added comments by William A. Warre, his great-great nephew.

Chapter 15

Colonel Colquhoun Grant

It was during the siege of Badajoz that, for the last time for a long period, I saw my late much lamented brother-in-law, Colonel Colquhoun Grant, who was chief of the intelligence department of the army and by no means the least distinguished for military talents of the many distinguished men who served with the Peninsular army. Equal to most officers of that army in military capacity, he far surpassed anyone I ever met for the milder virtues of the Christian soldier and for all that was amiable, kind and benevolent in disposition. Colonel Grant was devotedly fond of his profession. He entered the army at a very early age, having, I believe, hardly completed his fifteenth year. So desirous was he to be a soldier that his mother could no longer retain him at school. His friend, General James Grant, gave him an ensigncy in his regiment, the 11th Foot, and through his kindness he obtained leave of absence to complete his studies at an academy near London until he joined his regiment as a lieutenant.

Lord Wellington did not tarry long at Badajoz after its fall. During his absence the enemy had made an incursion on the other side of Portugal and he hastened in pursuit of him. Having got the British and Portuguese sick and wounded comfortably accommodated at Badajoz and Elvas – in both which places the purveyors had fitted up every church, monastery, convent and public building as hospitals – I followed the commander-in-chief; but before he departed, I accompanied him on a visit to the principal hospitals at Elvas, where our wounded were placed and, in going round, he spoke kindly to many of the poor fellows as I pointed out their cases to him, and expressed himself much satisfied with the degree of comfort and cleanliness in which we had got them placed so speedily, and under such adverse circumstances.

Of the officers, some were desperately wounded and were suffering much, particularly Sir George Walker, Sir James Kempt and Colonel Pakenham, the brother-in-law of Lord Wellington. Sir George Elder, who had led part of a division to the assault, was one of the severest sufferers.

When Lord Wellington proceeded to the north, he took all the army with him but the second division, which he left under Lord Hill. It was at this time, and when the French army under Soult was rapidly advancing upon Lord Hill's force which had covered the siege of Badajoz, that my late brother-in-law, Colonel Grant, was made prisoner by them on the frontier of Portugal while following his usual occupation of reconnoitring. As he himself more than once said to me, had he been in Spain instead of Portugal, he never should have been taken. Along the whole of the Spanish frontier, Colonel Grant was known, and wherever known, he was held in the greatest esteem. Of this I cannot here omit to mention a very singular instance. Employed on the same service, viz., that of the intelligence department, there was in singular coincidence another officer of the same name and rank. What the peculiar features of his character might have been, I cannot take upon me to describe, but he and Colonel Colquhoun Grant were at the opposite poles in the estimation of the Spaniards; the latter they designated, the 'Granto Bueno' the other the 'Granto Malo'.

Colonel Colquhoun Grant had a singular talent, not only for the acquisition of languages, but of the different dialects of languages. He was a proficient in those of all the provinces of Spain, was intimately acquainted with their customs, their songs, their music, and with all their habits and prejudices. He was moreover an enthusiastic admirer of the Spanish character, was well read in all their popular works and he danced even their national dances most admirably. With such qualifications and predilections so flattering to the national sentiment of the Spaniards, in union with a character of the most rigid morality, it will not be surprising that he was a favourite with them, particularly with their priests and peasantry, who spread his name and character so widely, and were so devotedly attached to him that, in the most critical situations and when surrounded by posts of the French army, he was at all times secure.

In collecting accurate information of the French army, as he informed me, and as was well known to Lord Wellington, he was occasionally in their rear, where he obtained exact intelligence, not only of their troops, the manner in which their cavalry was mounted, the number and equipment of their guns, the state of their supplies, &c. He was acquainted not only with the character of each superior officer, but of that of each commandant of battalion. The hair's breadth escapes which he had were numerous; sleeping frequently in the fields under any shelter, or as it frequently happened without any, and in all kinds of weather, which he had done for two or three years. But, as he said, he always felt secure when in Spain, where one padre or peasant passed him on to another, all emulous to serve and in admiration of the character of the 'Granto Bueno.' As I have said, however, he did not feel so secure in Portugal and, proceeding by the frontiers of that country to Spain to observe the state of the French army, when hastily retreating from the incursion which they made into Portugal, information was conveyed to Marshal Marmont that Grant, who had been so long formidable to him and whose capture had been so much desired, was concealed somewhere near him. Colonel Grant, finding that he was discovered and that parties were beating about near the house where he was concealed, mounted his horse, and made off, happily escaping many shots fired at him by some infantry. A party of cavalry was then sent in pursuit when, finding that they were nearing him, he got off his horse and betook him to some enclosures where, however, he was at length captured and the more readily as he wore his uniform. Their exultation was great on getting him into their hands and the French officers, who had heard of him and admired his character, crowded everywhere around him as he was brought to headquarters. They questioned him much about Lord Wellington, the English army, our losses at Badajoz and Lord Wellington's further plans; and the superior officers were greatly out of humour when found they could draw no information from him.

He was carried under a strong escort to Salamanca, the headquarters of Marmont, where, on its being required of him, Colonel Grant gave his parole. But when brought before Marshal Marmont, who was unable by sifting to get much information from him respecting the British army, the marshal treated him somewhat harshly and said, 'It is fortunate for you, sir, that you have that bit of red over your shoulders [meaning his uniform]. If you had not, I would have hung you on a gallows twenty feet high.' The colonel answered, 'Marshal, you know I am your prisoner, and recollect, I have given you my parole, but hitherto I have not been treated as an officer on parole.' The marshal desired the French officer, who had conveyed Colonel Grant to his presence, to lead him away, and he was brought to a quarter which had been assigned to him and was strictly guarded. Not only was a French sentinel placed at the door of his apartment, but an officer was placed in his room. Of this he complained greatly and the French officers, who were daily appointed for this duty, all felt for a gallant officer and did their duty lightly, leaving the apartment when anyone called upon him – and he was visited by several of the principal inhabitants of Salamanca to whom, either by character or personally, he was known. In fact, the whole population of Salamanca and its neighbourhood admired his deeds, his hair's breadth escapes and, of all things, the annoyance he had been to the French, whom they cordially hated. One of his most frequent visitors was Dr Curtis, head of the Irish college of Salamanca, from whom I had the particulars which I now detail. The frequent visits of Dr Curtis to Colonel Grant gave great offence to Marshal Marmont, who sent for the reverend gentleman. As Dr Curtis related to me, the marshal behaved very harshly to him and threatened him much if he did not reveal what he said he was in possession of, i.e. the secrets of Colonel Grant. He said, 'You frequently visit the English colonel.' He replied, ' I do.' 'How is it possible, sir, that you do so without having some purpose, some business therein?' He replied, 'The holy Catholic religion, which you, marshal and I profess, enjoins us to succour the distressed, to visit the sick and the prisoner and to administer comfort and consolation to them.' The marshal rejoined, 'He is not of your religion; he is a heretic; a Protestant.' Dr Curtis replied, 'We are both Christians; we follow the precepts of our Saviour and he is my countryman.' The marshal said, 'That is false. He is an *Ecossais* and you an *Irlandais*, and you shall immediately go to prison unless you reveal to me secrets which I am informed the English colonel has confided to you, and which it is material to the interests of the emperor that I should be put in possession of.'

He did not throw Dr Curtis into prison; but he treated him most harshly, expelled him from his college, and took possession of his furniture and a valuable library.

Even at this time, in Salamanca, Colonel Grant continued to convey much valuable information to Lord Wellington and in this manner. Whenever the weather was favourable, he was permitted to walk out. On such occasions, some of the Spanish peasants, who had long been employed by him, got near to him and he put into their hands, in small twisted pieces of paper, such information as he had collected, and they, as Lord Wellington afterwards informed me, carried these to headquarters where they always received handsome rewards. I have reason to believe that the priests organised these messengers, trustworthy, hardy fellows, for this very dangerous vocation.

Not long after this, although Colonel Grant had given his parole, so formidable did he appear from the attachment to him of the priests and peasantry, and so universally was he known and admired by the Spaniards, that when Marmont sent him off to Bayonne, it was with an escort of 300 men and six guns, so fearful was he that a rescue might be attempted by the guerrillas and peasantry.

However, to resume my narrative; I have said that Lord Wellington returned to the northward from whence he drove the enemy, who had made an incursion into Portugal while he was employed in the siege of Badajoz.

Having completed the arrangements for the wounded at Elvas and Badajoz so as to leave them tolerably comfortable in the hospitals, I, according to his orders, followed the commander-in-chief. At my first interview with him, he immediately entered on the subject of Grant's capture and blamed him much for having given his parole; as he told me, that before he had learned his having done so, he had offered a high reward to several of the guerrilla chiefs for his rescue, if they brought him in alive.

Two days afterwards, Lord Wellington again entered on the subject with me, which appeared much to engross him. He lamented his capture extremely; and said that the want of the valuable information with which Grant was wont to furnish him was an incalculable loss to him. He added, 'Sir, the loss of a brigade could scarcely have been more felt by me; I am quite in the dark about the movements of the enemy and as to the reinforcements which they expected.'

The day after this, and after my daily visit when I reported to him the state

Colonel Colquhoun Grant, C.B., (1780–1829). Head of Intelligence for the Duke of Wellington (McGrigor family portrait, photographed by Roy Summers)

of all the hospitals, he desired me to walk out with him. He then said, 'Grant is a very extraordinary fellow, a very remarkable character. What think you of him, at this moment, when a prisoner, sending me information?'

He showed me two twisted bits of paper which he said a Spanish peasant had brought in that morning, and he added; 'The information coming from Grant, I know it is correct and is most valuable.' He then read to me a courteous reply to a letter which he had written to Marshal Marmont requesting the exchange of Colonel Grant, for whom he had offered any officer of the rank of colonel, of whom he had several as prisoners. In his reply, the marshal promised it should be done and expatiated on the inexpressible pleasure it would give him to have an opportunity of doing anything that might be agreeable to such an illustrious character as Lord Wellington, of whom, of all others, he was the greatest admirer. I expressed great joy at this when he said sarcastically, 'Do you believe this? There is not a word of truth in his promise, for here I hold a French despatch from Marmont to the minister of war at Paris, which has been intercepted by Don Julian.' The despatch of the marshal to the minister of war expressed great joy at the capture of Colonel Grant, whom the marshal described as a singular man, who had for so long a period done infinite mischief, to whom the Spanish priests and peasantry were devotedly attached, and who could be deterred by no threats or punishment from communicating with him and supplying him with every information for Lord Wellington. He added that he had sent him off with a strong escort and recommended him to the strictest surveillance of the minister of the interior and police at Paris.

To the best of my recollection the despatch bore the same date with his letter to Lord Wellington, informing him of the pleasure he would have in sending Colonel Grant to his lordship in exchange for a French colonel. It was supposed that Marmont identified the Colonel Grant, who had sometimes visited his camp, and Colonel Colquhoun Grant as one and the same person, and that may in some measure justify his severity to the latter, but my brother-in-law Colonel Colquhoun Grant considered the treatment as undeserved and not in accordance with that of an officer who had given his parole, and that it justified his making his escape should opportunity occur.

The subsequent history of Colonel Grant is curious. As I have said, he was conveyed to Bayonne under an escort of 300 men with six guns. On the march he entertained the French officers with several of his exploits, and the manner of his escape, when some of his hearers were in pursuit of him at different places. Gallant men themselves, they admired his courage and address, but whether any of them connived at his escape or not, I never could learn from Colonel Grant; if they did, he might think himself in honour bound not to reveal it. However, when the party arrived at Bayonne, it was in the evening; they halted in a *place* or square and all busied themselves in procuring billets. Grant, finding himself alone, walked off, found his way to a place from whence the diligence started, took his place to Paris as an American, and soon after left Bayonne. When he was missed, he did not exactly know, but, as he afterwards heard, as soon as he was missed parties of horses and foot were sent in search of him; the police and infantry soldiers searched every corner of Bayonne and of the environs, and parties of light cavalry scoured the whole country in the direction of the Spanish frontier, being sure that he would endeavour to get through to Spain where he had so many friends. The search for him was long continued, but no Colonel Grant was to be found; he had, in the meantime, arrived in Paris, the last place in the world where they would have thought of looking for him.

On his arrival in Paris, he found his way to the house of Mr McPherson, an eminent jeweller and a worthy highlander, of whose kindness to his countrymen he had heard much. This old gentleman had been many years a resident in Paris. During the time of the Revolution, he had been thrown into a dungeon by Robespierre and had been doomed to the guillotine, but had escaped that death by the death of the monster Robespierre himself.

While with Mr McPherson, as an American and with an American passport, Grant moved freely about Paris, made it a point to be present at all the reviews and, by entering into conversation with various individuals, whom he met out of doors and at Mr McPherson's table, got correct information of the reinforcements sent to all the armies, particularly that of Portugal. At Mr McPherson's he frequently met a gentleman with whom he contracted some degree of intimacy. These two gentlemen, as acquaintances, became most acceptable to each other and Grant gained much very valuable information from him; and, extraordinary as it may appear, he continued to convey that information to Lord Wellington, which came to my knowledge in the following manner.

I do not exactly recollect where the British army was at this time in Spain, but one day, when I was with Lord Wellington on business, a day on which the mail for England was being made up at headquarters, Lord Wellington, addressing me, said, 'Your brother-in-law is certainly one of the most extraordinary men I ever met with; even now when he is in Paris he contrives to send me information of the greatest moment to our government. I am now sending information of his to ministers of the utmost value about the French armies in every quarter; information which will surprise them, and which they cannot by any possibility get in any other way and, what is more, which I am quite sure is perfectly correct. Go into the next room and desire Fitzroy[1] to show you the information from Grant enclosed in the despatch to Lord Bathurst.'[2]

About this time, his friends, whom he met at Mr McPherson's, told that gentleman to desire Grant to discontinue going to the reviews, and further, that he must remain quiet for some time, change his appearance if possible and get a different passport. All this was accomplished. He assumed a different appearance and got another American passport, that of an American gentleman recently deceased in Paris, but McPherson was further informed that the police were secretly making inquiries for him and it was decided that he must leave Paris. He did so and got to the coast, off which he learned that a British man-of-war was stationed. For ten *louis d'or* he engaged an old French fisherman and his son to take him out to sea, but they became alarmed and in the evening returned with him. As he told me, his situation then appeared to him more dangerous than it had been on any former occasion, for he was at the mercy of the two fishermen and he knew what his fate would have been had he been re-taken at that time. To heighten the unpleasantness of his situation, his stock of money was very nearly exhausted.

On being put ashore, he determined not to stay where he was. He learned that not many leagues from where he was a French marshal of Scottish descent, a relation of his mother's, had his seat and he determined to make for it. He travelled the whole of that night, and during the following day remained concealed in a dry ditch, overhung with weeds. He resumed his journey the following night and on the next day reached the mansion of the marshal. On obtaining an interview with him and explaining the object of his visit, the marshal immediately acknowledged the relationship and ordered refreshments for him, but said he did not think it would be safe for him to prolong his stay in his house. The marshal, however, lent him one hundred *louis*, with which he returned to the port he had left where he hired another fishing boat. While passing the mouth of the harbour, some suspicion being aroused, a shot was fired which brought the boat to until a party of soldiers could get on board to search. At this critical moment, when the sail was lowered to be coiled round the mast, [one] fisherman put Grant upright close to the mast, twisting the sail round him so that he was effectually concealed. The soldiers jumped on board, searched everywhere and even probed several parts with their swords. The men had a quantity of fish on board to conceal their object; the soldiers took some of them and desired the fishermen to proceed. On the following morning, the faithful fishermen conveyed him on board a British 74 and, as he informed me, his exultation on finding himself safe on the quarter-deck was considerable.

Great was my surprise on receiving a letter from him in London, wherein he complained much of the illiberality of the then Transport Board, and the difficulty he had in getting those two poor fishermen released from an English prison who had so faithfully conveyed him from a position of such extreme danger.

Colonel Grant soon returned to the headquarters of the army in the Peninsula and was most kindly welcomed by the duke and all the officers on his staff. He received promotion, served in the Peninsula during the remainder of the war, and was afterwards at the Battle of Waterloo, where he held a superior staff appointment. He died at Aix-la-Chapelle of disease contracted at Arracan, then part of Burmah, where he commanded a brigade. A monument is erected to his memory in the Protestant burying ground at Aix-la-Chapelle [see Appendix 6]. A notice of Colonel Grant will be found in the history of the Peninsular war by his friend, the historian, Colonel Napier. [3]

NOTES

1   Lord Fitzroy Somerset, afterwards Lord Raglan.

2   The letter to Lord Bathurst is mentioned in the Duke's despatches.

3   Ibid, Vol. IV, pp. 464-72.

*E*DITOR'S INTRODUCTION TO CHAPTER 16

McGrigor, at the beginning of this chapter, says that following the victory of Badajoz nothing much occurred until the beginning of June. However the *Journal* which, with the help of his clerks, he kept from the beginning of the campaign, proves that his system of management in the hospitals was proving singularly effective. It also describes the achievements of Dr Tier at Celerico, who, in circumstances of great danger as the French advanced, managed to save all his patients, as well as valuable hospital equipment.

9 April, 1812
Dr Charles Forbes was appointed to the charge of the general hospital established at Badajoz, but he was directed to retain no cases there which could without injury be removed, Staff Surgeon Burnel, along with other officers, was placed under the orders of Dr Forbes.

By a letter from Dr Tier of this date from Celerico, I hear that he has removed all the sick from Castaniera and was proceeding with the evacuation of Celerico on Coimbra as the enemy was fast advancing.

10 April, 1812
By an order of this day I directed no man was to be sent to the rear but stump cases which would eventually come before an invaliding board.

At this period all the new hospitals in the Alentejo were ordered to be provided with boards and trestles for the men to lie on.

21 April, 1812
I set off from Niza and that evening got to Castelo Branco. While we were engaged in the siege of Badajoz, Marmont advanced and made an incursion to this quarter. By the activity of Staff Surgeon Wood (with the aid of Captain Stewart, the Commandant), not only the whole of the sick but a great portion of the stores were removed and at this time we found them most useful when transport was procured with so much difficulty and many articles were scarce in the country.

On the 24th reached Tabrigal . . . I inspected our small miserable hospital . . . which henceforth was to remain a passing station between Castelo Branco and Celerico.

26 April, 1812
Orders given to Dr Tier to prepare Celerico again as an hospital station. The enemy suddenly had made their appearance near it and, but for the extraordinary exertions of Dr Tier, would have made a capture of the sick and a considerable body of hospital stores, which from the difficulty of transport and other circumstances

were unavailable in the country and were at the same time much required by the enemy.

From the wise precautions therefore which Dr Tier had taken, it was found practicable and speedy to re-establish Celerico, and fortunate it was that we were able to do this as it speedily became the station most [ ] to, being the nearest and most convenient for the greater part of the divisions of the army.

26 April

Dr Gray having reported the crowded state of Estremoz, I directed that no more cases should be sent from Elvas or Badajoz, but that these stations should be established as permanent hospital stations, to be fitted up accordingly and to be provided with medicines and stores.

Much Opthalmia came to Estremoz from the 2nd Division of the army.

It appears from the monthly return comprehending the period between 21 March and 20 April, and consequently the whole of the siege, that there were:

8,925	men in general hospitals
750	... in regimental
9,675	total in all hospitals
462	deaths, being the total which fell in this month.

Of that number, 122 died from dysentery, 161 from continued fever and 146 from wounds – 17 of them tetanus – and the rest from various causes.

These figures, which of course do not include the men killed in battle, prove nonetheless that, even when many were wounded in a bloody assault like Badajoz, dysentery and typhus remained the two greatest killers in the army of McGrigor's time. His *Journal* continues:

May 1812

At the commencement of this month the army was in cantonments in the north of Portugal, and on the course of the Douro ... [except] the corps of Lord Wellington which remained in front of Badajoz and watching Soult.

20 May

About this period the regiments of the 7th Division of the army appeared singularly unhealthy. Dr D. reports that their surgeons of the 51st and 68th Regiments state as the cause that this corps had served in Walcheren where they suffered extremely.

Reports from the doctors in charge of the other hospitals, prove that the prevailing diseases were Continued or Remittent fever [typhus] and Intermittent fever [malaria]. At Badajoz, where only wounded remained, men with compound fractures were suffering from tetanus ...

The fatalities at the large hospital at Coimbra were still a cause of anxiety, as McGrigor writes: 'Coimbra has been long a station productive of much mortality though much improvement has been effected in it during the last three months. A greater number of deaths has fallen on it ... than in any other station.'

A board of medical officers had been appointed to report on the reasons for this happening but they were, he complains, 'not very communicative as to the causes of the disease and the excessive mortality. I am, however, convinced from own observation at Coimbra as well as from a great deal of enquiry which I made on the spot that the great mortality was with the cases which they had and which most of them came from Ciudad Rodrigo, Castaniera and Celerico many in the last stages of fever and dysentery or with a complication of visceral disease.'

A later report from the doctor in charge of the Coimbria hospital states that: 'The fever [was] mostly of the typhoid form where purgation and cold affusions were found useful.'

Lisbon
There has been a great reduction affected of the great number of sick men and officers who were [ ] this station so desirable to them all.

June, 1812
As to the state of the hospital stations, Lisbon continues to be still further reduced.

CHAPTER 16

Retreat to Portugal

After the siege of Badajoz, I returned with headquarters to Freineda.

Nothing remarkable occurred till the movement of the army commenced in the beginning of June.

It had been for some time evident that preparations were making for an advance. The advance on Salamanca, the retreat of the French army thence, and their siege and capture of fortified convents, were all matters of great interest to me, and I was enabled to view them narrowly, being in the neighbourhood of the Irish college which I occupied as our largest hospital. A remarkable circumstance occurred at this time. We were daily keeping up a heavy fire on the strongly fortified convents and we had carried our works close up to them; the casualties to the besieging force were daily numerous and we lost many officers. The progress of the siege was best viewed from a window in the upper part of the Irish college. This window was often had recourse to by the engineer and the officers, but the enemy knew this and were very jealous of our inspection of them from it. There were constantly sharp shooters to pop at the window when anyone appeared to be near it. It was pierced with bullets in every direction. One afternoon, when I was taking a peep from the window, I observed an unusual bustle. I mentioned this circumstance to the engineer officer who immediately said, 'They are offering to surrender.' We all ran down the stairs together and the officer of engineers mentioned to Marshal Beresford, who happened to be near, that they had made a signal of desire to surrender. He immediately ordered a cessation of our firing and advancing with a few officers, of whom I was one, hoisted a white handkerchief, when the firing on both sides ceased. As no flag of truce approached from them, the marshal sent forward an officer bearing one. We followed at some paces distant when from threatening signals forbidding our further advance, we stopped and we saw that when our officer advanced to the gateway, they blindfolded him. We had not waited more than a very few minutes when we observed the officer returning, who informed us that they had neither the desire nor the intention to surrender for in two days we should be obliged to raise the siege, and further, that five minutes by the watch were allowed us to get back, at the expiration of which time precisely, they would re-open their fire. As may readily be believed, we were not tardy in retracing our steps; in fact, we plainly saw their preparations with the guns and, furthermore, their sharp shooters taking up their ground.

The enemy's army was for several days in position opposite to us, within a short distance of the city of Salamanca. Every day a general action was looked for, but beyond some slight changes of position, one day followed another without anything taking place. To me the situation was one of real interest and I daily rode out to our army, posted on a ridge of hills of no great elevation, that of the enemy being drawn out on an opposite range of heights, with a valley of little breadth between us in which the pickets were placed. At this time desertion from our army was not infrequent, particularly from the foreign corps in our service. One day I went to our pickets in the intervening valley with the field officer of the day, and while there I witnessed one of these desertions actually taking place. It was from the Chasseurs Britanniques, who were posted to the right of the 4th Division, with whose pickets I then was. I observed a man suddenly run forward; the cry was immediately, 'Deserter!' and several shots were instantly fired after him; but he ran hard and in less than two minutes was with the French picket, his countrymen, as I was told, and that he was a sergeant. The French picket fired a few shots in return to ours. This occasioned a great bustle, for the whole of the division, hearing as they thought the entire picket engaged and believing that the enemy were advancing, ran to arms. I was in the act of ascending the height from the valley when I met Sir Lowry Cole riding down to ascertain the state of affairs. He told us an action was about to commence and entreated me instantly to go to the rear, saying I was quite out of my place where I then was.

In a day or two after this, the French moved off from their position, the forts at Salamanca surrendered and we followed the enemy.

By the beginning of July we reached Rueda, where headquarters remained for some time after the battle of Salamanca.

After this great battle, my own labours, as well as those of all the medical officers, were very arduous.

By the desire of Lord Wellington, I repeatedly wrote to him on the state of the wounded and, particularly respecting the officers, the nature of their wounds and those likely to prove fatal. I received three letters from his lordship; in two of which he pressed me much to join headquarters, but in the third in such terms that I immediately set off.

At several places on my route I found considerable numbers of sick. Some of them were left by the parties of recruits proceeding to the army who had fallen ill in the long march from Lisbon; many others had been left sick by the divisions of the army on their march from Salamanca to Madrid. The causes of the diseases of the greater part of the soldiers were dissipation and drunkenness, but not a few officers were likewise sick at those places. Some of them who had been wounded in the battle of Salamanca, and would not be restrained from proceeding with their regiments, arrived at the Spanish capital. The situation of some of these parties, men and officers, was in many instances most deplorable. Not only without medicine and medical attendance, but also without provision of any kind, many of them were fast sinking into the last stage of disease, and not a few officers as well as men had died without having been seen by a medical man. I everywhere went round and visited them, but was powerless to help them.

I sent orders to the principal medical officer in Salamanca to despatch medical and purveying officers to each of those stations where I had found parties of sick and wounded officers and soldiers. At the same time I wrote to the deputy commissary-general of Salamanca, informing him of the destitute condition those stations were in, and I recommended him immediately to send a store of provisions to each place, with proper commissariat officers. In doing this, I felt that I was not only obeying the dictates of humanity, but another recollection came to my mind.

Major William Warre, writing to his father on 27 July, described the dreadful agonies of the soldiers wounded at Salamanca. [1] 'Owing to the enemy having advanced and the few means of transport, many of the wounded, particularly of the French, have suffered horribly, for, three days after, I saw a great many still lying, who had received no assistance nor were likely to until next day, and had lain scorching in the sun without a drop of water or the least shade. It was a most dreadful sight. These are the horrid miseries of war. No person who has not witnessed them can possibly form any idea of what they are. Humanity shudders at the very idea, and we turn with detestation and disgust to the sole author of such miseries. What punishment can be sufficient for him! Many of the poor creatures have crawled to this. Many made crutches of the barrels of their firelocks and their shoes. Cruel and villainous as they are themselves, and even were during the action of our people, one cannot help feeling for them and longing to be able to assist them. But our own people have suffered almost as much, and they are our first care.'

When, on my arrival at Madrid I waited on Lord Wellington, he received me in the kindest and warmest manner. He was sitting to a Spanish painter for his portrait and, after receiving me, he asked if I was not too much busied to sit down and give him the detail of the state of the wounded at Salamanca, with that of my journey thence. I related to him the number of sick I had met with at so many places and their miserable state. But when I came to inform him that for their relief I had ordered up purveying and commissariat officers, he started up and in a violent manner reprobated what I had done. It was to no purpose that I pleaded the number of seriously ill and dying I had met with, and that several men and some officers had died without ever having been seen by a medical officer. I even alluded to what had formerly occurred at Talavera and to the clamour raised in England when it was known that so many wounded and sick had been left to the mercy of the enemy. All was in vain. His lordship was in a passion, and the Spanish artist, ignorant of the English language, looked aghast, and at a loss to know what I had done to enrage his lordship so much. 'I shall be glad to know,' exclaimed his lordship, 'who is to command the army? I or you? I establish one route, one line of communication for the army; you establish another and order the commissariat and the supplies by that line. As long as you live, sir, never do so again; never do anything without my orders.' I pleaded that 'there was no time to consult him to save life.' He peremptorily desired me 'never again to act without his orders.' Hereupon I was about to take my leave, when in a lower tone of voice, he begged I would dine with him that day and of course I bowed assent.

At dinner, the duke showed me unusual civility and marked attention, desiring me to sit next to him on his left, the Prince of Orange always sitting on his right hand. The guerrilla chief, El Medico (in English 'The Doctor'), dined there that day. His lordship introduced us to each other and was very humorous, calling us brother of the profession of medicine, but said, 'I had not so much distinguished myself in a military capacity as my Spanish brother.'

We received rather sudden orders to march from Madrid. Our first night's halt, that of headquarters, was at the Escurial, from whence we moved to Burgos to which we laid siege and, as is well known, without sufficient means.

Our entrance into Valladolid was effected and I had to establish an hospital for our wounded. In doing this, I received anything but aid from the Bishop of Valladolid and we had a very angry contest. He appealed to Lord Wellington, who by no means approved of his want of humanity.

On the 19th September I arrived with my establishment at Burgos, the castle of which was then invested. I had a miserable quarter in a poor dilapidated house in the suburb, a few yards distant only from that occupied by Lord Wellington.

As is well known, we met with nothing but discomfiture in our attempts upon the castle of Burgos. We lost a number of men. The wounded were numerous, we were without adequate hospital accommodation and the cases were of the severest character.

In my usual morning visits to his lordship with reports of the sick and wounded of the army, when I met the heads of the departments and likewise the chief engineer (who had nothing but an unfavourable report to give), Lord Wellington was often in bad humour for everything went wrong with him. This, therefore, was the period of his life when fortune seemed to turn her back upon him. At length, after daily losses of numbers of men and officers, discontent was not silent even among the officers themselves for they saw that, without means, particularly in artillery, they were knocking their heads against stone walls without the least prospect of making any impression upon them. One morning, I was in his lordship's small apartment when two officers were there requesting leave to go to England. One of them, an officer in the Engineers – Captain **** – first made his request; he had received letters informing him that his wife was dangerously ill and that the whole of his family were sick. His lordship quickly replied, 'No, no, sir! I cannot at all spare you at this moment.' Captain ****, with a mournful face and submissive bow, retired. A general officer of a noble family, and who commanded a brigade at Burgos, next advanced, saying, 'My lord, I have of late been suffering much from rheumatism . . . ' Without allowing him time to proceed further, Lord Wellington rapidly said, 'and you must go to England to get cured of it. By all means. Go there immediately.' The general, surprised at his lordship's tone and manner, looked abashed while he made a profound bow, but to prevent his saying anything in explanation, his lordship immediately addressed me, inquiring the casualties of the preceding night and the nature of them.

I have said that the daily disappointment and the unfavourable morning reports of the result of our operations against the castle, while they at length raised a spirit of discontent, made his lordship fretful. This all felt who came in contact with him, but I escaped entirely – except on one occasion, in regard to my department when he expressed himself so hastily as to hurt my feelings. I felt it acutely because I felt that neither I nor the medical officers deserved it. On the evening of the day on which this occurred, he wrote me a note, requesting I would come up to him immediately as he wished much to speak to me. I felt unwell, so much so, indeed, that I had applied a few leeches to my head which relieved me by the time his note arrived. I could then have gone and waited upon him, but my pride had been wounded by him in the morning. I felt that I, personally, and the medical officers, had made extraordinary exertions, and that no part of the army was more warmly animated by zeal for the service than the medical officers. I therefore wrote an apology for not calling on him that evening.

Finding myself quite recovered in the morning, I went at an early hour to Lord Wellington's quarters, but found that he had set off, with the whole of his personal staff, for the army in advance, at two o'clock in the morning. I immediately proceeded after him and found the whole of our force in position, drawn out in line opposite to that of the enemy. Lord Wellington, surrounded by the staff, was in the act of using his glass when I came up, viewing narrowly the French line. On someone calling out my name he turned round and, taking me by the arm, took a turn to the rear with me. He said, 'We cannot keep Madrid. Hill is obliged by an overwhelming force to quit his position; he is in fact on the march toward us and I must leave this place this very night. But what is to become of our sick and wounded? I fear they are numerous, and of the wounded there are many who cannot be moved. What do you propose to do?' I replied I was happy to inform him our sick and wounded were not numerous, that, seeing how much his mind was occupied with the siege, I got from the commissary-general all the carts and mules that came up with provision for the army and by them, on their return, had daily sent back everyone who could be moved to the hospitals which I established at Valladolid. 'Very well, indeed,' said he. 'But how many have you now at Burgos hospital?' I replied that with the conveyance I expected that day, I hoped to have only about sixty men and officers, and those would be cases of severe wounds, recent amputation and fractures which would not bear movement. He quickly rejoined, 'Admirable! I shall be off to night. Make your own arrangements quietly and quickly: but be most careful not to let a syllable of my intention of moving escape you.' He then desired me to be off immediately and without communicating with anyone, though no doubt the group of officers had some curiosity to know what he had had to say to me which so urgently took him away from reconnoitring the instant he found I was near him. I should have said that he asked if I meant to take any steps with the cases to be left behind, when I informed him that I would attach two careful medical officers with a deputy purveyor, provided with a sum of money. I said also that I would write a letter to be given to the principal medical officer of the French army who might come in, recommending the wounded and our three officers to his kind care. All this he further approved of.

I immediately went back, saw all the wounded men and officers, selected those to be left behind and gave orders, towards evening, in written instructions to the two medical officers and the deputy purveyor to be left behind, so that the intention of removal remained a secret till it was nearly dark and we were all ready to march.

As soon as this was known, I was besieged by notes and messages from the wounded officers to be left behind, entreating me not to leave them. One of them, a gallant and distinguished officer, Colonel McKenzie Fraser of the Guards, the son of my excellent friend the late General McKenzie Fraser, was particularly importunate. Fraser's leg had been amputated by the late Mr Rose, surgeon of the Guards, but two days before; he was in no condition to be moved. He pressed me hard, however, said he was sure he should die if left behind, so that I was obliged to consent to his going and to endeavour to make up a litter on which he might be carried by some soldiers. But I feared he would sink by the way.

Having given final orders to the three medical officers who were to remain behind and started the cases to be sent on, I set off myself a little after dusk. We marched all night and halted about daylight in the morning when I visited as many of the cases as I could, receiving reports of the medical officers who accompanied them. I saw poor Fraser, who had got on better than I expected, and was able to take some tea which I had ordered to be made for him. The army did not commence its march till about midnight; the rear in passing near the castle of Burgos was fired upon and soon after the French army, having discovered that we were off, pursued us. As is well known, our retreat was disastrous enough – not the less so from the fire of a pursuing enemy than from the irregularities of our own men. The second night, I got under cover in a house which was occupied by, I believe, 400 or 500 men, who actually slept as close together as though packed in a barrel.

We reached Valladolid, where at one time I had more than 2,000 sick and wounded. I hastened the departure of all such as could march and of all that could bear conveyance to Salamanca, and sent pressing orders to the principal medical officers at Salamanca, Ciudad Rodrigo and the intermediate post to Oporto to hurry on the evacuation of those hospitals. These were in addition to orders to the same purport which I had issued from Burgos.

Lord Wellington, with headquarters, made a halt and encamped near Valladolid. He defended the bridge in front of Valladolid and held the passage there as long as he could that the army might be enabled to retreat in order.

With the late Dr James Forbes and the clerks of my establishment, I was encamped near Valladolid. The office was in full employment, as it always was on the march, or whenever I thought that I could command two or three hours to carry on the correspondence with the divisions of the army and with the hospital establishment, at this time widely spread over Spain and Portugal, when an orderly came with a note from Lord Wellington, desiring to see me as soon as possible. Mounting immediately, I rode very hard and found him at the post on the bridge against which a very heavy cannonade was kept up by the enemy. I found his lordship in the upper floor of a small house, which was riddled with shot. The house was on a small eminence, near the bridge. I found Mr Sydenham of the Madras Civil Service, a friend of Lord Wellington's, with him. On my entering he came quickly from a window with his glass in his hand and eagerly inquired about the hospitals in Valladolid, and the wounded there, saying: 'I fear our numbers are very great.' Indeed, they had lately amounted to 2,000. He proceeded: 'What is to be done? For, you see, we must be off from this place and conveyance there is none.' I said the number was small and when I told him that, officers and soldiers included, it did not exceed one hundred, for I had been daily laying hands on all the carts as well as the mule conveyance I could find to send them on to Salamanca, he rapidly replied, 'And you have made Salamanca choke full. I cannot stop there.' 'No,' I rejoined, 'they are in movement from Salamanca on Ciudad Rodrigo, and from that to the pisé hospital buildings which we erected near the Douro, and move from thence on Oporto, with instructions to the principal medical officer there to have them in readiness for embarkation, should that be necessary.' Turning quickly, he said, 'Sydenham, this is excellent. Now I care not how soon we are off.' I added, addressing him, 'My lord, you recollect how much you blamed me at Madrid for the steps which I took on coming up to the army, when I could not consult your lordship and acted for myself as I had done. Now, if I had not, what would the consequences have been?' He added, 'It is all right, as it has turned out, but I recommend you still to have my orders for what you do.' This was a singular feature of Lord Wellington.

It was near sunset when I left his lordship and I had not gone far before it became dark, when I lost my way and found myself in an encampment of Spaniards. This was not all, for my noble animal, my horse, poor Pat, to whom I was fondly attached, was quite knocked up. We had journeyed from morning till night; I had not got a particle of food for him and I myself felt sorely the cravings of hunger. At last, leading my horse, I reached at midnight the encampment I had left in the morning; but found, to my dismay, that everything – my clerks, servants, office establishment, baggage and horses – were all gone. I could see by the light of a bright moon the ashes of the fire I had left when I set off. From the noise which I heard, I could easily make out that the army was in full retreat. I was so near the river that I could distinctly hear the French who were encamped on the opposite side, but I had no means of moving, and even if I could crawl on myself, I could not bear the thought of leaving poor Pat behind, who had carried me so many hundreds of miles. Hungry and wearied, I endeavoured to collect some sticks in the wood with which to make a fire by stirring up the expiring embers. But it commenced raining and I found it impossible.

I tied poor Pat's bridle to a tree; he was much exhausted. I collected some grass, but he would not eat and I had no bread or biscuit to offer him. I laid me down in my cloak with my feet towards the ashes and embers. I heard a moan from Pat. I found him shivering; I put my cloak over him and laid myself down again upon the ground, but finding myself cold and chilly from the rain which fell, I resumed my cloak. In a short time, I found Pat shivering exceedingly. I again put my cloak over him and thought I could walk about, but I was extremely fatigued and faint from hunger. All this time, I could most distinctly hear the noise in the enemy's camp close by on the other side of the river and, by the sounds, I could distinguish that they were preparing to march. At length, daylight came and I found a great number of the followers of our army in full retreat. I learned from them that there was a post of ours about a league off. Leading Pat, who could move but slowly, I made for the post and reached it with some difficulty. I found a subaltern, with a veterinary surgeon and a few dragoons, stationed there in charge of the stores. After describing my situation to them, they in the kindest manner offered me breakfast. But first, I begged for Pat's necessities and the veterinary surgeon took him in hand. Both Pat and I got refreshment, and I went to sleep. In the forenoon I got up and the veterinary surgeon had by that time found that my servants, horses and baggage were but a few miles further on. I found that Pat could now get on and in the evening I got up to my baggage. I went to bed, but had not been asleep an hour when orders arrived for our moving on with all expedition. Our retreat continued to be a hurried one and, as is well known, very disorderly. We made little halt till we came to Salamanca. On the retreat thither, great were the disorder, insubordination and intemperance: I never witnessed the like! One day, I am sure, I saw five hundred men at least in a state of beastly intoxication. All subordination was gone, all alike – English, Scots and Irish – were equally the slaves of drunkenness and the consequent state of insubordination was awful. Had the enemy come upon us at the time we should have been an easy prey to him.

There was perhaps some excuse for them. They were in want of provisions and the commissariat was blamed (although, I think, without much reason). They had a difficult task at the moment of retreat and in one division at least, where the utmost disorder prevailed, it is said that they were provisioned on the march, but improvidently they made away with their provisions and in consequence were for some days without food. The extreme displeasure of Lord Wellington was loudly expressed against more than one quarter. He at one time forcibly said, 'The medical department is the only one which will obey orders; on them I can rely for doing their duty.' But at this time the duty of every department was unpleasant and most arduous.

After a short halt at Salamanca, we proceeded on our retreat. I found it necessary to leave about eighty cases of badly wounded in the hospital at Salamanca and left two medical officers with a purveyor provided with money in charge of them.

Soon after the passage of the bridge of Salamanca, having given my last directions to the senior medical officers (for the enemy was seen preparing to enter by one of the gates as we passed out the other), I received a most severe kick from a horse upon my knee, which I first thought had fractured the bones.

After several attempts to move forward with my horse, the pain was so intolerable, accompanied with sickness and faintness, that I felt constrained to dismount and to be laid upon the ground, where I became at length reconciled to remain and to being made a prisoner for the enemy were manoeuvring in pursuit of us. My friends about me, in particular Dr Forbes, went everywhere in search of a cart, being determined to construct some conveyance by which to carry me off and not to let me fall into the hands of the enemy. Lord Wellington heard of my situation and instantly ordered his carriage (the only one in the army) to take me up, and in the course of this day he came most kindly to make inquiry for me.

I suffered extreme pain, even from the motion of his comfortable easy carriage, but it was ascertained that no bone was broken, although inflammation ran very high. On the following day the Colonel of the Wagon

Corps provided one of the best of the spring wagons for me and accompanied me himself. By the time I reached Ciudad Rodrigo, though still lame, I could move about.

Lord Wellington sent for me as soon as he arrived at Ciudad Rodrigo.

I shall never forget the interview. I found him in a miserable small room, leaning over the fire. He was attentively reading some printed paper. He begged me to be seated. I could see that the paper he was reading was Cobbett's Register, just received with the letters from England. After perusing it for a few minutes, he threw it into the fire and anxiously inquired what reports I had of the sick and wounded. He was in very bad humour; he adverted in bitter language to the disorder of the retreat and indicated especially some divisions of the army and, also, some officers in particular. Inquiring of me then what accounts I could give him of the sick, he reverted anew to the disorder of the retreat and read to me a severe order, which he said he would issue to the army. This order subsequently made a great deal of noise, not only in the army, but throughout England.

After recounting to him that I had effected almost the complete evacuation of the hospitals at Burgos, Valladolid, Salamanca and even Ciudad Rodrigo, and that I had further directed the principal medical officer at Oporto to be prepared in case any sick should be sent there. I proposed stopping the further transport of the sick and also of such as might turn up. He replied quickly, 'No; I cannot say that we will stop here, or that the Aguadia will bring us up; they may pursue us further.' The enemy did not pursue us further. Headquarters were re-established at Freineda and I, with the medical staff and clerks attached to me, occupied our old quarters at Castelo Bom, where we remained for the winter, which proved a severe one.

In his *Journal of the Peninsular Campaign* (volume V), McGrigor writes:

The army during June as well as July was exposed to the direct influence of a burning sun, darting his rays through a sky without a single cloud. The troops marching and fighting during the day and bivouacking during the night in arid unsheltered plains. They felt at times extremes of heat and cold. The consequence was what might be expected in a retrograde movement taking place, a very severe and fatal sickness in the army.

August, 1812
DESCRIPTION OF THE FEVER: The symptoms in many were such as are met with in intertropical countries. The most obstinate costiveness attended with the most dreadful irritability of stomach continuing to the end of the existence of the patient. Vomiting of blood ... accompanied these symptoms.

Blood-letting from the arm and temporal artery, if early employed, seemed the most successful practice in conquering the irritability of the stomach. Blisters alone were unavailing and camomile guarded with opium was often useless . . .

Whenever the vomiting ceased, purging with camomile and jallop, and particularly with castor oil, produced the speediest solution of the disease and brought the patient into a state fit for exhibiting the Peruvian bark. All the hospitals at Salamanca were suddenly broken up and the sick hurried to the rear, their first stop was Ciudad Rodrigo [ ] leagues.

The situation of this place is by no means favourable: a town composed chiefly of ruins, with very narrow streets, most of them without a single inhabitant. The place had been so much the object of control and the site of hospitals with the continuing fever that was [ ] that bodies had been put in the earth on the [ ] of [ ] month.

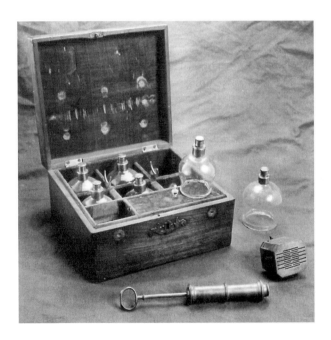

A set of cupping glasses showing a scarificator and an exhausting syringe used for blood-letting. One method involved opening a vein and allowing the blood to run into a bleeding-bowl. An alternative technique made use of the cupping glasses. In 'dry-cupping' the skin was not cut, whereas 'wet-cupping' meant using the metal scarificator (shown in front) to cut the skin. The glasses were warmed before use either by heating them over a small spirit lamp or by burning paper inside them. Once heated, they were applied to the patient's skin, where, due to the vacuum created by the cooling air, they would become firmly attached and draw blood to the patient's skin (by kind permission of Aberdeen Medico-Chirurgical Society, photographed by the Medical Illustrations Department, Aberdeen University)

Ciudad is situated close to the banks of what is in winter a rapid torrent but in summer a muddy sluggish stream, they are exposed to the influence of all the vapours arising from a clayey bed covered with a few inches of stagnant water.

The country around is an arid, and at present, barren plain without a hedge and almost without a tree. It is generally covered with a dry weed resembling mustard, to which the natives set fire, and thereby produce some ashes to serve for manure. In addition to the solar heat, this place for the last two months [has been] enveloped in clouds of ashes and smoke arising from entire tracks of country in the neighbourhood in a state of ignition. The atmosphere of a volcano . . . is almost cool in comparison.

The [city] formerly contained 2,000 inhabitants within the walls, now it had hardly 600 and about 30 of these died monthly. Within a short period, this city has been sacked and ravaged, the inhabitants linger under famine amidst the smoking ruins of their city.

30 September, 1812
Dr Emery, in a report of this date, tells the means he has taken in preparing Valladolid as an hospital site for 3,000 sick and wounded.

Wellington's despatches contain the following:

Flores de Avila
28 July, 1812, 2 p.m.

I have received your letter of yesterday at noon, and am very much obliged to you for the good account you have given me of the wounded. I assure you that I am very sensible of the diligence and attention of the medical department of which I have reported my sense to the Secretary of State.

Wellington's outburst of fury on discovering that McGrigor had instructed the deputy commisary general of Salamanca to send provisions to the sick and wounded men seems to have resulted from the physical and mental exhaustion produced by his command. William Warre states that he was amazed to find him well for he had 'scarce a moment's rest for mind or body.' [2]

McGrigor, writing from Madrid on 31 August, says, 'Lord Wellington has of late been unwell, but mends; I pursue a plan of treatment which in England Sir W. Farquhar had chalked out for his Lordship, and which in all his illnesses in this country he had found to serve him admirably.' [3]

McGrigor's understanding of the complex character of the Field Marshal – he is claimed to be 'the only man who ever stood up to him' – is proved by the incident on the bridge of Valladolid. Praised by Wellington for arranging transport in carts for the wounded, McGrigor seized the chance to remind him of his reprimand, for doing just that, after the battle of Salmanca. 'Now, if I had not, what would the consequences have been?'

'It is all right, as it has turned out' came the answer. Wellington could never be wrong! Likewise, in the case of the pre-fabricated hospitals he would not acquiesce immediately – the idea had to be his own!

NOTES

1   *Letters from the Peninsula 1808-1812*, by Lieut.-General Sir William Warre C.B., K.T.S., edited by his nephew the Rev. Edmond Warre D.D., C.B., M.V.O., with added comments by William A. Warre, his great-great nephew, p. 186.

2   Ibid, p. 175.

3   National Library of Scotland, MSS 3610, f. 220.

Editor's Introduction to Chapter 17

McGrigor records the events of 1 October, 1812:

'The weather was . . . very severe and we had very turbulent equinoctial [gales]. During the progress to Ciudad, to Celerico and other places, the sick were exposed to severe weather, heavy rain; this in their protracted journeys occasioned simple continued fever and Intermittents, to degenerate into typhus and dysenteries and to assume so malignant a character as to baffle the skill of the medical officer, the cases frequently proving fatal within a few days sometimes after their being committed to his care . . . Mr Burrows, at Celerico states that his hospital has been inundated with sick from Ciudad Rodrigo [in fact, 395 were transferred] and that "the heavy rain and bad weather which the sick met with in their progress . . . greatly aggravated their diseases."

'Many of those who had been lingering on for many weeks or months, went off within 8 days after the rain commenced, resembling the last leaves clinging to the boughs at the commencement of winter which fall on the first frosty night.'

From Coimbra, Dr Tier reports 'that the most prevailing disease is the sudden exhibition of Gangrene among the wounded.

'In many cases there occurred haemorrhages which could not be subdued . . . In all there were colliquation, discharges, rapid emaciation, sudden collapse and death. These symptoms were chiefly observed in French prisoners which came in numbers and in a very bad state to Coimbra . . . The treatment was by tonics and stimulants . . . I issued orders to all the Divisions to establish general hospitals; to get good Douro wine, rice and salt from the Commissariat; to repair hospital cantonments . . .

'In Mr Humphrey's report of the College of Arts, where the wounded French were placed, he lost many, but favours the application of Camphor dissolved in Ol Terebinth (Turpentine Tree).'

[From Vol. 7] 'It is reported that the French army lost 6,000 men in Ciudad in 14 months.

'Staff Surgeon Paddock, in his report on the Gracia hospital of which he is in charge, says that many intermittents yielded [to] solution in Quassia. Any tree of the Tropical American simarubaceous genus. [Also called *vermifuge*, i.e., to expel worms and now used in insecticides.]

'Dr Somers of Abrantes claimed that whenever he could attack dysentery early with the lancet . . . that he has in every instance succeeded.

'Mr [ ] states that in chronic cases of dysentery he has found benefit from a mixture of the balsam of Copaiba in gum arabic with infusion of Columba: using at the same time mercurial frictions, flannel bandages and a milk diet.

'His surgical division was filled with most aggravated sloughing wounds, several of them terminating fatally. This happened mostly in gunshot wounds, with amputations that had been moved under most disadvantageous circumstances . . . The men had been many days without being dressed, exhausted by wet and cold, suffering many severe privations. These induced extreme debility and predisposed them ... when crowded together in hospital, with clothing that had long been dirty ... to become the subjects of this frightful infection.

'Dr Charles Forbes, from Vizeu, reported that the Continued and Intermittent fevers showed a strong disposition to run into typhus of the worst kind ... The number of hospital servants who fell down showed the infectious nature of typhus which prevailed.

'Dr [ ]'s report is that he had many cases of typhus which was contagious. He found much benefit from sponging the men with warm water and spirits; he gave the bark liberally.' [1]

Chapter 17

The army in winter quarters at Freineda

Castelo Bom was, as I have already mentioned, a miserable place – a ruined castle with the remains of about fifty cottages. The inhabitants had formerly consisted of about 150 or 200 souls, but by famine and starvation, as I have said, their numbers had been greatly reduced; indeed, the place had a most melancholy and dilapidated appearance, there being only about twenty or thirty persons living in it. And they looked more dead than alive.

After we took up our abode, they improved in their appearance, owing, I really believe, to what we gave them in charity. There were only two individuals in the place with whom we could associate – the priest and the *juez de foro*, or magistrate – but neither of them had their minds much cultivated. The priest was a pious good man, who appeared to discharge his duties most scrupulously to his miserable flock. He frequently partook of my dinner. His abode was a miserable cottage of two rooms, inhabited by himself and his mother, an aged, wretched-looking female. One of the apartments was at the same time the dormitory of the priest and a kind of store for provisions, the other served both as a kitchen and the bedroom of the old lady. They had no servant and the domestic duties appeared to be performed by the poor old woman. She was without shoes and the earthen muddy floor was in different places imprinted with the shape of her large feet. I understood, however, that the males and females of the poor pastor's flock readily rendered any assistance that might be wanted by him and his mother. He told me that in the winter he and his mother lived entirely on bacon and chestnuts, and showed me where these were piled up in the corner of his dormitory. He received wine from his flock, when they had any. The pastor was a man of mild gentle manners; not so our only other associate here, the *juez de foro*, a very rough, coarse man in appearance and manner, but with all, very good-natured. Whenever he dined with me, I could not push the bottle too far with him. At length, some of my party wished to make the experiment how far they could do it, but in spite of every artifice, they did not succeed in finding out the profundity of his stomach; he drank bottle after bottle of port wine and he even qualified it with a glass or two of Scotch whisky, which he called *nuevo*, praising it much, but without betraying any symptoms of intoxication, and when the party broke up he showed but little inclination to take his departure.

Our party here consisted of Mr Gunning, the surgeon-in-chief of the army; Dr James Forbes; Mr James, the purveyor-general of the army; Mr Hodges, the purveyor; and Mr Croft who was at the head of my office; Mr Wallington; Mr Burney; and two other gentlemen attached to the office. Dr Hume, the surgeon at headquarters, and other officers frequently joined our party and I had visits from Dr Fergusson, Dr Robb, Dr Neale and the medical officers of divisions of the army.

After the retreat, and when the army had got into quarters, the duties of the medical officers were most arduous.

From the first returns made by the divisions of the army, the number of missing was prodigious. They were said to be sick, but I could give Lord Wellington no correct account of them, having received no reports of their having reached any hospital. The general belief was that they were in the hands of the enemy. However, in the course of a fortnight a greater number of stragglers than was expected turned up, but a very great number of men who, from intoxication, irregularities or fatigue, had dropped behind were found in a state of disease and incapable of movement. Not a few were found dead and, had not the enemy retired so soon, all these sick and stragglers would have fallen into their hands. The disasters of the retreat, and the general prevalence of disease and mortality, were not apparent till a considerable time afterwards. Contagious typhus fever seized a great portion of the army and our loss was great. It was even said by several of the officers, who had retreated with Sir John Moore to Corunna, that the retreat from Burgos, and its consequences, were not much less disastrous nor attended with less loss.

At the first interview which I had with Lord Wellington, on his arrival at Ciudad Rodrigo and after he had hastily committed Cobbett's Register to the flames, he said to me, when in much vexation about his retreat, 'I never knew till now, nor believed, how unjustly poor Moore had been dealt with in the outcry raised against him in England about his retreat. I consider him the worst used man that ever lived. Nothing is so unmanageable as a British army in retreat, or when foiled.'

At length, after parties had been sent out in various directions to collect the stragglers and I was able to ascertain the number of our sick, and to get them housed, I found the numbers were very great, and, from the causes which existed, would continue so for a long time, contagion spreading on every side. But I felt it my duty to lay all this fully before his lordship, together with the small number of medical officers compared with the formidable number of sick, especially as they were spread over such an extent of country. Another evil existed of no less moment, the absolute want of hospital accommodation of any description for a tenth part of our sick.

I suggested remedies for all those formidable evils, which Lord Wellington instantly adopted and with his wonted energy gave me every means of carrying into execution. He forwarded to England my demand for medical officers of every class and a requisition that every medical officer absent on leave should be instantly sent out.

As, however, a considerable time would necessarily elapse before this aid could reach us, I proposed taking into our pay all the Spanish medical officers I could find with such of the French medical officers, our prisoners of war, as would take employment, and I recommended the English pay instead of their own. This bait took, for I do not think one of those gentlemen refused, and I posted them to the hospitals in the rear that they might be out of the temptation of deserting to their countrymen. I had my friend Dr Thomas Araji, the Spanish professor of Valladolid, who was perfectly the master of the English language, as well as of the French, attached to my office as correspondent and to enlist his countrymen. Of these he obtained a few only, but they proved to be very useful. However, with the French and Spanish medical officers in our employment, the gap was filled up till a reinforcement of British medical officers arrived from England. Then, in regard to the absolute want of hospitals, I had an excellent opportunity of putting in full execution my long-cherished plan of regimental hospitals, which I had quietly introduced. This rendered it more easy now to establish them on a large scale and universally for a great many of the surgeons had been in the habit of establishing them temporarily on a small scale: they therefore had only to work on a more extensive one from a model which was familiar to them.[2]

Every corps, therefore, had orders from me to construct its own hospital under the superintendence of the staff surgeon of the brigade or division of the army to which the corps belonged. This was done in general in a most efficient manner and everywhere was to be seen a comfortable hospital for the sick; surgeon and commanding officer vying with each other who would construct the best and most comfortable hospital for his corps. I made the purveyor supply them with such stores as each regimental surgeon required and to each corps was sent an assortment of medicines and wine.

In a short time, the march of sick from regiments to the established hospitals in the rear was stopped and it was high time, for the number that died on the way, of those sent to the rear, was very great. When this was firmly established and each corps had its own hospital where all its sick were treated under its own medical officers, who were all acquainted with the character of each individual in the corps, I went on an inspection tour to visit them and I was particularly desirous to see the distant established general hospitals in Portugal, which I inspected at Guarda, Celerico, Viseu and Coimbra. From thence I made an excursion to the Tras os Montes and to Gimuerens, where were the famous baths and mineral wells of Caldas, which I desired to examine in order, that if required, I might establish an hospital for such cases as needed the baths or waters.

By this time the army of the enemy having likewise suffered much in their pursuit of us, and in partial small actions in a most inclement season, halted at Salamanca and both armies went into winter quarters upon which Lord Wellington proceeded to Cadiz.

During the time we were in quarters, the chief duty of the army fell on the medical officers, which was most laborious, in some cases overwhelming, and in a great many instances the medical officers fell a sacrifice to their zeal and humane exertions. Worn down by the harassing fatigue they underwent, they were seized frequently with the contagion of the typhus fever they were treating and too often they fell sacrifice to it.

At this time the chief duty of the military officer was to sit at court-martials upon officers and men, for irregularities during and after the retreat were numerous, and Lord Wellington had determined to curb them effectually.

On 28 November, 1812, McGrigor transcribes in his *Journal* the words of Wellington's 'Memorandum to Officers commanding Divisions and Brigades', which caused so much distress among his subordinates:

I am concerned to have to observe that the army under my command has fallen off in the respect of discipline in the late campaign, to a greater degree than any army with which I have ever served, or of which I have ever read ... It must be obvious to every officer that from the moment the troops commenced their retreat from the neighbourhood of Burgos on the one hand, and of Madrid on the other, the officers lost all control over their men. Irregularities and outrages were committed with impunity ... I have no hesitation in attributing these evils to the habitual inattention of the officers of the regiments to their duty ... In regard to the food of the soldier, I have frequently observed and lamented in the late campaign the facility and celerity with which the French cooked in comparison with our army. The cause of this disadvantage is the same with that of every other – want of attention of the officers to the orders of the army and the conduct of the men.

Wellington had, in fact, asked for smaller kettles to replace the vast Flanders cauldrons. The light tin camp-kettles, which could be 'got to boil without needing a whole tree of half a church door to warm them' proved a vast improvement when they eventually arrived in 1813.

Sir Charles Oman states that, while 'there was undoubtedly much to justify the strong language which Wellington used as to the grievous relaxation of discipline in some regiments', some had been wrongly maligned. The 'awful days' of 15–19 November took a terrible toll. On 20 November, one officer reported: 'During the whole of the retreat, from the fifteenth inclusive, not only has the weather been dreadfully severe, but the commissariat arrangements having failed, the troops have been mostly without any issue of rations, and have suffered the extremity of privation, having lived upon acorns and hogs killed occasionally in the woods. The natural result of this has been great disorder and confusion, and the roads in the rear of the columns of march are covered with exhausted stragglers left to the enemy. In fact, by some inconceivable blunder, which the quartermaster-general's department attribute to that of the commissary-general, and which the latter throw back on the former, the supplies of the army, which were adequate for much larger numbers, on the morning that we broke up from the Arapiles were sent down the Tormes, by Ledesma toward Almeida, while the army marched on Ciudad Rodrigo – *hinc illae lachrymae*.' [3]

The efficiency of the medical service following the retreat from Burgos wrung from Wellington the exclamation: 'The medical department is the only one which will obey orders; on them I can rely for doing their duty.' [4]

McGrigor's *Journal* continues to record:

15 November, 1812
Dishonesty amongst the local people, many of them nearly starving, obviously was rife. A barely legible letter reports the loss of a 'public mule' stolen from behind the writer's tent and McGrigor, writing to Colonel Gordon, Quartermaster-General, requests 'that you will be pleased to grant to Staff Surgeon Boatflower recently appointed to this staff, an order to the commisary-general for a public mule.' [5]

December, 1812
At this time . . . all that could bear removal to Celerico were sent thither. Celerico might be considered as an advanced hospital station.

January 1813
I myself inspected at the beginning of this month the principal hospital stations, Portuguese as well as English taking such corps and regimental hospitals as lay near my route. I visited Guarda, Celerico, Vizeu, Coimbra, Oppata Lamigo.

My first object in going to Celerico was the separation and dissipation of diseases, so necessary at all times, so necessary now. The sloughing sores were placed in an airy hospital by themselves . . . The utmost attention to ventilation, fumigation and cleanliness and, above all, a strict attention to the comfort and nourishment of enfeebled patients and to produce the greatest good.

I may say of the whole of our hospitals in the Peninsula as well of this station that at all times the utmost cleanliness of the wards and bedding and especially of the persons and linen of the patients have now been rigidly enforced. We regard cleanliness and ventilation not only as means of cure and of comfort but as essentially requisite to prevent contagion.

Mr Burton of the 36th says that the Continued Fever [typhus or typhoid] which prevails has been induced by excessive fatigue and privations during the retreat, the greater part of the men being destitute of shoes or stockings. The disease commenced in, and has been almost confined to, a draft from England of 86 men which joined them at Salamanca. They were raw recruits, many of them not more than 16 years of age and unequal to fatigue ...

The men of the 79th are in rags ... they are without great coats and many of them without blankets and he pronounces the regimental dress [kilt] a cause of rheumatism, sore legs, etc.

Cases of infection of the chest were very prevalent. Many of the most fatal cases admitted were those of complete exhaustion without any prominent symptoms of disease ... These men have simply complained of utter want of power to move the limbs and have died without being roused in the least by any stimulant ... largely but cautiously and gradually exhibited. Dissection made no discovery of the causes of the disease.

S. S. Cole in his report on the state of the 6th Division states that they have been very unhealthy since the retreat ... This division suffered particularly for want of clothing and blankets, with coats, shoes and stockings.

This, as well as some other Divisions, arrived in ruined and miserable villages assigned them as cantonments in the middle of winter. Unfortunately, the means of intoxication were everywhere at hand, wine being the only thing that was plentiful and cheap and the thoughtless soldier has never been . . . for his . . . or temperance ...

The subjects first attacked were those that had suffered at Walcheren.

S. S. Bone, who was in charge of the division at Fronteniers, says that the medical cases come from the front in a very debilitated state and the disease aggravated by the want of clothing and necessaries [see page 210]. From these cases he thinks typhus was propagated and he believes it to be contagious. From 11 January, when he took charge of the 20th, the ward mate, the washerwoman, surgery man, four orderlies, many convalescents and fifteen men from the depot caught the disease. The bedding is deficient and few patients have two sheets, many none.

February, 1813
At the commencement of this month, headquarters were still at Ficente Guinaldo, the army continued in cantonments – part of it on the line of the Douro and part

on the interior, the corps of General Hill occupying. I had only last month returned from my tour of Castelo Bom. The general hospitals are as follows: Lisbon, Santarem, Abrantes, Alto da Chao, Coimbra, Vizeu, Celerico, Ciudad Rodrigo.

Mr Nixon, in his letter of this date, states that so completely has the 1st Guards been cut up by the Fever that he has not yet (3 months) seen any individual fairly recovered . . .

Sometime back, the care of the French prisoners of war was thrown upon us by the Portuguese government and they are very unprovided. In a letter of this date from Lisbon, Mr Guthrie informs me that he is obliged to retain in hospital 300 of their convalescents because there is no clothing provided for them.

Pneumonia is very much the disease of soldiers . . . as it results from sudden or incautious exposure to cold, after breathing for some time the debilitatory exhausted atmosphere of a crowded narrow quarter or barrack room.

The important Ciudad Rodrigo, an unhealthy station for our hospital, no doubt. The river Agueda forms part of the circumference in which it is built . . . At Ciudad it has no bank sufficiently elevated to prevent its overflowing the neighbouring low ground . . . In almost any direction it communicates with many ravines on the same level and, stretching inwards among the hills, when its surface in any morning is covered with a dense vapour which continues until the sun acquires power to dispel it . . .

The loss in this hospital station, as may be imagined, was very great. The fever was of typhus and of hospital gangrene . . . in this crowded state ventilation was impossible as, for want of bedsteads, the sick were placed on the ground, which a stream of air could never be made to sweep. In short, the situation was very favourable to the production of Contagious Typhus . . . The French as well as Spanish Garrisons which occupied Ciudad Rodrigo suffered not less than the British there. The mortality among the native inhabitants was enormous – Dr Neale states that during the last twelve months 1,200, out of a population of 6,000, died of misery and the Marsh Fever.

The inspection I made of the large general hospitals was a very necessary one and much was to be done at each. Fever of a low type was the prevailing disease, indeed, it was general and the mortality was high. It was most prevalent in the large hospital at Celerico and among the troops quartered in that district, but in the Guards particularly.

Nothing could have been better devised for arresting its progress in the army than the establishment of separate regimental hospitals in the cantonments of each corps, instead of sending the sick to a large general hospital which would have been crowded and where, by concentration, the virulence of the contagion would have been increased.

During his absence at Cadiz and Lisbon, Lord Wellington desired that I would regularly forward to him the weekly state of our hospitals. The number of the army laid up was excessive and the mortality was so high as to make a demand for reinforcements from England absolutely necessary, and this his lordship pressed on the British ministry, as well as a great addition to our medical staff, although, as already stated, we had in pay a great many French, Spanish and Portuguese medical officers, but I found they by no means made up for the want of British physicians and surgeons.

Immediately on the return of Lord Wellington from Cadiz and Lisbon to headquarters, I was sent for by him, when he fully discussed all these matters and instantly agreed to my proposals. I stated to him my perfect satisfaction with the regimental hospitals, which were by that time established in every corps in the army, but I thought it my duty to state that if the operations in the ensuing campaign should be more extended, or even on the same scale as the last, and at a distance from large towns, we should feel sorely the want of buildings for general hospitals to receive such cases of disease or wounds as would not bear conveyance.

On my usual morning visit with my reports on the following day, he told me he had had some conversation with the chief engineer and that he had thought some temporary buildings might be constructed somewhere, at no great distance from the present headquarters, which, on the advance of the army, might be moved and that they might be constructed to contain 5,000 men, with the necessary buildings for a general hospital. I reminded his lordship of a quarter where there was a royal forest which would afford us abundance of wood for the construction and that, if the staff corps was made available, we could soon raise a village of buildings of proper construction for a temporary hospital, upon which I would consult with the chief engineer. He told me that if the forest was a royal one we might have recourse to it, but forbade all meddling with private property.

At this interview I stated to him that when I went to the West Indies with Sir Ralph Abercromby's expedition, government had sent out with us wooden buildings for hospitals, with framework, which on being landed, required only to be put together by carpenters and that a day might suffice to erect a strong wooden building. At the time he did not appear to pay much attention to the suggestion, but desired me on the following day to set out and survey the neighbouring country, taking with me the purveyor-general of hospitals, and to report to him the best site I could fine for erecting our hospitals. He directed my attention to two main points only - that it must be at no great distance from a wood (on account of our want of transport for the materials) and that it was necessary it should be at no great distance from the Douro, so that, if requisite, the hospital might be evacuated and the sick conveyed to the hospital at Oporto; and perhaps that some intermediate station might be advisable between our large hospital and Oporto. He desired me to consider this conversation as most strictly confidential; that I should enjoin silence upon the subject to Mr James, the purveyor-general, and communicate to him only so much as was absolutely necessary.

Before proceeding further respecting the formation of this hospital, I may here state that not long after this conversation, upon my going to him one morning at my usual hour with the reports of the sick, he asked me to walk out with him and after eagerly inquiring the number of the convalescents who I thought could be sent to their corps in a month, he said, 'By the bye, your hospitals are ordered out and may soon be expected. By a despatch from Lord Bathurst which I received by the English mail, sent to headquarters this morning, I find that they ordered them instantly and were embarking them in three vessels, with two master carpenters and twelve carpenters to put them up and take them down, and to teach our artificers how to do this; but they will be a vast expense to the country.' I was certainly surprised for, from all that had passed, I merely thought that my suggestion, which I had not pressed, had passed unheeded from his lordship's mind. He ended by saying, 'You must let me know at what places you would wish to have them: they will be landed at Oporto, but you must have them at no great distance from Douro for I have no conveyance to a distance.'

As ordered, I proceeded with Mr James, the purveyor, to look our for a place where an hospital could be constructed and I fixed on a spot within a short distance of the Douro, where stores, &c., could be brought up from Oporto. It was near Castelo Rodrigo. I consulted with the chief engineer, who got orders from Lord Wellington to construct it according to a plan which I gave in and, in fact, it was to consist of several streets of small houses or cottages of what are called 'pisé' buildings.

By the extraordinary exertions of the medical officers, particularly at the large general hospitals in Lisbon, Coimbra, Oporto, Viseu and Celerico, a very large body of sick were sent out of the hospitals cured; and the weather being fine after their march, they joined the divisions of the army in firm health. Lord Wellington was highly pleased, as the number sent from the hospitals fit for duty was so much greater by some thousands than he had expected. Reinforcements having likewise joined from England, he determined on instantly commencing the campaign.

The hospital reports make distressing reading, yet much was being achieved as the following entry reveals:

March, 1813
During this month were admitted independent of transfers:
   5,621 cases of disease into regimental hospitals

887 cases into general hospitals

In the same month last year, and from a much smaller army, including transfers:

4,503 were admitted into the regimental hospitals

5,980 into general hospitals

So that this year and after all our disasters had not half this amount of sickness as in former years ... The total deaths in all the hospitals, general as well as regimental and including prisoners of war, amount to 577, being 625 less than on the former month.

The state of health of the divisions of the army is this month likewise very favourable, the most sickly of them have greatly improved in health. The prevailing fever has assumed milder forms and dysentery, in fact, disappearing. The mortality likewise is greatly diminished, though nearly the whole of the sick has been treated by themselves in their own regimental hospitals.

Looking forward to the campaign opening early, I made dispositions accordingly for the medical department ... all completed in medicines, bedding and [ ] of any kind to keep a constant establishment. Besides the sherry wagons, they were early directed to complete themselves with a cart or two and all the [ ] staff were removed from the hospital stations and to different regiments or the divisions of the army. At the same time, corps were ordered to prepare to disencumber themselves of sick, Invaliding Boards were held in every division of the army and [ ] would be sent off.

8 April, 1913

By returns of this date, the total number of sick and wounded to be sent to the general hospitals, by the divisions of the army on their moving, will not exceed 1,600. When we consider that for the last two months no cases have been sent from regiments, the success of the regimental system will be strongly apparent.

11 April, 1813

At the commencement of this month, the army remained still in their cantonments, though preparations were very like preparations for a move. I sent inspecting officers to every division of the army and every corps was monthly inspected ... the reports are most satisfactory. These not only exhibited a view of the present state of every hospital, the number of men lost since the retreat, but the fitness they are in to commence another campaign.

Napier, in his *Peninsular War* (revised edition, Vol. IV), affirms that 'During the ten months from the siege of Burgos to the battle of Vittoria the total number of sick and wounded who passed through the hospitals was 95, 348. By the unremitting attention of Sir James McGrigor and the medical staff under his orders, the army took the field preparatory to the battle with a sick list under 5,000. For twenty successive days it marched towards the enemy and, in less than one month after it had defeated him, mustered, within thirty men, as strong as before, and this too without reinforcements from England, the ranks having been recruited by convalescents . . . the extraordinary exertions of the medical officers of the army might be said to have decided the day at Vittoria, for their exercise had undoubtedly added a full division to the strength of Lord Wellington's army and without those 4,000 or 5,000 men, it is more than doubtful if his Lordship, with all his unrivalled talents, could have carried the day.'

Notes

1　From McGrigor's *Journal of the Peninsular Campaign*, Vol. VI.

2　The wisdom of these measures is adverted to in the following words by the historian of the Peninsular War:

'Confidential officers, commissioned to detect abuses in the general hospitals and depots, those asylums for malingerers, discovered and drove many to their duty. The second division alone recovered six hundred bayonets in one month; and this salutary measure was rendered more efficient by the establishment of both permanent and ambulant regimental hospitals, a wise measure, and founded on a principle which cannot be too widely extended: for it is certain that, as the character of a battalion depends on its fitness for service, a moral force will always be brought to bear upon the execution of orders, under regimental control, which it is vain to look for elsewhere.' From Napier's *History of the Peninsular War*, Vol. V, p. 503.

3　From the private and unpublished diary of General D'Urban.

4　From article on Sir James McGrigor by Lieut. Col. M.W. Russell in *Journal* of the R.A.M.C., August 1909, Vol. XIII.

5　National Library of Scotland, MSS 15337, f. 36 & f. 52.

EDITOR'S INTRODUCTION TO CHAPTER 18

Letters both to and from Sir James McGrigor are held in the National Library of Scotland. Some are included in the 'Murray Papers': the correspondence of Lieutenant-Colonel (later General Sir George) Murray, the quartermaster-general of the British army during the Peninsular Campaign. They illustrate the enormous amount of preparation involved in moving soldiers, animals and equipment and of transferring wounded men, involved in a military manoeuvre across rivers and mountainous land.

On 29 April, 1813, Captain Power of the Royal Artillery received a communication from Lieut. Colonel Murray, Quartermaster-General (writing from Wellington's headquarters at Freineda), asking for a report on the 'state of preparation of the convoy to move'. [1]

On 4 May, 1813, McGrigor [2] received a memorandum from Colonel Murray to the effect that: 'Orders have been sent this day to the 7th Division and to the 14th Light Dragoons directing the removal of the sick of these corps to the hospital station at Celerico.' [3]

More exciting was the news that, 'The commander of the forces, having approved of the suggestion . . . respecting the making at Oporto of a part of the hospital furniture required for the establishments now preparing for sick at Escalhaó and its neighbourhood, I have requested the commissary-general to furnish the necessary means of conveyance by water for such articles of the description mentioned in Lt. Col. Dundas's letter as you shall order the purveyor to procure at Oporto.' [4]

It would seem, in fact, that work on the field hospital had begun and that conflict had resulted between those involved in its construction. On 3 May, Murray, writing to McGrigor at Castelo Bom, informs him, 'I have told Lt. Col. Dundas to write to the officer of the staff corps that the staff surgeon has, of course, 'nothing to do with the workmen, but that if he could suggest anything tending to expedite the work, or to render the accommodations better for the objects they are meant for, these suggestions should be attended to.'

On 7 May, Murray wrote to Dundas (Colonel the Hon. R. L. Dundas, Controller of the Royal Staff Corps) telling him that a force of cavalry, about 1,000 strong, would be crossing the ferry at Pocinho on the fourteenth, for which he must prepare. Also, that the 18th Brigade would cross the Douro on the twelfth. 'I beg you will see Sir Robert Kennedy upon the subject and obtain his authority for employing additional boats.' [5]

On the same day Murray wrote to McGrigor:

'By the route transmitted to me it appears that the sick of Sir Robert Hill's corps will reach Aldea da Porte upon the eleventh Inst. I believe the only division we can make of the route from there to Escalhaó will be as following [here, the manuscript is very faint]:

12th As Navas or Jun,ca

13th Villastorpim

14th Escalhaó

'I fear, however, the accommodation is very bad at the places above named for the 12th and 13th. It would be very desirable, therefore, that you would be good enough to send an officer of your department beforehand to these places, to make the best arrangements that circumstances allow of, to the accommodation of the number of sick expected.'

'Memorandum to Dr McGrigor [same date] Orders have been this day sent to the 1st Division for the removal of the sick to the hospital station at Vizeu.' [6]

'Memorandum to Dr McGrigor at Castelo Bom, Freineda, 12 May, 1813. Orders have been sent this day to the 4th and Light Divisions for the removal of the sick of these corps to the hospital station of Escalhaó.'

On 13 May, Colonel Murray writes to Captain Power: 'I have transmitted the enclosed route for the detachment of the waggon train which has marched to Vizeu.' [7] After which he addresses 'The officer in charge of the Pontoon train' [no date given], and requires him to 'make application to the nearest division of the army for such aid as may be necessary to forward the progress of the train where the difficulties of the road impede its march.' [8]

Murray again writes to McGrigor at Castelo Bom, Freineda, on 17 May: 'Lord Wellington directs that half the establishment of the 100 carts placed at your disposal may be sent to Ciudad Rodrigo, there to wait further orders; and that half may proceed by the way of Torre de Monsoruo, [   ] for the march of which a route will be issued on you application.'

The efficiency which resulted from McGrigor's reforms of the Army Medical Service appear from the returns in Volume 12 of his *Journal* of May 1813.

It appears that the total sick in the army amounts to 5,127. Of this number 1,503 are convalescents, leaving only 3,724 only actually sick, [9] the strength being about 57,000, being in the proportion of a healthy 1 in 15.

About the end of this month, at Oporto and at Escalar some of the movable hospitals sent out from England [arrived] for the accommodation of the sick. Whatever might be their merits or demerits, and there were faults in the construction of them, they gave us admirable means of separating typhus and hospital gangrene from other diseases and gave us the opportunity of classing diseases more perfectly than we were able heretofore to do.

Every corps was not only complete in its regular establishment of medical officers, but extra officers were added, and every division had likewise inspectorial officers, physicians or additional hospital surgeons attached to it.

Besides the spring wagons, it was recommended that each battalion, according to its strength, should start provided with one or two carts or tilted wagons.

Invaliding Boards having been held in each division, the invalids were sent off to ports of embarkation to England and the sick sent to the general hospitals.

On the whole, the divisions of the army now set out so complete in medical means and so well provided to meet variations of climate.

15 May, 1813
It continued to rain very heavily.

17 May, 1813

Very warm weather succeeds heavy rain and, but for this extraordinary attention paid to the health of the army, and the confirmed health which they have attained, much disease would have ensued on the march.

21 May

We set out from Castelo Bom by Almeida and got the first night to the Smelt.

25 May

We got this day to Tori de Moncoror.

26 May

Today Dr Fergusson formed a general hospital establishment at Salamanca.

29 May

We arrived at Miranda de Douro. [This was the day that Wellington crossed the Douro by the famous basket-rope bridge at Miranda and joined General Graham, who was near Carvajales. On 1 June, Graham entered Zamora and the French, after destroying the bridges, retreated.] [10]

Mr Hill thinks that the excessive heat of the weather after the first days of the month, will account for the numerous relapses of intermittent fever which he had in the division. He adds that the excesses committed by the men since receiving the bounty for re-enlistment account for much of the sickness of the 5th Division.

On the whole, the state of the divisions of the army is very healthy, notwithstanding the continuance of drunkenness and irregularity consequent to the men's receiving bounties for re-enlistment.

By the first week of June, 1813, Wellington had advanced to the Douro. By his brilliant strategy he had forced the French, with hardly a blow struck, to leave very strong positions on the Esla and Douro. Napoleon's bother, Joseph, whom he had created King of Spain, should have been able to defend these strongholds and, in failing to do so, laid himself open to attack. The battle of Vittoria, which McGrigor briefly describes, proved to be one of the most decisive victories of Wellington's Peninsula campaign.

The *Journal* of the R.A.M.C. reports as follows:

Altogether the picture of medical affairs in the later phases of the Peninsular War is one a medical officer likes to dwell on: a capable chief, in intimate relations with, and possessing the entire confidence of the supreme commander, with a body of officers devoted to him and to their work, eager and able to second him to the full in his endeavours to promote the fighting efficiency of the army. That much of the success was due to the personality of McGrigor cannot be gainsaid.

CHAPTER 18

Battles of Vittoria and Toulouse

The day before that on which headquarters were to advance, I had a very long interview with Lord Wellington on the arrangements for the medical department. I expressed an opinion strongly on some points, which, as he negatived, I deemed I had only to submit to the decision of the commander-in-chief and did not express a word more. On returning to my quarter, however, at Castelo Bom and when in bed, I received an orderly dragoon letter on two sheets of foolscap paper, giving in detail and in his own hand-writing his lordship's reasons for dissenting from me. I was not a little surprised at his sending any explanation for his decision on any point was final and it was my duty merely to carry his orders into execution. Again, this letter of such extraordinary length was written at a time when other business, the most important, was on his mind, previous to his moving the whole army against the enemy and opening the campaign. The provisioning of the army, the complicated details of conveyance, the raising of supplies, the different arrangements regarding the heavy artillery and engineer departments – all these and endless arrangements for so large an army, with those for our allies the Spanish and Portuguese, being upon his mind, it often astonished me that, on the very eve of his departure, he should have devoted so much time in writing a letter to me on points of less immediate consequence upon which I had ventured to submit opinions not in accordance with those he entertained.

At this time the army advanced on three lines: Lord Hill on one route to the right; Sir Thomas Graham, afterwards Lord Lynedoch, on another to the left; and Lord Wellington with the centre directly against Salamanca. For the first time, with the other civil departments, I was separated from headquarters and proceeded with the column which moved from the left. I think it was about the 22nd of May when we advanced.

Before the campaign was opened, the number of convalescents who joined their regiments was very considerable and, as I have said, astonished even Lord Wellington, who at this time felt how efficient was the body of medical officers we then had, how invaluable their experience, how unbounded their zeal and devotion to the service, and how high their professional talents. Their zeal had been much stimulated by the great promotion of deserving officers, which at my recommendation his lordship had carried out for them at home. But, even during the march, considerable bodies of the convalescents from our far-famed hospitals were daily joining their respective corps, and it was said with much truth by an eminent individual that he thought the extraordinary exertions of the medical officers of the army might be said to have decided the day at Vittoria, for their exertions had undoubtedly added a full division in strength to Lord Wellington's army and without those 4,000 or 5,000 men it is more than doubtful if his lordship, with all his unrivalled talents, could have carried the day. Perhaps, without that material addition to his force, he would not have risked an action.

After long and rapid marches through the north of Spain, and though a beautiful country, but with precipices and defiles almost impassable to troops, we came close to Vittoria, in the kingdom of Navarre.

From an early hour in the morning of the 21st of June till the commencement of the battle I witnessed closely every movement. A grand and all-interesting sight it was and I continued a close spectator till we galloped into Vittoria in the evening of that ever-memorable day, in company with my friend the judge advocate-general, Mr Larpent,[11] with whom I had a complete view of the whole action.

McGrigor does not describe the scene of wild confusion as the French fled from Vittoria. The road was completely blocked about a mile east from the town with hundreds of French vehicles, intermixed with guns, baggage, etc . . . The plunder made by the soldiers was immense in spite of the efforts of the officers to keep them in the ranks. Leach recounts how, an army of sixty or seventy thousand Frenchmen, which for years had been living on the country and plundering and levying contributions on the inhabitants, had naturally amassed many valuables and riches. These were seized upon by the victors. 'The French military chest fell into our hands and many of the men secured both gold and silver in large quantities. Unfortunately, as is ever the case, the great bulk of the booty was looted by the camp followers and thieves, as well as by the worst class of soldiers who had left their regiments to plunder.' Many dramatic captures were made: Jourdan's travelling carriage with his Field-Marshal's baton were taken by a private in the 87th, whilst King Joseph's travelling carriage in which every dish and toilet article was of solid silver was captured by the 14th Light Dragoons of the Light Division. (The chamber pot known as King Joseph has graced many a festive night on the anniversary of Vittoria.) [12]

Joseph himself had a narrow escape. An officer forced open the door of his carriage, but in the scrimmage he managed to scramble out on the other side, mount his horse and get away.

We continued our victorious pursuit of the enemy till we drove them beyond the Pyrenees and into what they called the sacred territory of France. Headquarters were established at St Jean de Luz, about the middle of November, in very stormy weather.

The fall of Bordeaux was followed by an advance on Toulouse and the final sanguinary battle which there ensued.

Until communication could be made across the river Garonne, headquarters were stationed at Grenade, where I was billeted in a large house in which the family was very numerous, I believe not less than thirty persons, including grandfather and grandmother; the son, who was the landlord; his wife; several of their brothers and sisters; and a very numerous family of the rising generation. At this house I became acquainted with the physician of the family, a sensible, well-informed man, and from him I learned an extraordinary fact. Speaking of the *vin du pays*, which to me appeared delicious, he said it had its bad effects for, though the population of Grenade did not exceed 3,000 souls, yet there were on average one hundred of all classes always laid up with gout. I had formerly believed that this disease was more prevalent in England than in any other country, but I subsequently acquired knowledge of facts in other parts of France, which established to my satisfaction that gout is perhaps a more prevalent disease in France than in England.

At length a bridge was thrown over the Garonne, headquarters were established and I joined Lord Wellington on the 9th of April. The following day, Easter Sunday, the battle of Toulouse was fought. My brother-in-law, Lieutenant-Colonel Colquhoun Grant, being engaged, I felt deeply interested and from nearly the commencement in the morning till the close of it in the afternoon I was a close spectator. So close indeed was I that it might almost be said I bore a part in it, as might in some measure be said upon other occasions: first, in Grenada in the West Indies in 1796; secondly, at the storming of Badajoz; thirdly, at the twice attempted storming of Burgos; fourthly, at the storming of St Sebastian: fifthly, at the battle of Vittoria; sixthly, at the battle of the Pyrenees; and seventhly, on the memorable day when we fully entered France after storming the whole chain of redoubts that came in our way to St Jean de Luz and when, more than on any other occasion, the whole allied army, British, Portuguese and Spanish was engaged in opposition to the French army commanded by Marshal Soult.

In proper execution of their duties, medical officers are frequently under fire and during the late war the cases of wounded medical officers were numerous. Some had been killed and not a few lost limbs in sieges or in battles. Yet it has been ignorantly advanced by some military men that the medical officers have no business in exposed situations and in this professed opinion they would deny the medical officer a pension for the loss of a limb. Yet it is well known that the cases are numerous wherein the lives of officers and soldiers have been saved by the zealous medical officers of their regiments being at hand to suppress haemorrhage. In alleviating pain, it is no small advantage to have the surgeon at hand to extract cloth, splinters, &c. Circumstances may subsequently prevent this being done till a long period afterwards, when the state of inflammation has been considerably advanced and when their extraction must necessarily be attended with infinitely more pain; whereas, by promptness, life or a limb might have been saved, especially the former, as at an early period amputation would have been successful.

Early in the morning, after the surrender of Toulouse, I waited on the Duke of Wellington to receive his orders as to the disposal of our numerous wounded; when I called, he had been but a very few hours in bed and I had to wait until he rose. On seeing him and reporting the average number of our wounded from the calculation I was then enable to form, he said it was desirable that I should immediately go into Toulouse to see the magistrates there, and as speedily as possible make the best provision I could for the wounded of the allied army. On arriving at our advanced posts, I found some difficulty in proceeding, as the officer in command had no orders to let anyone pass and had received no official communication that a capitulation had been signed. He informed me that two officers with some soldiers who had gone in had been kept prisoners. However, armed with Lord Wellington's orders, I pushed on. After passing the French sentinels I found considerable difficulty in passing the mounds and barricades opposite the gate. Once in, attended by my Portuguese orderly dragoon, I was greeted by the shouts of an immense multitude in the first and contiguous streets with their welcomes and '*Vivent les Anglais!*' from every window, crowded more especially with females. I passed in this triumphant manner through several streets, but the loud shouts of the populace rendered my horse and that of the Portuguese orderly dragoon who attended me very uneasy. At length, we reached a noble square, with a superb building in front of us, the Capitol. Here the shouts on our appearance were tremendous, for there were several thousands assembled who rent the air with their acclamations. Passage was with difficulty made for us through this immense mass by the civic officers who laid about them somewhat roughly. Arrived at the capitol, I dismounted, when I caught sight of a red coat and beheld an English officer standing before me, laughing excessively. I discovered it to be Sir Lowry Cole. After recognition, he told me I was a very great man and informed me that I had been mistaken for the Duke of Wellington and owed all the acclamations and my triumphant entry into Toulouse to that mistake of the people, to whom it had been announced from the gates. We laughed heartily at it and I enjoyed the joke as much as Sir Lowry, who accompanied me to the mayor, sitting in council with the magistrates. Coming out from them I met with Dr Thomas, a resident English physician, who recommended me to disregard what the magistrates had told me for that there was abundant accommodation for all our numerous wounded and that, being well acquainted with Toulouse, he would show me all the accommodation. For all this I immediately applied and subsequently gave a list thereof to Lord Wellington, who ordered that the buildings should be instantly delivered over to me.

From the very great number of wounded a the battle of Toulouse, the labours of the medical officers were exceedingly great, not only on the day of action, but for some weeks afterward for the duty devolved on them not only of dressing the wounds and attending to the British, but also of performing similar offices for our allies, the Portuguese and Spaniards, a greater number of whom came under our care than on any former occasion. Knowing the inadequacy of their own surgeons, their gratitude was expressed in warm terms to the English surgeons who sedulously attended them, and the wounded French prisoners appeared to be equally grateful. Their gratitude had been conspicuous on a former occasion when, during the absence of Lord Wellington to superintend the siege of St Sebastian, the French made a sortie and captured part of the headquarters, carrying off Sir John Waters and Mr Larpent, the judge-advocate-general.

In our rearward movement we had been obliged to leave some sick and wounded at a place which it was ascertained the enemy would soon occupy. I left a staff surgeon, Dr Murray, in charge of the men, with money to procure what might be necessary for them, and desired him to recommend the sick and wounded officers and men in his charge to the good offices of the superior French officer who might occupy the village we were about to leave. As Dr Murray informed me at a subsequent period, he discovered the approach of the enemy about two hours after I had left him and to his astonishment saw about twenty of our men suddenly appear, who had hitherto concealed themselves in the village after the departure of Lord Wellington and the headquarters. From the manner of the men as they conversed together, and from the marked caution evinced in the order of their approach, Murray suspected they were preparing to go over to the enemy. He then spoke to them in an authoritative tone and demanded what they were about, reviling them as rascals if they intended to go over to the enemy. They eyed him with sullen looks, when a sergeant from among them came up to him and cautioned him immediately to leave them alone, otherwise he would have a bullet through his head. In a minute afterwards, he saw those men run towards the approaching enemy.

As the French cautiously advanced, Murray met them with his handkerchief on his sword and requested to see the officer in command to solicit his protection for the men left under his charge. This was readily granted and for the few days they were in the village he received every courtesy from the officers. Once or twice the French soldiers entered the house where our wounded officers were and, on Murray's mentioning this to the general, Count

D'Erlon, I believe, he immediately ordered sentries to be placed over the house for their protection.

On first seeing Dr Murray, the count eagerly asked after his friend General Hill, hoping that he had not been hurt in the late affair and that he was in good health, adding that General Hill was a good man. The enemy did not retain possession of this village long. Their force, which followed our army in a few days, was beaten back, their rear attacked by our advance close to the village and they had a considerable number of wounded. Their surgeons were stationed outside the village, at a spot where the wounded were brought to them. Dr Murray then very properly offered his assistance and, placing himself among the French surgeons, dressed as many of the wounds and performed a good many operations throughout the day. Not a few of the French officers presented themselves to Murray, who was preferred by several of them to their own surgeons. This statement does not rest on the sole narration of Mr Murray, for a few days afterwards Count D'Erlon wrote to Lord Hill detailing the circumstances, and requesting that the great merits, skill and professional ability of Dr Murray might be brought to the notice of the Marquis of Wellington, whose thanks I at the time conveyed to Dr Murray; and at a subsequent period, I had the pleasure of promoting him in the service.[13]

But to return to the battle of Toulouse and its results. As I have said, the number of wounded of the British army, of our allies the Portuguese and Spaniards, and of our prisoners, was great. It exceeded 5,000, but after some days of toil, aided by Dr Thomas the English resident already averted to, who knew all the localities of Toulouse, I succeeded in getting them all housed, making use of the hospitals belonging to the city, besides occupying the convents, nunneries and churches, with several houses and an encampment outside the walls.

But several days passed before I was enabled, with the exertions of the experienced officers under me, to ascertain exactly the number of wounded and to classify them according to the nature of their wounds, stating those which were dangerous and unlikely to recover. I placed the whole in two great divisions of the city, one under the superintendence of Mr Guthrie and the other under the superintendence of Dr Murray, being two of the ablest and most experienced of our operating surgeons.

After none of the previous battles were more operations performed than after that of Toulouse and on no former occasion was more skilful surgery displayed. Great experience and reflection had at this time created among us a body of operators such as never were excelled, if ever before equalled, in the British army.

Although the navy has produced many eminent medical men, and I will not say of less eminence than the army – Lind, Blane and many others, to wit – yet the opportunities for correct and cool observation are not so favourable in the navy as in the army. In the practice of a physician in the navy, the opportunities for obtaining a correct knowledge of the diseases peculiar to our colonies and to warm climates are be no means so favourable as those enjoyed by medical officers of the army. Fleets or single ships touch only at the seaports of our foreign possessions and their stay is seldom lengthened; whereas the military medical officer, by being stationed from time to time in every part of the interior of some island or of the peninsula of India for a long series of years, is led by his observation of facts to very different conclusions in regard to the prevailing diseases from what he would have formed during a few weeks' residence only at a seaport, where the prevailing causes of disease did not fully exert their influence.

NOTES

1   National Library of Scotland, MSS 46.3.18. f. 94.

2   National Library of Scotland, MSS 46.3.18, f. 107.

3   Ibid.

4   National Library of Scotland, MSS 46.5.15, f. 82.

5   Ibid, f. 111.

6   Ibid.

7   Ibid, f. 116.

8   Ibid. f. 124.

9   Note that the arithmetic is inaccurate.

10   Verner Willoughby: *A History of the Rifle Brigade*, part II, p. 446.

11   'I got, with Dr McGrigor and a few others, on a hill about a mile from the French, which commanded nearly the whole scene,' from the *Journal of the Judge-Advocate-General*, Vol. I, p. 242.

12   Verner Willoughby, *History of The Rifle Brigade*, part 2, p. 446.

13   'The French under D'Erlon behaved very well to Colonel Fenwick who was left wounded; no one was allowed to go into his house . . . and every attention was paid both to him and the surgeon left with him. The latter became so popular that the French liked to be dressed by him better than their own surgeons.' From Larpent's *Journal*, Vol. II, p. 34.

Chapter 19

Visit to Montpellier

Very soon after our taking possession of Toulouse, the report of the downfall of Napoleon and of the allied army having marched into Paris became current. About the same time we received the disastrous account from Bayonne and of the capture of Sir John Hope. In a couple of days afterwards Colonel Cook arrived from Paris with the intelligence that the French capital was in possession of the allies. I was at dinner at the duke's table when Colonel Cook arrived; he also sat down to dinner and, as might be readily believed, all were desirous to listen to his account.

Previous to the receipt of this news, the entry of the British troops into Toulouse had been enthusiastically welcomed by the inhabitants, but their enthusiasm increased after this and in the theatre, and throughout the street, 'Henri Quatre' was constantly played. I happened at this time to dine with the duke; he had intended to go to the theatre in the evening and it so happened that I was the only one of his staff who was in the way to accompany him. I shall never forget the outburst of enthusiasm with which he was received when they discovered him in the stage box. The whole audience stood up, while the orchestra gave us our national air of 'God save the King'. After this, the audience, still standing, called for 'Henri Quatre', which was sung by the whole house, the duke repeatedly expressing to me his satisfaction with the feeling exhibited by the people.

Sir George Murray, our quartermaster-general, after the Duke of Wellington, perhaps the ablest officer in our army, met Marshals Soult and Suchet about this time to arrange the terms of an armistice, and in a day or two afterwards the two French marshals dined with the duke. I dined with him on the same day. As soon as peace appeared likely to take place, being desirous to see the French hospitals, their arrangement and economy before the armies were broken up, it now occurred to me that an introduction to the French marshals would greatly facilitate my object. I therefore took an opportunity in the course of the evening to mention it to the duke, who entirely approved of it and immediately presented me to Soult and to Suchet, who in warm terms offered me every facility to inspect them and begged the honour to have me for their guest when I visited the headquarters of the French army at Carcassonne.

In no long time afterwards, with a passport from Lord Wellington, I put my plan in execution. Having provided a carriage and all things necessary for the journey, accompanied by Don Thomas Arrajo, the Spanish physician attached to my office, dressed in the English uniform of a physician to the forces, I set out from Toulouse. Don Thomas was a liberal Spaniard; he had been expelled from his chair of chemistry in the university of Valladolid on account of his opinions, but he bore a deadly hatred to the French as the oppressors of his country. He was a man of extensive information, spoke French and English fluently, and had a thorough knowledge of the principal writers in both languages. He was so intimately acquainted with Hume and Gibbon, Milton, Pope and Shakespeare as to quote them frequently. Before setting out it was agreed that in our conversation together in company he should speak to me in English for, had he been discovered to be a Spaniard and in an English uniform in our service, the least we could expect would have been that he should be insulted.

We set out on our journey from Toulouse on a fine morning and after travelling a few leagues came to our outposts where, at the time, a Portuguese brigade was stationed. By this time, the Portuguese had been rendered excellent soldiers and might be relied upon with nearly the same confidence as the British soldier. In one respect they were his superiors: they were never seen drunk; their orderly and submissive conduct to officers was constantly remarked; and they were always most respectful to British officers whenever they met them. As I passed the advanced sentry, he very respectfully asked for my passport, which he gave to a sergeant who delivered it to his officer, when the latter, advancing politely, requested me to proceed. In this little interval, while eyeing the Portuguese soldiers around us, when I reflected that we were about to be separated from them, they to return to their own country and I to mine, it induced a somewhat melancholy reflection and I was really sorry at the thoughts of parting with those good men, who had so long shared our fortunes, whether prosperous or the reverse, without a murmur.

On advancing to the French outposts, they received us with courtesy, examined our passports and allowed us to proceed. We then continued our journey to Carcassonne, the headquarters of the French army, which we reached in the evening. We found the town excessively crowded with French troops and on inquiry found that both Marshals Soult and Suchet were absent from Carcassonne. Don Thomas had therefore recourse to the principal hotel, or rather auberge, which was crowded with French officers and soldiers. The host, however, proposed to accommodate us and he showed us a large room in the upper part of the house, the low roof of which nearly touched our heads. In this room, or loft, there were three rows of coarse bedsteads, without curtains, in number about one hundred and we fixed on two of the bedsteads for our accommodation for the night. Our host informed us that supper would be ready in about an hour and at that time we entered the supper room. We found a long table occupied on both sides by about a hundred officers. Upon our entrance into the room, all gazed at our English uniforms and, after we had taken our seats, we not only excited the attention of the whole table but appeared to form the principal subject of their conversation. We had nearly gone through the business of supper when two young officers seated immediately opposite me addressed some questions to me regarding the late battle of Toulouse. The appearance of my querists was by no means prepossessing, their manner was far from courteous and they were very unceremonious in putting their questions to me. They both became warm and impetuous in their interrogatories to me, and their demeanour put me on my guard so that I whispered to Don Thomas not to enter the discussion. One of them asked me the number of our killed and wounded. As respected the latter, I gave a direct reply. Both shook their heads with strong dissent, one of them saying that he had certain information of our number of wounded, as well as of our killed, being at the least double the number we stated. I then announced myself as inspector-general of the medical department of the army and told them I was responsible for the correctness of the number returned as wounded, that my general return was constructed from my own personal knowledge and from the returns rendered to me by the principal medical officer of each division of the army, who framed their returns from the return of the surgeon of each regiment and that, therefore, there could be no error in the return of the wounded. The two officers replied with vehemence that it was an untrue or incorrect account. On this, two officers of more advanced age, and more gentlemanly appearance, rose up and severely reprehended their conduct towards two strangers and English officers. Words repeatedly passed between them and they were uttered with vehemence and violent gesticulations. At length, both laid their hands on the hilts of their swords and I looked momentarily for nothing less than a personal conflict between the now contending parties. While both were vociferating loudly and with the most hostile gestures, a door behind, which I had not before seen, suddenly opened and forthwith entered a French general officer, with his sword drawn, who fiercely demanded the cause of the broil and tumult. Both parties spoke simultaneously. He instantly commanded the silence of the two junior officers and ordered the oldest of the officers to state what had happened. He, pointing to Don Thomas and me, explained that two British officers who supped there had been grossly insulted by the other two officers and that, to the disgrace of the French army, the rights of hospitality had been greatly violated. On this the general called up an adjutant who sat towards the bottom of the table and upon the two violent gentlemen attempting to explain, he stamped his foot, commanding them to be silent and to deliver up their swords to the adjutant. Bowing then to Don Thomas and to me, the general left the room. After what had passed I thought it prudent, with my friend, to do the same and, obtaining a light, proceeded to our huge dormitory. Here occurred another curious scene. Upon entering the elevated dormitory by several flights of stairs, we found that several of the beds in the three rows, which went longitudinally through the room, were occupied. Our beds, next to each other, were pointed out to us in the centre row but, to our surprise, we found two females had commenced undressing on two of the beds near to ours: one of them a young woman and the other considerably older, perhaps her mother or an aunt. The oddity of this tickled the fancy of my grave Spanish friend, as well as mine, and I believe we laughed or smiled to each other, upon which the two ladies, both of them of very respectable appearance, commenced to redress themselves and left the room.

At an early hour the next morning we left Carcassonne and in the evening arrived at Narbonne, where I found a letter had been left for me by my friend Colonel David Stuart of Garth, who, as the first English officer, had preceded us on the route and had promised to leave a letter for me with all the information which he could gain respecting our route. The letter was written from Montpellier and sent to the Mayor of Narbonne, who, on our arrival, called upon us. To my astonishment the Mayor of Narbonne accosted me in the Scottish dialect and I found that he was my countryman. He had been many years in that city, had a large family by a lady of Narbonne and had at length arrived at the high civic honour he then had. He was most courteous, but I had determined not to tarry there and to set off in the morning for Montepellier. In the street at Narbonne I met three of the French medical officers who had been our prisoners and to whom I had given employment in our army; they greeted me most cordially.

On our way to Montepellier I attempted to read and re-read the letter of my friend Colonel Stuart, whose handwriting was most extraordinary. At length, with the aid of Don Thomas, I got through the whole, except the name of an hotel which he desired me particularly to avoid. We exerted our utmost ingenuity to decipher this to us important word, but were obliged to give it up. After passing Cette, where there was a depot of Spaniards who had followed the fortunes of King Joseph, whom my friend Don Thomas execrated, we returned again and again to the letter to discover the name of the obnoxious hotel, but all in vain. At length, having gained the suburbs of Montepellier, we asked the names of the three principal hotels. On ascertaining which was said to be the best of the three, we drew up to it and, on inquiring its name, were answered that it was the Hotel du Nord. It immediately occurred to me that this must be the hotel which Colonel Stuart had desired us to avoid. On looking at the Colonel's letter, we at once discovered that it was so. By this time most of our luggage had been taken out and the waiters stood beckoning us to proceed. Though the exterior of the hotel was very promising, I at first declined, but after a minute's consideration entered and on being shown into an apartment I desired the landlord should be sent for. A fat, paunchy man entered, bowing. I informed him that in coming to his hotel we had committed a mistake, asked him if it was the Hotel du Nord and, taking out my letter, demanded if he had not had an English colonel who wore spectacles with him a few days ago. He answered the affirmative. Looking at the letter, I then said that on account of exorbitant charges imposed upon him, and the insolent treatment he had met with, he had written to the British army, where many officers were about to set out for Montpellier, to shun the Hotel du Nord on that account. The astonishment of my host was extreme; his countenance exhibited an extraordinary and ludicrous cast. He assured me that the colonel's account was untrue, entreated me to make a trial of his house, and reiterated again and again '*Mon Dieu! Mon Dieu!*'. I resumed saying that more than one hundred officers were about to proceed to Montpellier, many of them of the *Gardes du Corps*, very rich and sons of noblemen, but that on account of his treatment of Colonel Stuart a notice had been posted up at Toulouse warning all to avoid the 'Hotel du Nord'. He added another 'Mon Dieu!' earnestly assured me that the colonel had done him an injustice and again eagerly repeated his entreaties that I would make trial of his house, if only for one day. I consented, and Don Thomas and I never had more reasonable charges, nor better treatment in our lives. The attention paid to us was extreme and when by ourselves we enjoyed our ruse very much. I acceded to the entreaties of my host to write to Toulouse and honestly wrote to a friend at headquarters describing the delightful situation of Montpellier and announcing the Hotel du Nord to be a most comfortable inn.

There were several regiments both of cavalry and infantry at Montpellier, but we had little encouragement to inspect their hospitals. Indeed, the officers never met us without frowns and contemptuous looks at our British uniforms. This was evinced also at the theatre on the day of our arrival. Upon our entering, a considerable part of the audience greeted us with shouts of '*Vivent les Anglais!*' which was, I believe, a shout of the bourgeois in contempt of their own military. In the box opposite to us were three French generals who sent some gendarmes to clear the house of those who raised the cry. There was a great commotion and after the performance of the evening had been stopped for a considerable time, Don Thomas and I, considering ourselves the cause of the disturbance, left the theatre.

Finding it hopeless to obtain access to the military hospitals, we visited the civil hospitals and met several of the professors of the university going to their classes to deliver their lectures. Most of the medical professors visited us, and showed us the utmost attention and kindness. As we could not gain the information we desired, we proceeded to Nîmes and visited the valuable remains of antiquities there. Thence we went to Pont du Gard and passing the River Rhone, proceeded to Avignon, once the Papal residence. We went from thence to Vaucluse, where we admired everything around us and then made the best of our way back to Toulouse.[1]

I regretted to have to return with the object of my journey unaccomplished. From much conversation with the French medical officers employed by me in our service, from communication with the professors at Montpellier, together with the condition of the sick and wounded French, and some of the hospitals which fell into our hands, I can have no doubt of the hospitals which I proposed to visit having been in the inferior state that was generally represented; and consequently I believe that they had no desire to have them inspected by me. I think I have seen every edition of the regulations for conducting the French hospitals from the commencement of the revolution to the present time, and I am free to confess that I see very little to copy from them as an improvement on our own. But one part would certainly be an improvement; I mean the ambulances for the transport of their wounded and sick, particularly of the former. I once proposed our adoption of it in Spain to Lord Wellington but he would not hear of it, nor would he give the credit of humanity to Napoleon as the motive for his introduction of it into his army.

NOTES

1 'The Society of Medicine at Montpellier made the doctor a member with such fine speeches that, even though he only half understood them, they raised his blushes,' *Larpent's Journal*, Vol. III, p. 227.

CHAPTER 20

Return through France to England

On my return to the army at headquarters at Toulouse, I was surprised by a communication the most flattering to me and which I look upon as the most gratifying incident of my life. It was to the purport that the medical officers had entered into a subscription for a service of plate, which had been ordered and of which they requested my acceptance. Nothing could go more directly to my heart than the terms in which this was expressed, in a letter from the medical officers of the Peninsula army. This handsome gift of the value of nearly one thousand guineas was subsequently presented to me in London. What greatly enhanced the value of this gift was that it was voted and presented at a time when the donors of it ceased to be under my control, when they could expect neither further approbation nor advantage from serving under me; in fact, when the tie was broken between us and when we were about to be widely separated.

The army now moved to Bordeaux – part of it was destined for further service in America and was embarked there. The remainder of the infantry sailed for England and the cavalry marched through France to Calais on their way homeward.

In company with my friend, the late Dr Thomas Thompson, I proceeded to Paris where I saw Baron Larrey with whom I had commenced an acquaintance in Egypt, at the time when the French army surrendered.

I was very desirous to see the great military hospital in Paris, which was under the directorship of my friend Baron Larrey, with whom, after breakfasting together, I visited it. He showed me several remarkable cases in which he had operated successfully and they certainly displayed the best efforts of surgical science. The hospital was in good order and the patients appeared comfortable and well cared for.

I also visited Baron Desgenettes, who had served in Egypt, and among the professional gentlemen to whom I was introduced at Paris by my friends Barons Desgenettes and Larrey was Baron Percy, likewise a medical officer of the army. The appearance and manner of this gentleman were more pleasing than those of his *confrères*, and in giving information he had a singular appearance of openness and candour.

About this time, my wife, to whom I had intimated my return on the conclusion of the peace, wrote to me that she would immediately set off from Scotland in order to be in London by the time of my arrival there. I had previously arranged with Sir Charles Stuart, the ambassador (now Lord Stuart de Rothsay), that he would accompany me to the Duke d'Angoulême, who, when at St Jean de Luz, desired to see me on my coming to Paris that he might present me to the king, and Lord Stuart had urged me to go to the king's levee, remarking that he could present me in the event of the Duke d'Angoulême not being in Paris. However, on the receipt of my wife's letter I determined immediately to leave Paris and on the following day left by the diligence for Calais. On arriving there, I found my old friend Lord Blayney about to sail for England and after breakfasting with him and his daughter, I accompanied them on board. After clearing at the Custom House, I immediately proceeded to London where I had the happiness to find my wife and son had arrived in good health.

I was kindly received by the three members of the medical board, Mr Weir, Sir Charles Kerr and Sir William Franklin.

I had a most gracious reception from the Duke of York and most friendly receptions from Sir Willoughby Gordon, the quartermaster-general; Sir Harry Calvert, the adjutant-general; and from my old friend Sir Henry Torrens, the military secretary.

Upon waiting on the Duke of Wellington, who received me most cordially, he informed me that I must continue my duty as usual of being with him every morning, for he was constantly receiving papers respecting the hospital establishments, which he must refer to me in order to furnish replies. I accordingly continued that duty, as on the late service in the Peninsula. One morning, after the usual business, he said, 'Mac, we are now winding up all arrears with the government; I have asked them how you are to be disposed of and I am told you are to placed on half pay, but I consider your peculiar services will entitle you to a specific retirement. Before I enter on this subject with Lord Castlereagh, I wish to know your own sentiments.' I replied that the last and only case I knew was that of Dr Young, who had been inspector-general with Sir Ralph Abercromby, and who got 3l. per day as a retiring allowance. He suddenly replied, 'To that they can have no possible objection; the demand is moderate.'

On my next seeing him, I believe on the following morning, he said, 'Well, they have at once agreed to your retiring with 3l. per day and they propose conferring the honour of knighthood on you.' After a little pause I said, 'On a service of such magnitude and importance as that in which I have been employed, and after having been repeatedly honoured with your grace's approbation, expressed in your public despatches, I did hope that, if they conferred any honour upon me, it would be the permanent one of the baronetage.' He immediately replied, 'You are the best judge of what you will take; but I would recommend your taking the knighthood in the meantime.' I replied, 'I had no hesitation in following any course his grace might be pleased to recommend.'

In a day or two afterwards, I had a kind note from him, informing me he would meet me at the levee the following day and present me to the Prince Regent, who would confer the honour of knighthood on me. In the afternoon I received another note from his grace stating that, being obliged to meet Lord Castlereagh in the country, he could not be at the levee, but that he had desired Lord Bathurst, whom I should find there, to present me. I confess I felt a little disappointed for I would have preferred to have been presented by the duke, rather than by Lord Bathurst, whom I did not know. However, to the levee I went and I was in the first apartment after the entrance room when I saw Lord Bathurst, but in so earnest conversation with some gentlemen that I could not intrude upon him. Presently, someone entered who appeared to attract the notice of all. It was the duke who instantly made up to Lord Bathurst and I could hear him say, 'Have you seen my friend McGrigor, whom you are to present?' Lord Bathurst had barely time to reply 'No,' when the duke, turning sharply round, got hold of me and said to Lord Bathurst, 'Here he is, take care of him.' He then speedily vanished out of the room. He was in a travelling dress, got into a post chaise and, as I afterwards learned, was going on business to Lord Castlereagh, at his place near Foots Cray where he subsequently died.

There was in this act of the duke a benevolence of character of which I had observed many other instances and which those only who had been much near him could know. The duke knew that I had much natural shyness. He knew the disappointment I would feel in not having his support at the presentation, which he could not give, being summoned to meet Lord Castlereagh on business. He therefore called on his way at Carlton House determined to put me under the wing of Lord Bathurst. Subsequently, he said, 'I thought it was as well to place you under Lord Bathurst. You are a shy fellow and might not have found him out.'

I kept close to Lord Bathurst, who advanced with me slowly with the crowd at the levee, but he was constantly in conversation with someone or other. Arrived in the presence, he spoke to the Regent and I then heard him announce my name in presenting me. The Prince added, 'I know McGrigor very well,' and then added something complimentary in his unequalled, most kind and gracious manner. He then desired me to kneel, when he waived the sword over me and I left the presence complimented by many, some of whom I did not know.

I still continued my morning attendance on the duke to transact any business that presented itself regarding my late department in the Peninsula. Many demands came from Spain as well as Portugal for monies which had been paid, as I found by reference to the purveyor of hospitals, who had an office in town till all the accounts were wound up. In many instances they were able to produce the receipts of the parties who were claimants. In justice to the late Mr James, purveyor-general, I must say that never had the public a more honourable or faithful servant. Although I believe nearly half a million had passed through his hands, not a shilling of it stuck to them. So strictly honest was that gentleman that, with a large family, he found much difficulty in living in London and it required years of repeated application through the Duke of Wellington to obtain the addition of four shillings to the usual half-pay, which he could claim on retirement from the shortest service. This, as observed by many, was but slight encouragement for honour and strict integrity. Had he taken the usual advantage of his situation, which would not have been considered extraordinary, he might have retired in affluence and his large family would have been well provided for. Under similar circumstances another public officer suffered the same fate – Sir Robert Kennedy, the worthy and upright commissary-general in the Peninsula service.

The parsimony of the state, which pays badly the civilians of the army, is most injurious. None of them are paid in a way commensurate with the important duties committed to them. The commissariat are the liberally paid, yet looking to the immense sums which pass through their hands I consider them underpaid. The small pay of the purveyors and their deputies holds out a temptation to them to remunerate themselves out of what passes through their hands.

At this time, public dinners were given to the Duke of Wellington to some of which, as one of his staff, I was invited, particularly to a very splendid one given in the city at the Mansion House and also to another given by the East India Company, and to others by various public bodies.

The National Library of Scotland holds the following letter:

Army Medical Board
London, 18 October, 1826

Sir James McGrigor presents his compliments to Sir Walter Scott, and has the honour to present a letter from Baron Larrey with his works in four volumes.

Sir James McGrigor has known the Baron since the year 1800, when he left Egypt with the French army, and he believes him to be a man of the greatest integrity and honour.

The friendship between James McGrigor and Baron Larrey, remarkable in view of the fact that they held equivocal positions as enemies, continued to the end of their lives. McGrigor,

Contemporary engraving of Baron Larrey
(Galerie des Contemporains Illustres)

in a letter dated 13 December 1839 to his son, Charles, who was visiting Paris, wrote, 'I hope you called on Baron Larrey and his son.'

Such was the strength of their friendship, based on mutual regard, that McGrigor made Larrey an honorary member of the Aberdeen Medical and Chirurgical Society and continued to correspond with him for many years. Mr George McGrigor, grandson of Sir James, states that he, in fact, translated Larrey's autobiography, *The Memoir of Baron Larrey*, from the French.

'Napoleon's great surgeon, the Baron Larrey, initiated research into the surgical aspects of transportation. His introduction of light, fast-moving, two-wheeled ambulances [*ambulances volantes*] effected a more rapid evacuation of the wounded and sick. This, combined with his surgical skill, saved many lives.' [1]

'Baron Percy of the French army occupied, during the Peninsular War, much the same position as Sir James. To him, some of the success of the '*ambulances volantes*' was due as well as to Baron Larrey, Napoleon's Chief Medical Officer.' [2]

McGrigor, on his arrival in the Peninsula, found that there were 'no intermediate medical stations between the regiments and the general hospitals, no mobile field medical units and no dedicated medical evacuation transport. This situation undoubtedly caused increased mortality, slowed down recovery and thus delayed return to duty, and was wasteful in medical resources such, as they were. By comparison, Baron Larrey had introduced the concept of a flying ambulance or *ambulances volante* into the French army some years previously. This unit had an establishment of 113 officers and men, including fourteen surgeons all mounted and under the command of a surgeon-major of the First Class. It moved with the divisions and rapidly transported wounded to the rear. [3]

NOTES

1   From 'Original Communications', an article in *Journal* of the Royal Army Medical Corps, Vol. XCV1, Jan. 1951, by Lieut.-Colonel A.N.T. Menzies, Reader in Tropical Medicine, R.A.M. College.

2   Ibid.

3   From *The Aberdeen University Review*, Spring 1991. The McGrigor lecture delivered to the Aberdeen Medico-Chirurgical Society on 21 September, 1989, by Anthony J. Shaw.

CHAPTER 21

Appointed Director-General

Having settled the principal and most material part of the public business connected with the Peninsula and the numerous papers referred to me by the duke, Lady McGrigor and myself (accompanied by our son) prepared to visit our relations and friends in Scotland. I had the supreme happiness of renewing my acquaintance with many old and much regarded friends, and my dear wife enjoyed her meeting with her mother and family under happier and more cheerful circumstances than when she went to them after my departure for the Peninsula. Among the numerous kind friends from whom we received much attention none could surpass the Honourable General Sir Alexander Duff, my kind brother officer for years in the 88th Regiment and Sir David Baird, both of whom had been my companions in crossing the desert from Bombay to Egypt. How different were our situations then compared to what we were now enjoying in our native country. I had the pleasure of meeting another of my esteemed Bombay friends – Mr James Augustus Grant – who was secretary to the government of Bombay, but my Peninsula business not being quite finished we were obliged to return to London in October. We often had the pleasure of looking back on that visit to Scotland as one of the happiest periods of our lives.

Having been always fond of the study of my profession, I determined to re-study two of my favourite branches – anatomy and chemistry. For this purpose I returned to my old master, Mr Wilson, who lectured in the Hunterian School in Windmill Street, a gentleman whose pupil I had been upwards of twenty years before. Mr Brande had at this time commenced lecturing on chemistry. I liked his manner and immediately became his pupil also. I believe that neither Wilson nor Brande had in their classes a more assiduous pupil than myself.

I was not the only elderly disciple to be seen among the young students at these lectures. Several practitioners attended the anatomical lectures and many gentlemen of various professions attended the chemical lectures, which Mr Brande made very interesting. My old friend, Dr Helenus Scott of Bombay, who had returned from India with an ample fortune after a residence there of twenty-five years, learning from me the interest of these lectures, joined me as a student, became likewise the pupil of Messers Wilson and Bell and also of Mr

Brande, and his venerable figure was daily seen as the most attentive of students in both places.

I had business with the Duke of Wellington, the War Office, and the purveyor's department, in sanctioning charges and winding up accounts, which made it necessary for me to have an office, with one clerk, up to nearly the end of 1814, when I was placed upon half-pay, or rather, retired on an income given me for special services.

I now began to look about me and to see what future prospects I had. Numbers of my friends, military, particularly, urged my entering on the practice of my profession as a physician in the metropolis. It then appeared I could do this with every prospect of success, known as I was to the whole body of the officers who had been in the Peninsula and through them to their relatives in London, many of them of the aristocracy, or most opulent individuals; and having acquired a name from the late service I had been upon, I was assured that my success was not doubtful.

About this time the late Mr Weir, then director-general of the army medical department, was taken very ill and he soon afterwards resigned on account of his health. A body of my friends, mostly medical officers of the army, came forward and urged me to present myself as a candidate for the Board. But it appeared to me that I could claim a seat at the Board, only as the younger of the three members; and that Sir Charles Kerr, or Sir William Franklin, would have a claim to be the first, and to succeed Mr Weir as director-general. Soon after this I was sent for to the Horse Guards and informed by the late Sir Henry Torrens, the military secretary, that, finding there was no prospect of the recovery of Mr Weir, it was the intention of His Royal Highness the Duke of York to appoint me his successor. My ambition at once decided me to accede to this, although my friends were still apprehensive for my health. Further, I was strongly impressed with the irksome nature of the office I was about to undertake and the impossibility of my answering the expectations of many who, as my friends, would look up to me to promote them in the service, though with the certainty of converting many of them into enemies and malcontents, particularly at the conclusion of a war, when very many reductions would be insisted upon by the higher authorities in compliance with the outcry for retrenchment, which always occurs at the commencement of peace.

Dazzling as is the patronage of office, it is at the same time its most unsatisfactory and most annoying appendage, particularly when the candidates are in any degree literary; and I often found to my cost that the thin skin did not belong exclusively to poets and painters.

The feelings, therefore, with which I received this communication were by no means those of unmixed joy. The candidates for the office conferred on me were numerous and not confined to medical officers of the army. The disappointments were therefore equally numerous. I heeded none of these, however, except those of the two old and most respectable officers, who then held seats at the board. Their disappointment at not succeeding to the first seat and at being superseded by a much junior officer, was very natural, and I could readily enter into their feelings. I felt much awkwardness and reluctance to take my seat, delayed doing so for several days and, in the interval, made a call at the houses of Drs Kerr and Franklin.

When I had taken my seat those sentiments continued for some time, and if there existed feelings of my being unwelcome on the part of my colleagues, I readily admitted their being very natural. I believe I made the largest allowance for them and endeavoured so to conduct myself as to make myself as little unacceptable as possible. Dr Franklin, as noble minded an individual as I ever met with, and who to the mildness of his nature added the manners of a perfect gentleman, immediately acted in concert with me and met me cordially on every point of public business. We soon found that our general views of the service, and of the subjects which came before us, were the same, and we were almost always unanimous in opinion.

In a few months afterwards, Dr Kerr sought retirement from the service and obtained it. Dr William Somervillle was appointed in his stead, but he remained a few months only, government having decided on reducing the members of the board from three to two.

I had one inducement to enter the board, which had no small influence on my mind, though somewhat hesitating between the opinion of some of my friends to embark in practice and that of those who urged me to take office. This was my extreme desire, to accomplish fully the object which I had entertained for many years, viz., to turn the reports and returns rendered by the medical officers of the army to the account of science, and the improvement of the officers themselves, instead of devoting them, as was the fashion of the day, to the fiscal concerns of the department, to the economy and the minute expenditure on account of the hospitals, in fact, to pounds, shillings and pence, and that almost entirely. It was notorious in the army and had even become cause for ridicule among military officers, that the subject matter of the correspondence of the board, as shown by the correspondence book of the regimental medical officers, turned wholly upon those details.

Previously to Mr Knight's elevation to be a member of the army medical board, having Sir Lucas Pepys and Mr Keate as colleagues, he had been the surgeon of one of the regiments of guards and got credit there for introducing a system of economy in the management of the expenses of the hospital, which in the guards were then defrayed in a great measure from the stock purse of the regiment. The system, as applicable to a regiment of the guards, or to the hospital of any regiment, was extremely good; it established a thorough check upon the expenditure and when Mr Knight established it as the system for the hospitals of all regiments in the service, it worked so well that he was loudly and deservedly praised for it. But the system was carried by Mr Knight and some of his deputies to a ridiculous extent; by carrying on a lengthened correspondence with the officers about grains of salt, and ounces of oatmeal and soap; the smallest possible expense of a poultice, with the lowest prices of eggs, butter, potatoes and milk; the prices of the various qualities of these; and different petty grievances. The minute attention to this species of economy became, I said, ridiculous in the deputies of Mr Knight. But it was worse than trifling and ridiculous for it engaged the time and diverted the attention of medical officers from the proper objects of their profession.

When I now retrospectively estimate in all fairness this state of things, as they existed at that time, I am fain to confess that I was myself carried away in the vortex of the then prevailing routine. Although I did not go to the extreme, as did some of my brethren – the deputy inspectors of hospitals – I did enough, as I now think on looking back, which I consider absurd. But, like others, I was duly impelled to this by mandates from Mr Knight's deputies at the board, who directed my attention to the enormous expenditure in salt in the hospital of one regiment, of that in oatmeal in another, and in poultices in a third. In conclusion, suffice it to say, Mr Knight's system, when introduced, was much required in the service. It effectually checked profusion and extravagance in the regimental hospitals, which, with plunder by the hospital servants, had existed to a great extent, previously to its introduction. When pruned as it now is of its extravagances, I look upon the system as perfect and it would have been well for the service if, at the time it was introduced into the regimental hospitals, it had been likewise introduced into the general hospitals in as far as the established system and usages of the department admitted.

For a long time there had existed a difference of opinion respecting the value of general and of regimental hospitals. The members of the army medical board had themselves differed much on this subject and the officers of the department, ranging themselves under one or other of the members of the board, advocated and adopted their opinion; so that, in fact, the whole of the officers of the medical department of the army enlisted themselves in time under the two opposite factions. Eventually, the difference became more than calm differences of opinion at the council board on a point of public duty. It was whispered that animosities existed and that whatever other matters came before the board, they were discussed with anything but temper. This conflict of opinion, and these divisions in the board, had dated from far back; and it is generally understood that an altercation with one of his colleagues was the immediate cause of the death of the celebrated John Hunter.

When Mr Gunning joined Mr Keate and Sir Lucas Pepys in the board, it was reported that anything but unanimity prevailed among them. Mr Rush succeeded Mr Gunning, and Mr Knight succeeded Mr Rush. Still discord

Sir James McGrigor, Director-General of the Army Medical Department, holding reports dated 1839 (photographed by Gordon Ross Thomson)

prevailed and the interests of the public were ill looked after. This could scarcely be otherwise, when the materials and constitution of the board are considered. None of these gentlemen, the great John Hunter and Mr Rush excepted, had any knowledge of the habits of soldiers or of the diseases incidental to them, unless we admit those of them who had served as surgeons in a regiment of guards at home. Mr Rush had served for a short time as surgeon of a regiment in America. Besides, each of these gentlemen exercised his profession extensively in the metropolis and as this led to more emolument than his situation in the public service; it is fair to admit, he paid most attention to his private practice. Indeed, it was known, that the prospect of introduction to extensive private practice was the object of some in soliciting a seat at the board.

During the official reign of Sir Lucas Pepys, Mr Keate and Mr Knight, an occurrence brought this in glaring colours before the public at large, and laid the foundation of a total change in the constitution of the board. This was nothing less than the circumstance I have already once adverted to: viz., that after the fatal expedition to Walcheren took place, alarming accounts reached this country of the most frightful sickness and mortality in our army there. Upon this, government directed that one of the members of the board should be sent to Zealand to examine the state of affairs and report to them. But each of the three members excused himself and in an examination at the bar of the House of Commons, the physician general, Sir Lucas Pepys, excused himself there, on the plea of his advanced age and particularly on that of his unacquaintance with the diseases of soldiers [see Appendix 7].

In fact, not one of the three members had served with an army or had any practical knowledge of the arrangements. The public outcry was loud, and this state of things could no longer be tolerated. Accordingly, the Duke of York ordered a board of general officers to assemble, to investigate and report. The result was that a board should be formed of medical officers of long service in the army, of practical experience and who had served much abroad in various climates. The first recommendation was that this board should consist of five members, and I had the honour to be nominated one of the five; but after this project had been submitted to the ministry, they cut down the number to a board of three members. The three sufficiently advanced in life, and who had seen much service, were the late Mr Weir, Dr Kerr and Dr Theodore Gordon, senior; the two latter, active and able officers, particularly Dr Gordon, a man highly respected throughout the whole army, and who, from his known talents, possessed the entire confidence, as well as the respect, of the whole body of medical officers. In the service this very judicious and able officer had suffered much in his eyes: he had lost one and by the ardour with which he entered on his duties, the other eye became attacked with inflammation, which so much alarmed him, that he retired from the board. His successor was my own lamented friend, the late Sir William Franklin, and as the successor of Dr Theodore Gordon, a better selection, or a man more fitted of the situation, could not have been found in the British army. I am enabled to speak of him thus from a very long knowledge of him. For nearly twenty years we sat as colleagues at the same table, where matters of public business came daily before us for discussion There might occasionally be a little difference of opinion, but that did not last for five minutes and on no occasion did any unpleasant feeling exist for a second.

CONCLUSION

The preceding *Autobiography* terminates thus abruptly, at the period of Sir James McGrigor's appointment as Member of the Army Medical Board in 1815, a few months after which the Board was remodelled and he was placed at the head of it as Director-General.

That Sir James did not carry on the narrative of his life after his elevation to office arose doubtless from many causes, of which the following may in a great measure have contributed their influence.

His life had hitherto been passed with little intermission, in the midst of the varied and stirring events of active service in the field. It had been a career of arduous duty, zealously performed amid all the manifold dangers and vicissitudes incidental to service in distant climes, in which, in his medical capacity his personal risks and anxieties, like those of all the members of his profession, were considerable.

His great merits and acknowledged abilities had won for him another field of action; one in which, though the demands on his exertions were no less urgent, his labours no less uninterrupted and his responsibility was quite as great as before, yet it presented no longer the same constant succession of interesting circumstances for record. It proffered him a calmer sphere of physical exertion. It was one in which he could devote his mind with less interruption to the elaboration of those plans for the amendment of the executive and working systems of the medical department of the British army, the serious need of which he had long been impressed with, and which his experience and judgement had enabled him to devise.

Moreover, in his capacity as director-general of the department, most of the incidents and facts of his current official life were, in the strictest sense, official in all their relations. They were, so to say, the properties of his Office and as such demanded a discreet reserve, an honourable secrecy. It was not, therefore, likely that he would make them subjects of narrative; and it would have been unbecoming in him to have indited with his own pen a relation of the various improvements he effected, the eminent services he rendered to the interests of science as connected with the Army Medical Department and the numerous acts of beneficence which he performed throughout his long tenure of office in the interests of all immediately connected with the medical service of the army.

Lieutenant-General Sir Neil Cantlie, K.C.B., K.B.E., M.C., M.M.B., F.R.C.S., Director-General of what had by then become the R.A.M.C., sums up the difficulties with which his predecessor had to contend.

'At the end of the Napoleonic War there was a great reduction in the strength of the military forces and with it of the Army Medical Department. The Treasury exercised a strict financial control and new methods, new ideas, new hospitals, had no chance of being adopted or built. We have already seen how under the old Medical Board, and even later under Director-General Weir, emphasis had been put on economy in hospital expenses. Now under McGrigor the emphasis was to be on the care of the soldier in sickness and in health. As a result of the reduction in the strength of medical officers, McGrigor's policy was to weed out those whom he regarded as the less efficient and retain only the best. In 1816 a memorandum was issued which ushered in a new era of professional standards; he wrote, 'It is not only in the sense of humanity, but in that of a sound policy and good economy, that the state should provide able medical and surgical advice for the soldier when sick or wounded. I look upon it to be an implied part of the contract of citizens with the State that, whoever enters the service of his country as a soldier to fight its battles, should be provided with the same quality of medical aid, when sick or wounded, which he enjoyed when a citizen.'

He went on to say that 'a liberal education for candidates is indispensably requisite and the greater the attainment of the candidate in the various branches of science, in addition to competent professional knowledge, the more eligible he will be for promotion, as selections to fill vacancies will be guided more by reference to such requirements than to seniority.'

At this time candidates applying for a commission had to produce certificates of attendance at lectures for a period of three years and pass an examination at the College of Surgeons in London, Edinburgh or Dublin. Some candidates, as in the case of McGrigor, were university graduates, but this was not essential.

McGrigor now pressed his officers to improve their professional knowledge by post-graduate study at universities or schools and promised every facility to assist the grant of leave or half-pay – he set a good example by attending some lectures himself. Moreover, he created the first steps in specialism by asking officers to study eye diseases, mental diseases and midwifery. 'Medical officers,' he said, 'are encouraged and recommended to look forward to the appointment of Surgeon to the Forces, or Physician to the Forces and to endeavour especially to qualify themselves for either.' Promotion, he emphasised, would be based on professional knowledge rather than seniority and his powers of patronage in this respect were all powerful for he exercised complete independence in his own domain and was not responsible to any staff department.

The indifference which many regimental surgeons had hitherto displayed to professional attainments gave way to an awakening interest in the prospect of promotion by merit. The vindication of this policy came later when McGrigor, with no little pride, was able to observe: 'In the ranks of the medical officers, men are to be found upon a level at least with those in the College of Physicians and Surgeons of London, Edinburgh and Dublin. Taking the profession in civil life generally, there are comprised in the body of the medical officers of the army not fewer men of literary attainments and university education than in the ranks of civil life.'

The status of medical officers vis-a-vis their comrades of combatant rank was a matter of continual concern and argument. They were always, as a matter of form, addressed as 'doctor' for they held no executive but only relative rank. Although there is nothing more honourable than the title of doctor, rank in the army is everything, and the absence of military titles as borne by the combatant officers meant that their army and social status was regarded as inferior. No medical officer could preside at any Court of Enquiry or Board for he was regarded as junior to every recently joined ensign, although he might have twenty years' service. On social occasions, incidents had occurred when medical officers were debarred from attending functions.

It was felt strongly that the ranks of officers should be the same as that of combatant officers of corresponding rank, and it was stressed that although the medical officers were the proper advisers on measures necessary to keep medical practice abreast of scientific progress, the rank and status officially accorded to them did not bear this out. Their power to make their representations effective was thereby weakened. Sir George Napier voiced this feeling when he wrote, 'It is a very general but unjust idea to think slightly of the medical man, for few officers receive so good an education or are so generally acquainted with science and literature. I am bound to state that if one takes the conduct of the whole Medical Department of the army into consideration, one will find few such large bodies of men who are now distinguished for their kindness, skill and indefatigable exertions for the health and comfort of the sick and wounded; and, as to danger, the medical officers of the British army have, without exception, invariably shown an utter contempt for it either in the field of battle or, which requires a higher courage, in the hospitals of plague or yellow fever.'

This problem was only settled after years of constant striving and representation to overcome the prejudice of senior army officers, and this was many years after McGrigor had retired.

One of the Director-General's most cherished ambitions was to establish an army medical school where officers, on first joining, would undergo systematic instruction on all forms of army procedure and medical and sanitary administration as well as the diagnosis and treatment of the common diseases which afflicted the soldier. Such a school had been strongly advocated many years previously . . . But at the termination of a war, which had involved vast expense, any scheme which required financial expenditure was certain to be rejected, and the Government refused to entertain it. Nearly fifty years were to pass before it became a reality; McGrigor had to be content with what he regarded as the very inadequate instruction which the period of probation of a few weeks at the general hospital at Fort Pitt provided, where no systematic lectures by qualified instructors were possible, but in other ways he was able to promote the professional interest which was so dear to his heart.

Lieutenant-Colonel Russell states that 'he [McGrigor] gradually collected full statements and services of every individual medical officer in the army, which were drawn up and signed by each.'

Sir James had once remarked, 'The efficiency of an army must ever depend on the state of the health of the corps which comprise it, and no regiment will ever be found healthy when the internal economy is bad. It is a trite but true saying that a good C.O. will generally have a healthy and effective regiment. Whenever there was much attention paid to the discipline and exercise of the men, where they were well fed, personal cleanliness as well as that of the quarters kept up, the men's clothing repaired and the men regularly messed, that regiment was always invariably found healthy.'

The aptitude which he had evinced at an early period of his professional career for medical statistics, and the high estimation in which he held that branch of study, as presenting the most reliable data on which to establish directive regulations for the better preservation of the health of troops, and the treatment of the diseases incidental to the different climates in which they were stationed, were prominently shown soon after his accession to the directorship. Concurrently with the discharge of his official duties, he proceeded to carry out his long-cherished project of instituting a system of Medical Reports and Returns of a more statistical character than had hitherto been the custom, with the view to making them of permanent use to the service; and form therewith a collection of constantly available records, calculated to advance the interests of science and the general improvement of the medical officers of the army.

For this purpose he issued forms to the surgeons of all the regiments in Great Britain and Ireland, and to the heads of the medical staff at all the colonial stations, requiring their periodical transmission in the shape of half-yearly and annual reports to the Medical Board in London, detailing the health and condition of the troops, the diseases prevalent among them, and the modes of treatment pursued.

Whenever any of these reports contained matter of unusual interest, Sir James McGrigor transmitted queries to the officers who furnished them, in order to elicit further information on the subject. In these periodical returns, among other points of interest, information was furnished respecting the average duration of the life of the soldier in different climates; the probable or ascertained exciting causes of each disease; its most effectual treatment; and the mortality in particular years of yellow fever, cholera and epidemics generally. The effects of any new sanitary measure or treatment introduced for the purpose of preserving the health of the troops, or facilitating the recovery of the sick, were thus readily ascertained by comparison; and the extension of beneficial measures was promoted wherever the same results were to be anticipated.

Sir James McGrigor pursued this course with such persistent zeal during his long tenure of office that, when he resigned the Director-Generalship, he left behind him a vast and important collection of records, bound in folio volumes, each duly lettered with the name of the colony or district to which it related, and indexed. To this, which in itself constituted a medical library of the greatest practical value, every facility of access for reference was granted to members of the profession at the office of the Army Medical Board.

Dating from the year 1816 to 1850, this immense repetorium of authenticated medical facts comprised the following subjects:

Half-yearly and annual returns of sick of the troops at home and abroad
    (vol. 303)
Topography, with maps (vol. 7)
Reports on cholera (vol. 5)
Reports on syphilis (vol. 2)
Histories of epidemics; being replies to queries issued in 1825 (vol. 2)
Replies to queries on mortality, diseases, &c., issued in 1837 (vol. 3)
Replies to queries on barracks, hospitals, clothing, &c., issued in 1838
    (vol. 4)
Replies to queries on cases of small-pox which have occurred after
    vaccination
    (vol. 2)
Reports on delirium tremens (vol. 3)
Returns of phthisis pulmonalis from troops at home, 1840 to 1850
Epidemic in Gibraltar in 1816 and 1828 (vol. 1)
Abstract of quarterly returns of sick, from 1816 to 1850 (vol. 11)
Abstract of quarterly returns of sick from foreign stations (vol. 3)
Abstract of quarterly returns of sick from home stations (vol. 2)
Nominal quarterly and annual returns of insane patients from 1827 to
    1850
Annual return of recruits from 1826 to 1850

The importance of these returns, as furnishing correct and instructive data for the preservation of the health of the soldier, was not long in being recognised; and the contents of these volumes were eventually published, with the aid of the War Office.

Their value, and that of medical statistics generally, has since been ably set forth in an article published in the 'Statistical Journal' for the year 1856, entitled 'On the Mortality arising from Military Operations', in the course of which, the author says: 'Sir James McGrigor, well known for many years as the Director-General of the Army Medical Board, was at the head of the medical department of the Peninsular army during the latter part of the war, at the conclusion of which he wrote a sketch of the medical history of those campaigns in which he had served. It contains many valuable suggestions as to the preservation of the health of troops on service, and some important statistical returns, which have been found useful in determining points that would otherwise have been left in doubt.' The author subsequently states that 'Sir James McGrigor recorded the causes of all the deaths which took place in the Peninsula while he was at the head of the medical department' and makes numerous quotations from those records.[1]

The strong predilection evinced by Sir James McGrigor for the resort to detailed statistical forms for the surer elucidation of the science of diseases incidental to troops, and of their treatment, appears to have been imbibed from his study of the works of Sir John Pringle, an eminent military medical officer, physician to the military hospital in Flanders in 1742, and shortly afterwards appointed Physician-General to the British forces beyond seas.

Deeply impressed with the value of Sir John Pringle's 'Observations on the Diseases of the Army in Camp and in Quarters',[2] that, as early in his professional life as the Egyptian campaign, Sir James McGrigor emulated his countryman's example by giving to the public his *Medical Sketch of the Expedition to Egypt from India.*

His sense of the numerous defects in the system on which the Army Medical Board was constituted and governed acquired the fullest confirmation from the result of the examinations of the medical authorities before the House of Commons, after the deplorable expedition to Walcheren, and justified him yet more in his opinion, not only of the necessity of an improved system of administration of the medical department of the army, but of the advantages which would be derived by the service, from the requisition of periodical statistical reports and returns of a detailed character, from the medical officers on every station at home and abroad.

In the Peninsular War, Sir James McGrigor had availed himself of the opportunity afforded by his position to pursue the course marked out by the experience of John Pringle upwards of half a century before, and with such good effect as to confirm him yet more in his estimate of the labours of that eminent medical officer. The estimate formed by Sir James McGrigor's professional brethren of the service rendered by him to the science of medicine, by the institution of the system of periodical statistical reports adverted to, is shown in a brief but able sketch by Mr Pettigrew, who says: 'He rendered the most effective service to his country, not only by appointing to the army gentlemen of high professional attainments; but, also, in making available the results of their experience to future generations; the science of medicine being in no manner more truly advanced than by the accurate histories of diseases, and the faithful details of the practice adopted by enlightened men.'

In a letter from Field Marshal Lord Beresford, in 1838, to Sir James McGrigor, the opinion of that eminent soldier of the value of these reports is expressed in the following words:

Bidgebury Park
7 Nov., 1838

My dear McGrigor,

It is high time I should acknowledge yours of the 22nd ult., and thank you for the very valuable publications you have sent me on the comparative state of the healthiness to our profession of the several parts of the British Empire, which must be most valuable to the country, and most interesting indeed to all military people. Would such a compilation had been made before our time, that we might have had the benefit of it. The subject reminds me indeed of your country's expression of 'Auld lang syne' when you and I were often so anxious, and conversed over such subjects for the benefit of those under our care and protection. You have in this shown and continued the same uniform zeal, care and interest in the cause of humanity, which then so honourably distinguished you. Nor do I know how you could more excellently have crowned you exertions in that cause, than by the part (or rather the whole) you have taken in this most useful and beneficial work.

I shall be desirous of getting the remaining publications.

Believe me, my dear McGrigor,
Yours sincerely,
Beresford.

The first years of Sir James McGrigor's official life were marked no less by a devotion to the purposes of benevolence and science. In both these works he resumed and gave a wider indulgence to the kindly disposition of heart, and the desire to forward the scientific improvement of the medical officers of the army, which he had shown as early as 1810, when on duty at Portsmouth as inspector of the South West District.

He took early measures for the formation at Fort Pitt, Chatham, of the Museum of Anatomy and Natural History, bearing upon Military Surgery. To his unremitting exertions and liberality, that Museum is chiefly indebted for its prosperous condition. So assiduously and successfully did he use his influence with the medical officers of the army that they lost no opportunity of collecting and forwarding specimens to enrich it; the reception of which donations was always punctually acknowledged by Sir James.

This museum contains 6,000 specimens of important preparations; and, upon the retirement of Sir James McGrigor, the collection comprised 5,888 specimens in natural, morbid and comparative anatomy, and comparative physiology; 19,262 specimens of the three different classes of the animal kingdom; 8,561 specimens of the vegetable kingdom; 6,891 specimens in mineralogy and geology; and 988 works of art.

The collection of human crania exceeded 500 specimens and, in this respect, it has been asserted be several eminent individuals, who have visited every museum of importance in Europe, to be unrivalled.

About the year 1822, Sir James McGrigor attached a library to the museum he had founded to which he made repeated gifts of books, and on one occasion bestowed upon it about 1,500 volumes. Many members of the medical department of the army became also liberal contributors to the library. Among these may be mentioned Mr Bruce, Surgeon to the Military College; Dr Fergusson, Inspector of Hospitals; and Mr Wordsworth. The first, who was both an able surgeon and an accomplished scholar, bequeathed all his books to the library at Chatham; and the second, 275 volumes of medical works; while Mr Wordsworth specified in his will that the ecclesiastical and poetical works of his two relatives – the Rev. Christopher Wordsworth and the poet laureate – should be presented to this library 'in grateful remembrance of his obligations to that establishment'.

This valuable adjunct to the Museum founded by Sir James McGrigor has not been wanting in other aid. According to the catalogue of March 1852, it contained nearly 10,000 volumes, and since that period it has received many important augmentations. In this library of the medical officers is a portrait of Sir James painted by Sir David Wilkie. Another portrait, painted by J. Jackson, R.A., was presented by his brother officers to Lady McGrigor.

The fostering care extended by Sir James McGrigor, while Director-General, to the excellent institution he had founded in the cause of science, at so early a period of his career, was extended with no less solicitude to another foundation, in the cause of benevolence, which owed its origin to his exertions in 1816.

Deeply impressed with the frequent misery accruing upon the death of medical officers to their widows and families, for want of a provision against such a contingency, by the insurance of their lives at an early period of their entering the service, when the deductions from premiums would be less sensibly felt than at a later time of life; Sir James McGrigor used his influence among the officers of the department for the establishment of the Army

Medical Friendly Society. [An officer's widow received only £36 a year.]

The young assistant-surgeon was enjoined by Sir James McGrigor to subscribe annually to this Society, an amount which could scarcely be felt as a loss of income, while it might act as an incentive to economy. Married officers paid a larger annual amount than the unmarried, and their widows became entitled to their annuities, varying according to the rate of premium paid by their husbands during their lifetime.

Under good management, a large capital or principal was thus accumulated and safely invested under the Act of Parliament for the Friendly Societies of Great Britain; and such development had this institution acquired when its founder retired from office, that it was distributing incomes among 120 widows, and was possessed of a capital verging upon 80,000*l.*

Instances of distress, against which no rule of prudence can guard, were nevertheless numerous among the poorer families of deceased medical officers. To meet these, Sir James McGrigor then founded a second institution, called the Army Medical Benevolent Society. The object of this institution was the relief of the more necessitous families of medical officers, especially of orphans. Supported by donations from the more prosperous army medical officers, this humanely devised institution fully effected the objects of its founder. Sums of money were annually distributed among the necessitous by a committee of gentlemen, with as much privacy and delicacy as possible. By this timely aid, the children of medical officers were enabled to complete an education commenced in the more prosperous days of their parent's lifetime.

To this society Sir James McGrigor was a liberal contributor. On his retirement from office in 1850, the invested capital of this second benevolent institution of his founding amounted to nearly 15,000*l.*, and the sum given annually to the poorer families of medical officers, chiefly to orphans, was about 500*l.*

So great were the benefits conferred by these two institutions – one an insurance and the other a charity – that, in an interesting and gratifying address presented to the family of Sir James McGrigor after his death, they were characterised as monuments of his wisdom, charity and benevolence.

Sir James also did all that he could to help to young men of his clan. Early in his own career, on 15 October, 1800, he wrote to Sir John Murray (who later as Sir John Murray MacGregor became chief of Clan Gregor) concerning Murray's project to raise a fund in India to bring out annually one of the clan to that country. Then, from a camp between Alexandria and Rosetta, on 21 December, 1801, when he is struggling to subdue the plague, he mentions Sir John's plan of 'forming a purse in order to send out yearly, some young men of the clan to India,' averring that he 'will at all times be ready to contribute towards it, but hitherto has been too unsettled to help otherwise.'

Later, writing from Beverley, on 22 October, 1805, he says, 'In future ages I hope it will by all of us, and by the whole clan, be remembered with gratitude, how much we all owe to you as the means of our emerging from an obscurity and disgrace unmerited by, and illiberally thrown on the whole name as a race.'

McGrigor is here referring to the proscription of the Clan MacGregor imposed in 1775 and only lifted finally in 1804.

During his tenure of office as Director-General, Sir James McGrigor received numerous honours. He was made a Knight-Commander of the Tower and Sword of Portugal for his services in the Peninsular campaign; and was also permitted by his Sovereign to wear the Turkish Order of the Crescent for the part he bore in the Egyptian campaign.

In addition, a Knight of Guelph, a Hanoverian Order, was accorded to him after Waterloo.

Letters held in the British Museum prove that he wrote not only to the Prime Minister, Lord Liverpool and the Duke of York, but also to the latter's brother, King George IV, requesting the honour of a baronetcy largely for the benefit of his son. Liverpool was unhelpful, claiming title went only to landowners. McGrigor nonetheless persisted, pointing out that his predecessors in the office which he held, whose responsibility had been less arduous then his own, had received this award and, eventually, perseverance won.[3]

The records of the Eagle and British Insurance Company, founded in 1807, show that 'Sir James McGrigor' was appointed to the Directorate in 1827.

In 1831, he was created a Baronet, and in August 1850, invested with the Order of a Knight-Commander of the Bath. Besides these and other marks of royal favour, upon the institution of the London University, he was appointed by Government a member of its council. He was also a Fellow of the Royal Society of London and a member of various societies of Dublin and Edinburgh, and of several societies on the continent. His attachment to Marischal College, University of Aberdeen, where in 1788, he had graduated as A.M., was a sentiment which he never ceased to cherish. He had there taken his M.D. in 1804; and three times did his Alma Mater show the high esteem in which he was there held by electing him to the Lord-Rectorship in 1826, in 1827 and in 1841. So thoroughly had he won the esteem of the students that they presented to the university a portrait of Sir James by Mr Dyce, which is now in the public hall; and to identify himself yet more with that ancient seat of learning, he further presented prizes to be competed for by the students.[4] In the year 1826, when he was first elected Lord-Rector of the university of Aberdeen, the Town Council of Edinburgh, claiming him also as one of the alumni of its University (from his having shared in its medical instruction), honoured him with the freedom of their city.

Sir James McGrigor was also one of the founders of the Medico-Chirurgical Society of Aberdeen; of which his auxiliary support was so marked for so many years, that upon his death, resolutions were passed at a public meeting of the members, expressive of their high sense of his abilities, of his valuable services in the field and during his long tenure of office; as also of his estimable private worth, and of their condolence with Lady McGrigor and his family on their sad bereavement.

Such were the honours he received from his sovereigns, his brother-officers and his countrymen.

Throughout the tenure of his office, the habits of life of Sir James McGrigor were characterised by that order and precision which bespeak the man whose mind is constantly directed to a diligent and effective discharge of his duties. Winter and summer, through a long succession of years, he rose at a very early hour and, after taking a cup of coffee, transacted much business at his own residence for which the hours of office were insufficient. Upon repairing thither at ten o'clock in the morning, he almost invariably carried with him numerous letters, all ready for transmission; and, until five o'clock in the afternoon, his daily occupation there was unremitting.

In a letter to his youngest son, Walter, dated 25 May, 1838, McGrigor advises:

> I wish from my heart, my dearest Walter, I could get you to take a manly resolution to the rule which I recommended and stick firmly to the perseverance in it: not to be out of bed after 10 o'clock at night while at Cambridge, and to be out of bed by six o'clock by your watch. . . . take a ten-minute walk till your room is made, then read till the chapel hour and take breakfast on your return. After breakfast, keep your door shut for three hours' reading, and then walk or make calls till the dinner hour, but do not make late calls after dinner and be in bed by 10 o'clock.

He had brought to the exercise of his new office, attributes of character, abilities and experience such as had not been concentrated in one and the same individual at the Army Medical Board since its first establishment; and the advantages accruing to the service from his able administration of the department had long been attested by the improved sanitary condition of the troops throughout the Home stations, those of the Mediterranean and the Colonies. In the local measures adopted for the health of the garrisons, and the constantly maintained numerical sufficiency, as well as efficiency, of the medical staff at those stations where the contingencies of sickly seasons had never before been duly and systematically provided for, Sir James McGrigor evinced a judgment and forethought, the want of which, under former administrations, had entailed at sure and certain intervals an ever-recurring increased mortality among the troops. The intimate knowledge which he had acquired of the respective qualifications of the medical officers of the service enabled him to select judiciously for heads of the medical staff in each of the colonies, those best fitted by previous service and professional ability.

To cite one instance of the many that could be adduced of the advantages which accrued to the service and the cause of humanity from the judicious preference given by Sir James McGrigor to ability over every other consideration, in his appointment of chiefs of medical staff at stations visited periodically by epidemics, Gibraltar may be named. Though the regiments of the line in garrison in that fortress are generally more free from sickness than are the regiments of the Guards in London, yet Gibraltar is subject to the visitations of a fatal epidemic. The garrison being also usually large, the spread of disease at such seasons among the troops is very extensive.

During four sickly months which occurred a few years before Sir James McGrigor's accession to office, the deaths from the epidemic among the troops alone amounted to 1,082; though in the two preceding years they had not exceeded 91; the strength of the garrison being in both cases nearly the same.

Accordingly, Sir James McGrigor, in 1828, transferred Dr Hennan from the charge of the medical department in the Mediterranean to a similar post at Gibraltar. As Sir James knew, Dr Hennan was deeply read in the works of Sir William Pym, Dr Hook, Sir James Fellowes, Mr Amiel, Dr Playfair and others who had been stationed at Gibraltar during the previous epidemics, either of 1804, 1810, 1813 or 1814. When quartered at Gibraltar, Dr Hennan transmitted much valuable information in the form of reports to the Director-General's office; and so well did he apply his knowledge, that, when the fatal epidemic commenced its ravages, he rendered most efficient aid in checking them; but in his unceasing efforts to preserve the lives of both soldiers and civilians, he neglected his own safety. Even after he had been seized by the disease, that zealous medical officer still remained at his post of duty, and until the very day preceding his own untimely death, he persevered in his efforts to preserve the lives of others; affording another of the many instances of that self-immolation to duty, which has so often distinguished the medical officers of the army and which in more recent days distinguished Surgeon Thomson, of Crimean celebrity, to whose memory Sir James McGrigor erected an obelisk of granite in his native land.[5]

McGrigor maintained his friendship with Wellington throughout his life. Not above making use of his connections when required for a good cause he, together with the celebrated surgeon George James Gathrie, succeeded in getting the backing of both Wellington and the Duke of York in the founding of the Royal Westminster Ophthalmic Hospital. Reputedly, he also instigated the acquisition by the Army Medical Service of its splendid buildings at Millbank.

In 1848, after nearly thirty-three years' zealous discharge of the arduous labours of his office, Sir James McGrigor, yielding to that yearning for rest which with advancing years steals upon the most active mind – and deeming it both more graceful and befitting his well-earned repute to retire from a laborious post before his energies became impaired – expressed his wish for retirement to the Duke of Wellington, then Commander-in-Chief. The Duke made the answer: 'No, no, McGrigor; there is plenty of work in you yet.' [This should read, 'No, no, Mac; there is plenty of work in you yet.' (Wellington's actual words.)]

Thus overruled and encouraged by the Duke, Sir James McGrigor continued to discharge his duties of Director-General, though he occasionally reiterated his wish for retirement.

In the autumn of 1850, he, however, made an urgent application for permission to retire, which received the following gratifying reply:

Horse Guards
23 Sept., 1850

My dear Sir James,

I have availed myself of the earliest opportunity in my power to lay before the Duke of Wellington your letter marked 'private' of the 16th instant, stating that you are under the necessity of soliciting permission to retire from the Office you have held for thirty-five years with such credit to yourself and such advantage to the public.

His Grace deeply regrets that the state of your health should oblige you to pursue this course.

He has had the pleasure of being well acquainted with you since the commencement of your career in the service. He is aware of and can vouch for the truth of the statements made in your letter, and indeed was present at the several stations in which your exertions were called forth, with the exception of the West Indies and Walcheren.

Upon receiving your official application for retirement, the Duke of Wellington will feel it his duty to forward it to the Secretary at War, and will have great pleasure in bearing the fullest testimony to your merits and services.

Believe me,
Very faithfully yours,
(Signed)
Fitzroy Somerset.

On 4 December, 1850, Sir James McGrigor received another letter from Lord Raglan, then Lord Fitzroy Somerset, transmitting letters from the Treasury and the War Office. The following paragraph occurs in Lord Raglan's letter:

The Duke of Wellington has directed me to draw your attention to the expression by the Lords of the Treasury of their high approbation of your long, able, and most meritorious services, and to the testimony which Mr Fox Maule is desirous of bearing to your merits; and further, I am to convey to you His Grace's congratulations on receiving so unqualified an acknowledgement from such high quarters, of your unceasing and successful application of your best energies to the discharge of your duty during a long course of years.

Besides receiving this additional testimony of the high esteem of the commander-in-chief at the close of the year 1850, the merits of Sir James McGrigor were thus noticed by the financial head of the army, in bringing forward the army estimates in the year 1851. 'In the army medical department the service has lost by the retirement, not, I am happy to say, by the death, of Sir James McGrigor, an officer to whom the public is much indebted.' These words, as reported in the journals of the day, were received in the House of Commons with cheers.

When Sir James McGrigor's retirement became known to the officers of his own department, they determined on evincing their regard for him by the presentation of a costly testimonial. On hearing of their intention, Sir James McGrigor lost no time in acquainting them that he could on no account accept any such offering after their former munificence. Thus prevented form carrying out their first intention, they next resolved to present him with a valedictory address. Although Sir James McGrigor's retirement was not complete till the spring of 1851, yet before 31 of May, of the same year, the address was signed by upwards of 500 members of the department. On that day, 31 May, a meeting of the medical officers was held at the Thatched House Tavern, St James's Street, where an able address, indicating many of the benefits which Sir James McGrigor had conferred on the department, was unanimously adopted. A deputation of officers then proceeded to the residence of Sir James McGrigor, where the address was read by Dr Skey, Inspector-General of Hospitals, in presence of a large circle of friends. The good opinion of more than 500 honourable and well-educated gentlemen, impartially expressed, after all connection between them and their chief had been dissolved, was indeed a testimony of honour very gratifying to the feelings of Sir James McGrigor, at such a moment; and as gratefully appreciated by the members of his family and personal friends.

In the army estimates for 1851 it was stated, 'In the army medical department the Service has lost by the retirement of Sir James McGrigor, an officer to whom the public is much indebted,' and the Treasury approved 'his long, able and most meritorious services.'

Sir Neil Cantlie, in recording this, adds, 'But one of the highest tributes in which he would have rejoiced was the statement that "he rendered the most effective service to his country by appointing to the army gentlemen of high professional attainments".'

Thus, in 1851, began Sir James McGrigor's retirement. Entering the army as surgeon of the Connaught Rangers in 1793, he quitted it as director-general in 1851. He had spent nearly fifty-seven years of his life in active employment. As night succeeds day, so rest must sooner or later succeed labour, and more than half a century of labour did certainly need repose. About seven years of life still remained to Sir James McGrigor, during which, though in the course of nature greatly enfeebled in bodily health, he enjoyed that piece of mind which was doubtless the result of a conscientious discharge of all his duties. The urbanity of his manners, the benevolence of his disposition and the simplicity of his heart, drew around him for the remaining years of his life a circle of friends, in whose cheering kindness and attentive solicitude, as in the devoted affection of the members of his family, he found enjoyment. Thus the current of those later years was calm and tranquil. Few men had seen pain, disease and death under more violent and hideous aspects than Sir James McGrigor; he had personally passed through many perils of shipwreck, siege and battle; yet, by the blessing of good general health combined with a sound mind, of an equanimity seldom ruffled; under the beneficent will of a Higher Power, the long current of his life ran itself gradually out, becoming even more smooth towards its close.

He died in London on 2 April, 1858, about seven days before the completion of his eighty-eighth year; without pain and almost without disease; for the gradual extinction of the powers of nature can scarcely be called disease.

The last illness . . . was only of a few days' duration and a fatal termination was not anticipated till within a day of his death.

Surrounded by his attached family, consisting of Lady McGrigor, whose watchful care was incessant, his only and much-loved daughter, Mrs Phillips, and his two sons, the venerable man gently fell asleep, whispering with emphasis and clearness, "I am happy." [6]

Thus closed the life of Sir James McGrigor; and little now remains to mention but a few of those instances of posthumous honour which proceeded from a sense of his public and private virtues. A few days after his death, committees of the two societies, which he had founded for the benefit of the army medical officers, were held in order to inscribe on their minutes expressions highly honourable to Sir James McGrigor's memory. Many tributes of respect were paid in other quarters, but they need not here be enumerated, although to his own immediate relatives they can never cease to be valuable. Exception, however, must be made in favour of a letter from the Treasury, Whitehall, in September, 1859, stating that, in the college which had recently been founded in honour of the memory of the Duke of Wellington, niches and places had been provided for the reception of the statues or busts of the principal officers, contemporary statesmen and personal friends of the late Duke of Wellington, and that the name of Sir James McGrigor had been selected for this distinction.

The only other honour of a posthumous nature which may here be adverted to is that of a subscription for a public monument, originated by Mr Wyatt, one of the surgeons of the Guards, a gentleman quite unconnected with Scotland, and therefore wholly unbiased by any national prejudices in favour of the country to which Sir James McGrigor belonged. The subscribers to the proposed monument, both among military men and civilians, were numerous. In January, 1861, application for a site was made to government which readily promised to give a place in some 'central part of London, where the statue intended to commemorate the distinguished services of Sir James McGrigor might occupy such a position as was desired by the subscribers'. In April of the same year, it was decided by the Board of Works that the statue of Sir James McGrigor should be erected on a piece of ground near to Westminster Abbey and the Houses of Parliament. This graceful acknowledgement of past services may be viewed as an useful encouragement hereafter to a zealous performance of duty. It may be viewed also as a just tribute to the memory of an officer who, during fifty-seven years of arduous service abroad and at home, gave all his thoughts and energies to his public duties; and whose highest ambition was to leave behind him a 'good' and honoured 'name'.

The life of Sir James McGrigor is one which by any standards must be called successful. Honoured in many countries for his services in times of peace and war, he seems to have been almost universally esteemed by the medical practitioners of his own and later times.

Lieutenant-Colonel M. W. Russell of the R.A.M.C. claimed that, 'He raised the Medical Service from a very slough of despond to a plane such as it had never seemed likely to attain.' Later, Sir Neil Cantlie wrote, 'Above all he was a man of principle and action – fair-minded and trustworthy. He had a clear and determined sense of duty, an inherent faculty of organisation, untiring zeal and general courtesy of manner with an aptitude of tact and conciliation, and a reputation of being one of the ablest and most energetic officers in the Service.'

Renowned as he was for his methodical and conscientious approach to all the aspects of his profession, it was nonetheless his humanity which won him both such universal regard.

'As proof of the respect in which Sir James is held by the military officers of all ranks, we may quote the following, which is but one of many such incidents with which we are acquainted. A few days hence, a professional gentleman, a friend of our own, visited a major suffering from a severe affection of the chest, to which he had been subject periodically since the lungs were severely wounded by a musket-ball at the storming of Badajoz. The officer, after relating his sufferings and remarking on the nature of the injury he had sustained, suddenly inquired, "How is Sir James McGrigor?" Being informed he was tolerably well, the major observed: "We of the old times worshiped that man!" The last words were uttered in a faltering tone, and followed by a flow of tears. When the nerve and firmness of the veteran returned, he added, "I love him, I love him!"

'They must have been no common qualities which could impress a youth of sixteen so forcibly, for the officer in question, though now grey in the service, was a boy of that age when indebted to the services of Sir James.'

NOTES

1 While alluding to this article in the 'Statistical Journal' it is worthy of remark that the writer, in adverting therein to the condition of the British troops during the Crimean War, for want of proper clothing, and of medical and other requisites, points to it as the result of a mismanagement similar to that which was evinced in the early part of the peninsular War; when Admiral Berkeley, who commanded on the Lisbon Station, wrote to Earl Temple on 10 September, 1809, saying that stores of things sent from England 'were rotting and spoiling in the Tagus'.

2 Published in 1752 and translated into several languages.

3 'Liverpool Papers' (British Museum), Add. MSS 43190; 'McGrigor Letters', Add. MSS 38301.

4 An obelisk of polished granite, seventy-two-feet high, stands in the Quadrangle of Marischal College as a memorial to Sir James McGrigor.

5 In commemoration of the self-devotion of Dr Hennan to arrest the epidemic of 1828 at Gibraltar, a monument was erected to his memory at the expense of Sir George Don, the Governor, and many of the inhabitants.

6 From obituary in the *Edinburgh Medical Journal*, Vol. III, July 1857–June 1858.

Appendix 1

The reason for this sudden counter-order is thus given in the *Life of Sir David Baird*: 'The arrival of this overland despatch changed the whole course of events, and while General Baird was anxiously expecting some alteration merely in his final instructions for the reduction of Batavia, he received the following letter from Colonel Kirkpatrick:

[Secret]

Calcutta
10 February, 1801, 3 p.m.

My dear General, Lord Wellesley desires me to inform you that your new instructions are nearly ready. I am in hopes that they will be despatched either tonight or early tomorrow. The overland packet from England has made it necessary for his Lordship to change his whole plans and you are now to assist Sir Ralph Abercromby in driving the French from Egypt, instead of seizing on Batavia.

I am, my dear General,
Yours most faithfully,

Wm. Kirkpatrick

By a sudden attack of illness, Colonel Wellesley, the future Duke of Wellington, was prevented from taking a command in this expedition, and in a letter to Sir David Baird, dated 9 April, 1801, expressed his disappointment at being obliged to relinquish his share therein. To his brother, the Hon. H. Wellesley, he had said in a previous letter in reference thereto, 'I have been a slave to it to this moment notwithstanding I was sick.

'The objects proposed by Mr Dundas, and by the Governor-General, in the expedition to the Red Sea, are:

'Firstly, to get possession of the forts and posts which the French may have on its shores.

'Secondly, to urge and encourage the natives of Upper Egypt (Mamelukes and Arabs) to commence hostilities against them.

'Thirdly, to assist the operations of the natives by giving them arms and ammunition; or by a junction with them, either of part or of the whole of the force.

'The advanced state of the season renders it probable that it will be so difficult to reach Suez that the object is not attainable. It is possible, however, that the force which left Bombay in December last, under the orders of Admiral Blanquet, may have succeeded in effecting the objects in view when it was fitted out, as far as they relate to Suez. Cosseir will then be the first object of attention, and the operations of the army ought to be directed, in the first instance, to gain possession of that place.

'It is needless to enter into a statement of the difficulties to be apprehended in crossing the desert; they are certainly great, but I imagine not insurmountable.

'But if it is not certain that the army or detachments which may cross the desert, will partake of the plenty of the banks of the Nile when they reach them; if they should be certain of having water only, and such forage as their cattle should be able to pick up; I apprehend that the difficulty will become so great that the expedition ought not to be attempted,' and further, weighing the probabilities in favour of and against the expedition, the late Duke adds, 'Upon the whole, I am decidedly of the opinion that, if the Mamelukes are not on our side, no attempt ought to be made to cross the desert.'

The actual difficulties which had to be surmounted by the expedition justified fully the conception formed of them by Colonel Wellesley.

It sailed from India in December 1800, and having to contend with the monsoon which had set in before it arrived at the entrance of the Red Sea, it was unable to reach Cosseir so soon as anticipated. That effected, the troops, with but short respite, prepared to march across the 'long desert' from Cosseir on the Red Sea to Kenna on the Nile. During this march, accompanied with dangers and fatigues of so novel a character to British troops, the 88th (Connaught Rangers) formed the van of Sir David Baird's army, and thus had the honour of being, by a day's march, the first British regiment to tread that perilous route.[1]

In fourteen days the gallant little army completed the passage of 140 miles. Its pathway was chiefly as in a defile – through ravines and between hills, varying in height from five to 1,500 feet. Not a trace of vegetation could be discovered; the eye rested everywhere upon bare and naked rocks or upon sands and gravel. The thermometer by day stood at 115 degrees of Fahrenheit in the shade, and the nights even – the time of march – were oppressively sultry. The thirst suffered by the troops was unquenchable with the brackish water of the wells dug by the Arabs, and it found relief only in a little diluted vinegar. Upon reaching Kenna, it was with indescribable transport that the troops laved their parched lips in the waters of the Nile; and forgetting then all their toils, they embarked on boats upon its bosom, reached Grand Cairo at length, and effected a junction with their countrymen under the command of Major-General (afterwards Lord) Hutchinson.

NOTES

1   From the *Historical Records of the Connaught Rangers*.

APPENDIX 2

In the *Historical Record of the 88th Regiment of Foot*, page 6, the following honourable mention is made of the veteran General Reid, here referred to by Sir James McGrigor:

'Among the measures of defence taken at this time by the government to secure the country against the invasion with which it was threatened by Buonaparte, a general order was issued from the Horse Guards on the 2nd of December, 1803, commanding that (in case of enemy's effecting a landing in any part of the United Kingdom) all officers below the rank of general officers, and not attached to any particular regiment, should report themselves in person to the general officer commanding the district in which they might happen to reside; and requesting all general officers not employed on the staff to transmit immediately their addresses to the adjutant-general. The colonel of the 88th, the veteran General Reid, was then in his eighty-second year, yet he immediately obeyed the summons and transmitted his address in a letter so spirited as to deserve a place in the memoirs of the regiment which he commanded, and upon which his gallantry reflected honour.

London
6 December, 1803
To the Adjutant-general

Sir,
In obedience to the orders of His Royal Highness the Commander-in-Chief, expressed in the London *Gazette* of Saturday last, for all general officers not employed on the staff to report to you their address, I have the honour to inform you that I am to be found at No. 7, Woodstock Street, near Oxford Street; that I am an old man, in the eighty-second year of my age, and have become very deaf and infirm, but I am still ready, if my services will be accepted, to use my feeble arm in the defence of my King and country; having had the good fortune on former occasions to have been repeatedly successful in action against our

perfidious enemies, on whom, I thank God, I never turned my back.
I have, &c.

(signed)
John Reid, General,
Colonel of the 88th Regiment

Appendix 3

Though Sir James McGrigor refers thus lightly to his literary labours, they were in reality more numerous and of greater value to science and the public service than might be deemed from this his passing allusion thereto. In 1801, he had already presented to the Bombay Medical Board a 'Memoir on the State of Health of the 88th Regiment, and of the Corps attached to it from June 1800 to May 1801'. In the year 1808, he published a letter of reply to Dr Bancroft, who had published some scrictures on the Fifth Report of the Commissioners of Military Inquiry. In 1810, he published in the sixth volume of the 'Edinburgh Medical and Surgical Journal' some valuable observations on the fever which appeared in the army on its return from Spain to England in 1809. His next publication of importance was a folio volume (in 1838) entitled, 'Statistical Reports on the Sickness, Mortality and Invaliding among the Troops in the West Indies', prepared from the records of the boards of the Army Medical Department and War Office returns. In the following year he published 'Statistical Reports on the Sickness, Mortality and Invaliding among the Troops in the United Kingdom, the Mediterranean and British America'. This also was in folio.

His next, and perhaps most interesting publication, is a paper which appeared in the sixth volume of the *Medico-Chirurgical Transactions*, being a 'Sketch of the Medical History of the British Armies in the Peninsula of Spain and Portugal during those Campaigns'. But it may be justly said that the later labours of his long Directorship of the Medical Department of the Army were of a literary character, if the labours of the pen may be so designated, for it was during his zealous administration of that arduous office that the 'Medical Army Reports', which will always hold a high place in medical literature, owed to him their creation.

APPENDIX 4

The Parliamentary investigation referred to by Sir James McGrigor formed no exception to the general character of many of our State trials. Mr Hallam observes that 'the State trials of England exhibit the most appalling accumulation of judicial iniquity, which is to be found in any age or country of the world; and far exceeding in atrocity anything recorded of legal injustice in the annals even of Eastern despotism. The reason,' as he justly adds, 'is that the monarch could not wreak his vengeance, or the contending nobles or parties destroy each other, as in other states, by open outrage or undisguised violence; and that the courts of law were the theatre, and State prosecutions the engines by which the oppression was perpetrated, and these contests of faction conducted.'

The debates in Parliament on the Walcheren expedition were much in the same spirit, although there were the strongest grounds for the indignation of the country, and therefore for the prosecution of enquiries upon the calamitous issue of the expedition. But far beyond these, it was made in Parliament an instrument of political partisanship by the Opposition. It was alleged that the whole blame of the failure of the expedition rested with ministers, and ministers alone; that from the very first, success was unattainable; that Antwerp was injudiciously selected as the point of attack; that the forces were ill-directed; and last, not least, that sanitary laws and provisions had been grossly overlooked.

As bearing on the last charge only, that on which Sir James McGrigor gave his evidence, the following extract from the Parliamentary records of the day will enable the reader to form some estimate of the inquiries addressed to him.

'Martis, 6 die Martii, 1810
The Right Honourable Sir John Anstruther, Bart. in the Chair
James McGrigor, M.D. was called in. Examined by the committee:

'Did you succeed Mr Webb as Chief of the Medical Staff of the Island of Walcheren?'

'I did.'

'At what date did you take upon you the charge of the department?'

'I arrived on 29 September, and took charge two days afterwards.'

'Did you continue in charge of the department till the evacuation of the island?'

'I did.'

'Did the sick of the army during your superintendence experience any want of medicines and particularly of bark?'

'They did not.'

'Did they experience any want of medical comforts, and particularly of wine and porter?'

'I know they did not.'

'Did the hospitals during the time you were in charge, experience any want of bedding, or were the sick well accommodated?'

'The sick did not experience want of bedding; there were in a few instances two men in a bed from want of room.'

'Was there any material want experienced of medical officers?'

'The soldiers in the island, I believe, had at all times medical attendance, though the duty was excessively severe upon the medical officers.'

'Did you call in the assistance of the medical people of the island, and with what effect?'

'I did; I called in I think four, and attached them to the two battalions of the German Legion.'

'Did you find the arrangement succeed?'

'They were very usefully employed with those battalions.'

'Do you apprehend that if the army had been landed to carry on operations against Antwerp, it would have been exposed in the neighbourhood of Antwerp to any extraordinary sickness?'

'I never was at Antwerp myself; I have understood from the French officers that the country near Antwerp was healthy.'

'Was there a sufficiency of medical assistance during the time of the sickness in Walcheren?'

'I have said that I know no instance of the soldiers wanting attendance, though the duty was so excessively severe as to occasion the illness of the officers.'

'Can you state whether there would have been any considerable difficulty in obtaining an additional number of medical assistants from England if they had been required?'

'I have understood there was great difficulty found in England in getting medical assistants.'

'Can you state to the Committee from what cause; whether from a want of giving them proper encouragement, or that they were not to be found?'

'I should think that if they had proper encouragement a sufficient number might be found.'

'Have you had any experience of the effect of a fumigation by nitrous acid, in preventing contagion?'

'I have.'

'State to the Committee what the result of that experience has been.'

'It has been favourable to the use of the fumigation.'

'Was it constantly used in the different hospitals in Walcheren over which you had the superintendence?'

'It was not in every hospital, because there were no appearances of contagion existing; I directed it to be used in several.'

'Was it not generally of the gaol distemper or typhus fever our men died on the island of Walcheren?'

'It was not generally.'

'Do you know of the stock of bark in store at Walcheren being reduced so low as three hundred pounds at any time?'

'I forwarded to the surgeon-general a representation from the purveyor on 3 October, stating that he had in store bark only for two days.'

'When was any additional supply received from England?'

'To the best of my recollection no supply came after my arrival till about the eleventh of October.'

'How was the bark obtained in the meantime for the use of the hospital?'

'By purchase in the island. I understood from an adventurer, a man who came out with bark for sale.'

'What do you mean by an adventurer?'

'A man who came out to offer bark for sale.'

'From this country?'

'I understood so, but I never saw the man.'

'It was by accidental circumstance of that kind that bark was obtained till further supplies came from England?'

'I find by my notes that fourteen hundred and sixty pounds of bark were purchased.'

'Supposing that adventurer had not had a quantity of bark for sale, the hospitals would have been without any supply?'

'I believe they would.'

'In that case, might not a supply of bark, more than sufficient to cover the interval, have been procured from the navy?'

'I cannot certainly say the quantity of bark that might have been procured from the navy; I have understood that the quantity the navy had was not large.'

'Did the treatment of the sick differ from that of your predecessor?'

'My duty was not the immediate treatment of the sick; that was left to the physicians and surgeons of the army. My duty was that of the general superintendence of the hospital and the medical department.'

'Have you formed any opinion of the nature of the disease at Walcheren?'

'I have.'

'Have you the same opinion of the disease now which you had before you went to Walcheren?'

'I have, as I had been in the country at a former period.'

'Did not General Whetham, at Portsmouth, make every distribution in his power for the accommodation of the sick?'

'I know that he did before I went out.'

'Relative to the admittance of a number of sick into a certain hospital or barrack at Portsmouth?'

'I do not know what particular hospitals.'

'Did General Whetham admit, as far as his means allowed him, a competent number of sick into a barrack at Portsmouth, which was the subject of a request made by the surgeon-general of the army?'

'General Whetham provided the fullest accommodations for all the sick that offered.'

'On what day did you take charge of the hospitals in Walcheren?'

'Two days after my arrival in the island, which was the 29th of September.'

'Do you recollect about that period a recommendation from some medical officer in that island, that a certain quantity of port wine should be allowed to the convalescents?'

'I know that my predecessor did make that recommendation.'

'Do you mean to say that Mr Webb made that recommendation?'

'After Mr Webb's illness, Mr Burrows, for a short period, acted as inspector till I took charge.'

'Did you approve of that recommendation?'

'As far as it was practicable.'

'Was it practicable?'

'It was practicable to all the convalescents who were in the hospital.'

'What was the number of convalescents at that time?'

'I can only answer that by saying that the total sick of the army, including convalescents, when I arrived was 9,800, including officers.'

'How many of the 9,800 were allowed port wine, and in what quantity were they allowed it?'

'I cannot from recollection say the exact number, though it was the greater part of that number, perhaps about 9,000 of those.'

'Was that about the number that was under hospital treatment at the time?'

'About the number I cannot say exactly, without reference to returns, which I could produce.'

'Is the Committee to understand that there were 9,000 persons who were allowed port wine?'

'Certainly not; many of those cases did not require port wine, some of them had porter, some of them required neither the one nor the other.'

'Was there port wine enough for those that required it?'

'I believe there never was at any time after my arrival any want of port wine.'

The witness was directed to withdraw.

The chairman was directed to report progress, and ask leave to sit again.

APPENDIX 5

How faithfully and generously Lord Wellington fulfilled that promise is attested by the following letter to the Earl of Liverpool, Secretary of State:[1]

Camp at Badajoz
8 April, 1812
The Earl of Liverpool

My Lord,
It gives me great pleasure to inform your Lordship that our numerous officers and soldiers are doing well.

I have had great reason to be satisfied with the attention paid to them by Mr McGrigor, the Inspector-General of Hospitals, and the medical gentlemen under his direction and I trust that the loss to the service upon this occasion, will not eventually be great.

I have the honour to be, &c.
Wellington

NOTES

1   Of this the duke appraised Sir James, in the following letter:

Elvas de Avila

25 July, 1812, 2 p.m.

Dr McGrigor

My Dear Sir,

I have received your letter of yesterday at noon, and I am very much obliged to you for the good accounts which you have given me of our wounded. I assure you that I am very sensible of the diligence and attention of the Medical Department of which I have reported my sense to the Secretary of State.

I think you will do well to send to Ciudad Rodrigo only those whose wounds are not likely ever to recover and the movement of whom will not be prejudicial to them, as we must get the men to their regiments again as soon as we can.

Ever yours most faithfully,

Wellington

APPENDIX 6

We are privileged to furnish here the following unpublished memorandum from the pen of the historian of the Peninsular War, in further notice of Colonel Colquhoun Grant. Its form is that of a record of the Colonel's services submitted to His Royal Highness the Duke of Cambridge, dated 1 September, 1857:

> The late Brigadier-General Colquhoun Grant was an intimate friend of mine, which enables me to make the following statement with a sure knowledge; but for the estimation in which he was held by the Duke of Wellington, I doubt not that a reference to Lord Seaton, Lord Downes, and Sir George Scovell, will obtain a corroboration of my assertions.
>
> Grant served as a regimental officer in the West Indies – real service against an enemy; and also on the staff of Sir George Prevost, who very highly esteemed him.
>
> In the Peninsula he was soon selected by the Duke of Wellington, as one of his exploring officers, men of whom the Duke in aftertimes said to me, 'No army in the world ever produced the like,' and he particularly dwelt upon the merits of Colquhoun Grant and Waters. I say exploring officers, because Grant was also employed to conduct a great portion of the secret intelligence; and it might be erroneously supposed he acted personally as a spy. There was a Grant who did so, and a very remarkable man he was in his line, but Colquhoun Grant, though he repeatedly penetrated the enemy's line, and even passed days in their cantonments, was always in uniform, trusting entirely to his personal resources, and with reason, for his sagacity, courage and quickness were truly remarkable, scarcely to be matched. A curious adventure, illustrating at once his qualities and his services, has been by me related at length in my history of the war. As conductor of the secret intelligence, Grant, besides his own personal exploits, displayed a surprising skill. I have seen letters from Alcaldes, and other agents of his from all parts of Spain, conveying intelligence rare and useful; and it is worth noticing, that he told me his

best, and indeed his only sure spies, were men who acted from patriotism and would not accept money. His talent in discovering them was not the least of his merits. There are indications of the man's character, but my object is to draw His Royal Highness's attention to points little known, where Colquhoun Grant's efforts in the public service were eminently advantageous.

When Marmont came down on Beiro in 1812, the Duke of Wellington's operations and designs were seriously affected, because, from the Spaniards' conduct, Ciudad Rodrigo was in great danger of being taken by a coup de main, and Almeida also, from its weakness, was in a like danger. The rapidity necessary to succour these places was very embarrassing. In this difficulty, Colquhoun Grant, as shown in my history, daringly entered the enemy's cantonments, and then perseveringly hung upon his flank watching his every movement; counting his numbers; and finally ascertaining that his scaling-ladders were left in Tamames; he assured the Duke that no coup de main was designed, and that Marmont's force was not such as to menace a serious invasion of Portugal. Thus time was given for arrangements, and a regular movement was made, which accident alone prevented being fatal to the French army.

When Napoleon returned from Elba, the Duke instantly called Grant from the Military College at Farnham to Belgium, to take charge of the Intelligence Department. Before a week had elapsed, he discovered and engaged a man and his wife, people particularly fitted for his purpose, to go to Paris as spies. From thence they transmitted constant and sure intelligence, having by some means access to the French Bureau de la Guerre. On 15 June, the man sent a note, which I have seen, noted thus by the Duke of Wellington in his own hand: 'received for Grant, June the 18th, eleven o'clock'. That is to say, just as the battle of Waterloo was commencing; and this document and its story are remarkable. Had it been received, as it ought to have been, two days before the battle, no surprise of the Allies could have happened, and the great battle would have been fought and won on the banks of the Sambre. The contents were in substance, and I think nearly in words, besides a great deal of minor information, thus: '*Les routes sont encombrées de troupes et de matériel, les officiers de toutes grades parlent haut que la grande bataille sera livrée avant trois jours.*' Why was this important notice withheld from the Duke until it was too late? Grant was too far in advance of the British outposts to be near his agents; other agents were employed by the Duke in various directions; and to ensure the regular transmission of their reports, General Dornberg was placed at Conde, I think, as an intermediate authority. That general mistook his position and fancied he was to judge of the importance and value of the reports; hence on receiving Grant's important letter he sent it back, saying that so far from convincing him that the Emperor was advancing for battle, it assured him of the contrary. Grant instantly conveyed his letter direct to the Duke, but it only reached him on the field of Waterloo, too late to be useful, but furnishing a convincing proof of Grant's great talents for never was intelligence more important, more exact or more complete, procured for a general in such grave circumstances. At Paris, after the battle, Grant's services were again very important to the army. The Allies, as happens in most armies, were very diligent in appropriating the spoils of war, without much regarding the British rights. The troops were aware of this and discontented, thinking their interests were neglected by the Duke; but secretly Grant was put upon the watch and he and his agents were everywhere taking notes of all guns and stores improperly removed from the British stock. I was with him when he in person detected guns being carried away in boats on the Seine; he thus enabled the Duke to obtain restitution, in money, I believe, and so saved the army from loss. After this European war, Grant went to India, and served as Brigadier-General in the first Burmese war in command of a moveable column upon Arracan; there he was stricken by fever, which brought him home and soon after sent him to his grave.

Signed

William Napier, Lieut.-General.

In this place it will perhaps be considered an interesting and graceful act by his countrymen to couple with the name of Colonel Colquhoun Grant that of his brother Colonel Alexander Grant, who so much distinguished himself in those Indian wars – particularly that of the Mahratta – which were the foundation of the fame of the Duke of Wellington. Passing over many of the numerous actions and assaults in which he gained the applause of his superior officers, and the confidence of his soldiers, it may be remarked that the military tact and individual exploits of Brigadier-Major Grant were specially conspicuous; and at the Battle of Assaye they have been widely admitted to have contributed in no small degree to the decision of that memorable day. It was at his suggestion that the decisive charge of cavalry was made which saved the gallant 74th Regiment from being annihilated, and his subsequent ubiquity in the field, together with his personal exertions wherever the enemy appeared to be collecting, obtained for him the admiration of all who witnessed them. In the heat of the action, and in competition with the gallant Captain Seale of the 19th Dragoons, he was the first to come up to the German officer Pholman, a favourite leader in Scindiah's army, and cut him off his horse. On his return to England he received from his sovereign the dignity of C.B., but died prematurely, his constitution, though naturally vigorous, being broken down by his numerous campaigns.

APPENDIX 7

Jovis, 8 die Martii, 1810
The Right Hon. Sir John Anstruther, Bart. in the Chair.
Sir Lucas Pepys, Bart. again called in. Examined by the Committee:

'Having stated in your former examination that you were ordered, about the 10th of September last, to go to Harwich, to investigate the disease of those who had returned from Walcheren, and that you went accordingly; and having stated what you conceive to be the nature of the disease, with which you said you were previously perfectly acquainted, explain to the Committee on what grounds it was that in your letter to the Secretary at War, on the 27th of September, you stated as a reason for desiring to be excused from proceeding to Walcheren, that you knew nothing of the investigation of camp and contagious diseases?'

'It would not be supposed, after my letters to the Secretary of War, of the 11th and 13th of September, in which I gave a detailed account of the disease, that I could be unacquainted with it, or have no knowledge of it. I conceived, therefore, that as they were in possession of that, they merely wanted the duties of an inspectorial investigation to take place; by which I understand that of attending to the distribution of the sick, that they should have proper billets, and not, as was then reported, be deposited in damp places, in churches, and ill-aired warehouses; that they should particularly have attention paid to the embarkation of the sick for England; that no dying person should be sent on board the transports; that every transport should have a medical officer on board. Those I considered to be inspectorial duties and, as such, declared myself not competent to them, not having ever been in the habit of them. But, as to the knowledge of the diseases, it is perfectly clear I must have understood them from the letters of the 11th and 13th of September, which, if not before the House, I should hope will be before the House; those will plainly show that I perfectly understood the nature of the disease.'

APPENDIX 8

'The medical treatment of patients was severely limited because of lack of accurate knowledge of the cause of the disease, and because few effective drugs were available. Much emphasis was placed on diet, cleanliness and 'the goodness of the air'. Prominent in the minutes is the treatment known as "salivations of mercury", for which special warm rooms were provided. In 1750, three patients were admitted for whom mercury was thought to be the only hope of cure. They suffered from, respectively, a bad sore throat, warts and itch and scrofula.

'Salivations was an unpleasant treatment in which mercury was administered until what we now know to be the symptoms of poisoning occurred. Absorption of the element, applied as an ointment to the skin, was more rapid when the skin was warm, hence the need for heated rooms. Increased secretion of saliva was produced, two or three pints a day being thought to be ideal. This was often accompanied by ulcers on the tongue and mouth, loss of weight, weakness and tremor. It was believed at the time that the evil humours of the disease were excreted in the saliva and so a cure was achieved. One hundred years later, the method was confined to the treatment of syphilis, in which it may have been effective.' [1]

In the following extract, McGrigor sets out his reasons for using alternatives to mercury, previously the only known cure, not only for venereal disease but for hepatitis and dysentery as well.

Till within these few years, mercury was the only remedy to which we could fly in these diseases and, when early had recourse to, the relief from it is speedy and certain. But the irreparable injury done to the constitution, by repeated courses of mercury, at length becomes in that climate [that of India] a disease of itself . . . Too often, the practitioner is more to blame than the remedy; sometimes the indiscriminate, sometimes the injudicious use of the material proves as hurtful as the original disease.

The new remedies, in particular, the nitric acid,[2] after an experience of ten years has been found to be free of these faults; they do not injure, they rather amend the general health. Like mercury, they excite the salivary secretion and, like mercury they produce a healthy action in the liver . . . in upwards of five hundred cases of hepatitis and dysentery we have used these remedies, one in general [nitric acid] with great success . . .

All the oxygenating remedies appear to possess some properties in common and to have similar effects on the patient; they were: an increased frequency of pulse, a keen appetite and increase of all the excretions, in many of the secretions of saliva, and sometimes of the biliary juices, an increased irritability and a great flow of spirits.

The nitric acid was the pleasantest and the remedy which we have had patients frequently call for.

We frequently conjoined the external use of the nitric acid with [oxy-muriate of soda], and by this union, we more speedily affected the mouth, than by any other means. We gave it in liquid form and found milk the best vehicle for it . . .

The greater number by far of our trials have been with the nitric acid, we commenced with it in May 1799, and we think it does possess some advantages over the nitrous acid . . . a nauseous medicine and often producing unpleasant symptoms as gripping diarrhoea and costiveness. The pale-coloured nitric acid . . . was distilled from a mixture of alum and niter, it seldom disagrees with the patient.[3]

Though some of our cases were by the bath alone, our general practice was to continue the external and internal use of the acid. The medicine dose was from four to six drachms by measure in the twenty-four hours. This was diluted with one or two quarts of water and sucked by the patient thro' a glass tube, so as not to act on the patient's teeth, gums or mouth. Some patients could not at first take more than two drachms of the acid daily, many took as much as ten . . . two there were who went the length of eighteen. One of these, Charles Wood, for several days persevered in taking this large quantity in the twenty-four hours, it was, of course, very largely diluted. Some may think us censurable for giving what they may think an enormous quantity of corrosive acid, but this patient was in the most wretched situation, and the very worst symptoms of this loathsome disease yielded to this large quantity and but for this, the patient most probably would not have been today as he is, in the most perfect health. The addition of opiates, mucilages or barminatives remedied the common inconveniences of the acid, but it was not very often that laudanum, gumarabic or peppermint were required to be added to the acid mixture.

In most cases, the acid bath was general and was made hot, the patient went into it from one to four times in the day, remaining each time from five to forty minutes. Our custom was, to make it so strong, as just to fret the patient's skin, in a few days it turned the soles of the feet and the hands of a yellow colour, produced eruptions like that from mercurial inunction.

After keeping the patient on a course of the external and internal use of the acid from eight to twenty days, we intermitted its use for five or seven, then went on with a second, a third or a fourth course . . . In some cases changing the remedy, and having recourse to the oxy-muriate,[4] as to mercury speedily answered and, after failing before, we have alternately succeeded various combinations of these remedies. The peculiarity of habits, or other circumstances, causing these differences, I am unable to determine but that the new remedies effect some change in the animal . . .

In several cases, the patients themselves demanded what they called the 'sour medicine'. In another particular, we likewise did mercury the same justice which we did the new remedies, we generally used the blue pill (a mercurial pill) and unguentum hydrargyri . . .

Very often the warm bath was exhibited in the beginning and the cold in the last stages, or towards a cure . . .

The state of the gums and mouth were very carefully observed, and the quantity of saliva ejected each day was regularly measured; and that the new remedies do effect the salivary secretion we no longer doubt. We have examined many cases (not less than eight or nine hundred) that we cannot possibly be deceived, the quantity of saliva ejected was often one pint, sometimes two, and sometimes three or more in the day.

However, salivation is certainly not a constant effect of the use of the new remedies, by no means so much, as from the use of mercury. [Salivation is a symptom of mercury poisoning.] We do not recollect any case where the . . . ulceration of the gums, which follow the use of mercury, was remarked. The use of the nitric bath for a few days very frequently occasions a redness and swelling of the gums, and it never fails to hasten the flow of saliva when the mercury is used; as we have often seen in desperate cases of hepatitis and dysentery.

The period under treatment is always marked on the tables. There is a column for the quantity of the medicine taken, this is, in general, very considerable and we would particularly indicate this, that to the quantity exhibited, we attribute much of our success; that the quantity prescribed was exhibited the medical gentlemen who lived in the hospital for the time always saw.

There never was any auxiliary treatment that could interfere with the new remedies, or render their effects doubtful. In Chancres the only application was a lotion of acetated lead and simple cerate, or the blue vitriol as an escrotic [sic]. To buboes phymoses and paraphymoses, leeches, astringent lotions of lead, fomentations and cataplasms [poultices] were applied as required . . .

However, we often found, after minute enquiry, that our patients had been re-infected, and whether from the predominance of particular poisons, or from their greater susceptibility to the venereal virus, every surgeon must have observed that there are some men in any ship's company, or in every regiment, that are more frequently under their hands for these complaints; some men are never out of the hospital.'

James McGrigor, having given several examples of the success and in some cases failure of his new forms of treatment, admits that, 'Some advantages are possessed by mercury, which we have not yet found in the new remedies; the practice with mercurial pills and ointment as so much more easy, and these remedies are so portable, that in many cases especially in the navy and army this will give them the preference.'

Despite these reservations, he nonetheless concludes by saying:

. . . Being so much more friendly to the constitution and general health, the advantages are incalculable from the new remedies, and perhaps greater in some diseases than the venereal. The introduction of them, we think, [is one] of the greatest improvements of modern times . . . the science of medicine [is due] the gratitude . . . of mankind.'

NOTES

1 From a short description of 'Salivations of Mercury' by Mr Alec Adam F.R.C.S. in *Aberdeen Royal Infirmary*, edited by I. Levack & H. Dudley (Bailliere Tindall, 1992).

2 ACIDUM NITRICUM. Nitric Acid. L.E.D.- Liquid Nitric Acid is a heavy, colourless fluid, emitting, when exposed to the air, dense, disagreeable fumes; its taste is intensely acid and corrosive; and when applied to the skin, it tinges it of an indelible yellow colour, destroying the cuticle, which, in a few days, peels off. Its specific gravity is 1,513 to water as 1,000. It has a great affinity for water and attracts it from the air; and when water and the acid are suddenly mixed, heat is evolved.

3 'As a medicinal agent, nitric acid is never administered unless largely diluted. It is less powerful as a general tonic than sulphuric acid and it differs from it in undergoing decomposition in its passage through the circulation; operating consequently, rather by affording oxygen to the system than as a tonic in its entire state . . . It is also admirably adapted for keeping up the tone of the system under the irritation of a mercurial course as it does not interfere with, but rather favours, the action set up by the mercury . . . it proves highly beneficial in alternative courses of mercurials on obstinate ulceration of the legs and in cases of impetigo. I have frequently administered the chloride of mercury dissolved in nitric acid without observing any inconvenience to result from the

combination . . . nitric acid can be administered only when largely diluted . . . the London College orders the acid to be kept in a diluted state . . . nitric acid, taken in a concentrated state, is a most virulent poison. The stomach pump should be used and a mixture of magnesia and water, and mucilaginous drinks administered. If the symptoms be not relieved, death generally ensues within twenty-four hours from taking the poison.' From 'Elements of Materia Medica and Therapeutics', an article by Anthony Todd Thomson, M.D. F.L.S. 1835.

4 'Muriatic or hydrochloric acid is prepared by acting on common salt (chloride of sodium) by an equal weight of sulphuric acid. In conducting the pharmaceutical operation to obtain medicinal muriatic acid, it is necessary to dilute the sulphuric acid before pouring it upon the salt . . . to prevent the violent action which takes place when it is used in a concentrated state. Water dissolves 464 times its volume of muriatic acid gas to form liquid muriatic acid . . . Muriatic acid is a powerful tonic, and as such is frequently and advantageously employed in typhus and other fevers of a similar type. I can bear ample testimony to its efficacy in malignant ulcerated sore throat, such as frequently epidemic in the metropolis . . . it is an excellent application to gangrenous ulcers.' Extract from *Aberdeen Royal Infirmary*, edited by I. Levack & H. Dudley (Bailliere Tindall, 1992), pp. 542-3.

Appendix 9

Medical Sketch of the Expedition to Egypt from India

by James McGrigor, A.M.,
Member of the Royal College of Surgeons, of London;
Surgeon to the Royal Regiment of Horse Guards; and lately
Superintending Surgeon to the Indian Army in Egypt.

1804

This is an abridged version. Some explanations of the causes and treatment of disease are given by Colonel S. Lyle Cummins (referred to by the initials S.L.C.).

Introduction

In consequence of orders, from the Court of Directors to the government in India, it became my duty to give some account of the health of the troops employed on the late expedition from India to Egypt, and to describe the prevailing diseases.

The sources of information, to which I had recourse, were the reports made to me, and an extensive correspondence with the medical gentlemen of the army; particularly those employed in the pest-establishments. Besides these to which my situation, at the head of the medical department of the army of India, gave me access, other sources of information regarding the plague were open to me as a Member of the Board of Health in Egypt . . . From materials in my possession, I could have enlarged most parts of it . . . but when I drew up the following account in India, it never occurred to me that my imperfect Memoir would be the only account of the Egyptian expedition . . .

In the execution of my duty, during a long and perilous voyage, and after the most fatiguing marches, I sometimes laboured under difficulties, but my duty was in every instance much facilitated . . . I acknowledge my obligations to all the medical gentlemen of the Indian army, by whom I was most cordially and well seconded in all that I undertook.

From the nature of the prevailing diseases, the campaign in Egypt was, in a particular degree, a service of danger. To their regret, the Indian army arrived too late in Egypt to share in any other dangers than those arising from the diseases of the country; and here the medical gentlemen had the post of honour. The zeal, attention and perseverance displayed, particularly by those employed in the plague-establishments, deserve every praise. Nothing can so powerfully incite the exertions of medical men, in such circumstances of danger, as the consciousness of co-operating with the best and most enlightened of mankind, for the alleviation of human misery. Intrepidity is more a military than a medical virtue, but seldom, I believe, has there been a greater display of it than among the medical officers in Egypt, whose duty it became to reside in the pest-houses.[1]

There are two names which I cannot pass over with general praise. At a period of universal alarm, and of real danger, when the plague was committing the greatest ravages, two gentlemen stepped forward and generously volunteered their services in the pest-houses. It so happened, too, that from their acquirements, these two were the best calculated of any in the army to succeed in this dangerous duty. Dr Buchan had acquired a perfect knowledge of the disease in the former year, and while on duty at the pest-house, at Aboukir, had got the infection there, soon after the memorable landing of Sir Ralph Abercromby. Mr Price had made the history of the plague his particular study and, from his acquaintance with the oriental languages, was peculiarly calculated to be master of everything relating to it. As will be seen hereafter, in the execution of his duty at El-Hammed, he, likewise, caught the infection. To the exertions of these two gentlemen, the service owes much; their country very much . . .

Dr Shapter, who was for some time in charge of the medical department of the Indian army, and who succeeded Mr Young as head of the medical staff of the English army, deserves our thanks for his very ready accommodation on every occasion, and compliance with every request for assistance . . .

On the causes of diseases, I have dwelt a shorter time than to some may have appeared necessary . . . All that appeared necessary for me to do was to assign the extraordinary causes – those incidental to the expedition, or peculiar to Egypt . . .

Finally, in justice to myself, I must mention that, when they were preparing for the press, I laboured under many and very considerable disadvantages. I was on duty in a remote corner of the kingdom and have been, necessarily from the same reason, at a distance from the press, since and while printing went on: circumstances which, I hope, will conciliate the indulgence of readers in general and shield me from the severity of criticism.

PART I

Journal of the Indian Expedition to Egypt

In complying with the orders of government in India, I have sincere pleasure in being able, from original documents, to present them with a correct account of the diseases and mortality which occurred in their army during the late expedition to Egypt. From the period of the first sailing of the expedition and my appointment to the medical superintendence of it, I retained both the reports of the different medical gentlemen employed in it, and my own memorandums written on the spot . . .

The Indian government has ever been peculiarly anxious about everything that related to the health of their troops . . .

During an uncommonly long voyage, in a march over extensive deserts, and in a country and climate described as the most inimical to the human race, the Indian army enjoyed a considerable degree of health, and suffered but a small mortality. The causes of this I shall attempt to develop; the investigation may be useful.

The prevention of disease is usually the province, and is mostly in the power, of the military officer; the cure lies with the medical. In the expedition to Egypt very much was done by both . . .

In no army, perhaps, was the health of every soldier in it more the care of every officer from the general downwards, than in the Indian army.

It would be doing violence to my feelings not to mention how much my duty was abridged by having such a commander-in-chief as General Baird. His military abilities are well known. His extreme attention to everything which regarded the health and comfort of the soldier, I must mention, was a principal cause of the great degree of health enjoyed by the army.

To Brigadier-General Beresford the army owes very much likewise . . . under circumstances the most discouraging [he] led the advance over the desert . . . the British army, as well as that from India, were indebted to him, as President of the Board of Health, and as Commandant of Alexandria. The excellent police established by him gave security to the army as well as to the inhabitants and, more than any other circumstance, tended to the exclusion of the plague from Alexandria.

The route which we took from India to Egypt is remarkable for having been that by which, in the earliest ages, the commerce of Asia, its spices, its gums, its perfumes and all the luxuries of the East were conveyed to Tyre, Sidon, Carthage, Rome, Marseilles and, in a word, to all the coasts of the Mediterranean, from Egypt . . .

[The army] penetrated Egypt by a route over the desert of Thebes, a route unattempted by any army for perhaps two or three thousand years . . .

On one account the situation of the Indian army in Egypt is not a little curious. It consisted of about eight thousand men, of which number about one-half were natives of India and the other half Europeans. We have often seen the changes effected on a European habit by a removal to a tropical or to a warm climate, but not, till now, the changes in the constitution of an Asiatic army brought to a cold climate; for such were the bleak shores of the Mediterranean to the feeble Indian . . .

The voyage from India to Egypt is related in Chapter 7, where Sir James describes how the vessels of the fleet of transports anchored opposite Cosseir. Here, he remembers the place in most unflattering terms.

At Cosseir there is a fort and a town, if they deserve the name. They are built of mud and the Arabs inhabit them only at the season when caravans arrive with the pilgrims for Mecca, and with corn for that and the other ports on the opposite Arabian coast.

Like every other place described by Mr Bruce [Nile explorer] that we have seen, we found Cosseir most accurately laid down by that traveller in lat. 26 degrees 7', and long. 34 degrees 4'.

Cosseir is situated on the western coast of the Red Sea. Here, vessels for the expedition were daily arriving and the troops, in general, landed in a very healthy condition.

JUNE, 1801

At the beginning of this month we were in camp near the village of Cosseir. Soon after the arrival of the troops at Cosseir, all were attacked with a diarrhoea, occasioned by the water, which contained much sulphate of magnesia. At first, it greatly debilitated the men, but, as they became used to it, the water ceased to affect the bowels. On the whole, it appeared to have produced salutary effects and the army was, for some time, uncommonly healthy.

On 19 June, the 88th, with two companies of the 80th Regiment, under the command of Colonel Beresford, as the advance of the army, commenced the march across the desert. Having the digging of wells and other duties to perform, the advance did not reach the banks of the Nile until the next month . . . The course which we took was nearly that travelled by Mr Bruce. For a considerable way after we left Cosseir, the road had the strongest resemblance to the bed of a river . . . On the march, a very hot suffocating wind from the west set in about ten and continued to three o'clock . . .

On the 29th, at Le Gita, in my tent at 3 p.m., the mercury stood at 114 degrees. In the soldiers' tents it could not have been less than 118 degrees . . . In other places on the march the degree of heat must have been greater. Le Gita is not a situation favourable to the concentration of heat; it is situated in a large open plain of many miles extent.

There was but little sickness in this month and yet almost every exciting cause existed. The heat was intense. In the currents of dust, much of it went into the stomach and lungs, and occasioned nausea, which was likewise occasioned by the destructive hot wind. To this the Arabs and even the camels always turn their backs . . . The fatigue on the march has perhaps never been exceeded by any army . . .

JULY

During almost the whole of this month, the army was encamped on the banks of the Nile, which now began to overflow its banks, near Ghenné. On the opposite bank are the magnificent ruins of Tentyra, or Dendira, and the fine temple of Isis. The situation of the army near Ghenné was very healthy. There was excellent water, and an abundant market of vegetables, of fruit and of the best provisions. We prepared to move and detachments of the army went up to Thebes, Luxor and to the cataracts, to press all the boats. About the end of the month, the army began to move to Lower Egypt. The 10th Regiment marched to Girgé, the capital of Upper Egypt, sixty miles below Ghenné.

On the 27th and following days, the rest of the army embarked in boats . . . In the open air the heat was from 70 degrees to 115 degrees. There was more sickness than in the last month . . . In the beginning a considerable number of cases of fever appeared, and not a few of ophthalmia and pneumonia, but all these soon did well after being removed to a good hospital. The Catchief, the officer next in rank to the Bey, gave up his own house for an hospital, and General Baird likewise gave up his quarters to the sick.

AUGUST

By the 12th of this month, the greater part of the army, after a navigation of the Nile, of nearly four hundred miles, arrived at Ghiza, where we found one regiment of the English army, the 89th, and a general hospital under charge of Dr Franks, the inspector. The troops at first were put into quarters there, but an encampment was afterwards formed on Rhoda, a small island made by the

Nile, very nearly in the centre between Cairo and Ghiza. The Nilometer is on this island.

As they landed, the troops were uncommonly healthy. Most of the hepatic and dysenteric sick had recovered on the passage . . . This state of health continued but a very short time after landing. In the course of the first week, most of the corps sent one-twelfth and some one-tenth of their strength to the hospital.

In three weeks, the sick of the army exceeded one thousand. A considerable number of ophthalmic cases appeared, but the prevailing disease was fever. In every corps it prevailed, and very few escaped it. In general it was of short duration – of two, three, or five days at most – and rarely proved fatal. Ghiza appeared then to have been an unhealthy quarter and the ground of the encampment was found to be swampy . . .

The sick of the army was sent into Ibrahim Bey fort, pleasantly situated on the bank of the river on the Cairo side. It had been occupied by the enemy as an hospital and had been completely fitted up by them for the purpose. But it was neither . . . a healthy or a safe situation. A little before our arrival, the French had some cases of the plague in a ward of this hospital. On hearing this, every measure of precaution was taken and the disease did not appear; it was remarked, that those sent to the hospital, ill of ophthalmia, dysentery and hepatitis, rarely left it without an attack of the prevailing fever . . .

During the month the wind was most frequently from the north. The thermometer on the Nile, from the 1st to the 8th, was higher than we had found it in Ghenné. In the fort of Ibrahim Bey it moved from 80 degrees to 90 degrees. The sickness of the month was very considerable . . . Much of the sickness, and many of the deaths which subsequently occurred, we could trace to the situation near Cairo.

SEPTEMBER

Early in this month, the greater part of the army was encamped in the neighbourhood of Rosetta. The 86th Regiment and two companies of the 7th Bombay Regiment went into garrison at Ghiza. Separate regimental hospitals were provided for every corps in Rosetta, but the number of sick appeared to be gaining ground, particularly the cases of ophthalmia, which disease was nearly confined to the 10th and 88th Regiments. The number occurring in the artillery, 61st and 80th Regiments was inconsiderable, and the disease was rarely seen among the Sepoys. Dysentery and hepatitis prevailed very generally in every corps, but the appearance of another disease occasioned the greatest alarm throughout the army.

On the morning of the 14th, I discovered a case of the plague in the hospital of the 88th Regiment: Antonio, one of the hospital cooks, who had for thirty hours laboured under febrile symptoms, shewed me two buboes in his groins.

He had no venereal appearance and the fever was now attended with extreme irritability of the stomach. At the same time, I was shewn another hospital servant, a Hallancore, who lay next to Antonio. The Hallancore had been attacked in the night-time and, when I saw him, had much fever and pain in the axilla, though I could discover no swelling of the glands.

As speedily as possible these two men, and six other hospital servants who slept in the same apartment, were removed to a house at the extremity of the town. A room was immediately allotted, in the hospital of the 88th Regiment, for cases under observation.

To this every soldier, or follower, with febrile symptoms was sent the instant that the symptoms were discovered. A minute examination was made on the evening of the 14th of all of the men in the hospital, amounting then to 162, in order to discover whether any laboured under suspicious symptoms, but nothing was observed.

On the morning of the 15th, I discovered six men with fever, most of them had been attacked in the night-time; they were sent without delay into the observation room and most strictly guarded. By frequent observation, in the course of the day, I discovered buboes in one and pain in the axillary and femoral glands of all the others: all were therefore sent to the pest-house, which was now established.

Early on the morning of the 16th, the cook and Hallancore, first attacked, died. It was found necessary in the course of the day to send nine more men into the observation room, where the nitrous fumigation was very liberally used. After an emetic, I gave mercury very liberally to the whole nine, but the symptoms, on the morning of the 18th, were so unequivocal, that I sent them all to the pest-house.

It was the age of heroic treatments, and mercury, following the germs into the lymphatic glands, may have had some effect in lessening their activity. At any rate, McGrigor appears to have had some success with it. (S.L.C.)

Our situation now became very alarming. There were the clearest proofs of the hospital which the 88th Regiment occupied being thoroughly infected, consisting of about fourteen or fifteen rooms, but all the cases had hitherto come only from three of the rooms. Lamps for the nitrous fumigation were kept constantly burning both in them and in the observation room. A very large building was procured near Rosetta and, with all possible haste, the men were moved to it.

No man left the old hospital till all his clothes were washed, his hair was cut short and himself bathed. On coming to the outside walls of the new hospital, every man stripped himself naked and went into a warm bath before his reception into the hospital. He was then provided with new clothing and bedding; the clothing brought with him was received by a non-commissioned officer, who saw it repeatedly washed and baked, after which it was received into the hospital store-room. On the evening of the 18th, I sent four more men into the observation room and on the 21st three of them were sent into the pest-house. The other did well in the observation room.

On the 23rd, Littlejohn, a boy, was sent in the morning to the observation room, having been attacked the night before with rigors. On the 25th, Egan, another suspicious case, was also sent there. In both of them a severe ptyalism was excited in less than forty-eight hours by mercury and nitric acid, and they afterwards did well.

On the 28th, Craig, with febrile symptoms, was sent from the new hospital to the observation room of the old. His gums were speedily affected; but it was found necessary to send him to the pest-house. This was the only instance of the plague which appeared in the 88th Regiment after their removal to the new hospital.

The six native followers, first sent off, had no symptoms of the disease for eight days after their arrival at the pest-house; but on the ninth and tenth days after, all of them were attacked, and none survived the attack three days. Four more of the Indian servants, sent to the pest-house to attend the others, shared the same fate. The case of the Mukadum [sic] of the dooliebearers was the most rapid.

On the 17th, he was attacked about nine o'clock in the morning with rigors, and died before four o'clock. No instances of the plague appeared in any other corps of the army during this month. Though they attempted to conceal it, we discovered that some 'accidents' (as they call it) had occurred about the beginning of September among the people of the town . . .

After the plague, the most formidable disease in the army . . . was ophthalmia . . . The total number [of cases] in the army exceeded six hundred. Dysentery and hepatitis prevailed very generally among all the European corps, and the mortality of the month was very considerable.

OCTOBER

. . . As the men recovered, they were sent to a convalescent camp . . . and precautions were taken to prevent the men from intermingling with the inhabitants of Rosetta.

Thatched regimental hospitals were built in the camp and, though in the middle of a desert, the sick soldier had a warm, comfortable and well-ventilated apartment, and was liberally provided with everything conducive to his recovery.

During the month, a case of the plague appeared in the 61st Regiment. He had been a patient in the regimental hospital in Rosetta and caught the disease from straggling through the town. The only other case which occurred was a follower of the commissariat department.

NOVEMBER

At the commencement of this month, the army was encamped at El Hammed . . . On the 8th, we were again alarmed at the appearance of a case of the plague, in the department of the commissary of cattle, which was immediately put under quarantine. On the 12th, symptoms of the disease appeared in a Sepoy of the Bengal battalion, who was in the hospital of that corps. On the 13th, five more cases were discovered in the same hospital, which was ordered to be burnt, the sick having been removed into a large house near Rosetta, where the same precautions were used as with the 88th Regiment, when the disease first broke out. After their removal, no case appeared in that battalion. On the 12th, a case of small-pox was discovered in the hospital of the 10th Regiment and, in the course of two days more, four cases appeared in the same hospital. The first, a Portuguese servant, died. At the end of the month, the number of sick was reduced. In the weekly return from the 20th to the 26th, there were 632 Europeans and 380 Sepoys, making a total of 1,012.

None of the tents kept the rain well out, which was often heavy. The sand, however, quickly absorbed it in most places. The fever was, in several instances, similar to a type which we had been little used to, viz., the typhoid.

DECEMBER

Early in this month, part of the army marched to Alexandria and, by the end of it, all the army, with the exception of the Horse-Artillery, the 7th Bombay Regiment and the department of the commissary of cattle was collected there . . . The plague now gained on us.

On the 1st of the month, Corporal Francis of the 88th Regiment, who had been on the pest-house guard the day before, complained of slight febrile symptoms and giddiness. He had a vibex on the seat of the inguinal glands on one side, with some pain, but no swelling there. I shewed him to Mr Price, who was in charge of the pest-house, and he had no doubt of its being a case of the plague. Very soon after his admission into the pest-house, a bubo appeared in his groin and his fever increased. Mercury was thrown in rapidly, his mouth became affected and, the bubo suppurating, he recovered.

———

McGrigor goes on to describe other cases which were treated in the same way.

———

JANUARY, 1802

With the exceptions already mentioned, all the army, during this month, was in Alexandria, where they attained a degree of health they never had at Rosetta. No case of the plague had ever been known at Alexandria when the Indian army arrived there, and the strictest precautions were taken to cut off the communication with Rosetta and the 7th Regiment.

In the beginning of the month the weather was extremely boisterous . . . the thermometer was once below 60 degrees, and never above 70 degrees . . . On the 1st [January], Mr Price, who was in charge of the pest-house near Rosetta, was himself attacked with the disease, which with him proved very violent.

On the following day, three of six Arabs, who acted as in-servants to the pest-house near Rosetta, were also attacked.

On the 6th, a Sepoy of the 1st Bombay Regiment died suddenly in the hospital of the corps at Alexandria; the sick of this corps having arrived from Rosetta but a few days before.

On the 7th, two cases of the plague, from the same regiment, were detected in the camp at Alexandria.

On the 8th, the 1st and 7th Bombay Regiment marched to, and encamped at, Aboukir-bay, where a pest-establishment was placed for them.

On the 2nd, symptoms of the plague were discovered on Dr Whyte, who the day before had inoculated himself, and he died on the 9th . . . There occurred this month 72 cases of the plague in the Indian army, viz:

Officers: Dr Whyte and Mr Price
2 cases in the 10th Regiment
1 case .. .. 61st Regiment
22 .. .. 1st Bombay Regiment
30 .. .. 7th ditto
4 .. ... department of the commissary of cattle
1 .. .. Pioneer corps
10 .. .. Arab servants
Total: 72

FEBRUARY

This was a very cold and wet month, yet the number of sick continued to decrease, except in the 1st and 7th Regiments, in which corps the plague continued to rage . . . Till this day no native of India, who had entered the pest-house, ever returned. But so much was the dread of the distemper now lessened, that a volunteer in-steward, for the pest-house at Aboukir, came forward from the 7th Regiment.

On the 24th, the commissary's clerk at Rosetta got the disease. Of five Europeans, whom we had left at Rosetta, two caught it and died. The disease here raged with the utmost violence.

On the 28th, Signor Positti, an Italian, came from Rosetta and lodged at the house of Mr Fantouchi, the Swedish consul in Alexandria. It was discovered two days after that he had the plague, and he, with the surgeon attending him, was immediately sent to the Lazaretto. Signor Positti died on the day of his admission. Almost all the cases of plague, which subsequently appeared in Alexandria, could be traced to this case as a source . . .

On the whole, in the course of this month, there was a decrease in sickness.

MARCH

The spreading of the diseases rendered it necessary to multiply our pest-establishments. In addition to those of Alexandria, Rosetta and Aboukir, one was formed at Ghiza, and one at Rahamania, situated on an island at that part of the Nile where the canal of Alexandria formerly took its rise. Between Aboukir and Rosetta, a sergeant and twelve men of the 26th Dragoons, were stationed to prevent communication between Alexandria and Rosetta. Nine of these were attacked with the disease during this month. Within the walls of the pest side, or that part of the Lazaretto appropriated for the reception of cases of the plague, at Alexandria, a sergeant and twelve men were also posted as a guard to preserve order. Eleven of them caught the disease in the present, and the rest in the following, month. They were volunteers from the 10th, 61st and 88th Regiments . . . The source of this disease appeared to be . . . Signor Positti. Four of the Arab servants who attended him were seized, and the Board of Health obtained an order that no more soldiers should be sent on so dangerous a duty.

On the 2nd, a deserter from the Queen's German regiment, taken up in Alexandria, was sent to the provost's guard. He had only come to Alexandria a few minutes before he was discovered. He complained of being ill and, on being visited by Mr Blackwell, inspecting surgeon of plague-cases to the Board of Health, it was found that his disease was the plague. He was immediately conveyed to the Lazaretto and all the prisoners at the provost's guard were brought to the observation ground, and the provost with his guard were sent to the quarantine-ground. The deserter died a few minutes after his arrival in the pest-house. His case was one of the most inveterate.

On the 14th, Broughman O'Neal, one of the prisoners sent from the provost's guard, having symptoms of the plague, was sent by Mr Cloran, who was in charge of the observation-side, in to Mr Price, who was in charge of the pest-side, of the Lazaretto. On the 17th a case of the plague was detected in the hospital of the regiment De Roll. The infection could not be traced; however, the surgeon and the sick in the hospital were put under quarantine.

On the 19th, a case was detected in the hospital of Dillon's regiment and the hospital of that corps was also put under quarantine.

On the 16th, one of nine Lascars, attached to Major Falconer, deputy quartermaster general, was attacked with the plague at Rahamania. The major had only arrived there from Rosetta a few days before. Subsequently, the remaining eight Lascars, and two of the major's servants, caught the contagion, and every one of them died. On the 26th, a private of De Roll's regiment was sent from the observation to the pest side of the Lazaretto; and, on the same day, a sailor, belonging to the agent of transports near Aboukir, was sent into the pest-house, as was also a man of the Royal Artillery from Aboukir castle.

Of fever there occurred but a very few cases during the month, and the disease was a very mild one.

Of five cases of small-pox, two died, both of which were natives of India. Of hepatitis and dysentery there appear fewer cases, and of the total number more than one half were from the 61st Regiment, and all the severest cases were of that corps. Of ulcers the number still continued to be considerable and increasing.

APRIL

At the commencement of this month affairs wore a very unfavourable aspect. The plague, which first appeared in Rosetta and had hitherto, with little exception, been confined to that place, at the present period had travelled as far as Aboukir on the one side, and as far as Rahamania on the other side, of Alexandria; and we had information that most of the intermediate stages, betwixt us and these two places, were infected. With so much severity did the disease rage at Rosetta that, at the end of last month, it was found necessary to withdraw the commandant and every person from it, and the inhabitants shut themselves up. From information received by the Board of Health, they likewise found it necessary to place all those coming from Cairo and Ghiza under quarantine.

It was well known that in Upper Egypt, the plague was making dreadful ravages among the Mamelukes. The few cases which occurred in Alexandria made everyone alert there and a very strict police was kept up in the town by the commandant and by the Scorbatchie . . .

Both Mr Price and Mr Rice, who dissected the body of Signor Positti in the Lazaretto, had been ill ever since, and this day they were so ill that Dr Buchan was sent in to relieve Mr Price, and Mr Moss to relieve Mr Rice.

On the 3rd, a case of the plague appeared at Ghiza on a private follower, and another case was detected in the hospital of the 26th Dragoons at Alexandria.

On the evening of the 14th, Mr O'Farrel, who had charge of the pest-house at Aboukir, was attacked with the disease. This day all the hospitals were moved out of town and encamped under the walls of Alexandria.

On the 6th, a Jewess dropped down dead in the streets of the city and it was discovered that she had been ill for four days of the plague. Her husband, who concealed it from the Board of Health, was bastinadoed and afterwards was sent, with his whole family, into quarantine. On the same evening an Arab's family reported that one of them was ill of the plague. The person affected was sent to the pest-house and the rest of the family to the observation ground of the Lazaretto.

On the 7th, Mr Dyson, who on the 4th went to Aboukir to relieve Mr O'Farrel, discovered a bubo and symptoms of the plague in himself.

On the 10th, a sergeant of the 61st, who had had the disease last month, and who, after recovering, officiated as in-steward of the pest-house in Alexandria, was again attacked with the plague.

On the 11th, Mr Angle died, being the fourteenth day of his disease. He, three weeks before, went to assist Dr Buchan in the Lazaretto.

On the 14th, symptoms of the disease were first discovered on Mr Moss in the Lazaretto. Of the Jewish family sent to the observation ground on the 6th, which amounted to seven persons, two were sent today to the pest-house.

On the 15th, the husband of the Jewess died in an observation tent, having glandular swellings, which were not discovered till after his death. He did not appear to be ill. Mr Cloran was accustomed, once a day or oftener, to examine those under observation, but nothing was discovered to ail this man.

On the 16th, he discovered some symptoms of the disease in another of the same family, and sent him in to Dr Buchan.

On the 17th, a deserter from the 61st Regiment, sent to the regimental guard-house, where he was discovered to have the plague, was sent to the Lazaretto, and the guard – amounting to nineteen persons – into the observation ground of the Lazaretto. This man confessed that he had slept one night near the pest-house at Aboukir. On the 19th Mr Moss died. On the 24th the plague was discovered in another Jewish family. The plague of the Indian army, during the month, was as follows:

assistant-surgeons – 4
61st Regiment – 4
80th ditto – 1
7th Bombay ditto – 5
departments – 12
Total: 26

On the whole, it was a pleasing circumstance to see so little of the disease among the native corps as, when it did occur, it proved so much more fatal to them.

MAY
At the commencement of this month the principal part of the army was still

encamped at Alexandria. On the last day of April, orders arrived from England to General Baird, to return with his army to India, and to detach the 10th, 61st and 88th Regiments, which were placed on the British establishment.

On the 3rd, the Indian army began the march to Ghiza, where it remained encamped by the pyramids for some days, until water and the passage over the desert were reported to be ready. At length, the march commenced with the sick.

We crossed the river, encamped at Boulac [sic], set off from Cairo and, passing the ruins of Heliopolis, made B El Hadje our first stage. Our marches over the desert of Suez, as in crossing the great desert, were all performed during the night, and we always encamped by sunrise in the morning. Luckily, much rain had fallen before we marched and at one place in the middle of the desert, and again at Suez, we found large collections of rainwater, from which all were well supplied.

By the end of the month, the whole corps, except the 7th Bombay Regiment, had crossed the desert and arrived at Suez. Part of the army was encamped near the town of Suez and part at the Wells of Moses, nine miles on the eastern side of the Red Sea. The march over the desert of Suez was performed with much greater ease than that over the desert at Thebes . . . At the time of our arrival we found Suez very healthy. Though the plague had travelled as far as Cairo and all the neighbouring villages, it had not reached Suez till the arrival of the army . . .

JUNE
On the 2nd the embarkation commenced and by the 15th the whole army was embarked, and had sailed for the different presidencies, except the 7th Regiment, which, on account of the plague still prevailing in it after the rest of the army had embarked, was ordered to remain two months. Most of the corps in the army embarked in the most healthy state. There was hardly a sick man, except a few cases of the venereal disease which had resisted mercury. To conclude, never, perhaps, was there an army embarked for any service more healthy than the Indian army was when it re-embarked on its return from Egypt.

PART II

Of the Causes of the Diseases which Prevailed in the Indian Army

Perhaps it may be thought that I have descended to a great degree of minuteness. However, I conceive that, from the facts stated, important and useful deductions may be made. I think it is a matter of regret that such journals are not more frequently kept. With a little industry on the part of the profession, they might always be so. Had such records been always faithfully kept, many practical points would not, as they now are, be involved in doubt and uncertainty.

The health of each regiment on board ship and on arriving in Egypt is given in detail. The doctor's awareness of swampy ground being conducive of disease is evident throughout his narrative.

The pioneer-corps were uncommonly healthy till they came to El Hammed. Here they had much severe duty. They were employed in building the hospitals and very often in cutting reeds by the riverside or in conveying them through marshes. A very considerable share of the intermittents that prevailed in the army was from this corps . . .

I am decidedly of the opinion that, in the peculiar soil and climate of Egypt, we are to look for the principal causes of the diseases which prevailed the most in that country. On grounds that appear not slight, we suspected that several of these diseases were propagated by contagion. But I have no intention of entering on the discussion of the theories of contagion; an obscure subject, and on which I do not presume to think that I could throw any new light. If ever the veil which covers it be removed, the late discoveries in chemistry bid fair to do it. The accurate knowledge which we have acquired of the composition of bodies, and in particular of the constituent parts of the atmosphere, have opened new fields of enquiry to the philosopher and the physician. The successful application of these discoveries to the practice of physic by the Drs Beddoes and Thornton, and by Dr Rollo, Mr Cruikshank, Dr Wittman and other eminent surgeons of the artillery, and more particularly by the philanthropic Mr Scott, of India, deserve the gratitude of the profession and of mankind at large. Hereafter, most probably, and when introduced into general practice, they will be looked upon as the greatest improvements that the healing art has received in modern days . . .

The cultivated parts of Egypt, particularly the Delta, is a very rich country . . . after the subsiding of the Nile . . . there is a great exhalation from the mud and from the putrid animal and vegetable matters left behind. The effluvia of these substances . . . will readily account for much disease. If we add to these the extreme filth of the inhabitants of Egypt, their poor diet, their narrow, close and ill-ventilated apartments . . . we will not be astonished if a fever, at first intermittent [malaria] or remittent [typhoid or typhus] should have symptoms denominated malignant, superadded to the more ordinary symptoms of the disease. If an imported contagion should make its appearance at the same time, and under the above circumstances, we expect a most terrible disease.

The dry parching wind, which comes over the desert . . . was often severely felt by the army on their march . . .

The dews, which fall in Egypt, I always heard were very heavy, and were a cause of the diseases of the country . . . After weighing the matter carefully, I took a quantity of lint, twelve inches square, exposed it for a night to the dew, and, by weighing it in the morning again, ascertained the quantity it had gained . . . I learned from it that in the island off Bombay, on the Red Sea, and in Lower Egypt, the quantity of dew which falls is nearly equal.

It ought to be mentioned, that, during the year we were in Egypt, the season was not the usual one. There was a greater overflow of the Nile . . . The season of the plague set in much earlier than usual.[2]

Ghiza, the ancient Memphis, at the time the army disembarked there from Upper Egypt, we found to be a very unhealthy quarter. For a considerable time, and immediately before the arrival of the Indian army, it had been the station of large armies – alternately of Turks, Mamelukes, French and English. From all these armies a number died at Ghiza, and there was much filth and noxious effluvia . . . Whether this was or was not the cause of the fever which prevailed, I will not attempt to decide . . . The same objections are to be made at Rhoda that are applicable to any marshy situation . . .

Rosetta is not a healthy quarter. It is one of the largest and worst built towns in Egypt . . . It is, on two sides, surrounded by swamps. The river is in the front, and behind, it is nearly encompassed with burying grounds.

The place of the encampment at El Hammed was an unhealthy spot . . . but there was no choice: it was necessary to camp where there was water.

As a station for the army, Alexandria had every recommendation. It is built on a peninsula which formed the ancient harbour, on a fine dry and open situation . . . Its numerous mosques afforded us large and airy hospitals and barracks . . .

In the difference of Upper Egypt in June, and El Hammed and Rosetta in December . . . there was a change of climate and heat from 108 degrees to 49 degrees of the thermometer. We have said that, in many instances, the causes of disease at El Hammed could be traced to the march across the desert and the encampment at Rhoda. Very much, however, was likewise to be attributed to the change of weather experienced in November and December . . . I have repeatedly observed the sick-list of European corps more than doubled by the third week after the setting in of the monsoon . . .

One reason may, with probability, be brought forward to account for the very great difference, in point of health, between European and Indian corps, viz., the great intemperance of the European in eating and drinking. A native of India is astonished, at first, to see the meals of animal food devoured, and the quantity of spirits drunk, by Europeans. There can be little doubt, that the nearer we approach to the mode of living of the natives, the more nearly we shall attain their state of health . . .

The eight or ten days that followed the payment of the men, on the twenty fourth of every month, regularly produced much sickness.

The soldiers pay . . . allows him at times to indulge in excess. He is most amply supplied with meat and bread, and generally has a portion of vegetables; but the allowance of spirits issued to him is too great. In the dry season it is a quarter of a pint daily, and in the rainy months it is double this quantity. As the price of arrack is low, the soldier very often procures as much as he can use; besides which, he often has access to farrey, or toddy, the fermented juice of the coconut tree . . . Intemperance had hitherto always appeared as a principal cause of the diseases which have prevailed . . .

We received still farther confirmation of the very great influence which intemperance has as a cause of disease. We had demonstration how very little spirits are required, in a hot climate, to enable the soldier to bear fatigue, and how necessary a regular diet is.

At Ghenné, and on the voyage down the Nile (on account of the difficulty of at first conveying it across the desert), the men had no spirits delivered out to them . . . From two gums, or boats, the soldiers one day strayed into a village, where the Arabs gave them as much of the spirit which they distil from the juice of the date-tree, as induced a kind of furious intoxication. It was remarked, that, for three months after, a considerable number of these men were in the hospitals . . .

One of our medical gentlemen persevered in an opinion that the plague was not contagious. He made the first, and we sincerely hope the last, experiment of the kind to determine this question. Dr Whyte fell a victim to his own temerity.

Never were the effects of fear, in the treatment of diseases, more felt than at one period in the Indian army in Egypt . . . They exclaimed that they were sent to the pest-houses merely to die; and some of them refused every kind of medicine or sustenance.

I shall now advert to some of the principal measures of prevention of disease in general . . . Within the last thirty or forty years, the improvements made in the means of preserving the health of seamen have been great . . . but much remains to be done for the soldier, especially when embarked for service . . .

The clothing of the Indian army conduced much, in our opinion, to their healthiness. They landed with their white cotton dresses, which were admirably adapted to the warm season in which we came to Egypt; favourable to cleanliness; and, by consequence, to the exclusion of pestilential contagion.

From the time of the army first landing at Cosseir . . . bathing was enjoined throughout the army. In every corps it was regularly done under the inspection of a commissioned officer, and any neglect of cleanliness was most severely punished. In any country or climate, attention to cleanliness will be found a principal means of preserving the health of the troops, but, in Egypt, where contagion was lurking in every corner, it became indispensably necessary.

In the cold season, and while we were in Lower Egypt, warm comfortable clothing and bedding were provided, not only for the soldier or Sepoy, but likewise for the women and children, and all the numerous followers of the army.

The simple diet of the Hindu is well suited to a warm climate. It is seldom more than rice with aromatics, or clarified butter with a kind of pea, to which the luxury of a little salt-fish, of preserved tamarinds, or some fresh fruit, is occasionally added. As far as it could be done, the Europeans were made to conform to this diet; and we are convinced that it was with much advantage to them . . .

In the cold season it was found necessary to make some changes in the diet of the Sepoys. In the month of January they suffered so much from the severity of the weather . . . that a portion of animal food, as well as of wine, was ordered to be issued to them,

The prejudices of country, religion, and of the different castes of Gentoos, were first overcome in the Bombay regiments. At length, the most austere yielded and, finally, even the severe Brahmin, as well as the rigid Muslim, gave way to the necessity inspired by their situation in a foreign country . . .

McGrigor concludes this section of his narrative by appealing on behalf of the many chronic cases of illness among the soldiers for whom he felt deep concern.

One point remains still, and I know no finer place to introduce it than here. It has been mentioned, that liver complaints rarely recovered in Egypt, and, likewise, that cases of hepatitis and flux, which, in India, had long remained obstinate, here yielded themselves without medicine. This fact leads me to the suggestion of a measure, which, I conceive, would save many useful lives. It is:

whenever a case of fever, dysentery, or liver complaint, in India, is obstinate . . . to send such cases to sea or to Europe . . . In India, when patients, whose situation in life permits them to take a voyage to Europe, are in this state, they never fail to take it, and, most commonly are recovered by it, but there is no hope for the poor soldier or sailor there.

The same benefit might, however, be acquired for the soldier . . . Were the cruisers of the Company or the king's ships from time to time to take on board some of these chronic cases, for one cruise, the men would frequently be recovered by it . . . The prospect of this, by removing that despondency which, in chronic diseases is a never-failing attendant, and which we have too often found baffle every mode of treatment, would cheer the patient and of itself do infinite good.

Humanity, as well as policy, loudly calls for something to be done.

Part III

Of the Diseases of the Indian Army in Egypt; of the Plague

I begin with the plague; a disease of which accounts have been handed down to us from the earliest ages of history or of physic. The consideration of it is important, not only on account of its frequent and fatal occurrence, but as being, perhaps, the most formidable disease that the art of physic has to encounter . . .

The plague made its first appearance, in the army in India, in the middle of September, 1801. From its early appearance the natives were very much alarmed and prophesied a dreadful season of plague. They have observed that, when it breaks out before December, they always have a generally prevailing and a very destructive disease . . .

Though the contagion is seldom or never, I believe, out of the country, the natives of Egypt denominate the season of plague from November or December of one year, to June of the year following; they observe, that the disease constantly stops at the period of the summer solstice . . .

In the pest-houses of the army, thirteen medical gentlemen did duty, who in the Indian army might be said to have had the post of honour. They were: Mr Thomas, Mr Price, Mr Rice, Dr Whyte, Mr Grysdale, Mr Adrian, Mr O'Farrel, Mr White, Mr Dyson, Mr Angle, Mr Moss, Dr Buchan and Dr Henderson.[3] Besides these, Mr Cloran was in charge of the cases under observation, and Mr Bell of cases under quarantine. Mr Blackwell, surgeon on the staff of the English army, acted as inspecting surgeon to the Board of Health. He visited every case in the first instance and, as he judged it necessary, sent them to the quarantine, to the observation ground, or to the pest-house; to Mr Blackwell's unceasing attention and discriminating knowledge of the pestilential symptoms, we owed no small share of our safety in Alexandria.

Besides the above gentlemen, we had two Greeks, the barber-doctors usually employed in Egypt, who visited the inhabitants and before internment narrowly examined every body. These two made a daily report to the Board of Health of the number of deaths and of their inspection of the bodies; they likewise did other duties under Mr Blackwell.

In order to take from our medical gentlemen, in the pest-houses, some of the most dangerous part of the duty, it was my wish to procure some of the Greek doctors of the country to reside in the pest-houses, to feel the pulses there, draw blood, open and dress buboes, &c. The most diligent search was made for these people, and very high pay was promised to them, but we could tempt none of them to live in our pest-houses – a plain proof of the opinion which they entertain of the contagious nature of the disease.

The thirteen gentlemen first mentioned were those only that were directly in the way of contagion, for it became their duty to come into contact with the infected, and seven of them caught the infection and four died . . .

Dr Whyte entered the pest-house at El Hammed on the evening of the 2nd of January, 1802. In a letter of that date he writes to me, 'I just now inoculated myself, by friction, with bubonic matter on the left thigh.' On the 3rd, he says, 'I have this morning inoculated myself by incision on the right forearm.' Mr Rice, then doing duty in the pest-house at El Hammed, gives the whole of the case. In a letter on the 3rd of January, he writes to me, 'Dr Whyte came here last night. Soon after he came in, he rubbed some matter from the bubo of a woman on the inside of his thighs. The next morning, he inoculated himself in the wrist with a lancet, with matter taken from the running bubo of a Sepoy; he appears now very well.'

In subsequent letters, Mr Rice says, 'that Dr Whyte continued in good health on the 5th and all day on the 6th, till the evening, when he was attacked with rigors and other febrile symptoms. He said himself that it was the attack of an intermittent; and it bore a great resemblance to it. After sweating profusely, he was better in the morning of the 7th, but in the afternoon the shivering returned and when it had continued 30 minutes, a severe hot stage came on, then a profuse sweating followed, but with it much affection of the head, tremor of the limbs, particularly of the upper extremities, tongue black and dry, skin hot, pulse hard and irregular, thirst great, prostration of strength and anxiety. The head was the only place that he complained of and it seemed to be the principal seat of his disease; he still persisted that the disease was not the plague; he would not allow his groin or armpits to be examined and he refused all medical assistance.' He asked for a purgative, which Mr Rice gave him, and he requested to be bled. This Mr Rice thought the state of the symptoms would not justify him in doing. On the 8th, these symptoms continued, and there was some delirium; he begged to be removed from the pest-house at El Hammed to the old pest-house at Rosetta, under the charge of Arabs. He was removed on the morning of the 9th and died in the afternoon of that day very delirious.

'Unfortunately for himself he had no conception of the necessity of the precautions now taken to see that the inoculated material is 'dead' . . . It is tragic to recall that it is by inoculation of plague germs that the disease is now successfully prevented; dead plague germs. Unfortunately, his gallant attempt was with the living.' (S.L.C.)

Dr McGrigor then describes the illnesses of five other men who served in the pest-house, three of whom eventually recovered while the other two died. Writing that 'It is useless to detail more cases,' he adds that 'I cannot, however, without some notice, pass over three cases where mercury, early and liberally exhibited, had very remarkable effects.' He expands thus:

On the breaking out of the disease in the crowded hospital of the 88th Regiment every man in the hospital was examined at different periods of the day . . . At this time, I gave to each of three of the men, placed in the observation ward of the hospital . . . two grains of camomile and the sixth of a grain of opium every hour, and made them rub into the inside of the legs, thighs, arms and neck, half an ounce of the strong mercurial ointment three times a day. I, at the same time, made them each take half an ounce of nitric acid diluted in their drink during the day, and put their feet and hands, three times during the day, into a strong nitric bath, In about twenty-four hours, their mouths became severely affected, a tenderness in their armpits and groins went off, and the severest febrile symptoms yielded. The men were, however, extremely debilitated and remained a very long time convalescent . . . I thought it prudent to keep them in quarantine, being fully convinced that they had had an attack of the plague, the progress of which had been arrested, and the disease cut short by the above treatment . . .

The duration of the disease in different persons was very different. In several instances, the effect of the pestilential contagion was the immediate extinction of life and we had several instances of the patient surviving but a few hours the first sensation of illness.

The muccadum [sic] of the dooliebearers of the 88th Regiment, about nine in the morning, exhibited the symptoms of fever. About twelve, a bubo appeared and he died before four o'clock. In some instances, again, the patient lived till the thirteenth and seventeenth day of the illness; however, these cases were rare.

Prognosis. We found that the greatest caution was requisite in giving an opinion as to the probable event of cases: in no disease was the practitioner oftener deceived. In several instances, patients who had recovered from the fever, whose buboes were doing well, and people who were convalescent, suddenly dropped down and expired. Whether this was from re-infection, or whether it was a feature of the disease, will be difficult to determine.

On the 24th of December, one of the Arab servants, convalescent from the disease . . . while smoking his pipe suddenly expired. In no disease do patients bear motion worse than in this. The least motion[4] induced indeed syncope or death.

In the treatment of this disease, a variety of modes were put in practice, but so little success attended them that some were inclined to despair of success from any. Though, with it, even many were lost, yet oxygenation and particularly the use of mercury had the most success . . .

So much dejection prevailed among the natives of India that, from the moment of the attack, they gave themselves up and said they were sent to the pest-house to die. They never could be prevailed upon to swallow a morsel of food nor any medicine, and some actually starved themselves . . .

The general practice at last was, to begin by giving a purge of camomile, and the general remark was, that, if it operated briskly, the head was relieved and the skin became soft . . . Nitric acid was given internally and, where the patients would drink it, it shewed good effects . . .

The second indication most generally agreed upon was the inducing of ptyalism and perspiration. As offering the fairest prospect of effecting both at once, Mr Price proposed using the warm nitric-acid bath, but unfortunately our stock of nitric acid was insufficient to do this, otherwise than on a small scale. Mr Price got a little of the acid at El Hammed . . . he writes: 'On three of my patients, whose gums I could not readily affect with mercury, I determined to try the nitric-acid bath. It has shewn wonderful effects – ptyalism has been produced in all three – but the cold has regularly induced rigors and severe attacks of fever, and I shall lose my patients.'

Mr Price thought well of nitric acid. In some of the Arabs he effected cures by this, and by a bath of strong vinegar. Both Mr Rice and Mr Price were in the habit of washing their patients with vinegar and sponging them with it, as strong as it could be procured, or with lime-juice. They dipped rags in the acids and kept them constantly applied to the buboes. The head and the stomach were relieved by wet cloths being kept to the scrotum.

The third indication was to obviate the debility which appeared always to be very great. With this view, bark, wine and opium were largely given and, at a certain stage, the cold bath . . . I regret that, in this disease, we did not give a full and more fair trial to cold bathing. The extraordinary circumstance of the escape of the Lascar from the Rosetta pest-house, and the great benefit which I have seen from it in the yellow-fever, to which the plague bears no slight resemblance, would induce me to give it a full trial in plague.

I have, I believe, recounted the principal part of the treatment, and that which was most generally agreed upon. Other modes received a trial, but, from an experience of their inefficacy, they were all deserted.

Dr Whyte used the lancet very freely, but every one of his patients died . . . Mr Price bled one patient. The blood appeared very dark and dissolved; this patient died and Mr Price never repeated the operation on any other . . .

Some gentlemen, attached to the Brunonian system, put the stimulating plan to the test. By Messieurs Adrian and White patients were for some time kept under the influence of wine and opium; but this practice was never successful and they deserted it. At length it was the practice of Mr Adrian to unite stimulants and mercurials.

Seldom before, I believe, have the bodies of those who died of this disease been dissected. The first was a Sepoy, by Mr Price alone; the second by Messieurs Price and Rice; and in the last subject, viz., Signor Posetti, the Italian merchant, so severely affected were both of these gentlemen that it put a stop to this mode of investigation. The general appearances seen on the subjects were a perfectly diseased state of the glandular system. In the liver, no matter was found; but it was much enlarged and greatly diseased. Signor Posetti had only one bubo; the femoral gland was sixteen times the natural size and weight; and the blood from the femoral artery flowed black, pitchy and dissolved in texture.

I now come to the last and most pleasing part of the subject:

Prevention. If, in the treatment of the disease, we were not successful, we assuredly were completely so in the prevention . . . At length, this became so generally known that . . . the natives . . . no longer entertained the dread of the pest-houses. We, at length, even found volunteers from the natives for duty in the pest-houses.

McGrigor then lists the orders of General Baird to the army, which he also mentions in his *Autobiography* (see Chapter 7). In conclusion, he states that 'Much is to be attributed to the nitrous fumigation . . . The lamps, with this, were kept constantly burning in the observation rooms and in the rooms from which the cases of the plague had come. Vessels, with the materials for the fumigation, were likewise placed under the beds and in the corners of the rooms. When our stock of nitric was at length exhausted, we substituted marine salt for it, but this fumigation could not be kept up in rooms where the patients were all confined to their beds.'

Of the Ophthalmia of Egypt

Several gentlemen thought that this disease, in Egypt, was contagious . . . I believe that several diseases are contagious, which are not suspected to arise from such a cause; the theory of contagion is but very imperfectly understood . . .

The appearance which the disease put on . . . was nearly what we have seen in other parts of the world; except that the symptoms advanced with alarming rapidity to the highest inflammatory stages. In most cases the attack was sudden and very generally at night. Speedily, the patient complained of a burning heat of the eyeball, or of a sensation of needles being passed through the eye. There was considerable swelling of the ball of the eye, of the eyelids and sometimes of the neighbouring parts. Almost always, there was a copious flow of tears, which felt hot and scalding, and, as they flowed, excoriated the face down. Very frequently there was a racking headache and general fever. Oedema of the eyelids was frequently met with in the early stages of the disease, and inversion of the cilia in the last stages . . .

The practice of the natives was to apply, in the first stage, emollient decoctions of their plants and poultices of the kali. In the last stage, they rely much on the frequently bathing of the eye in the cold water of the Nile. They are likewise very fond of bleeding; and I understand that sometimes they use the actual cautery, burning behind the ear where we usually apply blisters.

The practice, which appeared to be by far the most successful, was the following:

For the first twenty-four or thirty-six hours after admission, the eyes of every patient were carefully syringed with tepid water, which had been filtered carefully. The syringing was performed from three to six times in the day, the light was carefully excluded, the patient kept cool and every other part of the antiphlogistic regimen strictly enforced. After the above period, a weak solution of sugar of lead, or of camphor, or vitriolated zinc, was applied. Where the pain was much complained of, a solution of opium was added to the collyrium: opium was applied in a cataplasm, or two or three drops of laudanum were let fall into the eye . . .

To remove the fever and to alleviate the distressing pain, we often gave opium internally in a considerable quantity, and with great advantage.

Setons in the neck and the free use of bark appeared to be of the greatest service, when the disease was of long standing . . .

As a collyrium in Egypt, I often gave with considerable benefit what I found in the hands of the black doctors in India, viz., a teaspoonful of lime-juice, four tablespoonfuls of water, or a teaspoonful of arrack to two tablespoonfuls of water. In the first stage I would have applied leeches, but never could procure them . . . In Persia, Dr Short informs me that he was very successful in the general use of an ointment, composed of white vitriol, tutty and cinnabar, after the application of leeches and scarification.

From the days of Prosper Alpinus, the salts contained in the soil of Egypt have been supposed to be among the principal causes of the ophthalmia of the country . . .

In the ophthalmia of Egypt, as in the plague, it would appear, that very much may be done in the prevention.

It could not escape observation, how rarely officers were the subjects of this disease. In accounting for this, I lay most stress on the attention which officers pay to cleanliness. In the 88th Regiment, where, I believe, forty men did not escape an attack, only two officers out of thirty had ophthalmia.

The exemption of the officers from the ophthalmia gives more weight to the opinion, that in Egypt this disease is communicated by contagion.

Part III of Dr McGrigor's narrative, 'Of the diseases of the Indian Army in Egypt', continues with a description of the other illnesses to which the soldiers of his time were prone. Points of particular interest include his assertion that 'the effects of the solo-lunar influence, so remarkable in fever, hepatitis and dysentery in India, were in Egypt likewise very observable. In the treatment of these diseases the practitioner found his account in attending to the periods of the moon; at the full and the change, paroxysms would frequently supervene, if not anticipated, and, at these periods, convalescents would frequently suffer a relapse.'

His treatment of most fevers has been already described in his treatise on 'The New or the Oxygenated Remedies in Syphilitic Complaints' in Appendix 8.

For dysentery, which he describes as 'by far the most generally prevailing, as well as the most fatal disease in the army', he writes that 'the best treatment appeared to be, after a dose of castor oil, to give opium liberally by the mouth, and by clyster, and to make the patient drink very freely of gum arabic at the same time. In some of these cases I have likewise given diluted nitric acid. A constriction of the vessels discharging mucus was in this way affected; the incessant discharge was stopped, and time given for a secretion of mucus to cover the abraded gut.'

Describing the treatment of Guinea-worm which disabled so many men on the *Fancy* that she had to return to Bombay, he writes:

It required force to detach it from the parts underneath. When detached with the forceps, we twisted round a ligature a piece of lint, and thus, often on the first day, succeeded in extracting a foot, or even two, of the worm . . . We continued daily, extracting as much of it as we could with gentle pulling. It was always dangerous to pull strongly, for fear of breaking the worm; it then occasioned the most acute pain, and there followed much swelling, with inflammation of the neighbouring parts, sometimes of two or three weeks' continuance, when the worm would show itself at another part, as at first, with itching and a blister . . .

I have good reason to think that the spreading of the Guinea-worm may be stopped . . . Extreme attention to cleanliness is indispensably necessary.

In India, the native doctors are much more successful in getting out the worms than the Europeans. After long feeling with their fingers, for the body of the worm, they make an incision as nearly as they can judge over its middle, and, pulling the worm by a duplicature of it, draw out both ends of the worm as the same time . . . Passing an electrical shot through the part had no effect.

It was only after sailing from Ceylon that the disease broke out; but it became a very serious matter in a few weeks, 161 being affected out of a total of 360 . . .

We now know the explanation. The embryos, escaping from the worm which has emerged from a human case into the water of places where a certain cyclops abounds, swarm into the bodies of the cyclopes and, there, undergo the changes preparatory to re-entrance into humans and, the water containing the infected cyclopes having been drunk, once more set up the disease . . . The time necessary for the whole change . . . is about a year.[5]

McGrigor then describes the remarkable cure of a sailor, who, having trod on a copper nail, was suffering from tetanus. 'The jaws were firmly locked . . . a bath was made from fat, or what is on ship-board called the "slush". The patient was immersed four times a day for half an hour at a time and 'after he came out, his whole body was rubbed with mercurial ointment.' McGrigor notes that the symptoms yielded slowly, yet recover he apparently did.

Following a long dissertation on the treatment of yellow fever, a disease which he believed had much similarity to the plague, he advocates the use of cold bathing, or sponging. 'By the use of the cold bathing, my life was saved in Jersey, in 1794, when I was ill of typhus fever . . . This I conceive to be one of the greatest improvements which the practice of physic has received in modern times.'

NOTES

1   A plan established in the army proved so useful, that I will here mention it. The letters and reports of the medical gentlemen in the pest-houses, I constantly sewed together, made them up in monthly volumes, and kept them at my quarters, where every medical gentleman in the army was invited to come and daily peruse them. The disease became the subject of daily discussion; and, from these discussions, I was enabled daily to propose queries in my letters to the

gentlemen in the pest-houses. Thus, the history of the disease, in most of its points, came to be investigated; and, previously to entering a pest-house, before his tour of duty came round, every gentleman had acquired some knowledge of the plague, and of the success of other practitioners.

2   These circumstances I learned from a member of the French Institute, and from the *Pharmacien en Chéf* to the French army, who often related to me the order which Buonaparte gave to him to poison the wounded with opium.

[A note in the margin of a copy of this book, held by the Royal Society of Medicine, states that the Chief Physician of the French Army, Desgenettes, said that Buonaparte did say that opium might be given them that they might not be tortured by the Turks, into whose hands they must fall in a few hours. Desgenettes said that the men were *in articulo*. Larry (Napoleon's own physician and later McGrigor's friend) said the same. S.L.C.]

3   Dr Buchan was on the staff of the British army, but twice nobly volunteered his services, and twice did duty in the Lazaretto of Alexandria, at this period common both to the English and Indian armies.

4   This remark we found to be particularly applicable to the last stage of the illness. In the beginning of the season, one case occurred that gave rise to much conversation in the army. From having come into contact with a case of plague, a Lascar, in the department of the commissary of cattle, was sent into the observation room of the pest-house of Rosetta; he was brought there much against his will, and contrived to make his escape from it on the evening of the day on which he was admitted, though fired at by the dragoon sentries placed round the establishment. Ineffectual search was made for him everywhere in the neighbourhood of Rosetta, and we could hear nothing of him for about five weeks, when he was discovered at Boulac. On being brought down to Rosetta, I examined him with Mr Guild, the surgeon of his corps. We found him then well, but certainly he had had the disease, for we saw an axillary bubo not quite healed. He told us, that he remained concealed for a great deal of the time among the rushes by the side of the river. On mentioning this case to Dr Currie, of Liverpool, I think he said he had heard of similar cures.

BIBLIOGRAPHY

Blanco, Richard L., *Wellington's Surgeon General – Sir James McGrigor* (Duke University Press, Durham)

Cantlie, Lieut. General Sir Neil, K.C.B., K.B.E., M.C., MB, Ch.B., F.R.C.S., *A History of the Army Medical Department* (Churchill Livingstone, Edinburgh & London), 1974

Cummins, Colonel S. Lyle, 'Echoes from the Past - Sir James McGrigor Bt.', pub. in *The Lancet* (Contemporary Medical Archives Centre), 1850, Vol. II

Dudley, H. & I. Levack, *Aberdeen Royal Infirmary* (Bailliere Tindall, London) 1992

Gaffney, Victor, *The Lordship of Strathavon* (Aberdeen University Press), 1960

Haley, Arthur H., *Our Davy: General Sir David Baird, 1757–1829* (Bullfinch Publications, Liverpool)

Haswell, J. *The First Respectable Spy* (Hamish Hamilton, London) 1969

Hibbert, Hibbert (ed.), *The Recollections of Rifleman Harris* (Windrush Press, Gloucester), 1996

Hill Burton Rodger, E., *Aberdeen Doctors at Home & Abroad* (Edinburgh), 1893

Keate, Thomas, F.R.S. *Observations of the Fifth Report of the Commissioners of Military Enquiry* (London), 1808

Keith, A., *A Thousand Years of Aberdeen*

MacDonald, Ian R., *Aberdeen and the Highland Church (1785–1900)* (St Andrew Press, Edinburgh), 2000

McGregor, A. M., *A History of Clan Gregor* (William Brown, Edinburgh), 1901

McGrigor, James, *The Autobiography & Services of Sir James McGrigor Bt., Late Director-General of the Army Medical Department* (Longman, Green, Longman & Roberts, London), 1861

McGrigor, James, *Journal of the Peninsular Campaign: 1812–1814* (13 vols) Aberdeen Medico-Chirurgical Library

McGrigor, James, *Letters* (British Museum), Add. Mss 38301

McGrigor, James, *Letters* (National Library of Scotland), Add. Mss 3903

McGrigor, James, *Medical Sketch of the Expedition to Egypt from India* (London), 1804

McGrigor, James, *Papers* (Aberdeen Medico-Chirurgical Library)

Murray, General Sir George, *Murray Papers: 46.1.1 – 46.10.2* (National Library of Scotland)

Milne, George P. (ed.), *Aberdeen Medico-Chirurgical Society: A Bicentennial History, 1789–1989* (Aberdeen University Press), 1989

Morland Simpson, H.F., M.A., F.S.A. (Scot) Rector (ed.), *Bon Accord – Records and Reminiscences of Aberdeen Grammar School* (Ballantyne Press, Aberdeen), 1906

'Obituary of Sir James McGrigor' in *Edinburgh Medical Journal*, (Sutherland and Knox, Edinburgh), Vol. III, July 1857–June 1858

Oman, Sir Charles, *A History of the Peninsular War* (A.M.S. Press, New York), Vols V & VI

Paget, Sir Julian, Bt. C.V.O., *Wellington's Peninsular War: Battles and Battlefields* (Leo Cooper, London), 1990

Rhys, W.J. ST. E-G., 'Mentioned in Dispatches' (Paper delivered to the International Congress on the History of Medicine, Glasgow), 1994

Shaw, Anthony J. 'Sir James McGrigor - An Appreciation' (Lecture delivered to the Aberdeen Medico-Chirurgical Society, 21 September 1989), *Aberdeen University Review*

Warre, Lieut.-General Sir William, *The Journal of the Royal Army Medical Corps*, Vol. XIII, No. 2; Vol CXVII, No. 2; Vol XCV1, No. 1

Warre, Revd Edmund Warre, D.D., C.B., M.V.O. and William A. Warre (eds.), *Letters from the Peninsula: 1808–12 from Lieut.-General Sir William Warre* (Spellmount, Staplehurst), 1999

Willoughby, Verner, *History & Campaigns of the Rifle Brigade: Part II: 1809–13* (John Bale, Sons & Danielsson Ltd., London), 1919